MAN, THE MASTER—
OR MAN, THE SLAVE?

Do we have the power to arrive at truth through the independent workings of our intellects? Or are we total prisoners of our sensory apparatus, our knowledge of reality a passive product of our sensations?

Is there any firm basis for standards of conduct in a world that does not recognize the authority of religion? Or are we doomed to moral anarchy without divine guidelines?

Does anything really distinguish man from the animals? Of what worth are the mental powers of which he is so proud?

These are among the timeless questions that Immanuel Kant faced as he built a philosophy that stands as one of the most ruthlessly questioning and ultimately inspiring statements of the human condition ever to profoundly shape man's vision of himself.

ARNULF ZWEIG was born in Essen, Germany, and educated at the University of Rochester (B.A., 1952), Yale University, and Stanford University (Ph.D. in Philosophy and Humanities, 1960).
He has had visiting professorships at M.I.T. and Harvard. Since 1956 he has taught at the University of Oregon and is at present head of their Department of Philosophy.
Besides numerous papers in Philosophical studies, analysis, and ethics, his publications include a translation of Kant's Philosophical Correspondence: 1759-99, and many articles on German philosophers in the Encyclopedia of Philosophy.

MENTOR Titles of Related Interest

The Essential Kant

EDITED WITH AN INTRODUCTION
BY ARNULF ZWEIG

*Prepared under the editorial supervision
of* ROBERT PAUL WOLFF

A MENTOR BOOK from
NEW AMERICAN LIBRARY
TIMES MIRROR
New York and Toronto
The New English Library Limited, London

MENTOR TRADEMARK REG. U.S. PAT. OFF. AND FOREIGN COUNTRIES
REGISTERED TRADEMARK—MARCA REGISTRADA
HECHO EN CHICAGO, U.S.A.

SIGNET, SIGNET CLASSICS, MENTOR AND PLUME
BOOKS are published by
The New American Library, Inc.,
1301 Avenue of the Americas, New York, New York 10019

First Printing, July, 1970

PRINTED IN THE UNITED STATES OF AMERICA

Contents

A Note on This Text and Sources

The letters to Herz and to Lavater are taken from Kant's *Philosophical Correspondence: 1759–1799*, translated and edited by Arnulf Zweig (Chicago: University of Chicago Press, 1967).

Selections from the *Critique of Pure Reason* are taken from the translation by Friedrich Maximilian Müller, first published in 1881. The "A" and "B" paginations refer approximately to the paginations of Kant's first and second editions respectively (A=1781, B=1787), with material new to the second edition printed in italics. Material from A, deleted in B, is reprinted in square brackets, followed in italics by the material substituted for it in B. The translator's footnotes are included, but footnotes marked with asterisks are Kant's own.

The excerpts constitute more than half of the *Critique* and include the most important arguments of that work. The Introduction summarizes Kant's problems. The Transcendental Aesthetic, which contains his theory of space and time, is reprinted in its entirety. The Transcendental Logic is represented by the most vital parts of the Transcendental Analytic, viz., the Transcendental Deduction of the categories (as formulated in both editions), the Schematism, where Kant argues the need for empirical criteria of application for *a priori* concepts, and the Analogies of Experience, in which Kant specifically defends the categories of substance, causality, and interaction ("community"). Kant's clearest attempt to answer Hume's account of causality is found in the arguments of the Second Analogy. A brief but important section on the distinction between phenomena and noumena is also included. Omitted are Kant's arguments concerning the other *a priori* principles, the "postulates of empirical thought in general," and the "anticipations of perception." A few other pages and paragraphs not essential to the main arguments have been excised.

The third main part of the *Critique* is the Transcendental Dialectic, which Kant's needlessly elaborate and confusing system of headings places under the Transcendental Logic. The Dialectic contains Kant's criticism of traditional metaphysics. Included in this anthology is the third of the Antinomies, the most important of the four, according to Kant himself. It deals with the conflict between freedom and determinism. Kant's famous attack on the Ontological Argument for the existence of God is also included, but not his discussions of the other classical arguments for God, since Kant maintains that they all depend on the Ontological Argument at some point or other, so that his refutation of that argument is supposed to destroy rational theology once and for all.

The Paralogisms criticize rationalistic proofs concerning the existence and immortality of the soul. Because of the great interest in philosophy of mind today, some of Kant's discussion is included here, though its interest might at first sight appear to be merely historical.

Kant's defense of the Ideas of Reason (e.g., God) as ideals having a legitimate "regulative" use is also included.

The *Fundamental Principles of the Metaphysics of Morals* (*Grundlegung zur Metaphysik der Sitten*, 1785) is reprinted in its entirety. The translation is by Thomas K. Abbott.

The selection from the *Critique of Practical Reason* (1788), translated by Thomas K. Abbott, continues the discussion of freedom begun in the *Critique of Pure Reason* (the Third Antinomy) and carried forward in the third part of the *Fundamental Principles*. Kant defends the idea that a person can be motivated by purely rational principles without any feeling or inclination being presupposed. (Contrast Hume's claim that "reason is and ought to be the slave of the passions.") This self-determination of the will, a freedom from all desires and sensuous impulses, Kant thinks essential to the possibility of morality. The *Critique of Pure Reason* argued that freedom is at least a logical possibility; the *Critique of Practical Reason* tries to show that it is more than that. The reality of freedom is proved by the moral law.

The Preface and Introduction to Kant's third critique, the *Critique of Judgement*, present a short statement of Kant's conception of a philosophical system and a fair summary of his views about Judgement, a faculty distinct from Reason and Understanding. He explains it as the faculty concerned with the *application* of concepts, and tries to show how this ability is tied up with the idea of purposiveness in nature. The translation is by James Creed Meredith (Oxford: The Clarendon Press, 1952).

A brief excerpt from the *Metaphysics of Morals* (1797) is included, just to show how Kant's account of duty is both more complicated and more flexible than one would gather from reading only the *Fundamental Principles*. The translation is by James Ellington and is taken from Kant's *Metaphysical Principles of Virtue* (Indianapolis and New York: Bobbs-Merrill Co., Inc., 1964).

The Essential Kant

I. Introduction

The German poet Heinrich Heine once said of Immanuel Kant that the history of his life would be hard to write, since Kant had neither life nor history. There is a certain truth in this. Kant's life was that of a scholar, a life devoid of personal or political adventures.[1] He was born in Königsberg in 1724, and, except for seven years spent as a private tutor, he lived there until his death in 1804. "All change frightens me," he once wrote to a friend, declining an offer to leave Königsberg for a more lucrative and exciting position at another university. The rigidity of his daily routine was proverbial. As Heine describes it: "Rising from bed, coffee-drinking [Heine is not quite accurate—Kant was a tea drinker], writing, lecturing, eating, walking, everything had its fixed time; and the neighbors knew that it must be exactly half past four when they saw Professor Kant in his grey coat with his cane in his hand step out of his house door . . . Strange contrast between the outer life of the man and his world-destroying thoughts."

Kant's "world-destroying thoughts" were not developed until rather late in his career. In 1770, after years of poverty, Kant was finally awarded a professorship at the University of Königsberg. Though his writings were known to the leading intellectuals of his time, the work for which he is now famous had not yet begun. His early interests had been as much in physics as philosophy and his publications included a number of purely scientific essays, among them an attempt to account

---

[1] Had he been less easily intimidated by established authority, Kant might have had more involvement with politics. His religious views got him into trouble with the reactionary government of Friedrich Wilhelm II, but Kant meekly complied with the latter's censorship edict, although his friends urged him to put up a fight.

for the origin and evolution of the solar system in purely secular terms, using the mechanistic principles of Newtonian physics but avoiding Newton's appeal to "the hand of God." Kant advocated the so-called "nebular hypothesis," which the physicist Laplace formulated independently of him some forty years later.[2] Kant's philosophical writings before 1770 dealt with a number of the problems discussed again in his later work: proofs of the existence of God, the difference between mathematics and philosophy as regards the proper method of investigation for each discipline, the problem of absolute versus relative space (a problem debated by Newton and Leibniz), the legitimacy of appeals to teleology or purposiveness in scientific explanation, the distinction between causal connections and logical connections. On several occasions Kant expressed skepticism about metaphysics, a science that offered interminable wrangling instead of the progress seen in other intellectual disciplines, and he spoke of the need for a reconstruction of metaphysics to make it respectable again. But Kant did not see the interrelatedness of these questions and the need for a wholly new approach to them until after 1770. In 1772 he first mentions his work on a "critique of pure reason," and he questions the "dogmatism" of his earlier rationalistic assumptions.

When Kant uses the term "dogmatism" he means an attempt to derive conclusions about what the world must be like from an analysis of "mere concepts," without any preliminary inquiry as to the *possibility* of such *a priori* knowledge. An inquiry of the latter kind, an attempt to show what sort of knowledge is possible for minds like ours, is called a "critical" investigation, and Kant's mature position is often called the Critical Philosophy.[3] Kant's main task is to show what human reason can and cannot hope to accomplish, independently of sense experience.

The "dogmatic" philosophers were those who took for granted the competence of human reason to construct metaphysical systems that would survey and demonstrate *a priori* the basic furniture of Heaven and Earth. The task of such a

[2] Kant's *General History of Nature and Theory of the Heavens* appeared in 1755, Laplace's *Exposition du Systeme du Monde* in 1796.
[3] His major "critical" works are the *Critique of Pure Reason*, 1781 and 1787; the *Fundamenal Principles of the Metaphysics of Morals*, 1785; the *Critique of Practical Reason*, 1788; and the *Critique of Judgment*, 1790. These are by no means all of Kant's mature writings, but they are the most important. In addition one should mention the *Prolegomena to Any Possible Future Metaphysics*, 1783; *Metaphysical Elements of Natural Science*, 1786; the *Metaphysics of Ethics*, 1797; and *Religion Within the Limits of Reason Alone*, 1797. Kant also wrote numerous essays on topics ranging from international politics (*Perpetual Peace*, 1795, is his best known work here) to the philosophy of history.

metaphysics was to deduce the *necessary* features of reality, features that reason alone could certify; metaphysics was not out to describe the contingent, variable "appearances" that our senses disclose. Most philosophers on the Continent (e.g., Descartes, Spinoza, Leibniz) were agreed that sense experience could provide at best a "confused and obscure" representation of reality. Pure reason, however, could transcend the realm of sense experience and prove the existence of God, the nature of the soul, and the origin and ultimate constituents of the world as a whole. The sciences of Rational Theology, Rational Psychology, and Rational Cosmology were the branches of metaphysics that were supposed to answer these questions.

Now one of the sources of Kant's loss of faith in the "dogmatic procedure of reason" was his discovery of the Antinomies, four pairs of conflicting *a priori* arguments, a discovery that made a farce of Rational Cosmology. Kant found that equally good arguments could be given in favor of opposing cosmological theses. It was possible to prove that the world must have had a beginning in time and that it couldn't have had a beginning, that it is limited in space and that it cannot be limited, that indivisible units or "atoms" are logically necessary and that such simple substances are impossible, that a "Necessary Being" must be assumed and that such a being cannot be assumed either as part or as cause of the world. Finally—and most significantly—it could be argued that freedom must exist, but also, with equal cogency, that determinism must hold throughout nature. The conflict between freedom and determinism was especially disturbing, since it was not merely a theoretical or cognitive issue but a practical one, an issue that affected human conduct, indeed the very foundations of ethics: If determinism were true of the human will, a large part of our ordinary moral discourse would have to be viewed as unintelligible. The existence of the Antinomies was therefore "a scandal of pure reason" and one that pointed dramatically to the need for a thorough inquiry into what the proper tasks and the limits of reason might be. It was this scandal, Kant says, that first "aroused me from my dogmatic slumber and drove me to the critique of reason itself."[4]

Kant's *Critique of Pure Reason* is such a difficult work that scholars have devoted their lives to understanding it, and even now there is no total agreement among them as to its main arguments. Kant often apologized for his literary limitations (though he could write clearly and eloquently on topics outside

---

[4] So Kant wrote in a letter to the philosopher Christian Garve in 1798. A better known passage in the *Prolegomena* credits David Hume with "awake" Kane from dogmatism.

of technical philosophy) and for the lack of readability of the *Critique*. He explained that he had put the book together hastily, after working on it for over a decade. Granting that it was painful to read (the philosopher Moses Mendelssohn called it "this nerve-juice consuming book"), Kant thought that some of this pain was unavoidable, for his position could not be stated without the barrage of technical terms and distinctions which he had introduced. People would eventually recover from their numbness, a numbness that his innovations made inevitable, Kant said. He challenged anyone to restate his thoughts in an untechnical, popular style, so as to discover for himself how impossible this was. Kant thought that he had invented a wholly new science, and from the looks of it he must have believed that a philosopher was truly "scientific" only if he presented his system with an impressive array of divisions, distinctions, classifications, tables, and the like, all couched in an obscure jargon. Still, Kant sometimes expressed the hope that his followers would succeed in explaining his work to the general reading public, and once or twice he even suggested how this might be done.[5]

Kant's objectives and motivations are enormously complex. His negative task is to expose the confusions of metaphysics and show how impossible it is for anyone to know anything about matters that transcend the world of experience. His arguments against metaphysics are found mainly in the Transcendental Dialectic, the third main portion of the *Critique*. Metaphysical theories are misguided; in many cases we cannot even state intelligibly the questions they propose to answer. If someone asks, "What is the cause of the world as a whole?" he must be using the notion of "cause" in a way that is utterly different from its use *within* the world of experience. We can understand "What is the cause of such and such a phenomenon?" but perhaps the word "cause" is meaningless, when used in the metaphysical question. Kant takes up the traditional proofs of God and the immortality of the soul and tries to show that these concepts too are suspicious, for God and the soul are not in any ordinary sense "objects," and the attempts to provide metaphysical knowledge of them involve fallacies and confusions—natural, even inevitable, misuses of reason. The analysis of these misuses, in the Transcendental Dialectic, shows the "sciences" of Rational Theology, Rational Psychology, and Rational Cosmology to be pseudosciences and the logic employed in them an illusion.

[5] See his letters to Mendelssohn, Garve, and J. Beck, in *Philosophical Correspondence: 1759–1799* (Chicago: University of Chicago Press, 1967).

But Kant's attitude towards metaphysics was not as unfavorable as these negative conclusions suggest. Sometimes he does go so far as to say that our concepts are meaningless when applied to "objects" beyond all possible experience. Usually, however, his position is more charitable: We can *think* about matters that are not *knowable*. Metaphysics is "the completion of the whole culture of human reason," Kant writes at the end of the *Critique*; it is the highest and most indispensable of sciences. The point is not to destroy it but to reform it. If we are ignorant of transcendent entities such as God and the soul, that need not be fatal, for knowledge itself is not the only important concern of human beings. Metaphysical concepts may be defended as "ideals of reason," serving a useful purpose in guiding our inquiries and actions. The belief that the world is the product of intelligent design, for example, is one that cannot be *known* to be true, either by empirical evidence or through logical demonstration; it is nevertheless useful to approach the world *as if* it were designed, for this encourages us to *look for* order and simplicity in seeking out the laws of nature. We then use the idea of design as a "regulative" principle, even though we do not know that it is "constitutive" of the world. Kant is not really skeptical about the "objects" of theology. In the *Critique of Practical Reason*, he tries to show that belief in God and in the immortality of the soul are "postulates" that are not only useful but indispensable in rendering the moral life meaningful. The limits of knowledge do not coincide with the limits of intelligibility, and the interest we have in knowledge-getting must sometimes be subordinated to the demands of action.

Kant's goal is thus not purely or mainly destructive, though his attack on the arguments of other philosophers earned him the title of "the Prussian Hume." His aim is to lay the groundwork for a rehabilitated, intellectually respectable metaphysics, one that would secure the foundations of natural science, mathematics, and morality and show how the principles underlying each of these fields could be compatible. That they *are* justified and compatible, Kant never doubted. In a flight of eloquence rare in Kant's writing, he states: "Two things fill the mind with ever new and increasing admiration and awe, the oftener and more steadily they are contemplated: the starry heavens above me, and the moral law within me."[6] The starry heavens had been conquered by Newton's mathematical physics; Kant intends to show how we know the fundamental principles of Newton's science to be necessarily true. The moral

[6] *Critique of Practical Reason*, Conclusion.

law, Kant felt, was recognized by every sinner, however unrepentant, and however unsophisticated and inarticulate his conscience. The philosopher's job is therefore not to teach people the meaning of freedom, duty, guilt, temptation, right and wrong, but to examine these concepts and to show how they can be defended against the seemingly hostile principles and laws of natural science.

The positive goal of Kant's philosophy is the defense of *a priori* concepts and *a priori* synthetic principles. Kant thinks that mathematics, physics, morality, and even our everyday experience all involve such principles. We must try to see how Kant uses the words "*a priori*" and "synthetic." By "*a priori*" Kant means "independent of experience," but this does not mean innate or temporally prior to experience—there are no innate concepts, Kant insists, and no inborn or divinely implanted items of knowledge. There are, however, certain inevitable ways of sensing and thinking, of receiving and conceptualizing the data of experience; there are concepts which do not depend on any *particular* experience but which are required by *any* experience; and there are certain "invulnerable" principles in the sciences, laws which assert more than any finite number of observations could possibly warrant, and which are treated as necessarily and universally true, in the sense that no possible observations are taken to be evidence against them. Such truths could not be mere generalizations from experience and yet possess necessity and universality, for experience tells us only what is or has been the case, not what *must* be. Examples of *a priori* principles from the foundations of natural science, according to Kant, are the laws of motion (e.g., every action has an equal and opposite reaction), the principle of causality (every alteration has a cause), and the conservation of matter or "substance." These laws were not treated by scientists as empirical summaries or inductive generalizations. Their status was privileged; they were immune to refutation by empirical findings. If an experiment seemed to go against such a law, the experiment rather than the law was thrown out. A scientist investigating the causes of some phenomenon would not interpret his failure to discover a cause as evidence that the phenomenon had no cause, but as showing some inadequacy in his investigation. Of course all the detailed laws of nature could not be known independently of experiments, and Kant did not maintain that they could. The principles and laws he regards as *a priori* are in many cases specifications of what to *look for*, rather than of what we shall *find*, in scientific inquiry. On the other hand, some of his examples are quite specifically Newtonian and would undoubtedly be rejected or reinterpreted in the light of subsequent developments in physics that Kant could not have foreseen.

Given Kant's conception of "*a priori*," we must try to see what he means by "synthetic." The distinction between "analytic" and "synthetic" judgments was, Kant thought, the essential first step in understanding his problem. For *a priori* judgments may be of two very different sorts: *analytic a priori* judgments are those the denial of which would be self-contradictory; their truth can therefore be established simply by reference to what they mean and to the law of contradiction. "All triangles have three sides" is an example of such a judgment. I only need to analyze the concept of a triangle or reflect on what I mean by the word "triangle" to find that the idea of having three sides is included in it. The denial of "All triangles have three sides" violates the law of contradiction. A *synthetic* judgment, on the other hand, is one that is not analytic, i.e., its truth or falsity cannot be determined merely by analysis, and its denial is not self-contradictory. All empirical judgments are synthetic; I could not determine analytically that eating candy is likely to produce cavities or that aspirin relieves headaches. The denial of such a judgment may be false, but it is not logically self-contradictory. The central problem of the *Critique* arises out of the fact that some *a priori* judgments are synthetic too: Every alteration has a cause, two straight lines cannot enclose a space, the shortest distance between two points on a plane is a straight line, are three of Kant's examples. Kant is not troubled by the existence of empirical synthetic judgments. But how are *a priori* synthetic judgments to be defended?

He is not worried (as perhaps he should have been) about analytic *a priori* judgments either. Kant disagrees with his rationalistic predecessors who thought that important metaphysical truths could be established analytically. He holds that analytic judgments are in a sense empty; they "explicate" or clarify what we already think, but they do not add to our knowledge. That is why there is no mystery about how we can determine their truth independently of experience. The predicate of an analytic judgment only makes explicit what is already thought, perhaps obscurely, in the subject. In a synthetic *a priori* judgment, however, verification requires more than an analysis of the constituent concepts or an appeal to the law of contradiction. I cannot determine that the shortest distance between two points on a plane is a straight line just by thinking about what I mean by "shortest distance" and "straight." There is no self-contradiction involved in supposing this judgment false. Similarly it would not be self-contradictory to imagine a change taking place without a cause, as it would be to think of a triangle without three sides. The problem is: what gives us the *right* to assert such synthetic *a priori* judgments as "Every change has a cause" and "The shortest distance between two points is a straight line"? In the case of empirical judgments, the "synthesis" or connection of subject and predicate concepts is justified by a "third thing," namely, an experience. But what "third thing" is there to warrant the connection of distinct concepts when the judgment is *not* empirical? This then is the sense of Kant's question, "How are synthetic *a priori* judgments possible?"

The problem of justifying synthetic *a priori* judgments is sometimes treated by Kant as a problem concerning *a priori concepts*, the so-called "Categories," or "pure concepts of the understanding." To understand why he should see the problem in this way, one has to see some of its historical sources. The controversy between empiricists and rationalists is one such source. "Rationalism" and "empiricism" generally signify competing theories as to (1) the origin, or (2) the justification, of human knowledge. These two distinct issues—the origin of our ideas and beliefs, and their justification—have not always been clearly separated. Psychological questions and philosophical questions have tended to be confused with each other. It is quite common in the eighteenth century to find philosophers insisting on a connection between the origin and the validity of ideas. Kant, for example, often writes as though having an "origin" in experience will relegate a concept to a kind of second-class citizenship, while Hume explicitly argues that without such an origin, an idea is meaningless.

According to Hume, we are merely the passive recipients of information received through our senses, and all our concepts and beliefs are generated mechanically out of that information. Rationalists such as Plato, Descartes, and Leibniz, on the other hand, had regarded the human mind as not purely passive and thus limited; the intellect, unlike the senses, is "spontaneous" and creative in knowledge-getting. It has a stock of innate concepts and principles that enable it to construct a clearer representation of reality than can be got from the senses. This was close to Kant's own position, in the Inaugural Dissertation of 1770. Despite his earlier misgivings about metaphysics, he there defends the Platonistic thesis that reason is equipped with "intellectual representations" that enable the philosopher to know an "intelligible" realm of things in themselves, distinct from the world of "appearance" presented to our senses.

In 1772, in a letter to his friend and former student Marcus Herz, Kant first expressed doubts about "intellectual representations" or *a priori* concepts. He asks, "What reason do we have for thinking that intellectual representations, the basic concepts of our understanding, have any necessary relationship to the world?" If there are indeed unavoidable ways in which human beings think or structure reality, why should the world be kind enough to correspond to these ideas? Some philosophers had asserted that there is a "pre-established harmony" between our fundamental concepts and the world, but Kant scorns this move as a philosophical *deus ex machina*, the greatest absurdity one can imagine in the theory of knowledge.

The problem of *a priori* concepts was thus construed by Kant as one of insuring that such concepts are not mere figments of the brain, *Hirngespinster*. For example, the concept of cause and effect is the concept of a necessary connection between distinct events. But we never observe any such connection. That is what David Hume pointed out: In searching for the "origin" of our idea of cause and effect, Hume found only that our experience of the so-called cause has been invariably (or very often) followed by an experience of the so-called effect. We never observe a connection, much less a necessary connection—"All events seem entirely loose and separate."[7] Therefore such a connection cannot be part of what we mean by "A causes B." Yet Hume and Kant both see that "B because of A" means more than "B always after A." Hume locates this "something more" in the observer and not in the events themselves. The necessary connection between a cause and its effect is only a subjective necessity. We develop a certain *habit* of anticipating one event when we experience another, a habit due to repeated association of two classes of events in our experience. Hume says that we transfer a "determination of thought" (i.e., a mental state) to the external objects; we do this, but in fact the "necessity" belongs only in our minds.[8]

Now the concept of cause and effect was one of the categories or "intellectual representations" whose legitimacy Kant had earlier taken for granted. The effect of Hume's argument was to reinforce Kant's dawning suspicions of this dogmatic position. If the concept of cause and effect was only the empirically derived concept that Hume held it to be, then the "necessity" which a scientist attributes to causal connections is really only a subjective, psychological necessity. On the other hand, if the concept is not based on experience, how can it be shown to have any objective reference?

Kant's solution to this dilemma is extraordinarily difficult to

[7] *Inquiry Concerning Human Understanding*, Section VII, Part II.
[8] *Treatise of Human Nature*, Book I, Part III, section xiv.

summarize. It involves a kind of mediation between empiricists and rationalists. However, this is a terrible oversimplification—it would be more accurate to say that Kant repudiates both views as inadequate, and that he throws out the problem of finding an "object" corresponding to *a priori* concepts. Kant agrees with the rationalists that the mind is indeed active and not merely a blank slate or a complex recording device. Its active character shows itself when we think, judge, recognize, discern, infer, understanding anything.[9] But reason's creative power is limited to supplying the "forms" of experience and knowledge; for "content" it needs data. The empiricist is thus not altogether wrong: Forms without content are not knowledge.

The metaphor of form and content is a favorite Kantian device. By "form" he usually means some invariant or inevitable feature of experience. Space and time are the "forms" of our sense experience—i.e., regardless of what particular items may or may not turn up in perceptions, our perceptions will inevitably be temporally and (in the case of "outer" sense) spatially related. This theory is spelled out in the first main portion of the *Critique*, the Transcendental Aesthetic.[10] There are "forms" of judging as well as forms of sensing: The "categories" or pure (nonempirical) concepts of the understanding are those forms, reflecting the basic kinds of statements or judgments that are possible. They are defended in the second main portion of the *Critique*, the Transcendental Analytic.

Scientific knowledge and even everyday experience require the cooperation of *two* distinct powers or "faculties": The "understanding" is the faculty that supplies concepts, *Begriffe*, which Kant thinks of as rules or criteria for unifying and interpreting experience; a concept is always of something *general*, i.e., a kind or species of things. The faculty called "sensibility" is the ability to represent *particulars*, i.e., *instances* of concepts. Sensibility supplies a diversity of data in space and time, a diversity which needs to be put together (*Zusammensetzung* is Kant's word for all the various ways in which the understanding puts together or "synthesizes" the manifold of sense impressions) in order to form connected experience. Without the "spontaneity" of the intellect, we would have a mere "rhap-

[9] Outside the sphere of knowledge-getting, the mind is "spontaneous" also in moral action, namely, in a man's freely determining the principles on which he shall act.

[10] The theory of space and time as mind-contributed forms is essential to Kant's explanation of how we can know mathematics *a priori*. Geometrical objects, e.g., are *a priori* constructions in space. Since they are the mathematician's own creations, it is comprehensible how their properties can be known independently of sense experience.

sody of sensations," lacking even the coherence of a dream. Without the understanding, I could not even be aware that I was having a particular experience, for I need the ability to discern, recall, distinguish, make a unity out of the data of sensibility. Yet without sensibility itself, I should be left with thoughts that are merely formal—generalities without reference. In a famous passage Kant writes: "Thoughts without contents are empty, intuitions without concepts are blind."[11] By "intuition" (*Anschauung*) Kant means a direct apprehension of some particular thing; intuitions may be empirical (as in apprehending a patch of color or a sound or smell) or they may be pure (as when a student in geometry, trying to prove a theorem, imagines a line drawn parallel to a given line). Empiricists are mistaken in regarding human knowledge as the result of a succession of "intuitions" or sense impressions, for the data of experience do not themselves tell us how they are to be combined and interpreted. It is the understanding that gives sense to sensation. But the work of the understanding would be empty if we did not have actual perceptual situations on which to apply our categories. Apart from a possible application to experience, the nonempirical concepts of the intellect lack determinate meaning.[12]

It was almost a decade before Kant completed work on his defense of this position. The most difficult part of his argument is the "deduction" or justification of *a priori* concepts. The heart of it is the claim that the categories are validly applicable to all objects of experience because they make connected experience itself possible. The idea of a "possible experience" and its presuppositions is the key to Kant's revolution in metaphysics. By "experience" Kant does not mean a mere stream of consciousness or a succession of images, sensations, and thoughts. "Experience" is for him a synonym for "empirical knowledge." It is the representation of objective events and public objects. An essential feature of experience, in this sense, is that it be *communicable* to others. Kant's search for the *a priori* conditions on which the "possibility of experience" rests is therefore comparable to the search for a kind of universal grammar.[13]

[11] A 51 = B 75. (References to the *Critique of Pure Reason* are usually given in this way. A 51 refers to p. 51 of the first edition, B 75 refers to p. 75 of the second edition.)

[12] The translation of the categories into concepts with empirical meaning is discussed in the section of Transcendental Analytic called The Schematism.

[13] This is an analogy that he himself suggests in the *Prolegomena*, § 39, where he compares discovering the categories with "detecting in a language the rules of the actual use of words generally."

Experience presupposes the *unity* of the experiencer, i.e., the possibility of connecting a diversity of representations in a single consciousness. Some examples might help. What intellectual abilities must be assumed, if I am to count the strokes of a bell and hear the seventh stroke as seventh? I must apprehend each individual stroke, perhaps focus my consciousness on it (discarding irrelevant data, the other sounds, aromas, sights, and so on that may be available in my perceptual field) and I must be able to reproduce the earlier strokes in my imagination and combine the present event with the past ones. This is what is needed in order to judge that the clock is striking seven. Or suppose that I am trying to understand a long and complicated German sentence (one of Kant's, for example): I must be able to "hang on" to the earlier nouns and prepositions and subordinate clauses and *combine* them with the verb that comes at the end. It is not sufficient to hear or read each individual word, if I am to make sense of the sentence. A "synthesis" is needed. And this presupposes that the mind that is performing the synthesis is the same consciousness that started out and that finished the sentence. This is what Kant refers to by his terrifyingly ponderous phrase, "the transcendental unity of apperception." Kant warns that this "transcendental unity" is not a *thing*, not a substantial ego; we are not justified in asserting the existence of a thinking substance or soul, as Descartes would have us do. The unity is only a certain *possibility* of connecting, the possibility, as Kant puts it, of saying "I think" or "I am aware that" to every item of my experience. The unity is "transcendental" rather than empirical, because of course I cannot *observe* my mind's continuity through a sequence of perceptions.

The Categories are, Kant argues, the basic rules for synthesizing, for making a unity out of a manifold of data. How do we know that they apply to the world? If the world—the world of phenomena, of things as they appear *to us*—did not conform to the categories of our understanding, it would not *be* a world for us. This is Kant's "Copernican Revolution" in philosophy: We know *a priori* how the world is ordered, for we have *imposed* that order upon it. The "object" which corresponds to our theories, the object of scientific inquiry, is not an unobservable thing-in-itself; it is a construction of our own.

This reinterpretation of what is to be meant by "an object corresponding to our concepts" has the double merit of showing how mathematics and the foundations of natural science can be defended against the skeptical attack of empiricists and, at the same time, leaving open the possibility that "things in themselves" might *not* obey the same laws as do objects-as-appearances. It is important to see this double motive in Kant's work: The *limitation* of our knowledge is not a misfortune; it is essentially required, in order that we may believe in freedom, the dignity and autonomy of the moral agent and yet, when doing science, believe in a deterministic universe that seems to rule out any such possibility. The conflict between freedom and determinism was, as we have seen, one of the main goads to Kant's analysis. Determinism, the thesis that every event in nature is governed by causal laws, was regarded by Kant as one of the *a priori* demands of the understanding, a principle essential to the possibility of science, indeed of any coherent experience.[14] But freedom in the sense of a power to initiate new causal sequences is something we take for granted in all of our moral discourse. (Praise and blame apply to *actions*, not events.) Freedom, in still another sense of the word, the sense in which a moral agent can make a decision independently of *any* personal desires—not only veto one impulse or desire by considering another—is what makes us *persons* rather than *things*. From the point of view of science, Kant maintains, there is no freedom: Every human action must be regarded as the predictable result of prior events, i.e., as part of a causal chain whose remote links were certainly beyond the agent's control. The character of a criminal, in so far as he is a specimen for sociological and psychological investigation, must be viewed as the product of events that are just as subject to the determinism of natural laws as is the motion of a ball rolling down an inclined plane.

From the standpoint of the agent himself, however, the problem is not to *predict* what he will do but to *decide*. His "determination of the will" can be of several kinds. He might simply let himself go, responding to whatever impulse or temptation happens to come along. On the other hand, he might decide to act, not on the basis of such desires, nor out of fear, but out of respect for the rightness of a certain policy. It is the possibility of such "autonomous" decision-making that Kant views as essential to the dignity of man, and it is freedom in this sense, autonomy, a radical sort of self-determination, that Kant aims to defend against the claims of determinism.

The distinction between phenomena and noumena is Kant's way out of the apparent conflict. He uses the word "noumenon" in two ways: In the negative sense, it is the world as

---

14 The argument that "every change has a cause" is an objectively valid principle and not, as Hume had argued, a merely subjective habit, appears in the Second Analogy of Experience. Kant tries to show that the existence of causal laws is a presupposition of our putting experiences in an objective temporal sequence.

it *might* be, apart from our experience, i.e., apart from the necessary demands of knowledge-getting. On the other hand, a noumenon in the positive sense would be the "object" of a nonsensuous (i.e., nonhuman) intuition—whatever that might be. The idea of a positive noumenon is an empty one, *ein Gedankending*, a mere creature of thought. But it is useful, indeed indispensable, that we think of the world as not exhausted by our scientific categories. It is not logically *impossible* that, from a standpoint other than that of the scientific investigator, the world might be interpreted so as to allow for a free causality. That is the (admittedly mysterious) possibility of noumenal freedom that Kant's *Critique of Pure Reason* leaves open, by limiting the scope of the categories to objects as "appearances."[15]

Freedom becomes more than a possibility as Kant turns his attention from "theoretical reason" to "practical reason." The reality of freedom is shown by the fact of morality. The "moral law" presupposes it. We could not make sense of having inescapable duties without it. That we have such duties, that the demands of morality are unconditional, is one of the starting points of Kant's ethics. The analysis he offers might be viewed as a secularized version of a "divine law" or natural law theory. Like the voice of God, the moral law *commands*; it does not coax and cajole. We can imagine a kind of being who would not experience the moral law as a command, a being whose inclinations were always perfectly in tune with the law (or who could not be said to have inclinations at all, who did not *want* anything). Such a fully "rational" being would have what Kant calls a "holy will" rather than a "good will." The idea of a holy will is a useful fiction; it helps us to see something important about our own sort of life, viz., that we human beings are not by nature inclined to do what we ought to do, and that our moral problems are therefore problems of obedience or submission to the voice of duty within us. If our desires are sometimes in accord with our duties, that is a precarious fact, not something to count on. A good will, one which tries to do what is right *because* it is right, requires more of us than natural feelings. As we have said, Kant thinks that the moral concepts

---

[15] Kant explains that by "appearance" (*Erscheinung*) he does not mean illusion (*Schein*). Though he does contrast "things as appearances" with "things as they are in themselves" (which sounds like "appearance" vs. "reality"), it would be less misleading if he spoke of things as *making* an appearance or as *presenting* themselves to us, to avoid the suggestion that, e.g., objects only *appear* or *seem to be* in space and time, causally related, and so forth, which is not at all what he intends to say.

and distinctions he aims to make explicit are already present in the minds and talk of ordinary people. They know what it is to have inescapable moral obligations; they recognize the difference between moral commandments and prudent advice and the difference between arbitrary or despotic laws and principles of justice. No philosopher is needed to explain to them what guilt is or temptation; and they recognize the difference between a man who treats men with dignity and justice and one who uses men efficiently to achieve his arbitrary goals.

Kant's "common man" who understands these things is obviously a man of the Judeo-Christian tradition. He is a man of the eighteenth century, who shares the humanistic values of the Enlightenment and believes in the dignity of all men (he may have doubts about women, and perhaps he hesitates when thinking of his house servants) and who believes in the equal application of laws to everyone. He is a humble man, who recognizes the great gulf that separates his own imperfect will from the moral ideal with which he constantly compares himself, and he is burdened with a sense of guilt, an awareness of his own selfishness and the ubiquity of temptation. He respects "man" and the Rights of Man, though he does not think much of people, believing them to be as weak and unlovable as he knows himself to be. The central fact of his moral experience is that there is something called the Moral Law. Its commands are "categorical," unconditional imperatives, not merely "hypothetical" imperatives, directions for the achievement of some arbitrary end. What it demands is something he may not wish to hear: That there is a radical difference between persons and things and that any policy that fails to take this difference into account is morally disgusting.

The supreme principle of ethics Kant calls *the* "Categorical Imperative." In his most famous formulation of it, Kant lays down the requirement of a kind of moral objectivity as essential to any morally respectable policy. "Act only on a maxim which you could consistently will to be a universal law," i.e., a law for all rational beings. This principle sets forth a bare minimum condition for moral action and for any system of justice. It tells us that laws and policies which discriminate arbitrarily between human beings cannot be morally acceptable. The requirement is that only those policies ("maxims") which every rational being could freely adopt as laws binding upon himself can have the status of legitimate lawfulness. Applied to jurisprudence, the intent is to insist that justice be blind, in the sense that what is lawful, criminal, right, or wrong does not depend on the particular likes and dislikes of individual men. If it is wrong to torture people in New York, it is wrong anywhere. It could not be morally right, in Kant's view, for a judge in one state to sentence a man to five years in jail while the same offense was punished by two years of probation elsewhere. It could not be just for a judge to vary the sentence, depending on how he liked the looks of the defendant. The condition of objectivity and impartiality is of course highly general; it does not tell us anything about the content of the law. But the condition is enormously important to Kant, so important that he is inclined to sound almost inhuman when he discusses the inexorability of objective laws, the demand for equal punishment of every similar offense, regardless of how much unhappiness it may bring. The equality of men before the law, or, to put it the other way around, the demand that laws and their administration treat all men equally, is the *sine qua non* of justice.

Another formulation of the Categorical Imperative reads: "Act so that you treat humanity, whether in your own person or in that of another, always as an "end," never as a means only." The idea that man is an "end," something whose worth is not dependent on what we can *use* him for, is the most important moral presupposition of all. Beings that have a relative worth, as mere means to some end, are called "things"; but rational beings, people, are designated "persons." They may not be used merely as devices for achieving some desired effect. They are objects of respect; they have a worth rather than a price. Their worth, Kant believes, is tied up with their freedom to determine what they do by considerations of principle and by the idea of lawfulness, so that morality and freedom, in the sense of "autonomy," are reciprocal notions. By his doctrine of "autonomy" Kant means to extend Rousseau's concept of political freedom (a state in which people are bound only by laws which they themselves have legislated) to the individual agent. A man has autonomy, a will of his own, when his decisions are not coerced by any power external to him. He is not the victim of arbitrary orders, not even those of God, nor is he a slave to his own passions and appetites, fears and desires.[16] He is his own man, *Selbstständig*, in the fullest sense.

The Categorical Imperative is defended in a little book entitled *Fundamental Principles of the Metaphysics of Morals.* At that title suggests, the foundations of ethics are not the whole story; the book was only to be the beginning of a "system" of ethics that would survey all that we can know *a priori*

---

[16] Kant thinks that basing ethics on religion is a mistake, if it means that a man conforms to moral demands out of fear of God's punishment or for the sake of a hoped-for reward. Such actions would be *in accord* with the moral law but would lack moral worth, since they would not be motivated by respect for morality as such.

about moral questions.[17] The application of such a system to specific questions as to what I should or should not do would require empirical information about human beings and their situations and would thus not be a part of philosophy proper.

The *a priori* principles which Kant defends in the *Fundamental Principles* do tell us enough to suggest some of the features of Kant's political philosophy. It is not surprising to find that he disagrees with earlier political theorists who regarded war as a legitimate instrument of national policy, the natural way to settle conflicts between states.[18] Kant contemptuously compares these men to Job's "irritating comforters." Their hope of civilizing the conduct of international relations is in vain, Kant argues, so long as there is no international government to end the Hobbesian "state of nature" in which each state jealously asserts its "savage freedom." And it is not surprising that he condemns standing armies as morally offensive: "To pay men to kill or be killed seems to entail using them as mere machines and tools in the hand of another [the state] and this is hardly compatible with the rights of mankind in our own person."[19] Kant's pacifism was not at all thoroughgoing, for he condones wars of self-defense against foreign aggression. But he speaks out forcefully against punitive wars (the idea that a state has the right to "punish" another is based on an incoherent master-servant assumption) and denounces wars of extermination as especially inhuman. He argues also against specific methods of warfare that even a just war could not justify: espionage, assassination, incitement to treason are some of his examples. They are forbidden because they would destroy the possibility of mutual confidence after hostilities are ended. Kant thinks that even one's enemies must be regarded

---

[17] It is important to notice that there is more to Kant's moral philosophy than the *Fundamental Principles (Grundlegung)*. The discussion of actual duties is found in the *Metaphysics of Morals*. It is divided into two main parts, *Metaphysical Principles of Virtue (Tugendlehre)* and *Metaphysical Elements of Justice*, or jurisprudence (*Rechtslehre*). Roughly, this division is between duties that cannot be enforced by the law and those that can. The excerpt from the *Tugendlehre* included in this anthology shows Kant to be far more flexible when it comes to the *application* of moral principles to actual situations than one might expect him to be if one read only the *Grundlegung*.

Another work, the *Critique of Practical Reason*, develops the arguments of the *Grundlegung*. It tries to explain how a man's will could be determined by "pure reason," independently of any "sensuous" motives. It also discusses God and immortality, arguing that they are legitimate objects of "rational faith."

[18] Theorists such as Hugo Grotius (1583–1645), Samuel von Pufendorf (1632–1694), Emerich de Vattel (1714–1767).

[19] "Perpetual Peace," in *Kant on History* (New York: Bobbs-Merrill, 1963), p. 87.

as human beings. Perhaps his most eloquent statement of this credo is in the *Fundamental Principles*: "Now I say man and in general every rational being exists as an end in himself and not merely as a means to be arbitrarily used by this or that will. In all his actions, whether they are directed to himself or to other rational beings, he must always be regarded as an end . . . [Nonrational beings] have only a relative worth as means and are therefore called "things"; on the other hand, rational beings are designated "persons" because their nature indicates that they are ends in themselves, i.e., things which may not be used merely as means. Such a being is thus an object of respect and, to that extent, restricts every possible choice. . . . In the realm of ends everything has either a *price* or a *dignity*. Whatever has a price can be replaced by something else as its equivalent; on the other hand, whatever is above all price, and therefore admits of no equivalent, has a dignity."

There is a great deal more to Kant's philosophy than has been mentioned in this Introduction. Kant's discussion of aesthetics, in the third of his critiques, the *Critique of Judgement*, is profound, even though Kant's own aesthetic appreciation was extraordinarily limited. We have hardly discussed Kant's philosophy of religion; his letter to Lavater, included in this anthology, gives a good picture of Kant's position. Kant's lifelong contempt for religious ceremonies, prayers, and other observances as totally irrelevant to the moral core of "rational belief" (*Vernunftglaube*) is forcefully stated in that letter. His philosophy of religion is developed more fully in *Religion within the Limits of Reason Alone*, a work that includes a profoundly pessimistic chapter, "On the Radical Evil in Human Nature," worthy of St. Augustine or John Calvin.[20] It is inevitable, with a thinker of Kant's depth and versatility, that the "essential Kant" should omit much that would be essential to a full portrait of this great philosopher. The works included do, I hope, provide more than just a taste of his arguments and more than a hint of his stature.

ARNULF ZWEIG
University of Oregon

[20] Kant's Pietistic upbringing shows itself again and again. *Religion* is available in a translation by T. M. Greene and H. H. Hudson (New York: Harper and Row, 1960) which includes a useful introductory essay by John Silber.

Selected Bibliography

Kant's commentators are often harder to read than Kant himself. Fortunately, there are some recent studies of his work that can be recommended to English language readers as first rate both in substance and in readability. Every serious student of Kant will want to read some of the following:

General Surveys:

L. W. Beck, *Early German Philosophy* (Cambridge, Mass.: Harvard University Press, 1969).

J. Kemp, *The Philosophy of Kant* (Oxford: Oxford University Press, 1968).

S. Körner, *Kant* (Baltimore: Penguin Books, 1955).

W. H. Walsh, "Kant," in *Encyclopedia of Philosophy* (Crowell Collier and Macmillan, 1966).

On the *Critique of Pure Reason:*

J. Bennett, *Kant's Analytic* (Cambridge University Press, 1966).

P. F. Strawson, *The Bounds of Sense* (London: Methuen, 1966).

H. J. Paton, *Kant's Metaphysics of Experience* (New York: Macmillan, 1936).

N. Kemp Smith, *A Commentary to Kant's Critique of Pure Reason* (London: Macmillan, 1918).

T. D. Weldon, *Kant's Critique of Pure Reason* (London: Oxford University Press, 1958).

R. P. Wolff, *Kant's Theory of Mental Activity* (Cambridge, Mass.: Harvard University Press, 1963).

On Kant's Moral Philosophy:

L. W. Beck, *A Commentary on Kant's Critique of Practical Reason* (Chicago: University of Chicago Press, 1960).

Mary J. Gregor, *Laws of Freedom* (New York: Barnes and Noble, 1963).

For some insights into Kant's personality, his relations to his contemporaries and his responses to critics, see Kant, *Philosophical Correspondence: 1759–1799,* edited and translated by by Arnulf Zweig (Chicago: University of Chicago Press, 1967).

Admirable translations of Kant's writings other than the most famous ones are now available in the Library of Liberal Arts, published by Bobbs-Merrill. For example:

The Metaphysical Elements of Justice, trans. by John Ladd, 1965.

Kant on History (a collection of several essays, including "What is Enlightenment?" and "Perpetual Peace," trans. by Lewis White Beck, 1963.

First Introduction to the Critique of Judgement, trans. by James Haden, 1965.

Analytic of the Beautiful (from the *Critique of Judgement*), trans. by Walter Cerf, 1963.

II. Kant's Letters to Marcus Herz
and J. C. Lavater

Letter to Marcus Herz, February 21, 1772

Noble sir,
Esteemed friend,
    You do me no injustice if you become indignant at the total
absence of my replies; but lest you draw any disagreeable conclusions from it, let me appeal to your understanding of the
way I think. Instead of excuses, I shall give you a brief account
of the kind of things that have occupied my thoughts and that
cause me to put off letter-writing in my idle hours. After your
departure from Königsberg I examined once more, in the inter-
vals between my professional duties and my sorely needed
relaxation, the project that we had debated, in order to adapt

it to the whole of philosophy and other knowledge and in order to understand its extent and limits. I had already previously made considerable progress in the effort to distinguish the sensible from the intellectual in the field of morals and the principles that spring therefrom. I had also long ago outlined, to my tolerable satisfaction, the principles of feeling, taste, and power of judgment, with their effects—the pleasant, the beautiful, and the good—and was then making plans for a work that might perhaps have the title, "The Limits of Sense and Reason." I planned to have it consist of two parts, a theoretical and a practical. The first part would have two sections, (1) general phenomenology and (2) metaphysics, but this only with regard to its nature and method. The second part likewise would have two sections, (1) the universal principles of feeling, taste, and sensuous desire and (2) the basic principles of morality. As I thought through the theoretical part, considering its whole scope and the reciprocal relations of all its parts, I noticed that I still lacked something essential, something that in my long metaphysical studies I, as well as others, had failed to pay attention to and that, in fact, constitutes the key to the whole secret of hitherto still obscure metaphysics. I asked myself: What is the ground of the relation of that in us which we call "representation" to the object? If a representation is only a way in which the subject is affected by the object, then it is easy to see how the representation is in conformity with this object, namely, as an effect in accord with its cause, and it is easy to see how this modification [*Bestimmung*] of our mind can *represent* something, that is, have an object. Thus the passive or sensuous representations have an understandable relationship to objects, and the principles that are derived from the nature of our soul have an understandable validity for all things insofar as those things are supposed to be objects of the senses. In the same way, if that in us which we call "representation" were active with regard to the object, that is, if the object itself were created by the representation (as when divine cognitions are conceived as the archetypes of all things), the conformity of these representations to their objects could be understood. Thus the possibility of both an *intellectus archetypi* (on whose intuition the things themselves would be grounded) and an *intellectus ectypi* (which would derive the data for its logical procedure from the sensuous intuition of things) is at least intelligible. However, our understanding, through its representations, is not the cause of the object (save in the case of moral ends), nor is the object [*Gegenstand*] the cause of the intellectual representations in the mind (*in sensu reali*). Therefore the pure concepts of the understanding must not be abstracted from sense perceptions, nor must they express the reception of representations through the senses; but though they must have their origin in the nature of the soul, they are neither caused by the object [Obiect] nor bring the object itself into being. In my dissertation I was content to explain the nature of intellectual representations in a merely negative way, namely, to state that they were not modifications of the soul brought about by the object. However, I silently passed over the further question of how a representation that refers to an object without being in any way affected by it can be possible. I had said: The sensuous representations present things as they appear, the intellectual representations present them as they are. But by what means are these things given to us, if not by the way in which they affect us? And if such intellectual representations depend on our inner activity, whence comes the agreement that they are supposed to have with objects—objects that are nevertheless not possibly produced thereby? And the axioms of pure reason concerning these objects—how do they agree with these objects, since the agreement has not been reached with the aid of experience? In mathematics this is possible, because the objects before us are quantities and can be represented as quantities only because it is possible for us to produce their mathematical representations (by taking numerical units a given number of times). Hence the concepts of the quantities can be spontaneous and their principles can be determined a priori. But in the case of relationships involving qualities—as to how my understanding may form for itself concepts of things completely a priori, with which concepts the things must necessarily agree, and as to how my understanding may formulate real principles concerning the possibility of such concepts, with which principles experience must be in exact agreement and which nevertheless are independent of experience—this question, of how the faculty of the understanding achieves this conformity with the things themselves, is still left in a state of obscurity.

Plato assumed a previous intuition of divinity as the primary source of the pure concepts of the understanding and of first principles. Mallebranche [sic] believed in a still-continuing perennial intuition of this primary being. Various moralists have accepted precisely this view with respect to basic moral laws. Crusius believed in certain implanted rules for the purpose of forming judgments and ready-made concepts that God implanted in the human soul just as they had to be in order to harmonize with things. Of these systems, one may call the former the influxum hyperphysicum and the latter the harmoniam praestabilitam intellectualem. But the deus ex machina is the greatest absurdity one could hit upon in the determination of the origin and validity of our knowledge. It has—besides its deceptive circle in the conclusion concerning our cognitions—also this additional disadvantage: it encourages all sorts of wild notions and every pious and speculative brainstorm.

While I was searching in such ways for the sources of intellectual knowledge, without which one cannot determine the nature and limits of metaphysics, I divided this science into its naturally distinct parts, and I sought to reduce the transcendental philosophy (that is to say, all concepts belonging to completely pure reason) to a certain number of categories, but not like Aristotle, who, in his ten predicaments, placed them side by side as he found them in a purely chance juxtaposition. On the contrary, I arranged them according to the way they classify themselves by their own nature, following a few fundamental laws of the understanding. Without going into details here about the whole series of investigations that has continued right down to this last goal, I can say that, so far as my essential purpose is concerned, I have succeeded and that now I am in a position to bring out a "Critique of Pure Reason" that will deal with the nature of theoretical as well as practical knowledge—insofar as the latter is purely intellectual. Of this, I will first work out the first part, which will deal with the sources of metaphysics, its methods and limits. After that I will work out the pure principles of morality. With respect to the first part, I should be in a position to publish it within three months.

In mental preoccupation of such delicate nature, nothing is more of a hindrance than to be occupied with thoughts that lie outside the scope of the field. Even though the mind is not always exerting itself, it must still, both in its relaxed and happy moments, remain uninterruptedly open to any chance suggestion that may present itself. Encouragements and diversions must serve to maintain the mind's powers of flexibility and mobility, whereby it is kept in readiness to view the subject matter from other sides all the time and to widen its horizon from a microscopic observation to a universal outlook in order that it may adopt all conceivable positions and that views from one may verify those from another. There has been no other reason than this, my worthy friend, for my delay in answering your pleasant letters—for you certainly don't want me to write you empty words.

With respect to your discerning and deeply thoughtful little work, several parts have exceeded my expectations.[1] However, for reasons already mentioned, I cannot let myself go in dis-

[1] Herz's *Betrachtungen aus der spekulativen Weltweisheit* (1771).

cussing details. But, my friend, the effect that an undertaking of this kind has on the status of the sciences among the educated public is such that when, because of the indisposition that threatens to interrupt its execution, I begin to feel anxious about my project (which I regard as my most important work, the greater part of which I have ready before me)—then I am frequently comforted by the thought that my work would be just as useless to the public if it is published as it would be if it remains forever unknown. For it takes a literary man with more reputation and eloquence than I have to stimulate his readers in such a way that they exert themselves to meditate on his writing.

I have found your essay reviewed in the Breslau paper and, just recently, in the Göttingen paper. If the public judges the spirit and principal intent of an essay in such a fashion, all effort is in vain. If the reviewer has taken pains to grasp the essential points of the effort, his criticism is more welcome to the author than all the excessive praise resulting from a superficial evaluation. The Göttingen reviewer dwells on several applications of the system that in themselves are trivial and with respect to which I myself have since changed my views— with the result, however, that my major purpose has only gained thereby. A single letter from Mendelssohn or Lambert means more to an author in terms of making him reexamine his theories than do ten such opinions from superficial pens. Honest Pastor Schultz, the best philosophical brain I know in this neighborhood, has grasped the points of the system very well; I wish that he might get busy on your little essay, too. There are two mistaken interpretations in his evaluation of the system that he is examining. The first one is the criticism that space, instead of being the pure form of sensuous appearance, might very well be a true intellectual intuition and thus might be objective. The obvious answer is that there is a reason why space is not given in advance as objective or as intellectual, namely, if we analyze fully the representation of space, we have in it neither a representation of things (as capable of existing only in space) nor a real connection (which cannot occur without things); that is to say, we have no effects, no relationships to regard as grounds, consequently no real representation of an object or anything real, nothing of what inheres in the thing, and therefore we must conclude that space is nothing objective.

The second misunderstanding leads him to an objection that has made me reflect considerably, because it seems to be the most serious objection that can be raised against the system, an objection that seems to occur naturally to everybody, and one that Mr. Lambert has raised.[2] It runs like this: Changes are something real (according to the testimony of inner sense). Now, they are possible only on the assumption of time; therefore time is something real that is involved in the determination of the things in themselves.

Then I asked myself: Why does one not accept the following parallel argument? Bodies are real (according to the testimony of outer sense). Now, bodies are possible only under the condition of space; therefore space is something objective and real that inheres in the things themselves. The reason lies in the fact that it is obvious, in regard to outer things, that one cannot infer the reality of the object from the reality of the representation, though in the case of inner sense the thinking or the existence of thought and the existence of my own self are one and the same. The key to this problem lies herein. There is no doubt that I must think my own state under the form of time and that therefore the form of the inner sensibility does give me the appearance of changes. I do not deny that changes are real, any more than I deny that bodies are real, even though by *real* I only mean that something real corresponds to the appearance. I can't even say that the inner appearance changes, for how would I observe this change if it doesn't appear to my inner sense? If one should say that it follows from this that everything in the world is objectively and in itself unchangeable, then I would reply: Things are neither changeable nor unchangeable. Just as Baumgarten states in his *Metaphysics*, paragraph 18: "The absolutely impossible is neither hypothetically possible nor impossible, for it cannot be considered under any condition," so also here, the things of the world are objectively or in themselves neither in one and the same state at different times nor in different states, for thus understood they are not in time at all.

But enough about this. It appears that one doesn't obtain a hearing by stating only negative propositions. One must rebuild on the plot where one has torn down, or at least, if one has cleared away the brainstorms, one must make the pure insights of the understanding dogmatically intelligible and delineate their limits. With this I am now occupied, and this is the reason why, often contrary to my own intent of answering friendly letters, I withhold from such tasks what free time my very frail constitution allows me for contemplation and give myself over to the net of my thoughts. And so long as you find me so negligent in replying, you should also give up the idea of repaying me and suffer me to go without your letters. Even so, I would

[2] See Lambert's letter of October 13, 1770.

count on your constant affection and friendship for me just as you may always remain assured of mine. If you will be satisfied with short answers then you shall have them in the future. Between us the assurance of the honest concern that we have for each other must take the place of formalities.

I await your next delightful letter as a token of your sincere reconciliation. And please fill it up with such accounts as you must have aplenty, living as you do at the very seat of the sciences, and please excuse my taking the liberty of asking for this. Greet Mr. Mendelssohn and Mr. Lambert, likewise Mr. Sultzer, and convey my apologies to these gentlemen for similar reasons.

Do remain forever my friend, just as I am yours!

I. KANT

Königsberg

Letter to J. C. Lavater, April 28, 1775

. . . You ask for my opinion of your discussion of faith and prayer. Do you realize whom you are asking? A man who believes that, in the final moment, only the purest candor concerning our most hidden inner convictions can stand the test and who, like Job, takes it to be sin to flatter God and make inner confessions, perhaps forced out by fear, that fail to agree with what we freely think. I distinguish the *teachings of Christ* from the *report* we have of those teachings. In order that the former may be seen in their purity, I seek above all to separate out the moral teachings from all the dogmas of the New Testament. These moral teachings are certainly the fundamental doctrine of the Gospels, and the remainder can only serve as an auxiliary to them. Dogmas tell us only what God has done to help us see our frailty in seeking justification before Him, whereas the moral law tells us what we must do to make ourselves worthy of justification. Suppose we were ignorant of what God does and suppose we were convinced only of this: that, because of the holiness of His law and the insuperable evil of our hearts, God must have hidden some supplement to our deficiencies somewhere in the depth of His decrees, something we could humbly rely on, if only we should do what is in our power, so as not to be unworthy of His law. If that were so, we should have all the guidance we need, whatever the manner of communication between the divine goodness and ourselves might be. Our trust in God is unconditional, that is, it is not accompanied by any inquisitive desire to know how His purposes will be achieved or, still less, by any presumptuous confidence that the soul's salvation will follow from our acceptance of certain Gospel disclosures. That is the meaning of the moral faith that I find in the Gospels, when I seek out the pure, fundamental teachings that underlie the mixture of facts and revelations there. Perhaps, in view of the opposition of Judaism, miracles and revelations were needed, in those days, to promulgate and disseminate a pure religion, one that would do away with all the world's dogmas. And perhaps it was necessary to have many *ad hominem* arguments, which would have great force in those times. But once the doctrine of the purity of conscience in faith and of the good transformation of our lives has been sufficiently propagated as the only true religion for man's salvation (the faith that God, in a manner we need not at all understand, will provide what our frail natures lack, without our seeking His aid by means of the so-called worship that religious fanaticism always demands)—when this true religious structure has been built up so that it can maintain itself in the world—then the scaffolding must be taken down. I respect the reports of the evangelists and apostles, and I put my humble trust in that means of reconciliation with God of which they have given us historical tidings—or in any other means that God, in his secret counsels, may have concealed. For I do not become in the least bit a better man if I know this, since it concerns only what God does; and I dare not be so presumptuous as to declare before God that this is the real means, the only means whereby I can attain my salvation and, so to speak, swear my soul and my salvation on it. For what those men give us are only their reports. I am not close enough to their times to be able to make such dangerous and audacious decisions. Moreover, even if I could be sure, it would not make me in any way more worthy of the good, were I to confess it, swear it, and fill up my soul with it, though that may be of help to some people. On the contrary, nothing is needed for my union with this divine force except my using my natural God-given powers in such a way as not to be unworthy of His aid or, if you prefer, unfit for it.

When I spoke of New Testament dogmas I meant to include everything of which one could become convinced only through historical reports, and I also had in mind those confessions or ceremonies that are enjoined as a supposed condition of salvation. By "moral faith" I mean the unconditional trust in divine aid, in achieving all the good that, even with our most sincere efforts, lies beyond our power. Anyone can be convinced of the correctness and necessity of moral faith, once it is made clear to him. The auxiliary historical devices are not necessary for this, even if some individuals would in fact not have reached this insight without the historical revelation. Now, considered as history, our New Testament writings can never be so esteemed as to make us dare to have unlimited trust in every word of them, and especially if this were to weaken our attentiveness to the one necessary thing, namely, the moral faith of the Gospels, whose excellence consists in just this: that all our striving for purity of conscience and the conscientious conversion of our lives toward the good are here drawn together. Yet all this is done in such a way that the holy law lies perpetually before our eyes and reproaches us continually for even the slightest deviation from the divine will, just as though we were condemned by a just and unrelenting judge. And no confession of faith, no appeal to holy names nor any observance of religious ceremonies can help—though the consoling hope is offered us that, if we do as much good as is in our power, trusting in the unknown and mysterious help of God, we shall (without meritorious "works" of any sort) partake of this divine supplement. Now, it is very clear that the apostles took this biblical doctrine of divine aid as the fundamental thesis of the Gospels, and whatever might be the actual *basis* of our salvation from God's point of view, the apostles took the essential requirement for salvation to be not the honoring of the holy teacher's religious doctrine of conduct but rather the veneration of this teacher himself and a sort of wooing of favor by means of ingratiation and encomium—the very things against which that teacher had so explicitly and repeatedly preached. Their procedure was in fact more suitable for those times (for which they were writing, without concern for later ages) than for our own. For in those days the old miracles had to be opposed by new miracles, and Jewish dogmas by Christian dogmas.

Here I must quickly break off, postponing the rest till my next letter (which I enclose). My most devoted compliments to your worthy friend Mr. Pfenniger.

Your sincere friend,
I. KANT

To J. C. Lavater [after April 28, 1775]
(Enclosed in the previous letter)

I would rather add something incomplete to my interrupted letter than nothing at all. My presupposition is that no book, whatever its authority might be—yes, even one based on the testimony of my own senses—can substitute for the religion of conscience. The latter tells me that the holy law within me has already made it my duty to answer for everything I do and that I must not dare to cram my soul with devotional testimonies, confessions, and so on, which do not spring from the unfeigned and unmistaking precepts of that law. For although statutes may bring about the performance of rituals, they cannot beget inner convictions. Because of this presupposition, I seek in the Gospels not the ground of my faith but its fortification, and I find in the moral spirit of the Gospels a clear distinction between what I am obligated to do and the manner in which this message is to be introduced into the world and disseminated, a distinction, in short, between my duty and that which God has done for me. The means of disclosure of my obligations may be what it will—nothing new is thereby provided for me, though my good convictions are given new strength and confidence. So much for the clarification of that part of my letter in which I spoke of the separation of two related but unequivalent parts of the holy scriptures and of their application to me.

As for your request that I give my opinion of the ideas on faith and prayer in your *Vermischte Schriften* ["Miscellaneous Writings" (1774)], the essential and most excellent part of the teachings of Christ is this: that righteousness is the sum of all religion and that we ought to seek it with all our might, having faith (that is, an unconditional trust) that God will then supplement our efforts and supply the good that is not in our power. This doctrine of faith forbids all our presumptuous curiosity about the manner in which God will do this, forbids the arrogance of supposing that one can know what means would be most in conformity with His wisdom; it forbids, too, all wooing of favor by the performing of rituals that someone has introduced. It allows no part of that endless religious madness to which people in all ages are inclined, save only the general and undefined trust that we shall partake of the good in some unknown way, if only we do not make ourselves unworthy of our share of it by our conduct.

III. Critique of Pure Reason

[A:1–2]

Introduction

I: THE IDEA OF TRANSCENDENTAL PHILOSOPHY

[Experience is no doubt the first product of our understanding, while employed in fashioning the raw material of our sensations. It is therefore our first instruction, and in its progress so rich in new lessons that the chain of all future generations will never be in want of new information that may be gathered on that field. Nevertheless, experience is by no means the only field to which our understanding can be confined. Experience tells us what is, but not that it must be necessarily as it is, and not otherwise. It therefore never gives us any really general truths, and our reason, which is particularly anxious for that class of knowledge, is roused by it rather than satisfied. General truths, which at the same time bear the character of an inward necessity, must be independent of experience—clear and certain by themselves. They are therefore called knowledge *a priori,* while what is simply taken from experience is said to be, in ordinary parlance, known *a posteriori* or empirically only.

Now it appears, and this is extremely curious, that even with our experiences different kinds of knowledge are mixed up, which must have their origin *a priori,* and which perhaps serve only to produce a certain connection between our sensuous

representations. For even if we remove from experience everything that belongs to the senses, there remain nevertheless
certain original concepts, and certain judgments derived from
them, which must have had their origin entirely *a priori*, and
independent of all experience, because it is owing to them that
we are able, or imagine we are able, to predicate more of the
objects of our senses than can be learnt from mere experience,
and that our propositions contain real generality and strict
necessity, such as mere empirical knowledge can never supply.]

1. OF THE DIFFERENCE BETWEEN PURE AND EMPIRICAL KNOWLEDGE

*That all our knowledge begins with experience there can be
no doubt. For how should the faculty of knowledge be called
into activity, if not by objects which affect our senses, and
which either produce representations by themselves, or rouse
the activity of our understanding to compare, to connect, or
to separate them; and thus to convert the raw material of our
sensuous impressions into a knowledge of objects, which we
call experience? In respect of time, therefore, no knowledge
within us is antecedent to experience, but all knowledge begins
with it.*

*But although all our knowledge begins with experience, it
does not follow that it arises from experience. For it is quite
possible that even our empirical experience is a compound of
that which we receive through impressions, and of that which
our own faculty of knowledge (incited only by sensuous impressions), supplies from itself, a supplement which we do
not distinguish from that raw material, until long practice has
roused our attention and rendered us capable of separating
one from the other.*

*It is therefore a question which deserves at least closer
investigation, and cannot be disposed of at first sight, whether
there exists a knowledge independent of experience, and even
of all impressions of the senses? Such* knowledge *is called*
a priori, *and distinguished from* empirical *knowledge, which
has its sources* a posteriori, *that is, in experience.*

This term a priori, *however, is not yet definite enough to
indicate the full meaning of our question. For people are wont
to say, even with regard to knowledge derived from experience, that we have it, or might have it,* a priori, *because we
derive it from experience, not* immediately, *but from a general
rule, which, however, has itself been derived from experience.*

Thus one would say of a person who undermines the foundations of his house, that he might have known a priori that it would tumble down, that is, that he need not wait for the experience of its really tumbling down. But still he could not know this entirely a priori, because he had first to learn from experience that bodies are heavy, and will fall when their supports are taken away.

We shall therefore, in what follows, understand by knowledge a priori knowledge which is absolutely independent of all experience, and not of this or that experience only. Opposed to this is empirical knowledge, or such as is possible a posteriori only, that is, by experience. Knowledge a priori, if mixed up with nothing empirical, is called pure. *Thus the proposition, for example, that every change has its cause, is a proposition a priori, but not pure: because change is a concept which can only be derived from experience.*

2. WE ARE IN POSSESSION OF CERTAIN COGNITIONS A PRIORI, AND EVEN THE ORDINARY UNDERSTANDING IS NEVER WITHOUT THEM

All depends here on a criterion, by which we may safely distinguish between pure and empirical knowledge. Now experience teaches us, no doubt, that something is so or so, but not that it cannot be different. First, then, if we have a proposition, which is thought, together with its necessity, we have a judgment a priori; and if, besides, it is not derived from any proposition, except such as is itself again considered as necessary, we have an absolutely a priori judgment. Secondly, experience never imparts to its judgments true or strict, but only assumed or relative universality (by means of induction), so that we ought always to say, so far as we have observed hitherto, there is no exception to this or that rule. If, therefore, a judgment is thought with strict universality, so that no exception is admitted as possible, it is not derived from experience, but valid absolutely a priori. Empirical universality, therefore, is only an arbitrary extension of a validity which applies to most cases, to one that applies to all: as, for instance, in the proposition, all bodies are heavy. If, on the contrary, strict universality is essential to a judgment, this always points to a special source of knowledge, namely, a faculty of knowledge a priori. Necessity, therefore, and strict universality are safe criteria of knowledge a priori, and are inseparable one from the other. As, however, in the use of the criteria, it is some-

*times easier to show the contingency than the empirical limita-
tion[1] of judgments, and as it is sometimes more convincing to
prove the unlimited universality which we attribute to a judgment than its necessity, it is advisable to use both criteria separately, each being by itself infallible.*

*That there really exist in our knowledge such necessary, and
in the strictest sense universal, and therefore pure judgments*
a priori, *is easy to show. If we want a scientific example, we
have only to look to any of the propositions of mathematics;
if we want one from the sphere of the ordinary understanding, such a proposition as that each change must have a cause,
will answer the purpose; nay, in the latter case, even the concept of cause contains so clearly the concept of the necessity
of its connection with an effect, and of the strict universality
of the rule, that it would be destroyed altogether if we attempted to derive it, as Hume does, from the frequent concomitancy of that which happens with that which precedes,
and from a habit arising thence (therefore from a purely subjective necessity), of connecting representations. It is possible
even, without having recourse to such examples in proof of the
reality of pure propositions* a priori *within our knowledge, to
prove their indispensability for the possibility of experience itself, thus proving it* a priori. *For whence should experience
take its certainty, if all the rules which it follows were always
again and again empirical, and therefore contingent and hardly
fit to serve as first principles? For the present, however, we
may be satisfied for having shown the pure employment of
the faculty of our knowledge as a matter of fact, with the
criteria of it.*

*Not only in judgments, however, but even in certain con-
cepts, can we show their origin* a priori. *Take away, for example, from the concept of a body, as supplied by experience,
everything that is empirical, one by one; such as colour, hardness or softness, weight, and even impenetrability, and there
still remains the space which the body (now entirely vanished)
occupied: that you cannot take away. And in the same manner, if you remove from your empirical concept of any object, corporeal or incorporeal, all properties which experience
has taught you, you cannot take away from it that property by
which you conceive it as a substance, or inherent in a substance (although such a concept contains more determinations
than that of an object in general). Convinced, therefore, by
the necessity with which that concept forces itself upon you,*

---

[1] According to an emendation adopted both by Vaihinger and
Adickes.

you will have to admit that it has its seat in your faculty of knowledge a priori.

But[2] what is still more extraordinary is this, that certain kinds of knowledge leave the field of all possible experience, and seem to enlarge the sphere of our judgments beyond the limits of experience by means of concepts to which experience can never supply any corresponding objects.

And it is in this very kind of knowledge which transcends the world of the senses, and where experience can neither guide nor correct us, that reason prosecutes its investigations, which by their importance we consider far more excellent and by their tendency far more elevated than anything the understanding can find in the sphere of phenomena. Nay, we risk rather anything, even at the peril of error, than that we should surrender such investigations, either on the ground of their uncertainty, or from any feeling of indifference or contempt. *These inevitable problems of pure reason itself are,* God, Freedom, *and* Immortality. *The science which with all its apparatus is really intended for the solution of these problems, is called* Metaphysic. *Its procedure is at first* dogmatic, *i.e. unchecked by a previous examination of what reason can and cannot do, before it engages confidently in so arduous an undertaking.*

Now it might seem natural that, after we have left the solid ground of experience, we should not at once proceed to erect an edifice with knowledge which we possess without knowing whence it came, and trust to principles the origin of which is unknown, without having made sure of the safety of the foundations by means of careful examination. It would seem natural, I say, that philosophers should first of all have asked the question how the mere understanding could arrive at all this knowledge *a priori,* and what extent, what truth, and what value it could possess. If we take natural to mean what is just and reasonable, then indeed nothing could be more natural. But if we understand by natural what takes place ordinarily, then, on the contrary, nothing is more natural and more intelligible than that this examination should have been neglected for so long a time. For one part of this knowledge, namely, the mathematical, has always been in possession of perfect trustworthiness; and thus produces a favourable presumption with regard to other parts also, although these may be of a totally different nature. Besides, once beyond the precincts of

    [2] The Second Edition gives here a new heading: III, Philosophy requires a science to determine the possibility, the principles, and the extent of all cognitions *a priori.*

experience, and we are certain that experience can never contradict us, while the charm of enlarging our knowledge is so
great that nothing will stop our progress until we encounter a
clear contradiction. This can be avoided if only we are cau-
tious in our imaginations, which nevertheless remain what they
are, imaginations only. How far we can advance independent
of all experience in *a priori* knowledge is shown by the brilliant example of mathematics. It is true they deal with objects
and knowledge so far only as they can be represented in intuition. But this is easily overlooked, because that intuition itself may be given *a priori,* and be difficult to distinguish from a
pure concept. Thus inspirited by a splendid proof of the power
of reason, the desire of enlarging our knowledge sees no limits.
The light dove, piercing in her easy flight the air and perceiving
its resistance, imagines that flight would be easier still in empty
space. It was thus that Plato left the world of sense, as opposing so many hindrances to our understanding, and ventured
beyond on the wings of his ideas into the empty space of pure
understanding. He did not perceive that he was making no
progress by these endeavours, because he had no resistance as
a fulcrum on which to rest or to apply his powers, in order to
cause the understanding to advance. It is indeed a very common fate of human reason first of all to finish its speculative
edifice as soon as possible, and then only to enquire whether
the foundation be sure. Then all sorts of excuses are made in
order to assure us as to its solidity, or to decline altogether
such a late and dangerous enquiry. The reason why during the
time of building we feel free from all anxiety and suspicion and
believe in the apparent solidity of our foundation, is this: A
great, perhaps the greatest portion of what our reason finds to
do consists in the analysis of our concepts of objects. This gives
us a great deal of knowledge which, though it consists in no
more than in simplifications and explanations of what is comprehended in our concepts (though in a confused manner), is
yet considered as equal, at least in form, to new knowledge.
It only separates and arranges our concepts, it does not enlarge them in matter or contents. As by this process we gain a
kind of real knowledge *a priori,* which progresses safely and
usefully, it happens that our reason, without being aware of
it, appropriates under that pretence propositions of a totally
different character, adding to given concepts new and strange
ones *a piori,* without knowing whence they come, nay without
even thinking of such a question. I shall therefore at the very
outset treat of the distinction between these two kinds of
knowledge.

4. OF THE DISTINCTION BETWEEN ANALYTICAL AND SYNTHETICAL JUDGMENTS

In all judgments in which there is a relation between subject and predicate (I speak of affirmative judgments only, the application to negative ones being easy), that relation can be of two kinds. Either the predicate B belongs to the subject A as something contained (though covertly) in the concept A; or B lies outside the sphere of the concept A, though somehow connected with it. In the former case I call the judgment analytical, in the latter synthetical. Analytical judgments (affirmative) are therefore those in which the connection of the predicate with the subject is conceived through identity, while others in which that connection is conceived without identity, may be called synthetical. The former might be called illustrating, the latter expanding judgments, because in the former nothing is added by the predicate to the concept of the subject, but the concept is only divided into its constituent concepts which were always conceived as existing within it, though confusedly; while the latter add to the concept of the subject a predicate not conceived as existing within it, and not to be extracted from it by any process of mere analysis. If I say, for instance, All bodies are extended, this is an analytical judgment. I need not go beyond the concept connected with the name of body, in order to find that extension is connected with it. I have only to analyse that concept and become conscious of the manifold elements always contained in it, in order to find that predicate. This is therefore an analytical judgment. But if I say, All bodies are heavy, the predicate is something quite different from what I think as the mere concept of body. The addition of such a predicate gives us a synthetical judgment.

[It becomes clear from this,

1. That our knowledge is in no way extended by analytical judgments, but that all they effect is to put the concepts which we possess into better order and render them more intelligible.

2. That in synthetical judgments I must have besides the concept of the subject something else (x) on which the understanding relies in order to know that a predicate, not contained in the concept, nevertheless belongs to it.

In empirical judgments this causes no difficulty, because this x is here simply the complete experience of an object which I conceive by the concept A, that concept forming one part only of my experience. For though I do not include the predicate of gravity in the general concept of body, that concept nevertheless indicates the complete experience through one of its parts, so that I may add other parts also of the same experience, all belonging to that concept. I may first, by an analytical process, realise the concept of body through the predicates of extension, impermeability, form, etc., all of which are contained in it. Afterwards I expand my knowledge, and looking back to the experience from which my concept of body was abstracted, I find gravity always connected with the before-mentioned predicates. Experience therefore is the *x* which lies beyond the concept A, and on which rests the possibility of a synthesis of the predicate of gravity B with the concept A.]

Empirical judgments, as such, are all synthetical; for it would be absurd to found an analytical judgment on experience, because, in order to form such a judgment, I need not at all step out of my concept, or appeal to the testimony of experience. That a body is extended, is a proposition perfectly certain a priori, and not an empirical judgment. For, before I call in experience, I am already in possession of all the conditions of my judgment in the concept of body itself. I have only to draw out from it, according to the principle of contradiction, the required predicate, and I thus become conscious, at the same time, of the necessity of the judgment, which experience could never teach me. But, though I do not include the predicate of gravity in the general concept of body, that concept, nevertheless, indicates an object of experience through one of its parts: so that I may add other parts also of the same experience, besides those which belonged to the former concept. I may, first, by an analytical process, realise the concept of body, through the predicates of extension, impermeability, form, etc., all of which are contained in it. Afterwards I expand my knowledge, and looking back to the experience from which my concept of body was abstracted, I find gravity always connected with the before-mentioned predicates, and therefore I add it synthetically to that concept as a predicate. It is, therefore, experience on which the possibility of the synthesis of the predicate of gravity with the concept of body is founded: because both concepts, though neither of them is contained in the other, belong to each other, though accidentally only, as parts of a whole, namely, of experience, which is itself a synthetical connection of intuitions.

In synthetical judgments *a priori,* however, that help is entirely wanting. If I want to go beyond the concept A in order to find another concept B connected with it, where is there anything on which I may rest and through which a synthesis might become possible, considering that I cannot have the advantage of looking about in the field of experience? Take the proposition that all which happens has its cause. In the concept of something that happens I no doubt conceive of something existing preceded by time, and from this certain analytical judgments may be deduced. But the concept of cause is entirely outside that concept, and indicates something different from that which happens, and is by no means contained in that representation. How can I venture then to predicate of that which happens something totally different from it, and to represent the concept of cause, though not contained in it, as belonging to it, and belonging to it by necessity? What is here the unknown *x,* on which the understanding may rest in order to find beyond the concept A a foreign predicate B, which nevertheless is believed to be connected with it? It cannot be experience, because the proposition that all which happens has its cause represents this second predicate as added to the subject not only with greater generality than experience can ever supply, but also with a character of necessity, and therefore purely *a priori,* and based on concepts. All our speculative knowledge *a priori* aims at and rests on such synthetical, i.e. expanding propositions, for the analytical are no doubt very important and necessary, yet only in order to arrive at that clearness of concepts which is requisite for a safe and wide synthesis, serving as a really new addition to what we possess already.

[We have here a certain mystery* before us, which must be cleared up before any advance into the unlimited field of a pure knowledge of the understanding can become safe and trustworthy. We must discover on the largest scale the ground of the possibility of synthetical judgments *a priori;* we must understand the conditions which render every class of them possible, and endeavour not only to indicate in a sketchy outline, but to define in its fulness and practical completeness, the whole of that knowledge, which forms a class by itself, systematically arranged according to its original sources, its

---

* If any the ancients had ever thought of asking this question, this alone would have formed a powerful barrier against all systems of pure reason to the present day, and would have saved many vain attempts undertaken blindly and without a true knowledge of the subject in hand.

divisions, its extent and its limits. So much for the present with regard to the peculiar character of synthetical judgments.]

5. IN ALL THEORETICAL SCIENCES OF REASON SYNTHETICAL JUDGMENTS A PRIORI ARE CONTAINED AS PRINCIPLES

1. All mathematical judgments are synthetical. This proposition, though incontestably certain, and very important to us for the future, seems to have hitherto escaped the observation of those who are engaged in the anatomy of human reason: nay, to be directly opposed to all their conjectures. For as it was found that all mathematical conclusions proceed according to the principle of contradiction (which is required by the nature of all apodictic certainty), it was supposed that the fundamental principles of mathematics also rested on the authority of the same principle of contradiction. This, however, was a mistake: for though a synthetical proposition may be understood according to the principle of contradiction, this can only be if another synthetical proposition is presupposed, from which the latter is deduced, but never by itself. First of all, we ought to observe, that mathematical propositions, properly so called, are always judgments a priori, *and not empirical, because they carry along with them necessity, which can never be deduced from experience. If people should object to this, I am quite willing to confine my statement to pure mathematics, the very concept of which implies that it does not contain empirical, but only pure knowledge* a priori.

At first sight one might suppose indeed that the proposition 7+5=12 *is merely analytical, following, according to the principle of contradiction, from the concept of a sum of 7 and 5. But, if we look more closely, we shall find that the concept of the sum of 7 and 5 contains nothing beyond the union of both sums into one, whereby nothing is told us as to what this single number may be which combines both. We by no means arrive at a concept of Twelve, by thinking that union of Seven and Five; and we may analyse our concept of such a possible sum as long as we will, still we shall never discover in it the concept of Twelve. We must go beyond these concepts, and call in the assistance of the intuition corresponding to one of the two, for instance, our five fingers, or, as Segner does in his arithmetic, five points, and so by degrees add the units of the Five, given in intuition, to the concept of the Seven. For I first take the number 7, and taking the intuition of the fingers of my hand, in order to form with it the concept of the 5, I gradually add the units, which I before took together, to make up the number 5, by means of the image of my hand, to the number 7, and I thus see the number 12 arising before me. That 5 should be added to 7 was no doubt implied in my concept of a sum 7 + 5, but not that that sum should be equal to 12. An arithmetical proposition is, therefore, always synthetical, which is seen more easily still by taking larger numbers, where we clearly perceive that, turn and twist our conceptions as we may, we could never, by means of the mere analysis of our concepts and without the help of intuition, arrive at the sum that is wanted.*

Nor is any proposition of pure geometry analytical. That the straight line between two points is the shortest, is a synthetical proposition. For my concept of straight *contains nothing of magnitude (quantity), but a quality only. The concept of the* shortest *is, therefore, purely adventitious, and cannot be deduced from the concept of the straight line by any analysis whatsoever. The aid of intuition, therefore, must be called in, by which alone the synthesis is possible.*

[It is true that some few propositions, presupposed by the geometrician, are really analytical, and depend on the principle of contradiction: but then they serve only, like identical propositions, to form the chain of the method, and not as principles. Such are the propositions, a=a, *the whole is equal to itself, or* (a+b)>a, *that the whole is greater than its part. And even these, though they are valid according to mere concepts, are only admitted in mathematics, because they can be represented in intuition.]*[3] *What often makes us believe that the predicate of such apodictic judgments is contained in our concept, and the judgment therefore analytical, is merely the ambiguous character of the expression. We are told that we* ought *to join in thought a certain predicate to a given concept, and this necessity is inherent in the concepts themselves. But the question is not what we* ought *to join to the given concept, but what we* really think *in it, though confusedly only, and then it becomes clear that the predicate is no doubt*

---

[3] This paragraph from *It is true* to *intuition* seems to have been a marginal note, as shown by Dr. Vaihinger.

inherent in those concepts by necessity, not, however, as thought in the concept itself, but by means of an intuition, which must be added to the concept.

2. Natural science (physica) contains synthetical judgments *a priori as principles. I shall adduce, as examples, a few propositions only, such as, that in all changes of the material world the quantity of matter always remains unchanged: or that in all communication of motion, action and reaction must always equal each other. It is clear not only that both convey necessity, and that, therefore, their origin is a priori, but also that they are synthetical propositions. For in the concept of matter I do not conceive its permanency, but only its presence in the space which it fills. I therefore go beyond the concept of matter in order to join something to it a priori, which I did not before conceive in it. The proposition is, therefore, not analytical, but synthetical, and yet a priori, and the same applies to the other propositions of the pure part of natural science.*

3. Metaphysic, *even if we look upon it as hitherto a tentative science only, which, however, is indispensable to us, owing to the very nature of human reason, is meant to* contain synthetical knowledge a priori. *Its object is not at all merely to analyse such concepts as we make to ourselves of things a priori, and thus to explain them analytically, but to expand our knowledge a priori. This we can only do by means of concepts which add something to a given concept that was not contained in it; nay, we even attempt, by means of synthetical judgments a priori, to go so far beyond a given concept that experience itself cannot follow us: as, for instance, in the proposition that the world must have a first beginning. Thus, according at least to its intentions, metaphysic consists merely of synthetical propositions a priori.*

6. THE GENERAL PROBLEM OF PURE REASON

Much is gained if we are able to bring a number of investigations under the formula of one single problem. For we thus not only facilitate our own work by defining it accurately, but enable also everybody else who likes to examine it to form a judgment, whether we have really done justice to our purpose or not. Now the real problem of pure reason is contained in the question, How are synthetical judgments *a priori* possible?

That metaphysic has hitherto remained in so vacillating a state of ignorance and contradiction is entirely due to people not having thought sooner of this problem, or perhaps even of a distinction between analytical *and* synthetical *judgments. The solution of this problem, or a sufficient proof that a possibility which is to be explained does in reality not exist at all, is the question of life or death to metaphysic.* David Hume, *who among all philosophers approached nearest to that problem, though he was far from conceiving it with sufficient definiteness and universality, confining his attention only to the synthetical proposition of the connection of an effect with its causes* (principium causalitatis), *arrived at the conclusion that such a proposition* a priori *is entirely impossible. According to his conclusions, everything which we call metaphysic would turn out to be a mere delusion of reason, fancying that it knows by itself what in reality is only borrowed from experience, and has assumed by mere habit the appearance of necessity. If he had grasped our problem in all its universality, he would never have thought of an assertion which destroys all pure philosophy, because he would have perceived that, according to his argument, no pure mathematical science was possible either, on account of its certainly containing synthetical propositions* a priori; *and from such an assertion his good sense would probably have saved him.*

On the solution of our problem depends, at the same time, the possibility of the pure employment of reason, in establishing and carrying out all sciences which contain a theoretical knowledge a priori *of objects, i.e. the answer to the questions*

How is pure mathematical science possible?

How is pure natural science possible?

As these sciences really exist, it is quite proper to ask, How *they are possible? for that* they must be possible, *is proved by their reality.**

But as to metaphysic, *the bad progress which it has hitherto made, and the impossibility of asserting of any of the metaphysical systems yet brought forward that it really exists, so*

---

* One might doubt this with regard to pure natural science; but one has only to consider the different propositions which stand at the beginning of real (empirical) physical science, those, for example, relating to the permanence of the same quantity of matter to the vis inertiae, *the equality of action and reaction, etc., in order to become convinced that they constitute a* physica pura, *or* rationalis, *which well deserves to stand by itself as an independent science, in its whole extent, whether narrow or wide.*

*far as its essential aim is concerned, must fill every one with
doubts as to its possibility.*

Yet, in a certain sense, this kind of knowledge *also must be
looked upon as given, and though not as a science, yet as a
natural disposition* (metaphysica naturalis) *metaphysic is real.
For human reason, without being moved merely by the con-
ceit of omniscience, advances irresistibly, and urged on by its
own need, to questions such as cannot be answered by any
empirical employment of reason, or by principles thence derived, so that we may really say, that all men, as soon as their
reason became ripe for speculation, have at all times possessed
some kind of metaphysic, and will always continue to possess
it. And now it will also have to answer the question*

How is metaphysic possible, as a natural disposition? *That
is, how does the nature of universal human reason give rise
to questions which pure reason proposes to itself, and which
it is urged on by its own need to answer as well as it can?*

*As, however, all attempts which have hitherto been made
at answering these natural questions (for instance, whether the
world has a beginning, or exists from all eternity) have always
led to inevitable contradictions, we cannot rest satisfied with
the mere natural disposition to metaphysic, that is, with the
pure faculty of reason itself, from which some kind of metaphysic (whatever it may be) always arises; but it must be possible to arrive with it at some certainty as to our either knowing or not knowing its objects; that is, we must either decide
that we can judge of the objects of these questions, or of the
power or want of power of reason, in deciding anything upon
them—therefore that we can either enlarge our pure reason
with certainty, or that we have to impose on it fixed and firm
limits. This last question, which arises out of the former more
general problem, would properly assume this form,*

How is metaphysic possible, as a science?

*The critique of reason leads, therefore, necessarily, to true
science, while its dogmatical use, without criticism, lands us
in groundless assertions, to which others, equally specious, can
always be opposed, that is, in* scepticism.

*Nor need this science be very formidable by its great pro-
lixity, for it has not to deal with the objects of reason, the
variety of which is infinite, but with reason only, and with
problems, suggested by reason and placed before it, not by
the nature of things, which are different from it, but by its
own nature; so that, if reason has only first completely understood its own power, with reference to objects given to it in
experience, it will have no difficulty in determining com-*

pletely and safely the extent and limits of its attempted application beyond the limits of all experience.

We may and must therefore regard all attempts which have hitherto been made at building up a metaphysic dogmatically, as non-avenu. For the mere analysis of the concepts that dwell in our reason a priori, which has been attempted in one or other of those metaphysical systems, is by no means the aim, but only a preparation for true metaphysic, namely, the answer to the question, how we can enlarge our knowledge a priori synthetically; nay, it is utterly useless for that purpose, because it only shows what is contained in those concepts, but not by what process a priori we arrive at them, in order thus to determine the validity of their employment with reference to all objects of knowledge in general. Nor does it require much self-denial to give up these pretensions, considering that the undeniable and, in the dogmatic procedure, inevitable contradictions of reason with itself, have long deprived every system of metaphysic of all authority. More firmness will be required in order not to be deterred by difficulties from within and resistance from without, from trying to advance a science, indispensable to human reason (a science of which we may lop off every branch, but will never be able to destroy the root), by a treatment entirely opposed to all former treatments, which promises, at last, to ensure the successful and fruitful growth of metaphysical science.

It will now be seen how there can be a special science serving as a critique of pure reason. [Every kind of knowledge is called pure, if not mixed with anything heterogeneous. But more particularly is that knowledge called absolutely pure, which is not mixed up with an experience or sensation, and is therefore possible entirely *a priori*.] Reason is the faculty which supplies the principles of knowledge *a priori*. Pure reason therefore is that faculty which supplies the principles of knowing anything entirely *a priori*. An Organum of pure reason ought to comprehend all the principles by which pure knowledge *a priori* can be acquired and fully established. A complete application of such an Organum would give us a System of Pure Reason. But as that would be a difficult task, and as at present it is still doubtful whether and when such an expansion of our knowledge is here possible, we may look on a mere criticism of pure reason, its sources and limits, as a kind of preparation for a complete system of pure reason. It should be called a critique, not a doctrine, of pure reason. Its usefulness would be negative only, serving for a purging rather than for an expansion of our reason, and, what after all is a considerable gain, guarding reason against errors.

I call all knowledge *transcendental* which is occupied not so much with objects, [as with our *a priori* concepts of objects,] *as with our manner of knowing objects, so far as this is meant to be possible* a priori. A system of such concepts might be called Transcendental Philosophy. But for the present this is again too great an undertaking. We should have to treat therein completely both of analytical knowledge, and of synthetical knowledge *a priori,* which is more than we intend to do, being satisfied to carry on the analysis so far only as is indispensably necessary in order to recognise in their whole extent the principles of synthesis *a priori,* which alone concern us. This investigation which should be called a transcendental critique, but not a systematic doctrine, is all we are occupied with at present. It is not meant to extend our knowledge, but only to rectify it, and to become the test of the value of all *a priori* knowledge. Such a critique therefore is a preparation for a New Organum, or, if that should not be possible, for a Canon at least, according to which hereafter a complete system of a philosophy of pure reason, whether it serve for any expansion or merely for a limitation of it, may be carried out, both analytically and synthetically. That such a system is possible, nay that it need not be so comprehensive as to prevent the hope of its completion, may be gathered from the fact that it would have to deal, not with the nature of things, which is endless, but with the understanding which judges of the nature of things, and this again so far only as its knowledge *a priori* is concerned. Whatever the understanding possesses *a priori,* as it has not to be looked for without, can hardly escape our notice, nor is there any reason to suppose that it will prove too extensive for a complete inventory, and for such a valuation as shall assign to it its true merits or demerits.

Still less ought we to except here a criticism on the books and systems treating of pure reason, but only on the faculty of pure reason itself. It is only if we are in possession of this, that we possess a safe criterion for estimating the philosophical value of old and new works on this subject. Otherwise, an unqualified historian and judge does nothing but criticise the groundless assertions of others by means of his own, which are equally groundless.

II. Division of Transcendental Philosophy

Transcendental Philosophy is with us an idea (of a science) only, for which the critique of pure reason should trace, according to fixed principles, an architectonic plan, guaranteeing the completeness and certainty of all parts of which the building consist. *It is a system of all principles of pure reason.* The reason why we do not call such a critique a transcendental philosophy in itself is simply this, that in order to be a complete system, it ought to contain likewise a complete analysis of the whole of human knowledge *a priori*. It is true that our critique must produce a complete list of all the fundamental concepts which constitute pure knowledge. But it need not give a detailed analysis of these concepts, nor a complete list of all derivative concepts. Such an analysis would be out of place, because it is not beset with the doubts and difficulties which are inherent in synthesis, and which alone necessitate a critique of pure reason. Nor would it answer our purpose to take the responsibility of the completeness of such an analysis and derivation. This completeness of analysis, however, and of derivation from such *a priori* concepts as we shall have to deal with presently, may easily be supplied, if only they have first been laid down as perfect principles of synthesis, and nothing is wanting to them in that respect.

All that constitutes transcendental philosophy belongs to the critique of pure reason, nay it is the complete idea of transcendental philosophy, but not yet the whole of that philosophy itself, because it carries the analysis so far only as is requisite for a complete examination of synthetical knowledge *a priori*.

The most important consideration in the arrangement of such a science is that no concepts should be admitted which contain anything empirical, and that the *a priori* knowledge shall be perfectly pure. Therefore, although the highest principles of morality and their fundamental concepts are *a priori* knowledge, they do not belong to transcendental philosophy, because the concepts of pleasure and pain, desire, inclination, free-will, etc., which are all of empirical origin, must here be presupposed. Transcendental philosophy is the wisdom of pure speculative reason. Everything practical, so far as it contains motives, has reference to sentiments, and these belong to empirical sources of knowledge.

If we wish to carry out a proper division of our science systematically, it must contain first *a doctrine of the elements*, secondly, *a doctrine of the method* of pure reason. Each of these principal divisions will have its subdivisions, the grounds of which cannot however be explained here. So much only seems necessary for previous information, that there are two stems of human knowledge, which perhaps may spring from a common root, unknown to us, viz. *sensibility* and the *understanding*, objects being given by the former and thought by the latter. If our sensibility should contain *a priori* representations, constituting conditions under which alone objects can be given, it would belong to transcendental philosophy, and the doctrine of this transcendental sense-perception would necessarily form the first part of the doctrine of elements, because the conditions under which alone objects of human knowledge can be given must precede those under which they are thought.

Transcendental Elements
First Part

TRANSCENDENTAL AESTHETIC

§ 1[4]

Whatever the process and the means may be by which knowledge reaches its objects, there is one that reaches them directly, and forms the ultimate material of all thought, viz. intuition (*Anschauung*). This is possible only when the object is given, and the object can be given only (to human beings at least) through a certain affection of the mind (*Gemüth*).

This faculty (receptivity) of receiving representations (*Vorstellungen*), according to the manner in which we are affected by objects, is called sensibility (*Sinnlichkeit*).

Objects therefore are given to us through our sensibility. Sensibility alone supplies us with intuitions (*Anschauungen*). These intuitions become thought through the understanding (*Verstand*), and hence arise conceptions (*Begriffe*). All thought therefore must, directly or indirectly, go back to intuitions (*Anschauungen*), i.e. to our sensibility, because in no other way can objects be given to us.

[4] These section numbers do not appear in the first edition.

The effect produced by an object upon the faculty of representation (*Vorstellungsfähigkeit*), so far as we are affected by it, is called sensation (*Empfindung*). An intuition (*Anschauung*) of an object, by means of sensation, is called empirical. The undefined object of such an empirical intuition is called phenomenon (*Erscheinung*).

In a phenomenon I call that which corresponds to the sensation its *matter;* but that which causes the manifold matter of the phenomenon to be perceived as arranged in a certain order, I call its *form.*

Now it is clear that it cannot be sensation again through which sensations are arranged and placed in certain forms. The matter only of all phenomena is given us *a posteriori;* but their form must be ready for them in the mind (*Gemüth*) *a priori,* and must therefore be capable of being considered as separate from all sensations.

I call all representations in which there is nothing that belongs to sensation, *pure* (in a transcendental sense). The pure form therefore of all sensuous intuitions, that form in which the manifold elements of the phenomena are seen in a certain order, must be found in the mind *a priori.* And this pure form of sensibility may be called the pure intuition (*Anschauung*).

Thus, if we deduct from the representation (*Vorstellung*) of a body what belongs to the thinking of the understanding, viz. substance, force, divisibility, etc., and likewise what belongs to sensation, viz. impermeability, hardness, colour, etc., there still remains something of that empirical intuition (*Anschauung*), viz. extension and form. These belong to pure intuition, which *a priori,* and even without a real object of the senses or of sensation, exists in the mind as a mere form of sensibility.

The science of all the principles of sensibility *a priori* I call *Transcendental Aesthetic.** There must be such a science, forming the first part of the Elements of Transcendentalism, as

---

* The Germans are the only people who at present (1781) use the word *aesthetic* for what others call criticism of taste. There is implied in that name a false hope, first conceived by the excellent analytical philosopher, Baumgarten, of bringing the critical judgment of the beautiful under rational principles, and to raise its rules to the rank of a science. But such endeavours are vain. For such rules or criteria are, according to their principal sources, empirical only, and can never serve as definite *a priori* rules for our judgment in matters of taste; on the contrary, our judgment is the real test of the truth of such rules. It would be advisable therefore to drop the name in that sense, and to apply it to a doctrine which is a real science, thus approaching more nearly to the language and meaning of the ancients with whom the division into αἰσθητὰ καὶ νοητά was very famous (or to share that name in common with speculative philosophy, and thus to use aesthetic sometimes in a transcendental, sometimes in a psychological sense).

opposed to that which treats of the principles of pure thought, and which should be called *Transcendental Logic*.

In Transcendental Aesthetic therefore we shall first isolate sensibility, by separating everything which the understanding adds by means of its concepts, so that nothing remains but empirical intuition (*Anschauung*).

Secondly, we shall separate from this all that belongs to sensation (*Empfindung*), so that nothing remains but pure intuition (*reine Anschauung*) or the mere form of the phenomena, which is the only thing which sensibility *a priori* can supply. In the course of this investigation it will appear that there are, as principles of *a priori* knowledge, two pure forms of sensuous intuition (*Anschauung*), namely, *Space* and *Time*. We now proceed to consider these more in detail.

FIRST SECTION OF THE TRANSCENDENTAL AESTHETIC

§ 2. OF SPACE

By means of our external sense, a property of our mind (*Gemüth*), we represent to ourselves objects as external or outside ourselves, and all of these in space. It is within space that their form, size, and relative position are fixed or can be fixed. The internal sense by means of which the mind perceives itself or its internal state, does not give an intuition (*Anschauung*) of the soul (*Seele*) itself, as an object, but it is nevertheless a fixed form under which alone an intuition of its internal state is possible, so that whatever belongs to its internal determinations (*Bestimmungen*) must be represented in relations of time. Time cannot be perceived (*angeschaut*) externally, as little as space can be perceived as something within us.

What then are space and time? Are they real beings? Or, if not that, are they determinations or relations of things, but such as would belong to them even if they were not perceived? Or lastly, are they determinations and relations which are inherent in the form of intuition only, and therefore in the subjective nature of our mind, without which such predicates as space and time would never be ascribed to anything?

In order to understand this more clearly, let us first consider space.

1. Space is not an empirical concept which has been derived from external experience. For in order that certain sensations should be referred to something outside myself, i.e. to something in a different part of space from that where I am; again, in order that I may be able to represent them (*vorstellen*) as side by side, that is, not only as different, but as in different places, the representation (*Vorstellung*) of space must already be there. Therefore the representation of space cannot be borrowed through experience from relations of external phenomena, but, on the contrary, this external experience becomes possible only by means of the representation of space.

2. Space is a necessary representation *a priori*, forming the very foundation of all external intuitions. It is impossible to imagine that there should be no space, though one might very well imagine that there should be space without objects to fill it. Space is therefore regarded as a condition of the possibility of phenomena, not as a determination produced by them; it is a representation *a priori* which necessarily precedes all external phenomena.

[3. On this necessity of an *a priori* representation of space rests the apodictic certainty of all geometrical principles, and the possibility of their construction *a priori*. For if the intuition of space were a concept gained *a posteriori*, borrowed from general external experience, the first principles of mathematical definition would be nothing but perceptions. They would be exposed to all the accidents of perception, and there being but one straight line between two points would not be a necessity, but only something taught in each case by experience. Whatever is derived from experience possesses a relative generality only, based on induction. We should therefore not be able to say more than that, so far as hitherto observed, no space has yet been found having more than three dimensions.]

4. (*3*) Space is not a discursive or so-called general concept of the relations of things in general, but a pure intuition. For, first of all, we can imagine one space only and if we speak of many spaces, we mean parts only of one and the same space. Nor can these parts be considered as antecedent to the one and all-embracing space and, as it were, its component parts out of which an aggregate is formed, but they can be thought of as existing within it only. Space is essentially one; its multiplicity, and therefore the general concept of spaces in general, arises entirely from limitations. Hence it follows that, with respect to space, an intuition *a priori*, which is not empirical, must form the foundation of all conceptions of space. In the same manner all geometrical principles, e.g. 'that in every triangle two sides together are greater than the third,' are never to be derived

from the general concepts of side and triangle, but from an intuition, and that *a priori*, with apodictic certainty.

[5. Space is represented as an infinite quantity. Now a general concept of space, which is found in a foot as well as in an ell, could tell us nothing in respect to the quantity of the space. If there were not infinity in the progression of intuition, no concept of relations of space could ever contain a principle of infinity.]

4. *Space is represented as an infinite given quantity. Now it is quite true that every concept is to be thought as a representation, which is contained in an infinite number of different possible representations (as their common characteristic), and therefore comprehends them: but no concept, as such, can be thought as if it contained in itself an infinite number of representations. Nevertheless, space is so thought (for all parts of infinite space exist simultaneously). Consequently, the original representation of space is an* intuition *a priori, and not a concept.*

§ 3. TRANSCENDENTAL EXPOSITION OF THE CONCEPT

OF SPACE

I understand by transcendental exposition (Erörterung), *the explanation of a concept, as of a principle by which the possibility of other synthetical cognitions a priori can be understood. For this purpose it is necessary, 1. That such cognitions really do flow from the given concept. 2. That they are possible only under the presupposition of a given mode of explanation of such concept.*

Geometry is a science which determines the properties of space synthetically, and yet a priori. *What then must be the representation of space, to render such a knowledge of it possible? It must be originally intuitive; for it is impossible from a mere concept to deduce propositions which go beyond that concept, as we do in geometry (Introduction, p. 52). That intuition, however, must be a priori, that is, it must exist within us before any perception of the object, and must therefore be pure, not empirical intuition. For all geometrical propositions are apodictic, that is, connected with the consciousness of their necessity, as for instance the proposition, that space has only three dimensions; and such propositions cannot be empirical judgments, nor conclusions from them (Introduction, p. 44).*

How then can an external intuition dwell in the mind anterior to the objects themselves, and in which the concept of objects can be determined a priori? *Evidently not otherwise than so far as it has its seat in the subject only, as the formal condition under which the subject is affected by the objects and thereby is receiving an* immediate representation, *that is,* intuition *of them; therefore as a form of the external sense in general.*

It is therefore by our explanation only that the possibility *of* geometry *as a synthetical science* a priori *becomes intelligible. Every other explanation, which fails to account for this possibility, can best be distinguished from our own by that criterion, although it may seem to have some similarity with it.*

Conclusions from the Foregoing Concepts

a. Space does not represent any quality of objects by themselves, or objects in their relation to one another; i.e. space does not represent any determination which is inherent in the objects themselves, and would remain, even if all subjective conditions of intuition were removed. For no determinations of objects, whether belonging to them absolutely or in relation to others, can enter into our intuition before the actual existence of the objects themselves, that is to say, they can never be intuitions *a priori.*

b. Space is nothing but the form of all phenomena of the external senses; it is the subjective condition of our sensibility, without which no external intuition is possible for us. If then we consider that the receptivity of the subject, its capacity of being affected by objects, must necessarily precede all intuition of objects, we shall understand how the form of all phenomena may be given before all real perceptions, may be, in fact, *a priori* in the soul, and may, as a pure intuition, by which all objects must be determined, contain, prior to all experience, principles regulating their relations.

It is therefore from the human standpoint only that we can speak of space, extended objects, etc. If we drop the subjective condition under which alone we can gain external intuition, that is, so far as we ourselves may be affected by objects, the representation of space means nothing. For this predicate is applied to objects only in so far as they appear to us, and are objects of our senses. The constant form of this receptivity, which we call sensibility, is a necessary condition of all relations in which objects, as without us, can be perceived; and, when abstraction is made of these objects, what remains is that pure intuition which we call space. As the peculiar conditions of our sensibility cannot be looked upon as conditions of the possibility of the objects themselves, but only of their appear-

ance as phenomena to us, we may say indeed that space comprehends all things which may appear to us externally, but not
all things by themselves, whether perceived by us or not, or by
any subject whatsoever. We cannot judge whether the intuitions of other thinking beings are subject to the same conditions which determine our intuition, and which for us are
generally binding. If we add the limitation of a judgment to a
subjective concept, the judgment gains absolute validity. The
proposition 'all things are beside each other in space,' is valid
only under the limitation that things are taken as objects of
our sensuous intuition (*Anschauung*). If I add that limitation
to the concept and say 'all things, as external phenomena, are
beside each other in space,' the rule obtains universal and unlimited validity. Our discussions teach therefore the reality,
i.e. the objective validity, of space with regard to all that can
come to us externally as an object, but likewise the *ideality* of
space with regard to things, when they are considered in themselves by our reason, and independent of the nature of our
senses. We maintain the empirical reality of space, so far as
every possible external experience is concerned, but at the same
time its transcendental ideality; that is to say, we maintain that
space is nothing, if we leave out of consideration the condition
of a possible experience, and accept it as something on which
things by themselves are in any way dependent.

With the exception of space there is no other subjective
representation (*Vorstellung*) referring to something external,
that would be called *a priori* objective. [This subjective condition of all external phenomena cannot therefore be compared
to any other. The taste of wine does not belong to the objective
determinations of wine, considered as an object, even as a phenomenal object, but to the peculiar nature of the sense belonging to the subject that tastes the wine. Colours are not qualities
of a body, though inherent in its intuition, but they are likewise
modifications only of the sense of sight, as it is affected in different ways by light. Space, on the contrary, as the very condition of external objects, is essential to their appearance or intuition. Taste and colour are by no means necessary conditions
under which alone things can become to us objects of sensuous
perception. They are connected with their appearance, as accidentally added effects only of our peculiar organisation. They
are not therefore representations *a priori,* but are dependent on
sensation (*Empfindung*), nay taste even on an affection (*Ge-
fühl*) of pleasure and pain, which is the result of a sensation.
No one can have *a priori*, an idea (*Vorstellung*) either of colour or of taste, but space refers to the pure form of intuition
only, and involves no kind of sensation, nothing empirical;

nay all kinds and determinations of space can and must be represented *a priori*, if concepts of forms and their relations are to arise. Through it alone is it possible that things should become external objects to us.]

With the exception of space there is no other subjective representation, referring to something external, that could be called a priori *objective. For from none of them can we derive synthetical propositions* a priori, *as we can from the intuition in space § 3. Strictly speaking, therefore, they can claim no ideality at all, though they agree with the representation of space in this, that they belong only to the subjective nature of sensibility, for instance, of sight, of hearing, and feeling, through the sensations of colours, sounds, and heat. All these, however, being sensations only, and not intuitions, do not help us by themselves to know any object, least of all* a priori.

My object in what I have said just now is only to prevent people from imagining that they can elucidate the ideality of space by illustrations which are altogether insufficient, such as colour, taste, etc., which should never be considered as qualities of things, but as modifications of the subject, and which therefore may be different with different people. For in this case that which originally is itself a phenomenon only, as for instance, a rose, is taken by the empirical understanding for a thing by itself, which nevertheless, with regard to colour, may appear different to every eye. The transcendental conception, on the contrary, of all phenomena in space, is a critical warning that nothing which is seen in space is a thing by itself, nor space a form of things supposed to belong to them by themselves, but that objects by themselves are not known to us at all, and that what we call external objects are nothing but representations of our senses, the form of which is space, and the true correlative of which, that is the thing by itself, is not known, nor can be known by these representations, nor do we care to know anything about it in our daily experience.

SECOND SECTION OF THE TRANSCENDENTAL AESTHETIC

§ 4. OF TIME[5]

I. Time is not an empirical concept deduced from any experience, for neither coexistence nor succession would enter into our perception, if the representation of time were not given *a priori*. Only when this representation *a priori* is given, can we imagine that certain things happen at the same time (simultaneously) or at different times (successively).

II. Time is a necessary representation on which all intuitions depend. We cannot take away time from phenomena in general, though we can well take away phenomena out of time. Time therefore is given *a priori*. In time alone is reality of phenomena possible. All phenomena may vanish, but time itself (as the general condition of their possibility) cannot be done away with.

III. On this *a priori* necessity depends also the possibility of apodictic principles of the relations of time, or of axioms of time in general. Time has one dimension only; different times are not simultaneous, but successive, while different spaces are never successive, but simultaneous. Such principles cannot be derived from experience, because experience could not impart to them absolute universality nor apodictic certainty. We should only be able to say that common experience teaches us that it is so, but not that it must be so. These principles are valid as rules under which alone experience is possible; they teach us before experience, not by means of experience.[6]

IV. Time is not a discursive, or what is called a general concept, but a pure form of sensuous intuition. Different times are parts only of one and the same time. Representation, which can be produced by a single object only, is called an intuition. The proposition that different times cannot exist at the same time cannot be deduced from any general concept. Such a proposition is synthetical, and cannot be deduced from concepts only.

---

[5] In the Second Edition the title is, Metaphysical exposition of the concept of time, with reference to par. 5, Transcendental exposition of the concept of time.

[6] I retain the reading of the First Edition, *vor derselben, nicht durch dieselbe*. *Von denselben*, the reading of later editions, is wrong; the emendation of Rosenkranz, *vor denselben, nicht durch dieselben*, unnecessary. The Second Edition has likewise *vor derselben*.

It is contained immediately in the intuition and representation of time.

V. To say that time is infinite means no more than that every definite quantity of time is possible only by limitations of one time which forms the foundation of all times. The original representation of time must therefore be given as unlimited. But when the parts themselves and every quantity of an object can be represented as determined by limitation only, the whole representation cannot be given by concepts (for in that case the partial representations come first), but it must be founded on immediate intuition.

§ 5. TRANSCENDENTAL EXPOSITION OF THE CONCEPT

OF TIME

I can here refer to [see footnote p. 46] where, for the sake of brevity, I have placed what is properly transcendental under the head of metaphysical exposition. Here I only add that the concept of change, and with it the concept of motion (as change of place), is possible only through and in the representation of time; and that, if this representation were not intuitive (internal) a priori, no concept, whatever it be, could make us understand the possibility of a change, that is, of a connection of contradictorily opposed predicates (for instance, the being and not-being of one and the same thing in one and the same place) in one and the same object. It is only in time that both contradictorily opposed determinations can be met with in the same object, that is, one after the other. Our concept of time, therefore, exhibits the possibility of as many synthetical cognitions a priori as are found in the general doctrine of motion, which is very rich in them.

Conclusions from the foregoing concepts

a. Time is not something existing by itself, or inherent in things as an objective determination of them, something therefore that might remain when abstraction is made of all subjective conditions of intuition. For in the former case it would be something real, without being a real object. In the latter it could not, as a determination or order inherent in things themselves, be antecedent to things as their condition, and be known and perceived by means of synthetical propositions *a priori*. All this is perfectly possible if time is nothing but a subjective condition under which alone[7] intuitions take place within us. For in that case this form of internal intuition can be represented prior to the objects themselves, that is, *a priori*.

b. Time is nothing but the form of the internal sense, that is, of our intuition of ourselves, and of our internal state. Time cannot be a determination peculiar to external phenomena. It refers neither to their shape, nor their position, etc., it only determines the relation of representations in our internal state. And exactly because this internal intuition supplies no shape, we try to make good this deficiency by means of analogies, and represent to ourselves the succession of time by a line progressing to infinity, in which the manifold constitutes a series of one dimension only; and we conclude from the properties of this line as to all the properties of time, with one exception, i.e. that the parts of the former are simultaneous, those of the latter successive. From this it becomes clear also, that the representation of time is itself an intuition, because all its relations can be expressed by means of an external intuition.

c. Time is the formal condition, *a priori*, of all phenomena whatsoever. Space, as the pure form of all external intuition, is a condition, *a priori*, of external phenomena only. But, as all representations, whether they have for their objects external things or not, belong by themselves, as determinations of the mind, to our inner state, and as this inner state falls under the formal conditions of internal intuition, and therefore of time, time is a condition, *a priori*, of all phenomena whatsoever, and is so directly as a condition of internal phenomena (of our mind) and thereby indirectly of external phenomena also. If I am able to say, *a priori*, that all external phenomena are in space, and are determined, *a priori*, according to the relations of space, I can, according to the principle of the internal sense, make the general assertion that all phenomena, that is, all objects of the senses, are in time, and stand necessarily in relations of time.

If we drop our manner of looking at ourselves internally, and of comprehending by means of that intuition all external intuitions also within our power of representation, and thus take objects as they may be by themselves, then time is nothing. Time has objective validity with reference to phenomena only, because these are themselves things which we accept as objects of our senses; but time is no longer objective, if we remove the sensuous character of our intuitions, that is to say, that mode of representation which is peculiar to ourselves, and speak of things in general. Time is therefore simply a subjec-

---

[7] Read *allein* instead of *alle*.

tive condition of our (human) intuition (which is always sensuous, that is so far as we are affected by objects), but by itself, apart from the subject, nothing. Nevertheless, with respect to all phenomena, that is, all things which can come within our experience, time is necessarily objective. We cannot say that all things are in time, because, if we speak of things in general, nothing is said about the manner of intuition, which is the real condition under which time enters into our representation of things. If therefore this condition is added to the concept, and if we say that all things as phenomena (as objects of sensuous intuition) are in time, then such a proposition has its full objective validity and *a priori* universality.

What we insist on therefore is the empirical reality of time, that is, its objective validity, with reference to all objects which can ever come before our senses. And as our intuition must at all times be sensuous, no object can ever fall under our experience that does not come under the conditions of time. What we deny is, that time has any claim on absolute reality, so that, without taking into account the form of our sensuous condition, it should by itself be a condition or quality inherent in things; for such qualities which belong to things by themselves can never be given to us through the senses. This is what constitutes the transcendental ideality of time, so that, if we take no account of the subjective conditions of our sensuous intuitions, time is nothing, and cannot be added to the objects by themselves (without their relation to our intuition) whether as subsisting or inherent. This ideality of time, however, as well as that of space, should not be confounded with the deceptions of our sensations, because in their case we always suppose that the phenomenon to which such predicates belong has objective reality, which is not at all the case here, except so far as this objective reality is purely empirical, that is, so far as the object itself is looked upon as a mere phenomenon. On this subject see a previous note, in section 2, on Space.

Explanation

Against this theory which claims empirical, but denies absolute and transcendental reality to time, even intelligent men have protested so unanimously, that I suppose that every reader who is unaccustomed to these considerations may naturally be of the same opinion. What they object to is this: Changes, they say, are real (this is proved by the change of our own representations, even if all external phenomena and their changes be denied). Changes, however, are possible in time only, and therefore time must be something real. The answer is easy enough. I grant the whole argument. Time certainly is something real, namely, the real form of our internal intuition. Time therefore has subjective reality with regard to internal experience: that is, I really have the representation of time and of my determinations in it. Time therefore is to be considered as real, not so far as it is an object, but so far as it is the representation of myself as an object. If either I myself or any other being could see me without this condition of sensibility, then these self-same determinations which we now represent to ourselves as changes, would give us a kind of knowledge in which the representation of time, and therefore of change also, would have no place. There remains therefore the empirical reality of time only, as the condition of all our experience, while absolute reality cannot, according to what has just been shown, be conceded to it. Time is nothing but the form of our own internal intuition.* Take away the peculiar condition of our sensibility, and the idea of time vanishes, because it is not inherent in the objects, but in the subject only that perceives them.

The reason why this objection is raised so unanimously, and even by those who have nothing very tangible to say against the doctrine of the ideality of space, is this. They could never hope to prove apodictically the absolute reality of space, because they are confronted by idealism, which has shown that the reality of external objects does not admit of strict proof, while the reality of the object of our internal perceptions (the perception of my own self and of my own status) is clear immediately through our consciousness. The former might be merely phenomenal, but the latter, according to their opinion, is undeniably something real. They did not see that both, without denying to them their reality as representations, belong nevertheless to the phenomenon only, which must always have two sides, the one when the object is considered by itself (without regard to the manner in which it is perceived, its quality therefore remaining always problematical), the other, when the form of the perception of the object is taken into consideration; this form belonging not to the object in itself, but to the subject which perceives it, though nevertheless belonging really and necessarily to the object as a phenomenon.

Time and space are therefore two sources of knowledge from which various *a priori* synthetical cognitions can be de-

---

* I can say indeed that my representations follow one another, but this means no more than that we are conscious of them as in a temporal succession, that is, according to the form of our own internal sense. Time, therefore, is nothing by itself, nor is it a determination inherent objectively in things.

rived. Of this pure mathematics give a splendid example in the case of our cognitions of space and its various relations. As they are both pure forms of sensuous intuition, they render synthetical propositions *a priori* possible. But these sources of knowledge *a priori* (being conditions of our sensibility only) fix their own limits, in that they can refer to objects only in so far as they are considered as phenomena, but cannot represent things as they are by themselves. That is the only field in which they are valid; beyond it they admit of no objective application. This ideality of space and time, however, leaves the truthfulness of our experience quite untouched, because we are equally sure of it, whether these forms are inherent in things by themselves, or by necessity in our intuition of them only. Those, on the contrary, who maintain the absolute reality of space and time, whether as subsisting or only as inherent, must come into conflict with the principles of experience itself. For if they admit space and time as subsisting (which is generally the view of mathematical students of nature) they have to admit two eternal infinite and self-subsisting nonentities (space and time), which exist without their being anything real, only in order to comprehend all that is real. If they take the second view (held by some metaphysical students of nature), and look upon space and time as relations of phenomena, simultaneous or successive, abstracted from experience, though represented confusedly in their abstracted form, they are obliged to deny to mathematical propositions *a priori* their validity with regard to real things (for instance in space), or at all events their apodictic certainty, which cannot take place *a posteriori,* while the *a priori* conceptions of space and time are, according to their opinion, creations of our imagination only. Their source, they hold, must really be looked for in experience, imagination framing out of the relations abstracted from experience something which contains the general character of these relations, but which cannot exist without the restrictions which nature has imposed on them. The former gain so much that they keep at least the sphere of phenomena free for mathematical propositions; but, as soon as the understanding endeavours to transcend that sphere, they become bewildered by these very conditions. The latter have this advantage that they are not bewildered by the representations of space and time when they wish to form judgments of objects, not as phenomena, but only as considered by the understanding; but they can neither account for the possibility of mathematical knowledge *a priori* (there being, according to them, no true and objectively valid intuition *a priori*), nor can they bring the laws of experience into true harmony with the *a priori* doctrines of mathematics.

According to our theory of the true character of these original forms of sensibility, both difficulties vanish.

Lastly, that transcendental aesthetic cannot contain more than these two elements, namely, space and time, becomes clear from the fact that all other concepts belonging to the senses, even that of motion, which combines both, presuppose something empirical. Motion presupposes the perception of something moving. In space, however, considered by itself, there is nothing that moves. Hence that which moves must be something which, as in space, can be given by experience only, therefore an empirical datum. On the same ground, transcendental aesthetic cannot count the concept of change among its *a priori* data, because time itself does not change, but only something which is in time. For this, the perception of something existing and of the succession of its determinations, in other words, experience, is required.

§ 8. GENERAL OBSERVATIONS ON TRANSCENDENTAL AESTHETIC

In order to avoid all misapprehensions it will be necessary, first of all, to declare, as clearly as possible, what is our view with regard to the fundamental nature of sensuous knowledge.

What we meant to say was this, that all our intuition is nothing but the representation of phenomena; that things which we see are not by themselves what we see, nor their relations by themselves such as they appear to us, so that, if we drop our subject or the subjective form of our senses, all qualities, all relations of objects in space and time, nay space and time themselves, would vanish. They cannot, as phenomena, exist by themselves, but in us only. It remains completely unknown to us what objects may be by themselves and apart from the receptivity of our senses. We know nothing but our manner of perceiving them, that manner being peculiar to us, and not necessarily shared in by every being, though, no doubt, by every human being. This is what alone concerns us. Space and time are pure forms of our intuition, while sensation forms its matter. What we can know *a priori*—before all real intuition, are the forms of space and time, which are therefore called pure intuition, while sensation is that which causes our knowledge to be called *a posteriori* knowledge, i.e. empirical intuition. Whatever our sensation may be, these forms are necessarily inherent in it, while sensations themselves may be of the most different character. Even if we could impart the highest degree of clearness to our intuition, we should not come one step nearer to the nature of objects by themselves. We should know our mode of intuition, i.e. our sensibility, more completely, but always under the indefeasible conditions of space and time. What the objects are by themselves would never become known to us, even through the clearest knowledge of that which alone is given us, the phenomenon.

It would vitiate the concept of sensibility and phenomena, and render our whole doctrine useless and empty, if we were to accept the view (of Leibniz and Wolf), that our whole sensibility is really but a confused representation of things, simply containing what belongs to them by themselves, though smothered under an accumulation of signs (Merkmal) and partial concepts, which we do not consciously disentangle. The distinction between confused and well-ordered representation is logical only, and does not touch the contents of our knowledge. Thus the concept of Right, as employed by people of common sense, contains neither more nor less than the subtlest speculation can draw out of it, only that in the ordinary practical use of the word we are not always conscious of the manifold ideas contained in that thought. But no one would say therefore that the ordinary concept of Right was sensuous, containing a mere phenomenon; for Right can never become a phenomenon, being a concept of the understanding, and representing a moral quality belonging to actions by themselves. The representation of a Body, on the contrary, contains nothing in intuition that could belong to an object by itself, but is merely the phenomenal appearance of something, and the manner in which we are affected by it. This receptivity of our knowledge is called sensibility. Even if we could see to the very bottom of a phenomenon, it would remain for ever altogether different from the knowledge of the thing by itself.

This shows that the philosophy of Leibniz and Wolf has given a totally wrong direction to all investigations into the nature and origin of our knowledge, by representing the difference between the sensible and the intelligible as logical only. That difference is in truth transcendental. It affects not the form only, as being more or less confused, but the origin and contents of our knowledge; so that by our sensibility we know the nature of things by themselves not confusedly only, but not at all. If we drop our subjective condition, the object, as represented with its qualities bestowed on it by sensuous intuition, is nowhere to be found, and cannot possibly be found; because its form, as phenomenal appearance, is determined by those very subjective conditions.

It has been the custom to distinguish in phenomena that

which is essentially inherent in their intuition and is recognised by every human being, from that which belongs to their intuition accidentally only, being valid not for sensibility in general, but only for a particular position and organisation of this or that sense. In that case the former kind of knowledge is said to represent the object by itself, the latter its appearance only. But that distinction is merely empirical. If, as generally happens, people are satisfied with that distinction, without again, as they ought, treating the first empirical intuition as purely phenomenal also, in which nothing can be found belonging to the thing by itself, our transcendental distinction is lost, and we believe that we know things by themselves, though in the world of sense, however far we may carry our investigation, we can never have anything before us but mere phenomena. To give an illustration. People might call the rainbow a mere phenomenal appearance during a sunny shower, but the rain itself the thing by itself. This would be quite right, physically speaking, and taking rain as something which, in our ordinary experience and under all possible relations to our senses, can be determined thus and thus only in our intuition. But if we take the empirical in general, and ask, without caring whether it is the same with every particular observer, whether it represents a thing by itself (not the drops of rain, for these are already, as phenomena, empirical objects), then the question as to the relation between the representation and the object becomes transcendental, and not only the drops are mere phenomena, but even their round shape, nay even the space in which they fall, are nothing by themselves, but only modifications or fundamental dispositions of our sensuous intuition, the transcendental object remaining unknown to us.

The second important point in our transcendental aesthetic is, that it should not only gain favour as a plausible hypothesis, but assume as certain and undoubted a character as can be demanded of any theory which is to serve as an organum. In order to make this certainty self-evident we shall select a case which will make its validity palpable.

Let us suppose that space and time are in themselves objective, and conditions of the possibility of things by themselves. Now there is with regard to both a large number of *a priori* apodictic and synthetical propositions, and particularly with regard to space, which for this reason we shall chiefly investigate here as an illustration. As the propositions of geometry are known synthetically *a priori*, and with apodictic certainty, I ask, whence do you take such propositions? and what does the understanding rely on in order to arrive at such absolutely necessary and universally valid truths? There is no other way but by concepts and intuitions, and both as given either *a priori* or *a posteriori*. The latter, namely empirical concepts, as well as the empirical intuition on which they are founded, cannot yield any synthetical propositions except such as are themselves also empirical only, that is, empirical propositions, which can never possess that necessity and absolute universality which are characteristic of all geometrical propositions. As to the other and only means of arriving at such knowledge through mere concepts or intuitions *a priori*, it must be clear that only analytical, but no synthetical knowledge can ever be derived from mere concepts. Take the proposition that two straight lines cannot enclose a space and cannot therefore form a figure, and try to deduce it from the concept of straight lines and the number two; or take the proposition that with three straight lines it is possible to form a figure, and try to deduce that from those concepts. All your labour will be lost, and in the end you will be obliged to have recourse to intuition, as is always done in geometry. You then give yourselves an object in intuition. But of what kind is it? Is it a pure intuition *a priori* or an empirical one? In the latter case, you would never arrive at a universally valid, still less at an apodictic proposition, because experience can never yield such. You must therefore take the object as given *a priori* in intuition, and found your synthetical proposition on that. If you did not possess in yourselves the power of *a priori* intuition, if that subjective condition were not at the same time, as to the form, the general condition *a priori* under which alone the object of that (external) intuition becomes possible, if, in fact, the object (the triangle) were something by itself without any reference to you as the subject, how could you say that what exists necessarily in your subjective conditions of constructing a triangle, belongs of necessity to the triangle itself? For you could not add something entirely new (the figure) to your concepts of three lines, something which should of necessity belong to the object, as that object is given before your knowledge of it, and not by it. If therefore space, and time also, were not pure forms of your intuition, which contains the *a priori* conditions under which alone things can become external objects to you, while, without that subjective condition, they are nothing, you could not predicate anything of external objects *a priori* and synthetically. It is therefore beyond the reach of doubt, and not possible only or probable, that space and time, as the necessary conditions of all experience, external and internal, are purely subjective conditions of our intuition, and that, with reference to them, all things are phenomena only, and not things thus existing by themselves in such or such wise. Hence, so far as their form is concerned, much may be predicated of them *a priori*, but nothing whatever of the things by themselves on which these phenomena may be grounded.

II. As a confirmation of this theory of the ideality both of the external and of the internal sense, and therefore of all objects of the senses as mere phenomena, we may particularly remark, that everything in our knowledge which belongs to intuition (excluding therefore the feelings of pain and pleasure, and the will, which are no knowledge at all) contains nothing but mere relations, namely, of the places in an intuition (extension), change of places (motion), and laws, according to which that change is determined (moving forces). Nothing is told us thereby as to what is present in the place, or what, besides the change of place, is active in the things. A thing by itself, however, cannot be known by mere relations, and we may, therefore, fairly conclude that, as the external sense gives us nothing but representations of relations, that sense can contain in its representation only the relation of an object to the subject, and not what is inside the object by itself. The same applies to internal intuition. Not only do the representations of the external senses constitute its proper material with which we fill our mind, but time, in which these representations are placed, and which precedes even our consciousness of them in experience, nay, forms the formal condition of the manner in which we place them in the mind, contains itself relations of succession, coexistence, and that which must be coexistent with succession, namely, the permanent. Now that which, as a representation, can precede every act of thinking something, is the intuition: and, if it contains nothing but relations, then the form of intuition. As this represents nothing except what is being placed in the mind, it can itself be the manner only in which the mind, through its own activity, that is, by this placing of its representation, is affected by itself, in other words, an internal sense with respect to its form. Whatever is represented by a sense is so far always phenomenal, and we should therefore have either to admit no internal sense at all, or the subject, which is its object, could be represented by it as phenomenal only, and not, as it might judge of itself, if its intuition were spontaneous only, that is, if it were intellectual. The difficulty here lies wholly in this, how a subject can have an internal intuition of itself: but this difficulty is common to every theory. The consciousness of self (apperception) is the simple representation of the ego, and if by it alone all the manifold (representations) in the subject were given spontaneously, the inner intuition would be intellectual. In man this consciousness requires internal perception of the manifold, which is previously given in the subject, and the manner in which this is given in the mind without spontaneity, must, on account of this difference, be called sensibility. If the faculty of self-consciousness is to seek for, that is, to apprehend, what lies in the mind, it must affect the mind, and can thus only produce an intuition of itself. The form of this, which lay antecedently in the mind, determines the manner in which the manifold exists together in the mind, namely, in the representation of time. The intuition of self, therefore, is not, as if it could represent itself immediately and as spontaneously and independently active, but according to the manner in which it is internally affected, consequently as it appears to itself, not as it is.

*III. If I say that the intuition of external objects and the self-intuition of the mind, represent both (viz. the objects and the mind) in space and time, as they affect our senses, that is, as they appear, I do not mean, that these objects are mere illusion. For the objects, as phenomena, nay, even the properties which we ascribe to them, are always looked upon as something really given: and all we do is, that, as their quality depends only on the manner of intuition on the part of the subject in relation to a given object, we distinguish the object, as phenomenon, from itself, as an object by itself. Thus, if I assert that the quality of space and time, according to which, as a condition of their existence, I accept both external objects and my own soul, lies in my manner of intuition and not in these objects by themselves, I do not mean to say that bodies seem only to exist outside me, or that my soul seems only to be given in my self-consciousness. It would be my own fault, if I changed that, which I ought to count as phenomenal, into mere illusion.**

This cannot happen, however, according to our principle of the ideality of all sensuous intuitions; on the contrary, it is only when we attribute objective reality to those forms of intuition

---

* *Phenomenal predicates can be attributed to the object in its relation to our sense: as for instance to the rose its red colour, and its scent. But what is merely illusion can never be attributed to an object as a predicate, for the simple reason that the illusion attributes to the object by itself something which belongs to it only in its relation to the senses, or to a subject in general: as for instance the two handles, which were formerly attributed to Saturn. That which is never to be found in the object itself, but always in its relation to a subject, and is inseparable from its representation by a subject, is phenomenal, and the predicates of space and time are therefore rightly attributed to objects of the senses, as such. In this there is no illusion. If, on the contrary, I were to attribute to the rose by itself redness, handles to Saturn, and extension to all external objects, without restricting my judgment to the relation of these objects to a subject, we should have illusion.*

that everything is changed inevitably into mere illusion. *For if
we take space and time as properties that ought to exist as
possible in things by themselves, and then survey the absurdi-
ties in which we should be involved in having to admit that
two infinite things, which are not substances, nor something
inherent in substances, but nevertheless must be something
existing, nay, the necessary condition of the existence of all
things, would remain, even if all existing things were removed,
we really cannot blame the good Bishop Berkeley for degrad-
ing bodies to mere illusion. Nay, it would follow that even our
own existence, which would thus be made dependent on the
independent reality of such a nonentity as time, must become
a mere illusion, an absurdity which hitherto no one has been
guilty of.*

*IV. In natural theology, where we think of an object which
not only can never be an object of intuition to us, but which
even to itself can never be an object of* sensuous *intuition,
great care is taken to remove all conditions of space and time
from its intuition (for all its knowledge must be intuitive, and
not* thought, *which always involves limitation). But how are we
justified in doing this, when we have first made space and time
forms of things by themselves, such as would remain as conditions of the existence of things a priori, even if the things
themselves had been removed? If conditions of all existence,
they would also be conditions of the existence of God. If we do
not wish to change space and time into objective forms of all
things, nothing remains but to accept them as subjective forms
of our external as well as internal intuition, which is called
sensuous, for the very reason that it is not originally spontaneous, that is such, that it could itself give us the existence of the
objects of intuition (such an intuition, so far as we can understand, can belong to the First Being only), but dependent on
the existence of objects, and therefore possible only, if the faculty of representation in the subject is affected by them.*

*It is not necessary, moreover, that we should limit this intui-
tion in space and time to the sensibility of man; it is quite
possible that all finite thinking beings must necessarily agree
with us on this point (though we cannot decide this). On account of this universal character, however, it does not cease
to be sensibility, for it always is, and remains derivative (intuitus derivativus), not original (intuitus originarius), and therefore not intellectual intuition. For the reason mentioned before,
the latter intuition seems only to belong to the First Being, and
never to one which is dependent, both in its existence and its
intuition (which intuition determines its existence with refer-*

ence to given objects). This latter remark, however, must only be taken as an illustration of our aesthetic theory, and not as a proof.

Conclusion of the Transcendental Aesthetic

Here, then, we have one of the requisites for the solution of the general problem of transcendental philosophy, How are synthetical propositions *a priori* possible? *namely, pure intuitions* a priori, *space and time. In them we find, if in a judgment* a priori *we want to go beyond a given concept, that which can be discovered* a priori, *not in the concept, but in the intuition corresponding to it, and can be connected with it synthetically. For this very reason, however, such judgments can never go beyond the objects of the senses, but are valid only for objects of possible experience.*

*Transcendental Elements
Second Part*

TRANSCENDENTAL LOGIC
INTRODUCTION. THE IDEA OF A TRANSCENDENTAL
LOGIC

I. OF LOGIC IN GENERAL

Our knowledge springs from two fundamental sources of our soul; the first receives representations (receptivity of impressions), the second is the power of knowing an object by these representations (spontaneity of concepts). By the first an object is *given* us, by the second the object is *thought,* in relation to that representation which is a mere determination of the soul. Intuition therefore and concepts constitute the elements of all our knowledge, so that neither concepts without an intuition corresponding to them, nor intuition without concepts can yield any real knowledge.

Both are either pure or empirical. They are empirical when sensation, presupposing the actual presence of the object, is contained in it. They are pure when no sensation is mixed up with the representation. The latter may be called the material of sensuous knowledge. Pure intuition therefore contains the form only by which something is seen, and pure conception the form only by which an object is thought. Pure intuitions and pure concepts only are possible *a priori,* empirical intuitions and empirical concepts *a posteriori.*

We call *sensibility* the *receptivity* of our soul, or its power of receiving representations whenever it is in any wise affected, while the *understanding,* on the contrary, is with us the power of producing representations, or the *spontaneity* of knowledge. We are so constituted that our intuition must always be sensuous, and consist of the mode in which we are affected by objects. What enables us to think the objects of our sensuous intuition is the understanding. Neither of these qualities or faculties is preferable to the other. Without sensibility objects would not be given to us, without understanding they would not be thought by us. *Thoughts without contents are empty, intuitions without concepts are blind.* Therefore it is equally necessary to make our concepts sensuous, i.e. to add to them their object in intuition, as to make our intuitions intelligible, i.e. to bring them under concepts. These two powers or faculties cannot exchange their functions. The understanding cannot see, the senses cannot think. By their union only can knowledge be produced. But this is no reason for confounding the share which belongs to each in the production of knowledge. On the contrary, they should always be carefully separated and distinguished, and we have therefore divided the science of the rules of sensibility in general, i.e. aesthetic, from the science of the rules of the understanding in general, i.e. logic.

Logic again can be taken in hand for two objects, either as logic of the general or of a particular use of the understanding. The former contains all necessary rules of thought without which the understanding cannot be used at all. It treats of the understanding without any regard to the different objects to which it may be directed. Logic of the particular use of the understanding contains rules how to think correctly on certain classes of objects. The former may be called *Elementary Logic,* the latter the *Organum* of this or that science. The latter is generally taught in the schools as a preparation for certain sciences, though, according to the real progress of the human understanding, it is the latest achievement, which does not become possible till the science itself is really made, and requires only a few touches for its correction and completion. For it is clear that the objects themselves must be very well known before it is possible to give rules according to which a science of them may be established.

General logic is either pure or applied. In the former no account is taken of any empirical conditions under which our understanding acts, i.e. of the influence of the senses, the play of imagination, the laws of memory, the force of habit, the inclinations, and therefore the sources of prejudice also, nor of anything which supplies or seems to supply particular kinds of knowledge; for all this applies to the understanding under certain circumstances of its application only, and requires experience as a condition of knowledge. General but pure logic has to deal with principles *a priori* only, and is a *canon of the understanding and of reason*, though with reference to its formal application only, irrespective of any contents, whether empirical or transcendental. General logic is called applied, if it refers to the rules of the use of our understanding under the subjective empirical conditions laid down in psychology. It therefore contains empirical principles, yet it is general, because referring to the use of the understanding, whatever its objects may be. It is neither a canon of the understanding in general nor an organum of any particular science, but simply a catharticon of the ordinary understanding.

In general logic, therefore, that part which is to constitute the science of pure reason must be entirely separated from that which forms applied, but for all that still general logic. The former alone is a real science, though short and dry, as a practical exposition of an elementary science of the understanding ought to be. In this logicians should never lose sight of two rules:

1. As general logic it takes no account of the contents of the knowledge of the understanding nor of the difference of its objects. It treats of nothing but the mere form of thought.

2. As pure logic it has nothing to do with empirical principles, and borrows nothing from psychology (as some have imagined); psychology, therefore, has no influence whatever on the canon of the understanding. It proceeds by way of demonstration, and everything in it must be completely *a priori*.

What I call applied logic (contrary to common usage according to which it contains certain exercises on the rules of pure logic) is a representation of the understanding and of the rules according to which it is necessarily applied *in concreto,* i.e. under the accidental conditions of the subject, which may hinder or help its application, and are all given empirically only. It treats of attention, its impediments and their consequences, the sources of error, the states of doubt, hesitation, and conviction, etc., and general and pure logic stands to it in the same relation as pure ethics, which treat only of the necessary moral laws of a free will, to applied ethics, which consider these laws as under the influence of sentiments, inclinations, and passions to which all human beings are more or less subject. This can never constitute a true and demonstrated science, because, like applied logic, it depends on empirical and psychological principles.

2. OF TRANSCENDENTAL LOGIC

General logic, as we saw, takes no account of the contents of knowledge, i.e. of any relation between it and its objects, and considers the logical form only in the relation of cognitions to each other, that is, it treats of the form of thought in general. But as we found, when treating of Transcendental Aesthetic, that there are pure as well as empirical intuitions, it is possible that a similar distinction might appear between pure and empirical thinking. In this case we should have a logic in which the contents of knowledge are not entirely ignored, for such a logic which should contain the rules of pure thought only, would exclude only all knowledge of a merely empirical character. It would also treat of the origin of our knowledge of objects, so far as that origin cannot be attributed to the objects, while general logic is not at all concerned with the origin of our knowledge, but only considers representations (whether existing originally *a priori* in ourselves or empirically given to us), according to the laws followed by the understanding, when thinking and treating them in their relation to each other. It is confined therefore to the form imparted by the understanding to the representations, whatever may be their origin.

And here I make a remark which should never be lost sight of, as it extends its influence on all that follows. Not every kind of knowledge *a priori* should be called transcendental (i.e. occupied with the possibility or the use of knowledge *a priori*), but that only by which we know that and how certain representations (intuitional or conceptual) can be used or are possible *a priori* only. Neither space nor any *a priori* geometrical determination of it is a transcendental representation; but that knowledge only is rightly called transcendental which teaches us that these representations cannot be of empirical origin, and how they can yet refer *a priori* to objects of experience. The application of space to objects in general would likewise be transcendental, but, if restricted to objects of sense, it is empirical. The distinction between transcendental and empirical belongs therefore to the critique of knowledge, and does not affect the relation of that knowledge to its objects.

On the supposition therefore that there may be concepts, having an *a priori* reference to objects, not as pure or sensuous intuitions, but as acts of pure thought, being concepts in fact, but neither of empirical nor aesthetic origin, we form by anticipation an idea of a science of that knowledge which belongs to the pure understanding and reason, and by which we may think objects entirely *a priori*. Such a science, which has to determine the origin, the extent, and the objective validity of such knowledge, might be called *Transcendental Logic*, having to deal with the laws of the understanding and reason in so far only as they refer *a priori* to objects, and not, as general logic, in so far as they refer promiscuously to the empirical as well as to the pure knowledge of reason.

3. OF THE DIVISION OF GENERAL LOGIC INTO ANALYTIC AND DIALECTIC

What is truth? is an old and famous question by which people thought they could drive logicians into a corner, and either make them take refuge in a mere circle,[8] or make them confess their ignorance and consequently the vanity of their whole art. The nominal definition of truth, that it is the agreement of the cognition with its object, is granted. What is wanted is to know a general and safe criterion of the truth of any and every kind of knowledge.

It is a great and necessary proof of wisdom and sagacity to know what questions may be reasonably asked. For if a question is absurd in itself and calls for an answer where there is no answer, it does not only throw disgrace on the questioner, but often tempts an uncautious listener into absurd answers, thus presenting, as the ancients said, the spectacle of one person milking a he-goat, and of another holding the sieve.

If truth consists in the agreement of knowledge with its object, that object must thereby be distinguished from other objects; for knowledge is untrue if it does not agree with its object, though it contains something which may be affirmed of other objects. A general criterium of truth ought really to be valid with regard to every kind of knowledge, whatever the objects may be. But it is clear, as no account is thus taken of the contents of knowledge (relation to its object), while truth

---

[8] The First Edition has *Diallele*, the Second, *Dialexe*.

concerns these very contents, that it is impossible and absurd to ask for a sign of the truth of the contents of that knowledge, and that therefore a sufficient and at the same time general mark of truth cannot possibly be found. As we have before called the contents of knowledge its material, it will be right to say that of the truth of the knowledge, so far as its material is concerned, no general mark can be demanded, because it would be self-contradictory.

But, when we speak of knowledge with reference to its form only, without taking account of its contents, it is equally clear that logic, as it propounds the general and necessary rules of the understanding, must furnish in these rules criteria of truth. For whatever contradicts those rules is false, because the understanding would thus contradict the general rules of thought, that is, itself. These criteria, however, refer only to the form of truth or of thought in general. They are quite correct so far, but they are not sufficient. For although our knowledge may be in accordance with logical rule, that is, may not contradict itself, it is quite possible that it may be in contradiction with its object. Therefore the purely logical criterium of truth, namely, the agreement of knowledge with the general and formal laws of the understanding and reason, is no doubt a *conditio sine qua non,* or a negative condition of all truth. But logic can go no further, and it has no test for discovering error with regard to the contents, and not the form, of a proposition.

General logic resolves the whole formal action of the understanding and reason into its elements, and exhibits them as principles for all logical criticism of our knowledge. This part of logic may therefore be called *Analytic,* and is at least a negative test of truth, because all knowledge must first be examined and estimated, so far as its form is concerned, according to these rules, before it is itself tested according to its contents, in order to see whether it contains positive truth with regard to its object. But as the mere form of knowledge, however much it may be in agreement with logical laws, is far from being sufficient to establish the material or objective truth of our knowledge, no one can venture with logic alone to judge of objects, or to make any assertion, without having first collected, apart from logic, trustworthy information, in order afterwards to attempt its application and connection in a coherent whole according to logical laws, or, still better, merely to test it by them. However, there is something so tempting in this specious art of giving to all our knowledge the form of the understanding, though being utterly ignorant as to the contents thereof, that general logic, which is meant to be a mere canon of criticism, has been employed as if it were an organum, for the real production of at least the semblance of objective assertions, or, more truly, has been misemployed for that purpose. This general logic, which assumes the semblance of an organum, is called *Dialectic*.

Different as are the significations in which the ancients used this name of a science or art, it is easy to gather from its actual employment that with them it was nothing but a logic of semblance. It was a sophistic art of giving to one's ignorance, nay, to one's intentional casuistry, the outward appearance of truth, by imitating the accurate method which logic always requires, and by using its topic as a cloak for every empty assertion. Now it may be taken as a sure and very useful warning that general logic, if treated as an organum, is always an illusive logic, that is, dialectical. For as logic teaches nothing with regard to the contents of knowledge, but lays down the formal conditions only of an agreement with the understanding, which, so far as the objects are concerned, are totally indifferent, any attempt at using it as an organum in order to extend and enlarge our knowledge, at least in appearance, can end in nothing but mere talk, by asserting with a certain plausibility anything one likes, or, if one likes, denying it.

Such instruction is quite beneath the dignity of philosophy. Therefore the title of Dialectic has rather been added to logic, as a critique of dialectical semblance; and it is in that sense that we also use it.

4. OF THE DIVISION OF TRANSCENDENTAL LOGIC INTO

TRANSCENDENTAL ANALYTIC AND DIALECTIC

In transcendental logic we isolate the understanding, as before in transcendental aesthetic the sensibility, and fix our attention on that part of thought only which has its origin entirely in the understanding. The application of this pure knowledge has for its condition that objects are given in intuition, to which it can be applied, for without intuition all our knowledge would be without objects, and it would therefore remain entirely empty. That part of transcendental logic therefore which teaches the elements of the pure knowledge of the understanding, and the principles without which no object can be thought, is transcendental Analytic, and at the same time a logic of truth. No knowledge can contradict it without losing at the same time all contents, that is, all relation to any object, and therefore all truth. But as it is very tempting to use this pure knowledge of the understanding and its principles by themselves, and even beyond the limits of all experience, which alone can supply the material or the objects to which those pure concepts of the understanding can be applied, the understanding runs the risk of making, through mere sophisms, a material use of the purely formal principles of the pure understanding, and thus of judging indiscriminately of objects which are not given to us, nay, perhaps can never be given. As it is properly meant to be a mere canon for criticising the empirical use of the understanding, it is a real abuse if it is allowed as an organum of its general and unlimited application, by our venturing, with the pure understanding alone, to judge synthetically of objects in general, or to affirm and decide anything about them. In this case the employment of the pure understanding would become dialectical.

The second part of transcendental logic must therefore form a critique of that dialectical semblance, and is called transcendental Dialectic, not as an art of producing dogmatically such semblance (an art but too popular with many metaphysical jugglers), but as a critique of the understanding and reason with regard to their hyperphysical employment, in order thus to lay bare the false semblance of its groundless pretensions, and to reduce its claims to discovery and expansion, which was to be achieved by means of transcendental principles only, to a mere critique, serving as a protection of the pure understanding against all sophistical illusions.

Transcendental Logic

First Division

TRANSCENDENTAL ANALYTIC

Transcendental Analytic consists in the dissection of all our knowledge *a priori* into the elements which constitute the knowledge of the pure understanding. Four points are here essential: first, that the concepts should be pure and not empirical; secondly, that they should not belong to intuition and sensibility, but to thought and understanding; thirdly, that the concepts should be elementary and carefully distinguished from derivative or composite concepts; fourthly, that our tables should be complete and that they should cover the whole field of the pure understanding.

This completeness of a science cannot be confidently accepted on the strength of a mere estimate, or by means of repeated experiments only; what is required for it is an idea of the totality of the *a priori* knowledge of the understanding, and a classification of the concepts based upon it; in fact, a systematic treatment. Pure understanding must be distinguished, not merely from all that is empirical, but even from all sensibility. It constitutes therefore a unity independent in itself, self-sufficient, and not to be increased by any additions from without. The sum of its knowledge must constitute a system, comprehended and determined by one idea, and its completeness and articulation must form the test of the correctness and genuineness of its component parts.

This part of transcendental logic consists of two books, the one containing the *concepts,* the other the *principles* of pure understanding.

Transcendental Analytic

BOOK I: ANALYTIC OF CONCEPTS

By Analytic of concepts I do not understand their analysis, or the ordinary process in philosophical disquisitions of dissecting any given concepts according to their contents, and thus rendering them more distinct; but a hitherto seldom attempted dissection of the faculty of the understanding itself, with the sole object of discovering the possibility of concepts *a priori,* by looking for them nowhere but in the understanding itself as their birthplace, and analysing the pure use of the understanding. This is the proper task of a transcendental philosophy, all the rest is mere logical treatment of concepts. We shall therefore follow up the pure concepts to their first germs and beginnings in the human understanding, in which they lie prepared, till at last, on the occasion of experience, they become developed, and are represented by the same understanding in their full purity, freed from all inherent empirical conditions.

Analytic of Concepts

CHAPTER II
METHOD OF DISCOVERING ALL PURE CONCEPTS OF THE UNDERSTANDING

When we watch any faculty of knowledge, different concepts, characteristic of that faculty, manifest themselves according to different circumstances, which, as the observation has been carried on for a longer or shorter time, or with more or less accuracy, may be gathered up into a more or less complete collection. Where this collection will be complete, it is impossible to say beforehand, when we follow this almost mechanical process. Concepts thus discovered fortuitously only, possess neither order nor systematic unity, but are paired in the end according to similarities, and, according to their contents, arranged as more or less complex in various series, which are nothing less than systematical, though to a certain extent put together methodically.

Transcendental philosophy has the advantage, but also the duty of discovering its concepts according to a fixed principle. As they spring pure and unmixed from the understanding as an absolutely unity, they must be connected with each other, according to *one* concept or idea. This connection supplies us at the same time with a rule, according to which the place of each pure concept of the understanding and the systematical completeness of all of them can be determined *a priori,* instead of being dependent on arbitrary choice or chance.

Transcendental Method of the Discovery of All Pure Concepts of the Understanding
Section I

OF THE LOGICAL USE OF THE UNDERSTANDING IN GENERAL

We have before defined the understanding negatively only, as a non-sensuous faculty of knowledge. As without sensibility we cannot have any intuition, it is clear that the understanding is not a faculty of intuition. Besides intuition, however, there is no other kind of knowledge except by means of concepts. The knowledge therefore of every understanding, or at least of the human understanding, must be by means of concepts, not intuitive, but discursive. All intuitions, being sensuous, depend on affections, concepts on functions. By this function I mean the unity of the act of arranging different representations under one common representation. Concepts are based therefore on the spontaneity of thought, sensuous intuitions on the receptivity of impressions. The only use which the understanding can make of these concepts is to form judgments by them. As no representation, except the intuitional, refers immediately to an object, no concept is ever referred to an object immediately, but to some other representation of it, whether it be an intuition, or itself a concept. A judgment is therefore a mediate knowledge of an object, or a representation of a representation of it. In every judgment we find a concept applying to many, and comprehending among the many one single representation, which is referred immediately to the object. Thus in the judgment that all bodies are divisible,[9] the concept of divisible applies to various other concepts, but is here applied in particular to the concept of body, and this concept of body to certain phenomena of our experience. These objects therefore are represented mediately by the concept of divisibility. All judgments therefore are functions of unity among our representations, the knowledge of an object being brought about, not by an immediate representation, but by a higher one, comprehending this and several others, so that many possible cognitions are collected into one. As all acts of the understanding can be reduced to judgments, the understanding may be defined as *the faculty of judging*. For we saw before that the understanding is the faculty of thinking, and

[9] *Veränderlich* in the First Edition is rightly corrected into *theilbar* in later editions, though in the Second it is still *veränderlich*.

thinking is knowledge by means of concepts, while concepts, as predicates of possible judgments, refer to some representations of an object yet undetermined. Thus the concept of body means something, for instance, metal, which can be known by that concept. It is only a concept, because it comprehends other representations, by means of which it can be referred to objects. It is therefore the predicate of a possible judgment, such as, that every metal is a body. Thus the functions of the understanding can be discovered in their completeness, if it is possible to represent the functions of unity in *judgments*. That this is possible will be seen in the following section.

METHOD OF THE DISCOVERY OF ALL PURE CONCEPTS OF THE UNDERSTANDING
SECTION II

§ 9. OF THE LOGICAL FUNCTION OF THE UNDERSTANDING IN JUDGMENTS

If we leave out of consideration the contents of any judgment and fix our attention on the mere form of the understanding, we find that the function of thought in a judgment can be brought under four heads, each of them with three subdivisions. They may be represented in the following table:

I

Quantity of Judgments

Universal.
Particular.
Singular.

II
Quality
Affirmative.
Negative.
Infinite.

III
Relation
Categorical.
Hypothetical.
Disjunctive.

IV
Modality
Problematical.
Assertory.
Apodictic.

As this classification may seem to differ in some, though not very essential points, from the usual technicalities of logicians, the following reservations against any possible misunderstanding will not be out of place.

1. Logicians are quite right in saying that in using judgments in syllogisms, singular judgments may be treated like universal ones. For as they have no extent at all, the predicate cannot refer to part only of that which is contained in the concept of the subject, and be excluded from the rest. The predicate is valid therefore of that concept, without any exception, as if it were a general concept, having an extent to the whole of which the predicate applies. But if we compare a singular with a general judgment, looking only at the quantity of knowledge conveyed by it, the singular judgment stands to the universal judgment as unity to infinity, and is therefore essentially different from it. It is therefore, when we consider a singular judgment (*judicium singulare*), not only according to its own validity, but according to the quantity of knowledge which it conveys, as compared with other kinds of knowledge, that we see how different it is from general judgments (*judicia communia*), and how well it deserves a separate place in a complete table of the varieties of thought in general, though not in a logic limited to the use of judgments in reference to each other.

2. In like manner infinite judgments must, in transcendental logic, be distinguished from affirmative ones, though in general logic they are properly classed together, and do not constitute a separate part in the classification. General logic takes no account of the contents of the predicate (though it be negative), it only asks whether the predicate be affirmed or denied. Transcendental logic, on the contrary, considers a judgment according to the value also or the contents of a logical affirmation by means of a purely negative predicate, and asks how much is gained by that affirmation, with reference to the sum total of knowledge. If I had said of the soul, that it is not mortal, I should, by means of a negative judgment, have at least warded off an error. Now it is true that, so far as the logical form is concerned, I have really affirmed by saying that the soul is non-mortal, because I thus place the soul in the unlimited sphere of non-mortal beings. As the mortal forms one part of the whole sphere of possible beings, the non-mortal the other, I have said no more by my proposition than that the soul is one of the infinite number of things which remain, when I take away all that is mortal. But by this the infinite sphere of all that is possible becomes limited only in so far that all that is mortal is excluded from it, and that afterwards the soul

is placed in the remaining part of its original extent. This part, however, even after its limitation, still remains infinite, and several more parts of it may be taken away without extending thereby in the least the concept of the soul, or affirmatively determining it. These judgments, therefore, though infinite in respect to their logical extent, are, with respect to their contents, limitative only, and cannot therefore be passed over in a transcendental table of all varieties of thought in judgments, it being quite possible that the function of the understanding exercised in them may become of great importance in the field of its pure *a priori* knowledge.

3. The following are all the relations of thought in judgments:

a. Relation of the predicate to the subject.

b. Relation of the cause to its effect.

c. Relation of subdivided knowledge, and of the collected members of the subdivision to each other.

In the first class of judgments we consider two concepts, in the second two judgments, in the third several judgments in their relation to each other. The hypothetical proposition, if perfect justice exists, the obstinately wicked is punished, contains really the relation of two propositions, namely, there is a perfect justice, and the obstinately wicked is punished. Whether both these propositions are true remains unsettled. It is only the consequence which is laid down by this judgment.

The disjunctive judgment contains the relation of two or more propositions to each other, but not as a consequence, but in the form of a logical opposition, the sphere of the one excluding the sphere of the other, and at the same time in the form of community, all the propositions together filling the whole sphere of the intended knowledge. The disjunctive judgment contains therefore a relation of the parts of the whole sphere of a given knowledge, in which the sphere of each part forms the complement of the sphere of the other, all being contained within the whole sphere of the subdivided knowledge. We may say, for instance, the world exists either by blind chance, or by internal necessity, or by an external cause. Each of these sentences occupies a part of the sphere of all possible knowledge with regard to the existence of the world, while all together occupy the whole sphere. To take away the knowledge from one of these spheres is the same as to place it into one of the other spheres, and to place it in one sphere is the same as to take it away from the others. There exists therefore in disjunctive judgments a certain community of the different divisions of knowledge, so that they mutually exclude each other, and yet thereby determine in their totality the true knowledge, because, if taken together, they constitute the whole contents of one given knowledge. This is all I have to observe here for the sake of what is to follow hereafter.

4. The modality of judgments is a very peculiar function, for it contributes nothing to the contents of a judgment (because, besides quantity, quality, and relation, there is nothing else that could constitute the contents of a judgment), but refers only to the nature of the copula in relation to thought in general. Problematical judgments are those in which affirmation or negation are taken as possible (optional) only, while in assertory judgments affirmation or negation is taken as real (true), in apodictic as necessary.* Thus the two judgments, the relation of which constitutes the hypothetical judgment (*antecedens et consequens*) and likewise the judgments the reciprocal relation of which forms the disjunctive judgment (members of subdivision), are always problematical only. In the example given above, the proposition, there exists a perfect justice, is not made as an assertory, but only as an optional judgment, which may be accepted or not, the consequence only being assertory. It is clear therefore that some of these judgments may be wrong, and may yet, if taken problematically, contain the conditions of the knowledge of truth. Thus, in our disjunctive judgment, one of its component judgments, namely, the world exists by blind chance, has a problematical meaning only, on the supposition that some one might for one moment take such a view, but serves, at the same time, like the indication of a false road among all the roads that might be taken, to find out the true one. The problematical proposition is therefore that which expresses logical (not objective) possibility only, that is, a free choice of admitting such a proposition, and a purely optional admission of it into the understanding. The assertory proposition implies logical reality or truth. Thus, for instance, in a hypothetical syllogism the *antecedens* in the major is problematical, in the minor assertory, showing that the proposition conforms to the understanding according to its laws. The apodictic proposition represents the assertory as determined by these very laws of the understanding, and therefore as asserting *a priori,* and thus expresses logical necessity. As in this way everything is arranged step by step in the understanding, inasmuch as we begin with judging problematically, then proceed to an assertory acceptation, and finally maintain our proposition as inseparably united with the understanding, that is as necessary and apodictic, we may be allowed to call

* As if in the first, thought were a function of the understanding, in the second, of the faculty of judgment, in the third, of reason; a remark which will receive its elucidation in the sequel.

these three functions of modality so many varieties or momenta of thought.

METHOD OF THE DISCOVERY OF ALL PURE CONCEPTS OF THE UNDERSTANDING
SECTION III

§ 10. OF THE PURE CONCEPTS OF THE UNDERSTANDING, OR OF THE CATEGORIES

General logic, as we have often said, takes no account of the contents of our knowledge, but expects that representations will come from elsewhere in order to be turned into concepts by an analytical process. Transcendental logic, on the contrary, has before it the manifold contents of sensibility *a priori*, supplied by transcendental aesthetic as the material for the concepts of the pure understanding, without which those concepts would be without any contents, therefore entirely empty. It is true that space and time contain what is manifold in the pure intuition *a priori*, but they belong also to the conditions of the receptivity of our mind under which alone it can receive representations of objects, and which therefore must affect the concepts of them also. The spontaneity of our thought requires that what is manifold in the pure intuition should first be in a certain way examined, received, and connected, in order to produce a knowledge of it. This act I call *synthesis*.

In its most general sense, I understand by synthesis the act of arranging different representations together, and of comprehending what is manifold in them under one form of knowledge. Such a synthesis is pure, if the manifold is not given empirically, but *a priori* (as in time and space). Before we can proceed to an analysis of our representations, these must first be given, and, as far as their contents are concerned, no concepts can arise analytically. Knowledge is first produced by the synthesis of what is manifold (whether given empirically or *a priori*). That knowledge may at first be crude and confused and in need of analysis, but it is synthesis which really collects the elements of knowledge, and unites them to a certain extent. It is therefore the first thing which we have to consider, if we want to form an opinion on the first origin of our knowledge.

We shall see hereafter that synthesis in general is the mere result of what I call the faculty of imagination, a blind but indispensable function of the soul, without which we should have no knowledge whatsoever, but of the existence of which we are scarcely conscious. But to reduce this synthesis to concepts is a function that belongs to the understanding, and by which the understanding supplies us for the first time with knowledge properly so called.

Pure synthesis in its most general meaning gives us the pure concept of the understanding. By this pure synthesis I mean that which rests on the foundation of what I call synthetical unity *a priori*. Thus our counting (as we best perceive when dealing with higher numbers) is a synthesis according to concepts, because resting on a common ground of unity, as for instance, the decade. The unity of the synthesis of the manifold becomes necessary under this concept.

By means of analysis different representations are brought under one concept, a task treated of in general logic; but how to bring, not the representations, but the pure synthesis of representations, under concepts, that is what transcendental logic means to teach. The first that must be given us *a priori* for the sake of knowledge of all objects, is the manifold in pure intuition. The second is, the synthesis of the manifold by means of imagination. But this does not yet produce true knowledge. The concepts which impart unity to this pure synthesis and consist entirely in the representation of this necessary synthetical unity, add the third contribution towards the knowledge of an object, and rest on the understanding.

The same function which imparts unity to various representations in one judgment imparts unity likewise to the mere synthesis of various representations in one intuition, which in a general way may be called the pure concept of the understanding. The same understanding, and by the same operations by which in concepts it achieves through analytical unity the logical form of a judgment, introduces also, through the synthetical unity of the manifold in intuition, a transcendental element into its representations. They are therefore called pure concepts of the understanding, and they refer *a priori* to objects, which would be quite impossible in general logic.

In this manner there arise exactly so many pure concepts of the understanding which refer *a priori* to objects of intuition in general, as there were in our table logical functions in all possible judgments, because those functions completely exhaust the understanding, and comprehend every one of its faculties. Borrowing a term of Aristotle, we shall call these concepts *categories,* our intention being originally the same as his, though widely diverging from it in its practical application.

Table of Categories

I
Of Quantity

Unity.
Plurality.
Totality.

II
Of Quality

Reality.
Negation.
Limitation.

III
Of Relation

Of Inherence and Subsistence (*substantia et accidens*).
Of Causality and Dependence (cause and effect).
Of Community (reciprocity between the active and the passive).

IV
Of Modality

Possibility.	Impossibility.
Existence.	Non-existence.
Necessity.	Contingency.

This then is a list of all original pure concepts of synthesis, which belong to the understanding *a priori,* and for which alone it is called pure understanding; for it is by them alone that it can understand something in the manifold of intuition, that is, think an object in it. The classification is systematical, and founded on a common principle, namely, the faculty of judging (which is the same as the faculty of thinking). It is not the result of a search after pure concepts undertaken at haphazard, the completeness of which, as based on induction only, could never be guaranteed. Nor could we otherwise understand why these concepts only, and no others, abide in the pure understanding. It was an enterprise worthy of an acute thinker like Aristotle to try to discover these fundamental concepts; but as he had no guiding principle he merely picked them up as they occurred to him, and at first gathered up ten of them, which he called *categories* or *predicaments.* Afterwards he thought he had discovered five more of them, which he added under the name of *post-predicaments.* But his table remained imperfect for all that, not to mention that we find in it some modes of pure sensibility (*quando, ubi, situs,* also *prius, simul*), also an empirical concept (*motus*), none of which can belong to this genealogical register of the understanding. Besides, there are some derivative concepts, counted among the fundamental concepts (*actio, passio*), while some of the latter are entirely wanting.

With regard to these, it should be remarked that the categories, as the true fundamental concepts of the pure understanding, have also their pure derivative concepts. These could not be passed over in a complete system of transcendental philosophy, but in a merely critical essay the mention of the fact may suffice.

I should like to be allowed to call these pure but derivative concepts of the understanding the *predicabilia,* in opposition to the *predicamenta* of the pure understanding. If we are once in possession of the fundamental and primitive concepts, it is easy to add the derivative and secondary, and thus to give a complete image of the genealogical tree of the pure understanding. As at present I am concerned not with the completeness, but only with the principles of a system, I leave this supplementary work for a future occasion. In order to carry it out, one need only consult any of the ontological manuals, and place, for instance, under the category of causality the *predicabilia* of force, of action, and of passion; under the category of community the *predicabilia* of presence and resistance; under the predicaments of modality the *predicabilia* of origin, extinction, change, etc. If we associate the categories among themselves or with the modes of pure sensibility, they yield us a large number of derivative concepts *a priori,* which it would be useful and interesting to mark and, if possible, to bring to a certain completeness, though this is not essential for our present purpose.

I intentionally omit here the definitions of these categories, though I may be in possession of them.[10] In the sequel I shall dissect these concepts so far as is sufficient for the purpose of the method which I am preparing. In a complete system of pure reason they might be justly demanded, but at present they would only make us lose sight of the principal object of our investigation, by rousing doubts and objections which, without injury to our essential object, may well be relegated to another time. The little I have said ought to be sufficient to show clearly that a complete dictionary of these concepts with all requisite explanations is not only possible, but easy. The compartments exist; they have only to be filled, and with a syste-

[10] See, however, Karl's remarks on p. 241 of First Edition.

matic topic like the present the proper place to which each concept belongs cannot easily be missed, nor compartments be passed over which are still empty.

§ *11*

This table of categories suggests some interesting considerations, which possibly may have important consequences with regard to the scientific form of all knowledge of reason. For it is clear that such a table will be extremely useful, nay, indispensable, in the theoretical part of philosophy, in order to trace the complete plan of a whole science, *so far as it rests on concepts* a priori, *and to divide it systematically* according to fixed principles, *because that table contains all elementary concepts of the understanding in their completeness, nay, even the form of a system of them in the human understanding, and indicates therefore all the* momenta *of a projected speculative science, nay, even their* order. *Of this I have given an example elsewhere.** *Here follow some of the considerations.*

The first is, *that this table, which contains four classes of the concepts of the understanding, may, in the first instance, be divided into two sections, the former of which refers to objects of intuition* (pure, as well as empirical), *the latter to the existence of those objects* (either in their relation to each other, or to the understanding).

The first section I shall call that of the mathematical, *the second, that of the* dynamical *categories. The first section has no correlates, which are met with in the second section only. Must not this difference have some ground in the nature of the understanding?*

Our second remark is, *that in every class there is the same number of categories, namely three, which again makes us ponder, because generally all division* a priori *by means of concepts must be dichotomy. It should be remarked also, that the third category always arises from the combination of the second with the first. Thus* totality *is nothing but plurality considered as unity;* limitation *nothing but reality connected with negation;* community *is the causality of a substance as determining another reciprocally;* lastly, necessity, *the existence which is given by possibility itself. It must not be supposed, however, that therefore the third category is only a derivative, and not a primary concept of the pure understanding. For the joining of the first and second concepts, in order to produce the third, requires an independent act of the understanding, which is not identical with the act that produces the first and*

* *Metaphysical Elements of Natural Science.*

second concepts. Thus the concept of a number (which belongs to the category of totality) is not always possible when we have the concepts of plurality and unity (for instance, in the concept of the infinite); nor can we understand by simply combining the concept of a cause *and that of a* substance, *the influence, that is, how a substance can become the cause of something in another substance. This shows that a separate act of the understanding is here required, and the same applies to all the rest.*

Third observation. *With regard to one category, namely, that of community, which is found in the third class, its accordance with the form of a disjunctive judgment, which corresponds to it in the table of logical functions, is not so evident as elsewhere.*

In order to become quite certain of that accordance, we must remark that in all disjunctive judgments their sphere (that is, all that is contained in them) is represented as a whole, divided into parts (the subordinate concepts), and that, as one of them cannot be contained under the other, they are conceived as co-ordinate, not as subordinate, determining each other, not in one direction only, as in a series, but reciprocally, as in an aggregate (if one member of the division is given, all the rest are excluded, and vice versa).

A similar connection is conceived in a whole of things, in which one, as effect, is not subordinated to another as the cause of its existence, but is co-ordinated with it, simultaneously and reciprocally, as cause of the determination of the other (as, for instance, in a body of which the parts reciprocally attract and repel each other). This is a kind of connection totally different from that which exists in a mere relation of cause to effect (of ground to consequence), for here the consequence does not reciprocally determine the ground again, nor (as in the case of the Creator and the creation) constitute with it a whole. The process of the understanding, in representing to itself the sphere of a divided concept, is the same as that by which it thinks a thing as divisible: and in the same manner in which, in the former, the members of a division exclude each other, and are yet connected in one sphere, the understanding represents to itself the parts of the latter as existing (as substances), each independent of the rest, and yet united in a whole.

§ 12

In the transcendental philosophy of the ancients there is another chapter containing concepts of the understanding which,

*though they are not counted among the categories, are yet
considered by them as concepts* a priori *of objects. If so, they
would increase the number of the categories, which cannot be.
They are set forth in the famous proposition of the Schoolmen,
'quodlibet ens est unum, verum, bonum.' Now, although the
inferences to be drawn from this principle (yielding nothing
but tautological propositions) were very meagre, so that modern metaphysicians mention it almost by courtesy only, a
thought which has maintained itself so long, however empty
it may seem, deserves an investigation with regard to its origin,
nay, leads us to suspect that it may have its foundation in some
rule of the understanding which, as often happens, has only
been wrongly interpreted. What are supposed to be transcendental predicates of things are nothing but logical requirements
and criteria of all knowledge of things in general, whereby that
knowledge is founded on the categories of quantity, namely,
unity, plurality, and totality. Only, instead of taking them as
materially belonging to the possibility of things by themselves,
they (the predicates, or rather those who employed them) used
them, in fact, in their formal meaning only, as forming a logical
requisite for every kind of knowledge, and yet incautiously
made these criteria of thought to be properties of the things
by themselves. In every cognition of an object there is* unity
of concept, which may be called qualitative unity, *so far as we
think by it only the unity in the comprehension of the manifold
material of our knowledge: as, for instance, the unity of the
subject in a play, or a speech, or a fable. Secondly, there is*
truth, *in respect to the deductions from it. The more true
deductions can be made from a given concept, the more criteria
are there of its objective reality. This might be called the* qualitative plurality *of criteria, which belong to a concept as their
common ground (but are not conceived in it, as quantity).
Thirdly, there is* completeness, *which consists in this, that the
plurality together leads back to the unity of the concept, according completely with this and with no other concept, which
may be called the* qualitative completeness (totality). *This
shows that these logical criteria of the possibility of knowledge
in general do nothing but change the three categories of quantity, in which the unity in the production of the quantum must
throughout be taken as* homogeneous, *for the purpose of connecting* heterogeneous *elements of knowledge also in one consciousness, by means of the quality of the cognition as the
principle of the connection. Thus the criterion of the possibility
of a concept (but not of its object) is the definition of it, in
which the* unity *of the concept, the* truth *of all that may be
immediately deduced from it, and lastly, the* completeness *of*

what has been deduced from it, supply all that is necessary for the constitution of the whole concept. In the same manner the criterion *of an hypothesis consists, first, in the intelligibility of the ground which has been admitted for the sake of explanation, or of its* unity (*without any auxiliary hypothesis*); *secondly, in the* truth *of the consequences to be deduced from it* (*their accordance with themselves and with experience*); *and lastly, in the* completeness *of the ground admitted for the explanation of these consequences, which point back to neither more nor less than what was admitted in the hypothesis, and agree in giving us again, analytically a posteriori, what had been thought synthetically a priori. The concepts of unity, truth, and perfection, therefore, do not supplement the transcendental table of the categories, as if it were imperfect, but they serve only, after the relation of these concepts to objects has been entirely set aside, to bring their employment under general logical rules, for the agreement of knowledge with itself.*

Transcendental Analytic

Chapter II
Of the Deduction of the Pure Concepts of the Understanding
Section 1

§ 13. OF THE PRINCIPLES OF A TRANSCENDENTAL DEDUCTION IN GENERAL

Jurists, when speaking of rights and claims, distinguish in every lawsuit the question of right (*quid juris*) from the question of fact (*quid facti*), and in demanding proof of both they call the former, which is to show the right or, it may be, the claim, the *deduction*. We, not being jurists, make use of a number of empirical concepts, without opposition from anybody, and consider ourselves justified, without any deduction, in attaching to them a sense or imaginary meaning, because we can always appeal to experience to prove their objective reality. There exist however illegitimate concepts also, such as, for instance, chance, or fate, which through an almost general indulgence are allowed to be current, but are yet from time to time challenged by the question *quid juris*. In that case we are greatly embarrassed in looking for their deduction, there being no clear legal title, whether from experience or from reason, on which their claim to employment could be clearly established

Among the many concepts, however, which enter into the complicated code of human knowledge, there are some which are destined for pure use *a priori*, independent of all experience, and such a claim requires at all times a deduction[11] because proofs from experience would not be sufficient to establish the legitimacy of such a use, though it is necessary to know how much concepts can refer to objects which they do not find in experience. I call the explanation of the manner how such concepts can *a priori* refer to objects their transcendental deduction, and distinguish it from the empirical deduction which shows the manner how a concept may be gained by experience and by reflection on experience; this does not touch the legitimacy, but only the fact whence the possession of the concept arose

We have already become acquainted with two totally distinct classes of concepts, which nevertheless agree in this, that they both refer *a priori* to objects, namely, the concepts of space and time as forms of sensibility, and the categories as concepts of the understanding. It would be labour lost to attempt an empirical deduction of them, because their distinguishing characteristic is that they refer to objects without having borrowed anything from experience for their representation. If therefore a deduction of them is necessary, it can only be transcendental.

It is possible, however, with regard to these concepts, as with regard to all knowledge, to try to discover in experience, if not the principle of their possibility, yet the contingent causes of their production. And here we see that the impressions of the senses give the first impulse to the whole faculty of knowledge with respect to them, and thus produce experience which consists of two very heterogeneous elements, namely, matter for knowledge, derived from the senses, and a certain form according to which it is arranged, derived from the internal source of pure intuition and pure thought, first brought into action by the former, and then producing

---

[11] That is a transcendental deduction.

concepts. Such an investigation of the first efforts of our faculty of knowledge, beginning with single perceptions and rising to general concepts, is no doubt very useful, and we have to thank the famous Locke for having been the first to open the way to it. A deduction of the pure concepts *a priori*, however, is quite impossible in that way. It lies in a different direction, because, with reference to their future use, which is to be entirely independent of experience, a very different certificate of birth will be required from that of mere descent from experience. We may call this attempted physiological derivation (which cannot properly be called deduction, because it refers to a *quaestio facti*), the explanation of the possession of pure knowledge. It is clear therefore that of these pure concepts *a priori* a transcendental deduction only is possible, and that to attempt an empirical deduction of them is mere waste of time, which no one would think of except those who have never understood the very peculiar nature of that kind of knowledge.

But though it may be admitted that the only possible deduction of pure knowledge *a priori* must be transcendental, it has not yet been proved that such a deduction is absolutely necessary. We have before, by means of a transcendental deduction, followed up the concepts of space and time to their very sources, and explained and defined their objective validity *a priori*. Geometry, however, moves along with a steady step, through every kind of knowledge *a priori*, without having to ask for a certificate from philosophy as to the pure legitimate descent of its fundamental concept of space. But it should be remarked that in geometry this concept is used with reference to the outer world of sense only, of which space is the pure form of intuition, and where geometrical knowledge, being based on *a priori* intuition, possesses immediate evidence, the objects being given, so far as their form is concerned, through their very knowledge *a priori* in intuition. When we come, however, to the pure concepts of the understanding, it becomes absolutely necessary to look for a transcendental deduction, not only for them, but for space also, because they, not being founded on experience, apply to objects generally, without any of the conditions of sensibility; and, speaking of objects, not through predicates of intuition and sensibility, but of pure thought *a priori*, are not able to produce in intuition *a priori* any object on which, previous to all experience, their synthesis was founded. These concepts of pure understanding, therefore, not only excite suspicion with regard to the objective validity and the limits of their own application, but render even the concept of space equivocal, because of an inclination to apply it beyond the conditions of sensuous intuition, which was the very reason that made a transcendental deduction of it, such as we gave before, necessary. Before the reader has made a single step in the field of pure reason, he must be convinced of the inevitable necessity of such a transcendental deduction, otherwise he would walk on blindly and, after having strayed in every direction, he would only return to the same ignorance from which he started. He must at the same time perceive the inevitable difficulty of such a deduction, so that he may not complain about obscurity where the object itself is obscure, or weary too soon with our removal of obstacles, the fact being that we have either to surrender altogether all claims to the knowledge of pure reason—the most favourite field of all philosophers, because extending beyond the limits of all possible experience —or to bring this critical investigation to perfection.

It was easy to show before, when treating of the concepts of space and time, how these, though being knowledge *a priori*, refer necessarily to objects, and how they make a synthetical knowledge of them possible, which is independent of all experience. For, as no object can appear to us, that is, become an object of empirical intuition, except through such pure forms of sensibility, space and time are pure intuitions which contain *a priori* the conditions of the possibility of objects as phenomena, and the synthesis in these intuitions possesses objective validity.

The categories of the understanding, on the contrary, are not conditions under which objects can be given in intuition, and it is quite possible therefore that objects should appear to us without any necessary reference to the functions of the understanding, thus showing that the understanding contains by no means any of their conditions *a priori*. There arises therefore here a difficulty, which we did not meet with in the field of sensibility, namely, how subjective conditions of thought can have objective validity, that is, become conditions of the possibility of the knowledge of objects. It cannot be denied that phenomena may be given in intuition without the functions of the understanding. For if we take, for instance, the concept of cause, which implies a peculiar kind of synthesis, consisting in placing according to a rule after something called A something totally different from it, B, we cannot say that it is *a priori* clear why phenomena should contain something of this kind. We cannot appeal for it to experience, because what has to be proved is the objective validity of this concept *a priori*. It would remain therefore *a priori* doubtful whether such a concept be not altogether empty, and without any corresponding object among phenomena. It is different with objects of sensuous intuition. They must conform to the formal conditions of sensibility existing *a priori* in the mind, because otherwise they could in no way be objects to us. But why besides this they should conform to the conditions which the understanding requires for the synthetical unity of thought, does not seem to follow quite so easily. For we could quite well imagine that phenomena might possibly be such that the understanding should not find them conforming to the conditions of its synthetical unity, and all might be in such confusion that nothing should appear in the succession of phenomena which could supply a rule of synthesis, and correspond, for instance, to the concept of cause and effect, so that this concept would thus be quite empty, null, and meaningless. With all this phenomena would offer objects to our intuition, because intuition by itself does not require the functions of thought.

It might be imagined that we could escape from the trouble of these investigations by saying that experience offers continually examples of such regularity of phenomena as to induce us to abstract from it the concept of cause, and it might be attempted to prove thereby the objective validity of such a concept. But it ought to be seen that in this way the concept of cause cannot possibly arise, and that such a concept ought either to be founded *a priori* in the understanding or be surrendered altogether as a mere hallucination. For this concept requires strictly that something, A, should be of such a nature that something else, B, follows from it necessarily and according to an absolutely universal rule. Phenomena no doubt supply us with cases from which a rule becomes possible according to which something happens usually, but never so that the result should be necessary. There is a dignity in the synthesis of cause and effect which cannot be expressed empirically, for it implies that the effect is not only an accessory to the cause, but given by it and springing from it. Nor is the absolute universality of the rule a quality inherent in empirical rules, which by means of induction cannot receive any but a relative universality, that is, a more or less extended applicability. If we were to treat the pure concepts of the understanding as merely empirical products, we should completely change their character and their use.

§ *14.* TRANSITION TO A TRANSCENDENTAL DEDUCTION

OF THE CATEGORIES

Two ways only are possible in which synthetical representations and their objects can agree, can refer to each other with necessity, and so to say meet each other. Either it is the object alone that makes the representation possible, or it is the representation alone that makes the object possible. In the former case their relation is empirical only, and the representation therefore never possible *a priori*. This applies to phenomena with reference to whatever in them belongs to sensation. In the latter case, though representation by itself (for we do not speak here of its[12] causality by means of the will) cannot produce its object so far as its existence is concerned, nevertheless the representation determines the object *a priori*, if through it alone it is possible to know anything as an object. To know a thing as an object is possible only under two conditions. First, there must be intuition by which the object is given us, though as a phenomenon only, secondly, there must be a concept by which an object is thought as corresponding to that intuition. From what we have said before it is clear that the first condition, namely, that under which alone objects can be seen, exists, so far as the form of intuition is concerned, in the soul *a priori*. All phenomena therefore must conform to that formal condition of sensibility, because it is through it alone that they appear, that is, that they are given and empirically seen.

Now the question arises whether there are not also antecedent concepts *a priori*, forming conditions under which alone something can be, if not seen, yet thought as an object in general; for in that case all empirical knowledge of objects would necessarily conform to such concepts, it being impossible that anything should become an object of experience without them. All experience contains, besides the intuition of the senses by which something is given, a concept also of the object, which is given in intuition as a phenomenon. Such concepts of objects in general therefore must form conditions *a priori* of all knowledge produced by experience, and the objective validity of the categories, as being such concepts *a priori*, rests on this very fact that by them alone, so far as the form of thought is concerned, experience becomes possible. If by them only it is possible to think any object of experience, it follows that they refer by necessity and *a priori* to all objects of experience.

There is therefore a principle for the transcendental deduction of all concepts *a priori* which must guide the whole of our investigation, namely, that all must be recognised as conditions *a priori* of the possibility of experience, whether of intuition, which is found in it, or of thought. Concepts which supply the objective ground of the possibility of ex-

[12] Read *deren* instead of *dessen*.

perience are for that very reason necessary. An analysis of the experience in which they are found would not be a deduction, but a mere illustration, because they would there have an accidental character only. Nay, without their original relation to all possible experience in which objects of knowledge occur, their relation to any single object would be quite incomprehensible.

[There are three original sources, or call them faculties or powers of the soul, which contain the conditions of the possibility of all experience, and which themselves cannot be derived from any other faculty, namely, sense, imagination, and apperception. On them is founded—

1. The synopsis of the manifold *a priori* through the senses.
2. The synthesis of this manifold through the imagination.
3. The unity of that synthesis by means of original apperception.

Besides their empirical use all these faculties have a transcendental use also, referring to the form only and possible *a priori*. With regard to the senses we have discussed that transcendental use in the first part, and we shall now proceed to an investigation of the remaining two, according to their true nature.]

Locke, for want of this reflection, and because he met with pure concepts of the understanding in experience, derived them also from experience, and yet acted so inconsistently that he attempted to use them for knowledge which far exceeds all limits of experience. David Hume saw that, in order to be able to do this, these concepts ought to have their origin a priori; *but as he could not explain how it was possible that the understanding should be constrained to think concepts, which by themselves are not united in the understanding, as necessarily united in the object, and never thought that possibly the understanding might itself, through these concepts, be the author of that experience in which its objects are found, he was driven by necessity to derive them from experience (namely, from a subjective necessity, produced by frequent association in experience, which at last is wrongly supposed to be* objective, *that is, from habit). He acted, however, very consistently, by declaring it to be impossible to go with these concepts, and with the principles arising from them, beyond the limits of experience. This empirical deduction, which was adopted by both philosophers, cannot be reconciled with the reality of our scientific knowledge* a priori, *namely, pure* mathematics *and* general natural science, *and is therefore refuted by facts. The former of these two celebrated*

men opened a wide door to fantastic extravagance, *because
reason, if it has once established such pretensions, can no
longer be checked by vague praises of moderation;* the other,
thinking that he had once discovered so general an illusion
of our faculty of knowledge, which had formerly been accepted as reason, gave himself over entirely to scepticism.
*We now intend to make the experiment whether it is not pos-
sible to conduct reason safely between these two rocks, to assign to her definite limits, and yet to keep open for her the
proper field for all her activities?*

I shall merely premise an explanation of what I mean by
the categories. *They are concepts of an object in general by
which its intuition is regarded as determined with reference to
one of the* logical functions *in judgments.* Thus the function
of the categorical judgment was that of the relation of the
subject to the predicate; for instance, *all bodies are divisible.*
Here, however, with reference to the pure logical employment of the understanding, it remained undetermined to which
of the two concepts the function of the subject, or the predicate, was to be assigned. For we could also say, *some divisible
is body.* But by bringing the concept of body under the category of substance, it is determined that its empirical intuition
in experience must always be considered as subject and never
as predicate only. The same applies to all other categories.

OF THE DEDUCTION OF THE PURE CONCEPTS OF THE UNDERSTANDING
SECOND SECTION
TRANSCENDENTAL DEDUCTION OF THE PURE CONCEPTS OF THE UNDERSTANDING

§ 15. OF THE POSSIBILITY OF CONNECTING (*conjunctio*) IN GENERAL

The manifold of representations may be given in an intuition which is purely sensuous, that is, nothing but receptivity, and the form of that intuition may lie a priori in our
faculty of representation, without being anything but the man-

ner in which a subject is affected. But the connection (con-junctio) *of anything manifold can never enter into us through the senses, and cannot be contained, therefore, already in the pure form of sensuous intuition, for it is a spontaneous act of the power of representation; and as, in order to distinguish this from sensibility, we must call it understanding, we see that all connecting, whether we are conscious of it or not, and whether we connect the manifold of intuition or several con-cepts together, and again, whether that intuition be sensuous or not sensuous, is an act of the understanding. This act we shall call by the general name of* synthesis, *in order to show that we cannot represent to ourselves anything as connected in the object, without having previously connected it ourselves, and that of all representations* connection *is the only one which cannot be given through the objects, but must be car-ried out by the subject itself, because it is an act of its spon-taneity. It can be easily perceived that this act must be origi-nally one and the same for every kind of connection, and that its dissolution, that is, the* analysis, *which seems to be its op-posite, does always presuppose it. For where the understand-ing has not previously connected, there is nothing for it to disconnect, because, as connected, it could only be given by the understanding to the faculty of representation.*

But the concept of connection includes, besides the concept of the manifold and the synthesis of it, the concept of the unity of the manifold also. Connection is representation of the synthetical *unity of the manifold.**

The representation of that unity cannot therefore be the re-sult of the connection; on the contrary, the concept of the con-nection becomes first possible by the representation of unity being added to the representation of the manifold. And this unity, which precedes a priori *all concepts of connection, must not be mistaken for that category of unity of which we spoke on p. 100; for all categories depend on logical functions in judgments, and in these we have already connection, and therefore unity of given concepts. The category, therefore, presupposes connection, and we must consequently look still higher for this unity as qualitative (see p. 100, § 12), in that, namely, which itself contains the ground for the unity of dif-*

---

* Whether the representations themselves are identical, and whether therefore one can be thought analytically by the other, is a matter of no consequence here. The consciousness *of the one has always to be distinguished from the consciousness of the other, so far as the mani-fold is concerned; and everything here depends on the synthesis only of this (possible) consciousness.*

ferent concepts in judgments, that is, the ground for the very possibility of the understanding, even in its logical employment.

§ 16. THE ORIGINAL SYNTHETICAL UNITY OF APPERCEPTION

It must be possible *that the* I think *should accompany all my representations: for otherwise something would be represented within me that could not be thought, in other words, the representation would either be impossible or nothing, at least so far as I am concerned. That representation which can be given before all thought, is called* intuition, *and all the manifold of intuition has therefore a necessary relation to the* I think *in the same subject in which that manifold of intuition is found. That representation, however (that* I think), *is an act of spontaneity, that is, it cannot be considered as belonging to sensibility. I call it* pure apperception, *in order to distinguish it from empirical apperception, or* original apperception *also, because it is that self-consciousness which by producing the representation,* I think *(which must be capable of accompanying all others, and is one and the same in every act of consciousness), cannot itself be accompanied by any other. I also call the unity of it the* transcendental unity of self-consciousness, *in order to indicate that it contains the possibility of knowledge* a priori.

For the manifold representations given in any intuition would not all be my *representations, if they did not all belong to one self-consciousness. What I mean is that, as my representations (even though I am not conscious of them as such), they must be in accordance with that condition, under which alone they can stand together in one common self-consciousness, because otherwise they would not all belong to me. From this original connection the following important conclusions can be deduced.*

The unbroken identity of apperception of the manifold that is given in intuition contains a synthesis of representations, and is possible only through the consciousness of that synthesis. The empirical consciousness, which accompanies various representations, is itself various and disunited, and without reference to the identity of the subject. Such a relation takes place, not by my simply accompanying every relation with consciousness, but by my adding *one to the other and being conscious of that act of adding, that is, of that synthesis. Only because I am able to connect the manifold of given representa-*

tions in one consciousness, *is it possible for me to represent to myself the* identity *of the* consciousness *in these* representations, *that is, only under the supposition of some synthetical unity of apperception does the analytical unity of apperception become possible.**

The thought that the representations given in intuition belong all of them to me, is therefore the same as that I connect them in one self-consciousness, or am able at least to do so; and though this is not yet the consciousness *of the* synthesis *of representations, it nevertheless presupposes the possibility of this synthesis. In other words, it is only because I am able to comprehend the manifold of representations in one consciousness, that I call them altogether my representations, for otherwise, I should have as manifold and various a self as I have representations of which I am conscious. The synthetical unity of the manifold of intuitions as given* a priori *is therefore the ground also of the identity of that apperception itself which precedes* a priori *all definite thought. Connection, however, does never lie in the objects, and cannot be borrowed from them by perception, and thus be taken into the understanding, but it is always an act of the understanding, which itself is nothing but a faculty of connecting* a priori, *and of bringing the manifold of given representations under the unity of apperception, which is, in fact, the highest principle of all human knowledge.*

It is true, no doubt, that this principle of the necessary unity of apperception is itself identical, and therefore an analytical proposition; but it shows, nevertheless, the necessity of a synthesis of the manifold which is given in intuition, without which synthesis it would be impossible to think the unbroken identity of self-consciousness. For through the Ego, *as a simple representation, nothing manifold is given; in the intuition, which is different from that, it can be given only, and then, by*

---

* *This analytical unity of consciousness belongs to all general concepts, as such. If, for instance, I think* red *in general, I represent to myself a property, which (as a characteristic mark) may be found in something, or can be connected with other representations; that is to say, only under a presupposed possible synthetical unity can I represent to myself the analytical. A representation which is to be thought as common to different representations, is looked upon as belonging to such as possess, besides it, something different. It must therefore have been thought in synthetical unity with other (though only possible) representations, before I can think in it that analytical unity of consciousness which makes it a* conceptus communis. *The synthetical unity of apperception is, therefore, the highest point with which all employment of the understanding, and even the whole of logic, and afterwards the whole of transcendental philosophy, must be connected; ay, that faculty is the understanding itself.*

connection, *be thought in one consciousness. An understanding in which, by its self-consciousness, all the manifold would be given at the same time, would possess* intuition; *our understanding can do nothing but think, and must seek for its intuition in the senses. I am conscious, therefore, of the identical self with respect to the manifold of the representations, which are given to me in an intuition, because I call them, altogether, my representations, as constituting* one. *This means, that I am conscious of a necessary synthesis of them* a priori, *which is called the original synthetical unity of apperception under which all representations given to me must stand, but have to be brought there, first, by means of a synthesis.*

§ 17. THE PRINCIPLE OF THE SYNTHETICAL UNITY OF APPERCEPTION IS THE HIGHEST PRINCIPLE OF ALL EMPLOYMENT OF THE UNDERSTANDING

The highest principle of the possibility of all intuition, in relation to sensibility, was, according to the transcendental Aesthetic, that all the manifold in it should be subject to the formal conditions of space and time. The highest principle of the same possibility in relation to the understanding is, that all the manifold in intuition must be subject to the conditions of the original synthetical unity of apperception.*

All the manifold representations of intuition, so far as they are given us, are subject to the former, so far as they must admit of being connected in one consciousness, to the latter; and without that nothing can be thought or known by them, because the given representations would not share the act of apperception (I think) in common, and could not be comprehended in one self-consciousness.

The understanding *in its most general sense is the faculty of* cognitions. *These consist in a definite relation of given representations to an object; and an* object *is that in the concept of which the manifold of a given intuition is connected. All*

---

* *Space and time, and all portions thereof, are* intuitions, *and consequently single representations with the manifold of their content. (See the transcendental Aesthetic.) They are not, therefore, mere concepts, through which the same consciousness, as existing in many representations, but intuitions through which many representations are brought to us, as contained in one and in its consciousness; this latter, therefore, is compounded, and these intuitions represent the unity of consciousness as* synthetical, *but yet as primitive. This character of* singleness *in them is practically of great importance (see § 25).*

such connection of representations requires of course the unity of the consciousness in their synthesis: consequently, the unity of consciousness is that which alone constitutes the relation of representations to an object, that is, their objective validity, and consequently their becoming cognitions, so that the very possibility of the understanding depends on it.

The first pure cognition of the understanding, therefore, on which all the rest of its employment is founded, and which at the same time is entirely independent of all conditions of sensuous intuition, is this very principle of the original synthetical unity of apperception. Space, the mere form of external sensuous intuition, is not yet cognition: it only supplies the manifold of intuition a priori for a possible cognition. In order to know anything in space, for instance, a line, I must draw it, and produce synthetically a certain connection of the manifold that is given, so that the unity of that act is at the same time the unity of the consciousness (in the concept of a line), and (so that) an object (a determinate space) is then only known for the first time. The synthetical unity of consciousness is, therefore, an objective condition of all knowledge; a condition, not necessary for myself only, in order to know an object, but one to which each intuition must be subject, in order to become an object for me, because the manifold could not become connected in one consciousness in any other way, and without such a synthesis.

No doubt, that proposition, as I said before, is itself analytical, though it makes synthetical unity a condition of all thought, for it really says no more than that all my representations in any given intuition must be subject to the condition under which alone I can ascribe them, as my representations, to the identical self, and therefore comprehend them, as synthetically connected, in one apperception through the general expression, I think.

And yet this need not be a principle for every possible understanding, but only for that which gives nothing manifold through its pure apperception in the representation, I am. An understanding which through its self-consciousness could give the manifold of intuition, and by whose representation the objects of that representation should at the same time exist, would not require a special act of the synthesis of the manifold for the unity of its consciousness, while the human understanding, which possesses the power of thought only, but not of intuition, requires such an act. To the human understanding that first principle is so indispensable that it really cannot form the least concept of any other possible understanding, whether it

*be intuitive by itself, or possessed of a sensuous intuition, dif-
ferent from that in space and time.*

§ *18.* WHAT IS THE OBJECTIVE UNITY OF SELF-CONSCIOUSNESS?

The transcendental unity *of apperception connects all the
manifold given in an intuition into a concept of an object. It is
therefore called* objective, *and must be distinguished from the*
subjective unity *of consciousness, which is a form of the* internal sense, *by which the manifold of intuition is empirically
given, to be thus connected. Whether I can become empirically
conscious of the manifold, as either simultaneous or successive, depends on circumstances, or empirical conditions. The
empirical unity of consciousness, therefore, through the association of representations, is itself phenomenal and wholly contingent, while the pure form of intuition in time, merely as
general intuition containing the manifold that is given, is subject to the original unity of the consciousness, through the necessary relation only of the manifold of intuition to the one,* I
think, *that is, through the pure synthesis of the understanding, which forms the* a priori *ground of the empirical synthesis. That unity alone is, therefore, valid objectively; the
empirical unity of apperception, which we do not consider
here, and which is only derived from the former, under given
conditions* in concreto, *has subjective validity only. One man
connects the representation of a word with one thing, another
with another, and the unity of consciousness, with regard to
what is empirical, is not necessary nor universally valid with
reference to that which is given.*

§ *19.* THE LOGICAL FORM OF ALL JUDGMENTS CONSISTS IN THE OBJECTIVE UNITY OF APPERCEPTION OF THE CONCEPTS CONTAINED THEREIN

*I could never feel satisfied with the definition of a judgment
in general, given by our logicians, who say that it is the representation of a relation between two concepts. Without disputing
with them in this place as to the defect of that explanation,
that it may possibly apply to categorical, but not to hypothetical and disjunctive judgments (the latter containing, not*

a relation of concepts, but of judgments themselves)—*though many tedious consequences have arisen from this mistake of logicians*—I must at least make this observation, that we are not told in what that relation consists.*

But, if I examine more closely the relation of given cognitions in every judgment, and distinguish it, as belonging to the understanding, from the relation according to the rules of reproductive imagination (which has subjective validity only), I find that a judgment is nothing but the mode of bringing given cognitions into the objective *unity* of apperception. This is what is intended by the copula is, which is meant to distinguish the objective unity of given representations from the subjective. It (the copula is) indicates their relation to the original appreciation, and their necessary unity, even though the judgment itself be empirical, and therefore contingent; as, for instance, bodies are heavy. By this I do not mean to say that these representations belong necessarily to each other, in the empirical intuition, but that they belong to each other by means of the necessary unity of apperception in the synthesis of intuitions, that is, according to the principles of the objective determination of all representations, so far as any cognition is to arise from them, these principles being all derived from the principle of the transcendental unity of apperception. Thus, and thus alone, does the relation become a judgment, that is, a relation that is valid objectively, and can thus be kept sufficiently distinct from the relation of the same representations, if it has subjective validity only, for instance, according to the laws of association. In the latter case, I could only say, that if I carry a body I feel the pressure of its weight, but not, that it, the body, is heavy, which is meant to say that these two representations are connected together in the object, whatever the state of the subject may be, and not only associated or conjoined in the perception, however often it may be repeated.

* *The lengthy doctrine of the four syllogistic figures concerns categorical syllogisms only, and though it is really nothing but a trick for obtaining the appearance of more modes of concluding than that of the first figure, by secretly introducing immediate conclusions* (consequentiae immediatae) *among the premisses of a pure syllogism, this would hardly have secured its great success, had not its authors succeeded, at the same time, in establishing the exclusive authority of categorical judgments, as those to which all others must be referred. This as we showed in § 9, p. 91 ff. is wrong.*

§ 20. ALL SENSUOUS INTUITIONS ARE SUBJECT TO THE CATEGORIES AS TO CONDITIONS UNDER WHICH ALONE THEIR MANIFOLD CONTENTS CAN COME TOGETHER IN ONE CONSCIOUSNESS

The manifold which is given us in a sensuous intuition is necessarily subject to the original synthetical unity of apperception, because by it alone the unity of intuition becomes possible (§ 17). That act of the understanding, further, by which the manifold of given representations (whether intuitions or concepts) is brought under one appreciation in general, is the logical function of a judgment (§ 19). The manifold, therefore, so far as it is given in an empirical intuition, is determined with regard to one of the logical functions of judgment, by which, indeed, it is brought to consciousness in general. The categories, however, are nothing but these functions of judgment, so far as the manifold of a given intuition is determined with respect to them (§ 13, p. 102 ff.). Therefore the manifold in any given intuition is naturally subject to the categories.

§ 21. NOTE

The manifold, contained in an intuition which I call my own, is represented through the synthesis of the understanding, as belonging to the necessary unity of self-consciousness, and this takes place through the category.*

This category indicates, therefore, that the empirical consciousness of the manifold, given in any intuition, is subject to a pure self-consciousness a priori, in the same manner as the empirical intuition is subject to a pure sensuous intuition which likewise takes place a priori.

In the above proposition a beginning is made of a deduction *of the pure concepts of the understanding. In this deduction, as the categories arise in the understanding only, independent of all sensibility, I ought not yet to take any account of the manner in which the manifold is given for an empirical intuition, but attend exclusively to the unity which, by means of the category, enters into the intuition through the understanding. In what follows (§ 26) we shall show, from the manner in*

---

* The proof of this rests on the represented unity of intuition, by which an object is given, and which always includes a synthesis of the manifold which is given for an intuition, and contains the relation of the latter to the unity of apperception.

which the empirical intuition is given in sensibility, that its unity is no other than that which is prescribed by the category (according to § 20) to the manifold of any given intuition. Thus only, that is, by showing their validity a priori with respect to all objects of our senses, the purpose of our deduction will be fully attained.

There is one thing, however, of which, in the above demonstration, I could not make abstraction: namely, that the manifold for an intuition must be given antecedently to the synthesis of the understanding, and independently of it; how, remains uncertain. For if I were to imagine an understanding, itself intuitive (for instance, a divine understanding, which should not represent to itself given objects, but produce them at once by his representation), the categories would have no meaning with respect to such cognition. They are merely rules for an understanding whose whole power consists in thinking, that is, in the act of bringing the synthesis of the manifold, which is given to it in intuition from elsewhere, to the unity of apperception; an understanding which therefore knows nothing by itself, but connects only and arranges the material for cognition, that is, the intuition which must be given to it by the object. This peculiarity of our understanding of producing unity of apperception a priori by means of the categories only, and again by such and so many, cannot be further explained, any more than why we have these and no other functions of judgment, and why time and space are the only forms of a possible intuition for us.

§ 22. THE CATEGORY ADMITS OF NO OTHER EMPLOYMENT

FOR THE COGNITION OF THINGS, BUT ITS APPLICATION

TO OBJECTS OF EXPERIENCE

We have seen that to think an object is not the same as to know an object. In order to know an object, we must have the concept by which any object is thought (the category), and likewise the intuition by which it is given. If no corresponding intuition could be given to a concept, it would still be a thought, so far as its form is concerned: but it would be without an object, and no knowledge of anything would be possible by it, because, so far as I know, there would be nothing, and there could be nothing, to which my thought could be referred. Now the only possible intuition for us is sensuous (see Aesthetic); the thought of any object, therefore, by means of a pure concept of the understanding, can with us become knowledge only, if it is referred to objects of the senses. Sensuous intuition is either pure (space and time), or empirical, i.e. if it is an intuition of that which is represented in space and time, through sensation as immediately real. By means of pure intuition we can gain knowledge a priori *of things as phenomena (in mathematics), but only so far as their form is concerned; but whether there are things which must be perceived, according to that form, remains unsettled. Mathematical concepts, by themselves, therefore, are not yet knowledge, except under the supposition that there are things which admit of being represented by us, according to the form of that pure sensuous intuition only. Consequently, as things in* space *and* time *are only given as perceptions (as representations accompanied by sensations), that is, through empirical representations, the pure concepts of the understanding, even if applied to intuitions* a priori, *as in mathematics, give us knowledge in so far only as these pure intuitions, and therefore through them the concepts of the understanding also, can be applied to empirical intuitions. Consequently the categories, by means of intuition, do not give us any knowledge of things, except under the supposition of their possible application to empirical intuition; they serve, in short, for the possibility of empirical* knowledge *only, which is called* experience. *From this it follows that the categories admit of no other employment for the cognition of things, except so far only as these are taken as objects of possible experience.*

§ 23

The foregoing proposition is of the greatest importance, for it determines the limits of the employment of the pure concepts of the understanding with reference to objects, in the same manner as the transcendental Aesthetic determined the limits of the employment of the pure form of our sensuous intuition. Space and time are conditions of the possibility of how objects can be given to us, so far only as objects of the senses, therefore of experience, are concerned. Beyond these limits they represent nothing, for they belong only to the senses, and have no reality beyond them. Pure concepts of the understanding are free from this limitation, and extend to objects of intuition in general, whether that intuition be like our own or not, if only it is sensuous and not intellectual. This further extension, however, of concepts beyond our sensuous intuition, is of no avail to us; for they are in that case empty concepts of objects, and the concepts do not even enable us to say, whether such objects be possible or not. They are mere forms of thought, without objective reality: because we have no intuition at hand to which the synthetical unity of apperception, which is contained in the concepts alone, could be applied, so that they might determine an object. Nothing can give them sense and meaning, except our sensuous and empirical intuition.

If, therefore, we assume an object of a non-sensuous intuition as given, we may, no doubt, determine it through all the predicates, which follow from the supposition that nothing belonging to sensuous intuition belongs to it, that, therefore, it is not extended, or not in space, that its duration is not time, that no change (succession of determinations in time) is to be met in it, etc. But we can hardly call this knowledge, if we only indicate how the intuition of an object is not, without being able to say what is contained in it, for, in that case, I have not represented the possibility of an object, corresponding to my pure concept of the understanding, because I could give no intuition corresponding to it, but could only say that our intuition did not apply to it. But what is the most important is this, that not even a single category could be applied to such a thing; as, for instance, the concept of substance, that is, of something that can exist as a subject only, but never as a mere predicate. For I do not know whether there can be anything corresponding to such a determination of thought, unless empirical intuition supplies the case for its application. Of this more hereafter.

§ 24. OF THE APPLICATION OF THE CATEGORIES TO OBJECTS OF THE SENSES IN GENERAL

The pure concepts of the understanding refer, through the mere understanding, to objects of intuition, whether it be our own, or any other, if only sensuous intuition, but they are, for that very reason, mere forms of thought, by which no definite object can be known. The synthesis, or connection of the manifold in them, referred only to the unity of apperception, and became thus the ground of the possibility of knowledge a priori, so far as it rests on the understanding, and is therefore not only transcendental, but also purely intellectual. Now as there exists in us a certain form of sensuous intuition a priori, which rests on the receptivity of the faculty of representation (sensibility), the understanding, as spontaneity, is able to determine the internal sense through the manifold of given representations, according to the synthetical unity of apperception, and can thus think synthetical unity of the apperception of the manifold of sensuous intuition a priori, as the condition to which all objects of our (human) intuition must necessarily be subject.

Thus the categories, though pure forms of thought, receive objective reality, that is, application to objects which can be given to us in intuition, but as phenomena only; for it is with reference to them alone that we are capable of intuition a priori.

This synthesis of the manifold of sensuous intuition, which is possible and necessary a priori, *may be called* figurative (synthesis speciosa), *in order to distinguish it from that which is thought in the mere category, with reference to the manifold of an intuition in general, and is called intellectual synthesis* (synthesis intellectualis). *Both are transcendental, not only because they themselves are carried out* a priori, *but because they establish also the possibility of other knowledge* a priori.

But this figurative synthesis, if it refers to the original synthetical unity of apperception only, that is, to that transcendental unity which is thought in the categories, must be called the transcendental synthesis of the faculty of imagination, in order thus to distinguish it from the purely intellectual synthesis. Imagination *is the faculty of representing an object even without its presence in intuition. As all our intuition is sensuous, the faculty of imagination belongs, on account of the subjective condition under which alone it can give a corresponding intuition to the concepts of the understanding, to our* sensibility. *As, however, its synthesis is an act of spontaneity, determining, and not, like the senses, determinable only, and therefore able to determine* a priori *the senses, so far as their form is concerned, according to the unity of apperception, the faculty of imagination is, so far, a faculty of determining our sensibility* a priori, *so that the synthesis of the intuitions, according to the* categories, *must be the transcendental synthesis of the faculty of imagination. This is an effect, produced by the understanding on our sensibility, and the first application of it (and at the same time the ground of all others) to objects of the intuition which is only possible to us. As figurative, it is distinguished from the intellectual synthesis, which takes place by the understanding only, without the aid of the faculty of imagination. In so far as imagination is spontaneity, I call it occasionally* productive *imagination: distinguishing it from the* reproductive, *which in its synthesis is subject to empirical laws only, namely, those of association, and which is of no help for the explanation of the possibility of knowledge* a priori, *belonging, therefore, to psychology, and not to transcendental philosophy.*

*   *   *

This is the proper place for trying to account for the paradox, which must have struck everybody in our exposition of the form of the internal sense; namely, how that sense represents to the consciousness even ourselves, not as we are by ourselves, but as we appear to ourselves, because we perceive ourselves only as we are affected internally. This seems to be contradictory, because we should thus be in a passive relation to ourselves; and for this reason the founders of the systems of psychology have preferred to represent the internal sense as identical with the faculty of apperception, while we have carefully distinguished the two.

What determines the internal sense is the understanding, and its original power of connecting the manifold of intuition, that is, of bringing it under one apperception, this being the very ground of the possibility of the understanding. As in us men the understanding is not itself an intuitive faculty, and could not, even if intuitions were given in our sensibility, take them into itself, in order to connect, as it were, the manifold of its own intuition, the synthesis of the understanding, if considered by itself alone, is nothing but the unity of action, of which it is conscious without sensibility also, but through which the understanding is able to determine that sensibility internally, with respect to the manifold which may be given to it (the understanding) according to the form of its intuition. The understanding, therefore, exercises its activity, under the name of a transcendental synthesis of the faculty of imagination, *on the passive subject to which it* belongs *as a faculty, and we are right in saying that the internal sense is affected by that activity. The apperception with its synthetical unity is so far from being identical with the internal sense, that, as the source of all synthesis, it rather applies, under the name of the categories, to the manifold of intuitions in general, that is, to objects in general before all sensuous intuition; while the internal sense, on the contrary, contains the mere form of intuition, but without any connection of the manifold in it, and therefore, as yet, no definite intuition, which becomes possible only through the consciousness of the determination of the internal sense by the transcendental act of the faculty of imagination (the synthetical influence of the understanding on the internal sense) which I have called the figurative synthesis.*

This we can always perceive in ourselves. We cannot think a line without drawing it in thought; we cannot think a circle without describing it; we cannot represent, at all, the three dimensions of space, without placing, from the same point, three lines perpendicularly on each other; nay, we cannot even represent time, except by attending, during our drawing a straight line (which is meant to be the external figurative representa-

tion of time) to the act of the synthesis of the manifold only by which we successively determine the internal sense, and thereby to the succession of that determination in it. It is really motion, as the act of the subject (not as the determination of an object*), therefore the synthesis of the manifold in space (abstraction being made of space, and our attention fixed on the act only by which we determine the internal sense, according to its form), which first produces the very concept of succession. The understanding does not, therefore, find in the internal sense such a connection of the manifold, but produces it by affecting the internal sense. It may seem difficult to understand how the thinking ego can be different from the ego which sees or perceives itself (other modes of intuition being at least conceivable), and yet identical with the latter as the same subject, and how, therefore, I can say: I, as intelligence and thinking subject, know myself as an object thought so far as being given to myself in intuition also, but like other phenomena, not as I am to the understanding, but only as I appear to myself. In reality, however, this is neither more nor less difficult than how I can be, to myself, an object, and, more especially, an object of intuition and of internal perceptions. But that this must really be so, can clearly be shown—if only we admit space to be merely a pure form of the phenomena of the external senses—by the fact that we cannot represent to ourselves time, which is no object of external intuition, in any other way than under the image of a line which we draw, a mode of representation without which we could not realise the unity of its dimension; or again by this other fact that we must always derive the determination of the length of time, or of points of time for all our internal perceptions, from that which is represented to us as changeable by external things, and have therefore to arrange the determinations of internal sense as phenomena in time, in exactly the same way in which we arrange the determinations of the external sense in space. If, then, with regard to the latter, we admit that by them we know objects so far only as we are affected externally, we must also admit, with regard to the internal sense, that by it we only are, or perceive ourselves, as we are internally affected by ourselves, in other

---

* Motion of an object in space does not belong to a pure science, consequently not to geometry, because the fact that a thing is moveable cannot be known a priori, but from experience only. Motion, however, considered as describing a space, is a pure act of successive synthesis of the manifold in external intuition in general by means of productive imagination, and belongs therefore, by right, not only to geometry, but even to transcendental philosophy.

words, that with regard to internal intuition we know our own self as a phenomenon only, and not as it is by itself. *

§ 25

In the transcendental synthesis, however, of the manifold of representations in general, and therefore in the original synthetical unity of apperception, I am conscious of myself, neither as I appear to myself, nor as I am by myself, but only that I am. This representation *is an act of* thought, *not of* intuition. *Now, in order to know ourselves, we require, besides the act of thinking, which brings the manifold of every possible intuition to the unity of apperception, a definite kind of intuition also by which that manifold is given, and thus, though my own existence is not phenomenal (much less a mere illusion), yet the determination of my existence† can only take place according to the form of the internal sense, and in that special manner in which the manifold, which I connect, is given in the internal intuition. This shows that I have no* knowledge *of myself as I am, but only as I appear to myself. The consciousness of oneself is therefore very far from being a knowledge of oneself, in spite of all the categories which constitute the thinking of an object in general, by means of the connection of the manifold in an apperception. As for the knowledge of an object different from myself I require, besides the thinking of an object in general (in a category), an intuition also, to determine that general concept, I require for the knowledge of my own*

---

* *I do not see how so much difficulty should be found in admitting that the internal sense is affected by ourselves. Every act of* attention *gives us an instance of it. In such an act the understanding always determines the internal sense, according to the connection which it thinks, to such an internal intuition as corresponds to the manifold in the synthesis of the understanding. How much the mind is commonly affected thereby anybody will be able to perceive in himself.*

† *The* I *think expresses the act of determining my own existence. What is thus given is the existence, but what is not yet given, is the manner in which I am to determine it, that is, in which I am to place within me the manifold belonging to it. For that purpose self-intuition is required, which depends on an a priori form, that is, on time, which is sensuous, and belongs to our receptivity of what is given to us as determinable. If, then, I have not another self-intuition which, likewise before the act of* determination, *gives the determining within me, of the spontaneity of which I am conscious only, as* time *gives the determinable, I cannot determine my existence as that of a spontaneously acting being, but I only represent to myself the spontaneity of my thinking, that is, of the act of determination, my existence remaining sensuous only, that is, determinable, as the existence of a phenomenon. It is, however, on account of this spontaneity that I call myself an* intelligence.

*self, besides consciousness, or besides my thinking myself, an
intuition also of the manifold in me, to determine that thought.
I exist, therefore, as such an intelligence, which is simply conscious of its power of connection, but with respect to the manifold that has to be connected, is subject to a limiting condition
which is called the internal sense, according to which that
connection can only become perceptible in relations of time,
which lie entirely outside the concepts of the understanding.
Such an intelligence, therefore, can only know itself as it appears to itself in an intuition (which cannot be intellectual and
given by the understanding itself), and not as it would know
itself, if its intuition were intellectual.*

§ 26. TRANSCENDENTAL DEDUCTION OF THE UNIVERSALLY POSSIBLE EMPLOYMENT OF THE PURE CONCEPTS OF THE UNDERSTANDING IN EXPERIENCE

In the metaphysical deduction *of the* categories *their* a priori
*origin was proved by their complete accordance with the gen-
eral logical functions of thought, while in their* transcendental
*deduction we established their possibility as knowledge a priori
of objects of an intuition in general (§ 20, 21). Now we have
to explain the possibility of our knowing a priori, by means of
the categories, whatever objects may* come before our senses,
*and this not according to the form of their intuition, but
according to the laws of their connection, and of our thus, as
it were, prescribing laws to nature, nay, making nature possible.
Unless they were adequate to that purpose, we could not understand how everything that may come before our senses must
be subject to laws which have their origin a priori in the understanding alone.*

First of all, I observe that by the synthesis of apprehension
*I understand the connection of the manifold in an empirical
intuition, by which perception, that is, empirical consciousness
of it (as phenomenal), becomes possible.*

*We have forms of the external as well as the internal intui-
tion* a priori, *in our representations of space and time: and to
these the synthesis of the apprehension of the manifold in
phenomena must always conform, because it can take place
according to that form only. Time and space, however, are
represented* a priori, *not only as forms of sensuous intuition,
but as intuitions themselves (containing a manifold), and therefore with the determination of the unity of that manifold in*

them (see transcendental Aesthetic.*). Therefore unity of the synthesis *of the manifold without or within us, and consequently a* connection *to which everything that is to be represented as determined in space and time must conform, is given* a priori *as the condition of the synthesis of all* apprehension simultaneously with *the intuitions, not* in *them, and that synthetical unity can be no other but that of the connection of the manifold of any* intuition whatsoever *in an original consciousness, according to the categories, only applied to our* sensuous intuition. *Consequently, all synthesis, without which even perception would be impossible, is subject to the categories; and as experience consists of knowledge by means of connected perceptions, the categories are conditions of the possibility of experience, and valid therefore* a priori *also for all objects of experience.*

* * *

If, for instance, I raise the empirical intuition of a house, through the apprehension of the manifold contained therein, into a perception, the necessary unity of space and of external sensuous intuition in general *is presupposed, and I draw, as it were, the shape of the house according to that synthetical unity of the manifold in space. But this very synthetical unity, if I make abstraction of the form of space, has its seat in the understanding, and is in fact the category of the* synthesis *of the* homogeneous *in intuition in general: that is, the category of* quantity, *to which that synthesis of apprehension, that is, the perception, must always conform.†*

Or if, to take another example, I perceive the freezing of water, I apprehend two states (that of fluidity and that of solidity), and these as standing to each other in a relation of time.

---

* *Space, represented as an object (as required in geometry), contains more than the mere form of intuition, namely, the comprehension of the manifold, which is given according to the form of sensibility, into a perceptible (intuitable) representation, so that the form of intuition gives the manifold only, while the formal intuition gives unity of representation. In the Aesthetic I had simply ascribed this unity to sensibility, in order to show that it precedes all concepts, though it presupposes a synthesis not belonging to the senses, and by which all concepts of space and time become first possible. For as by that synthesis (the understanding determining the sensibility) space and time are first given as intuitions, the unity of that intuition a priori belongs to space and time, and not to the concept of the understanding. (See § 24.)*

† *In this manner it is proved that the synthesis of apprehension, which is empirical, must necessarily conform to the synthesis of apperception, which is intellectual, and contained in the category entirely a priori. It is one and the same spontaneity, which there, under the name of imagination, and here, under the name of understanding, brings connection into the manifold of intuition.*

But in the time, which as internal intuition *I make the foundation of the phenomenon, I represent to myself necessarily synthetical* unity *of the manifold, without which that relation could not be given as* determined *in an intuition* (*with reference to the succession of time*). *That synthetical unity, however, as a condition* a priori, *under which I connect the manifold of* any *intuition, turns out to be, if I make abstraction of the permanent form of my intuition, namely, of time, the category of* cause, *through which, if I apply it to my sensibility, I determine* everything that happens, according to its relation in time. *Thus the apprehension in such an event, and that event itself considered as a possible perception, is subject to the concept of the* relation of cause and effect. *The same applies to all other cases.*

*   *   *

Categories are concepts which a priori *prescribe laws to all phenomena, and therefore to nature as the sum total of all phenomena* (natura materialiter spectata). *The question therefore arises, as these laws are not derived from nature, nor conform to it as their model* (*in which case they would be empirical only*), *how we can understand that nature should conform to them, that is, how they can determine* a priori *the connection of the manifold in nature, without taking that connection from nature. The solution of that riddle is this.*

It is no more surprising that the laws of phenomena in nature must agree with the understanding and its form a priori, *that is, with its power of* connecting *the manifold in general, than that the phenomena themselves must agree with the form of sensuous intuition* a priori. *For laws exist as little in phenomena themselves, but relatively only, with respect to the subject to which, so far as it has understanding, the phenomena belong, as phenomena exist by themselves, but relatively only, with respect to the same being so far as it has senses. Things by themselves would necessarily possess their conformity to the law, independent also of any understanding by which they are known. But phenomena are only representations of things, unknown as to what they may be by themselves. As mere representations they are subject to no law of connection, except that which is prescribed by the connecting faculty. Now that which connects the manifold of sensuous intuition is the faculty of imagination, which receives from the understanding the unity of its intellectual synthesis, and from sensibility the manifoldness of apprehension. Thus, as all possible perceptions depend on the synthesis of apprehension, and that synthesis itself, that empirical synthesis, depends on the transcendental, and,*

*therefore, on the categories, it follows that all possible percep-
tions, everything in fact that can come to the empirical consciousness, that is, all phenomena of nature, must, so far as
their connection is concerned, be subject to the categories. On
these categories, therefore, nature (considered as nature in
general) depends, as on the original ground of its necessary
conformity to law (as* natura formaliter spectata). *Beyond the
laws, on which* nature in general, *as a lawful order of phenomena in space and time depends, the pure faculty of the understanding is incapable of prescribing* a priori, *by means of mere
categories, laws to phenomena. Special laws, therefore, as they
refer to phenomena which are empirically determined, cannot
be completely derived from the categories, although they are
all subject to them. Experience must be superadded in order
to know such special laws: while those other* a priori *laws
inform us only with regard to experience in general, and what
can be known as an object of it.*

§ 27. RESULTS OF THIS DEDUCTION OF THE CONCEPTS OF
THE UNDERSTANDING

*We cannot think any object except by means of the cate-
gories; we cannot know any subject that has been thought,
except by means of intuitions, corresponding to those concepts.
Now all our intuitions are sensuous, and this knowledge, so far
as its object is given, is empirical. But empirical knowledge is
experience, and therefore no* knowledge a priori *is possible to
us, except of* objects *of possible* experience *only.**

*This knowledge, however, though limited to objects of ex-
perience, is not, therefore, entirely derived from experience,
for both the pure intuitions and the pure concepts of the understanding are elements of knowledge which exist in us* a priori.
*Now there are only two ways in which a necessary harmony of
experience with the concepts of its objects can be conceived;
either experience makes these concepts possible, or these con-*

---

* *Lest anybody should be unnecessarily frightened by the dangerous
consequences of this proposition, I shall only remark that the categories
are not limited for the purpose of* thought *by the conditions of our
sensuous intuition, but have really an unlimited field. It is only the
knowledge of that which we think, the determining of an object, that
requires intuition, and even in the absence of intuition, the thought of
the object may still have its true and useful consequences, so far as the
subjective use of reason is concerned. That use of reason, however, as it
is not always directed to the determination of the object, that is, to
knowledge, but also to the determination of the subject, and its volition,
cannot be treated of in this place.*

cepts make experience possible. The former will not hold good with respect to the categories (nor with pure sensuous intuition), for they are concepts a priori, and therefore independent of experience. To ascribe to them an empirical origin, would be to admit a kind of generatio aequivoca. *There remains, therefore, the second alternative only (a kind of system of the epigenesis of pure reason), namely, that the categories, on the part of the understanding, contain the grounds of the possibility of all experience in general. How they render experience possible, and what principles of the possibility of experience they supply in their employment on phenomena, will be shown more fully in the following chapter on the transcendental employment of the faculty of judgment.*

Some one might propose to adopt a middle way between the two, namely, that the categories are neither self-produced *first principles a priori of our knowledge, nor derived from experience, but subjective dispositions of thought, implanted in us with our existence, and so arranged by our Creator that their employment should accurately agree with the laws of nature, which determine experience (a kind of system of preformation of pure reason). But, in that case, not only would there be no end of such an hypothesis, so that no one could know how far the supposition of predetermined dispositions to future judgments might be carried, but there is this decided objection against that middle course that, by adopting it, the categories would lose that necessity which is essential to them. Thus the concept of cause, which asserts, under a presupposed condition, the necessity of an effect, would become false, if it rested only on some subjective necessity implanted in us of connecting certain empirical representations according to the rule of causal relation. I should not be able to say that the effect is connected with the cause in the object (that is, by necessity), but only, I am so constituted that I cannot think these representations as connected in any other way. This is exactly what the sceptic most desires, for in that case all our knowledge, resting on the supposed objective validity of our judgments, is nothing but mere illusion, nor would there be wanting people to say they know nothing of such subjective necessity (which can only be felt); and at all events we could not quarrel with anybody about what depends only on the manner in which his own subject is organised.*

Comprehensive View of this Deduction

The deduction of the pure concepts of the understanding (and with them of all theoretical knowledge a priori) consists

*in representing them as principles of the possibility of experi-
ence, and in representing experience as the* determination *of
phenomena in space and time, and, lastly, in representing that
determination as depending on the principle of the* original
*synthetical unity of apperception, as the form of the under-
standing, applied to space and time, as the original forms of
sensibility.*[13]

Deduction of the Pure Concepts
of the Understanding
Section II

OF THE A PRIORI GROUNDS FOR THE POSSIBILITY OF

EXPERIENCE

[That a concept should be produced entirely *a priori* and yet
refer to an object, though itself neither belonging to the sphere
of possible experience, nor consisting of the elements of such
an experience, is self-contradictory and impossible. It would
have no contents, because no intuition corresponds to it, and
intuitions by which objects are given to us constitute the whole
field or the complete object of possible experience. An *a priori*
concept therefore not referring to experience would be the
logical form only of a concept, but not the concept itself by
which something is thought.

If therefore there exist any pure concepts *a priori*, though
they cannot contain anything empirical, they must nevertheless
all be conditions *a priori* of a possible experience, on which
alone their objective reality depends.

If therefore we wish to know how pure concepts of the
understanding are possible, we must try to find out what are
the conditions *a priori* on which the possibility of experience
depends, nay, on which it is founded, apart from all that is
empirical in phenomena. A concept expressing this formal
and objective condition of experience with sufficient generality

[13] Kant does not carry the division into paragraphs in his second
edition further, because, as he says, he has to treat no more of elementary concepts, and prefers, in representing their employment, to adopt a
continuous treatment, without paragraphs.

might properly be called a pure concept of the understanding.
If we once have these pure concepts of the understanding, we
may also imagine objects which are either impossible, or, if not
impossible in themselves, yet can never be given in any experience. We have only in the connection of those concepts to
leave out something which necessarily belongs to the conditions
of a possible experience (concept of a spirit), or to extend
pure concepts of the understanding beyond what can be
reached by experience (concept of God). But the elements of
all knowledge *a priori,* even of gratuitous and preposterous
fancies, though not borrowed from experience (for in that
case they would not be knowledge *a priori*) must nevertheless
contain the pure conditions *a priori* of a possible experience
and its object, otherwise not only would nothing be thought
by them, but they themselves, being without data, could never
arise in our mind.

Such concepts, then, which comprehend the pure thinking
a priori involved in every experience, are discovered in the
categories, and it is really a sufficient deduction of them and a
justification of their objective validity, if we succeed in proving
that by them alone an object can be thought. But as in such
a process of thinking more is at work than the faculty of thinking only, namely, the understanding, and as the understanding,
as a faculty of knowledge which is meant to refer to objects,
requires quite as much an explanation as to the possibility of
such a reference, it is necessary for us to consider the subjective sources which form the foundation *a priori* for the
possibility of experience, not according to their empirical, but
according to their transcendental character.

If every single representation stood by itself, as if isolated
and separated from the others, nothing like what we call
knowledge could ever arise, because knowledge forms a whole
of representations connected and compared with each other.
If therefore I ascribe to the senses a synopsis, because in their
intuition they contain something manifold, there corresponds
to it always a synthesis, and receptivity can make knowledge
possible only when joined with spontaneity. This spontaneity,
now, appears as a threefold synthesis which must necessarily
take place in every kind of knowledge, namely, first, that of
the *apprehension* of representations as modifications of the
soul in intuition, secondly, of the *reproduction* of them in the
imagination, and, thirdly, that of their *recognition* in concepts.
This leads us to three subjective sources of knowledge which
render possible the understanding, and through it all experience
as an empirical product of the understanding.

Preliminary Remark

The deduction of the categories is beset with so many difficulties and obliges us to enter so deeply into the first grounds of the possibility of our knowledge in general, that I thought it more expedient, in order to avoid the lengthiness of a complete theory, and yet to omit nothing in so essential an investigation, to add the following four paragraphs with a view of preparing rather than instructing the reader. After that only I shall in the third section proceed to a systematical discussion of these elements of the understanding. Till then the reader must not allow himself to be frightened by a certain amount of obscurity which at first is inevitable on a road never trodden before, but which, when we come to that section, will give way, I hope, to a complete comprehension.

1. OF THE SYNTHESIS OF APPREHENSION IN INTUITION

Whatever the origin of our representations may be, whether they be due to the influence of external things or to internal causes, whether they have arisen *a priori* or empirically as phenomena, as modifications of the mind they must always belong to the internal sense, and all our knowledge must therefore finally be subject to the formal condition of that internal sense, namely, time, in which they are all arranged, joined, and brought into certain relations to each other. This is a general remark which must never be forgotten in all that follows.

Every representation contains something manifold, which could not be represented as such, unless the mind distinguished the time in the succession of one impression after another; for as contained in one moment, each representation can never be anything but absolute unity. In order to change this manifold into a unity of intuition (as, for instance, in the representation of space), it is necessary first to run through the manifold and then to hold it togther. It is this act which I call the synthesis of apprehension, because it refers directly to intuition which no doubt offers something manifold, but which, without a synthesis, can never make it such, as it is contained in *one* representation.

This synthesis of apprehension must itself be carried out *a priori* also, that is, with reference to representations which are not empirical. For without it we should never be able to have the representations either of space or time *a priori*, because these cannot be produced except by a synthesis of the manifold which the senses offer in their original receptivity.

It follows therefore that we have a pure synthesis of apprehension.

2. OF THE SYNTHESIS OF REPRODUCTION IN IMAGINATION

It is no doubt nothing but an empirical law according to which representations which have often followed or accompanied one another, become associated in the end and so closely united that, even without the presence of the object, one of these representations will, according to an invariable law, produce a transition of the mind to the other. This law of reproduction, however, presupposes that the phenomena themselves are really subject to such a rule, and that there is in the variety of these representations a sequence and concomitancy subject to certain rules; for without this the faculty of empirical imagination would never find anything to do that it is able to do, and remain therefore buried within our mind as a dead faculty, unknown to ourselves. If cinnabar were sometimes red and sometimes black, sometimes light and sometimes heavy, if a man could be changed now into this, now into another animal shape, if on the longest day the fields were sometimes covered with fruit, sometimes with ice and snow, the faculty of my empirical imagination would never be in a position, when representing red colour, to think of heavy cinnabar. Nor, if a certain name could be given sometimes to this, sometimes to that object, or if that the same object could sometimes be called by one, and sometimes by another name, without any rule to which representations are subject by themselves, would it be possible that any empirical synthesis of reproduction should ever take place.

There must therefore be something to make this reproduction of phenomena possible by being itself the foundation *a priori* of a necessary synthetical unity of them. This becomes clear if we only remember that all phenomena are not things by themselves, but only the play of our representations, all of which are in the end determinations only of the internal sense. If therefore we could prove that even our purest intuitions *a priori* give us no knowledge, unless they contain such a combination of the manifold as to render a constant synthesis of reproduction possible, it would follow that this synthesis of the imagination is, before all experience, founded on principles *a priori*, and that we must admit a pure transcendental synthesis of imagination which forms even the foundation of the possibility of all experience, such experience being impossible without the reproductibility of phenomena. Now, when I draw a line in thought, or if I think the time from one noon to another, or if I only represent to myself a certain number, it is clear that I must first necessarily apprehend one of these manifold representations after another. If I were to lose from my thoughts what precedes, whether the first parts of a line or the antecedent portions of time, or the numerical unities representing one after the other, and if, while I proceed to what follows, I were unable to reproduce what came before, there would never be a complete representation, and none of the before-mentioned thoughts, not even the first and purest representations of space and time, could ever arise within us.

The synthesis of apprehension is therefore inseparably connected with the synthesis of reproduction, and as the former constitutes the transcendental ground of the possibility of all knowledge in general (not only of empirical, but also of pure *a priori* knowledge), it follows that a reproductive synthesis of imagination belongs to the transcendental acts of the soul. We may therefore call this faculty the transcendental faculty of imagination.

3. OF THE SYNTHESIS OF RECOGNITION IN CONCEPTS

Without our being conscious that what we are thinking now is the same as what we thought a moment before, all reproduction in the series of representations would be vain. Each representation would, in its present state, be a new one, and in no wise belonging to the act by which it was to be produced by degrees, and the manifold in it would never form a whole, because deprived of that unity which consciousness alone can impart to it. If in counting I forget that the unities which now present themselves to my mind have been added gradually one to the other, I should not know the production of the quantity by the successive addition of one to one, nor should I know consequently the number, produced by the counting, this number being a concept consisting entirely in the consciousness of that unity of synthesis.

The very word of concept (*Begriff*) could have suggested this remark, for it is the *one* consciousness which unites the manifold that has been perceived successively, and afterwards reproduced into one representation. This consciousness may often be very faint, and we may connect it with the effect only, and not with the act itself, i.e. with the production of a representation. But in spite of this, that consciousness, though deficient in pointed clearness, must always be there, and without it, concepts, and with them, knowledge of objects are perfectly impossible.

And here we must needs arrive at a clear understanding of what we mean by an object of representations. We said before that phenomena are nothing but sensuous representations, which therefore by themselves must not be taken for objects outside our faculty of representation. What then do we mean if we speak of an object corresponding to, and therefore also different from our knowledge? It is easy to see that such an object can only be conceived as something in general = *x:* because, beside our knowledge, we have absolutely nothing which we could put down as corresponding to that knowledge.

Now we find that our conception of the relation of all knowledge to its object contains something of necessity, the object being looked upon as that which prevents our knowledge from being determined at haphazard, and causes it to be determined *a priori* in a certain way, because, as they are all to refer to an object, they must necessarily, with regard to that object, agree with each other, that is to say, possess that unity which constitutes the concept of an object.

It is clear also that, as we can only deal with the manifold in our representations, and as the *x* corresponding to them (the object), since it is to be something different from all our representations, is really nothing to us, it is clear, I say, that the unity, necessitated by the object, cannot be anything but the formal unity of our consciousness in the synthesis of the manifold in our representations. Then and then only do we say that we know an object, if we have produced synthetical unity in the manifold of intuition. Such unity is impossible, if the intuition could not be produced, according to a rule, by such a function of synthesis as makes the reproduction of the manifold *a priori* necessary, and a concept in which that manifold is united, possible. Thus we conceive a triangle as an object, if we are conscious of the combination of three straight lines, according to a rule, which renders such an intuition possible at all times. This *unity of rule* determines the manifold and limits it to conditions which render the unity of apperception possible, and the concept of that unity is really the representation of the object = *x*, which I think, by means of the predicates of a triangle.

No knowledge is possible without a concept, however obscure or imperfect it may be, and a concept is always, with regard to its form, something general, something that can serve as a rule. Thus the concept of body serves as a rule to our knowledge of external phenomena, according to the unity of

the manifold which is thought by it. It can only be such a rule
of intuitions because representing, in any given phenomena,
the necessary reproduction of their manifold elements, or the
synthetical unity in our consciousness of them. Thus the concept of body, whenever we perceive something outside us,
necessitates the representation of extension, and, with it, those
of impermeability, shape, etc.

Necessity is always founded on transcendental conditions.
There must be therefore a transcendental ground of the unity
of our consciousness in the synthesis of the manifold of all our
intuitions, and therefore also a transcendental ground of all
concepts of objects in general, and therefore again of all objects of experience, without which it would be impossible to
add to our intuitions the thought of an object, for the object
is no more than that something of which the concept predicates
such a necessity of synthesis.

That original and transcendental condition is nothing else
but what I call *transcendental apperception*. The consciousness
of oneself, according to the determinations of our state, is, with
all our internal perceptions, empirical only, and always tran-
sient. There can be no fixed or permanent self in that stream
of internal phenomena. It is generally called the *internal sense*,
or the empirical apperception. What is necessarily to be represented as numerically identical with itself, cannot be thought
as such by means of empirical data only. It must be a condition
which precedes all experience, and in fact renders it possible,
for thus only could such a transcendental supposition acquire
validity.

No knowledge can take place in us, no conjunction or unity
of one kind of knowledge with another, without that unity of
consciousness which precedes all data of intuition, and without
reference to which no representation of objects is possible.
This pure, original, and unchangeable consciousness I shall call
transcendental apperception. That it deserves such a name
may be seen from the fact that even the purest objective unity,
namely, that of the concepts *a priori* (space and time), is possible only by a reference of all intuitions to it. The numerical
unity of that apperception therefore forms the *a priori* condition of all concepts, as does the manifoldness of space and
time of the intuitions of the senses.

The same transcendental unity of apperception constitutes,
in all possible phenomena which may come together in our
experience, a connection of all these representations according
to laws. For that unity of consciousness would be impossible,
if the mind, in the knowledge of the manifold, could not
become conscious of the identity of function, by which it unites

the manifold synthetically in one knowledge. Therefore the original and necessary consciousness of the identity of oneself is at the same time a consciousness of an equally necessary unity of the synthesis of all phenomena according to concepts, that is, according to rules, which render them not only necessarily reproducible, but assign also to their intuition an object, that is, a concept of something in which they are necessarily united. The mind could never conceive the identity of itself in the manifoldness of its representations (and this *a priori*) if it did not clearly perceive the identity of its action, by which it subjects all synthesis of apprehension (which is empirical) to a transcendental unity, and thus renders its regular coherence *a priori* possible. When we have clearly perceived this, we shall be able to determine more accurately our concept of an object in general. All representations have, as representations, their object, and can themselves in turn become objects of other representations. The only objects which can be given to us immediately are phenomena, and whatever in them refers immediately to the object is called intuition. These phenomena, however, are not things in themselves, but representations only which have their object, but an object that can no longer be seen by us, and may therefore be called the not-empirical, that is, the transcendental object, $= x$.

The pure concept of such a transcendental object (which in reality in all our knowledge is always the same $= x$) is that which alone can give to all our empirical concepts a relation to an object or objective reality. That concept cannot contain any definite intuition, and can therefore refer to that unity only, which must be found in the manifold of our knowledge, so far as it stands in relation to an object. That relation is nothing else but a necessary unity of consciousness, and therefore also of the synthesis of the manifold, by a common function of the mind, which unites it in one representation. As that unity must be considered as *a priori* necessary (because, without it, our knowledge would be without an object), we may conclude that the relation to a transcendental object, that is, the objective reality of our empirical knowledge, rests on a transcendental law, that all phenomena, if they are to give us objects, must be subject to rules *a priori* of a synthetical unity of these objects, by which rules alone their mutual relation in an empirical intuition becomes possible: that is, they must be subject, in experience, to the conditions of the necessary unity of apperception quite as much as, in mere intuition, to the formal conditions of space and time. Without this no knowledge is possible.

4. PRELIMINARY EXPLANATION OF THE POSSIBILITY OF

THE CATEGORIES AS KNOWLEDGE A PRIORI

There is but one experience in which all perceptions are
represented as in permanent and regular connection, as there
is but one space and one time in which all forms of phenomena
and all relations of being or not being take place. If we speak
of different experiences, we only mean different perceptions so
far as they belong to one and the same general experience.
It is the permanent and synthetical unity of perceptions that
constitutes the form of experience, and experience is nothing
but the synthetical unity of phenomena according to concepts.

Unity of synthesis, according to empirical concepts, would
be purely accidental, nay, unless these were founded on a transcendental ground of unity, a whole crowd of phenomena
might rush into our soul, without ever forming real experience.
All relation between our knowledge and its objects would be
lost at the same time, because that knowledge would no longer
be held together by general and necessary laws; it would therefore become thoughtless intuition, never knowledge, and would
be to us the same as nothing.

The conditions *a priori* of any possible experience in general
are at the same time conditions of the possibility of any objects
of our experience. Now I maintain that the categories of which
we are speaking are nothing but the conditions of thought
which make experience possible, as much as space and time
contain the conditions of that intuition which forms experience. These categories therefore are also fundamental concepts by which we think objects in general for the phenomena,
and have therefore *a priori* objective validity. This is exactly
what we wish to prove.

The possibility, nay the necessity of these categories rests on
the relation between our whole sensibility, and therefore all
possible phenomena, and that original apperception in which
everything must be necessarily subject to the conditions of the
permanent unity of self-consciousness, that is, must submit to
the general functions of that synthesis which we call synthesis
according to concepts, by which alone our apperception can
prove its permanent and necessary identity *a priori*. Thus the
concept of cause is nothing but a synthesis of that which follows in temporal succession, with other phenomena, but a synthesis according to concepts: and without such a unity which
rests on a rule *a priori*, and subjects all phenomena to itself,
no permanent and general, and therefore necessary unity of
consciousness would be formed in the manifold of our per-

ceptions. Such perceptions would then belong to no experience at all, they would be without an object, a blind play of representations—less even than a dream.

All attempts therefore at deriving those pure concepts of the understanding from experience, and ascribing to them a purely empirical origin, are perfectly vain and useless. I shall not dwell here on the fact that a concept of cause, for instance, contains an element of necessity, which no experience can ever supply, because experience, though it teaches us that after one phenomenon something else follows habitually, can never teach us that it follows necessarily, nor that we could *a priori*, and without any limitation, derive from it, as a condition, any conclusion as to what must follow. And thus I ask with reference to that empirical rule of association, which must always be admitted if we say that everything in the succession of events is so entirely subject to rules that nothing ever happens without something preceding it on which it always follows— What does it rest on, if it is a law of nature, nay, how is that very association possible? You call the ground for the possibility of the association of the manifold, so far as it is contained in the objects themselves, the *affinity* of the manifold. I ask, therefore, how do you make that permanent affinity by which phenomena stand, nay, must stand, under permanent laws, conceivable to yourselves?

According to my principles it is easily conceivable. All possible phenomena belong, as representations, to the whole of our possible self-consciousness. From this, as a transcendental representation, numerical identity is inseparable and *a priori* certain, because nothing can become knowledge except by means of that original apperception. As this identity must necessarily enter into the synthesis of the whole of the manifold of phenomena, if that synthesis is to become empirical knowledge, it follows that the phenomena are subject to conditions *a priori* to which their synthesis (in apprehension) must always conform. The representation of a general condition according to which something manifold *can* be arranged (with uniformity) is called *a rule*, if it *must* be so arranged, *a law*. All phenomena therefore stand in a permanent connection according to necessary laws, and thus possess that transcendental affinity of which the empirical is a mere consequence.

It sounds no doubt very strange and absurd that nature should have to conform to our subjective ground of apperception, nay, be dependent on it, with respect to her laws. But if we consider that what we call nature is nothing but a whole of phenomena, not a thing by itself, but a number of representations in our soul, we shall no longer be surprised that we only see her through the fundamental faculty of all our knowledge, namely, the transcendental apperception, and in that unity without which it could not be called the object (or the whole) of all possible experience, that is, nature. We shall thus also understand why we can recognise this unity *a priori,* and therefore as necessary, which would be perfectly impossible if it were given by itself and independent of the first sources of our own thinking. In that case I could not tell whence we should take the synthetical propositions of such general unity of nature. They would have to be taken from the objects of nature themselves, and as this could be done empirically only, we could derive from it none but an accidental unity, which is very different from that necessary connection which we mean when speaking of nature.

DEDUCTION OF THE PURE CONCEPTS OF THE UNDERSTANDING
SECTION III

OF THE RELATION OF THE UNDERSTANDING TO OBJECTS IN GENERAL, AND THE POSSIBILITY OF KNOWING THEM A PRIORI

What in the preceding section we have discussed singly and separately we shall now try to treat in connection with each other and as a whole. We saw that there are three subjective sources of knowledge on which the possibility of all experience and of the knowledge of its objects depends, namely, *sense, imagination,* and *apperception.* Each of them may be considered as empirical in its application to given phenomena; all, however, are also elements or grounds *a priori* which render their empirical application possible. *Sense* represents phenomena empirically in *perception, imagination* in *association* (and reproduction), *apperception* in the *empirical consciousness* of the identity of these reproductive representations with the phenomena by which they were given; therefore in *recognition.*

The whole of our perception rests *a priori* on pure intuition (if the perception is regarded as representation, then on time, as the form of our internal intuition), the association of it (the whole) on the pure synthesis of imagination, and our empirical consciousness of it on pure apperception, that is, on the permanent identity of oneself in the midst of all possible representations.

If we wish to follow up the internal ground of this connection of representations to that point towards which they must all converge, and where they receive for the first time that unity of knowledge which is requisite for every possible experience, we must begin with pure apperception. Intuitions are nothing to us, and do not concern us in the least, if they cannot be received into our consciousness, into which they may enter either directly or indirectly. Knowledge is impossible in any other way. We are conscious *a priori* of our own permanent identity with regard to all representations that can ever belong to our knowledge, as forming a necessary condition of the possibility of all representations (because these could not represent anything in me, unless they belonged with everything else to one consciousness and could at least be connected within it). This principle stands firm *a priori,* and may be called the *transcendental principle of the unity* of all the manifold of our representations (therefore also of intuition). This unity of the manifold in one subject is synthetical; the pure apperception therefore supplies us with a principle of the synthetical unity of the manifold in all possible intuitions.*

This synthetical unity, however, presupposes or involves a synthesis, and if that unity is necessary *a priori,* the synthesis

* This point is of great importance and should be carefully considered. All representations have a necessary relation to some possible empirical consciousness, for if they did not possess that relation, and if it were entirely impossible to become conscious of them, this would be the same as if they did not exist. All empirical consciousness has a necessary relation to a transcendental consciousness, which precedes all single experiences, namely, the consciousness of my own self as the original apperception. It is absolutely necessary therefore that in my knowledge all consciousness should belong to one consciousness of my own self. Here we have a synthetical unity of the manifold (consciousness) which can be known *a priori,* and which may thus supply a foundation for synthetical propositions *a priori* concerning pure thinking in the same way as space and time supply a foundation for synthetical propositions which concern the form of mere intuition. The synthetical proposition that the different kinds of empirical consciousness must be connected in one self-consciousness, is the very first and synthetical foundation of all our thinking. It should be remembered that the mere representation of the Ego in reference to all other representations (the collective unity of which would be impossible without it) constitutes our transcendental consciousness. It does not matter whether that representation is clear (empirical consciousness) or confused, not even whether it is real; but the possibility of the logical form of all knowledge rests necessarily on the relation to this apperception *as a faculty.*

also must be *a priori*. The transcendental unity of apperception therefore refers to the pure synthesis of imagination as a condition *a priori* of the possibility of the manifold being united in one knowledge. Now there can take place *a priori* the productive synthesis of imagination only, because the reproductive rests on conditions of experience. The principle therefore of the necessary unity of the pure (productive) synthesis of imagination, before all apperception, constitutes the ground of the possibility of all knowledge, nay, of all experience.

The synthesis of the manifold in imagination is called transcendental, if, without reference to the difference of intuitions, it affects only the *a priori* conjunction of the manifold; and the unity of that synthesis is called transcendental if, with reference to the original unity of apperception, it is represented as *a priori* necessary. As the possibility of all knowledge depends on the unity of that apperception, it follows that the transcendental unity of the synthesis of imagination is the pure form of all possible knowledge through which therefore all objects of possible experience must be represented *a priori*.

This unity of apperception with reference to the synthesis of imagination is the *understanding,* and the same unity with reference to the transcendental synthesis of the imagination, the *pure understanding*. It must be admitted therefore that there exist in the understanding pure forms of knowledge *a priori*, which contain the necessary unity of the pure synthesis of the imagination in reference to all possible phenomena. These are the categories, that is, the pure concepts of the understanding. The empirical faculty of knowledge of man contains therefore by necessity an understanding which refers to all objects of the senses, though by intuition only, and by its synthesis through imagination, and all phenomena, as data of a possible experience, must conform to that understanding. As this relation of phenomena to a possible experience is likewise necessary (because, without it, we should receive no knowledge through them, and they would not in the least concern us), it follows that the pure understanding constitutes by the means of the categories a formal and synthetical principle of all experience, and that phenomena have thus a necessary relation to the understanding.

We shall now try to place the necessary connection of the understanding with the phenomena by means of the categories more clearly before the reader, by beginning with the beginning, namely, with the empirical.

The first that is given us is the *phenomenon,* which, if connected with consciousness, is called *perception*. (Without its relation to an at least possible consciousness, the phenomenon could never become to us an object of knowledge. It would therefore be nothing to us; and because it has no objective reality in itself, but exists only in being known, it would be nothing altogether.) As every phenomenon contains a manifold, and different perceptions are found in the mind singly and scattered, a connection of them is necessary, such as they cannot have in the senses by themselves. There exists therefore in us an active power for the synthesis of the manifold which we call imagination, and the function of which, as applied to perceptions, I call *apprehension*.* This imagination is meant to change the manifold of intuition into an image; it must therefore first receive the impressions into its activity, which I call *to apprehend*.

It must be clear, however, that even this apprehension of the manifold could not alone produce a coherence of impressions or an image, without some subjective power of calling one perception from which the mind has gone over to another back to that which follows, and thus forming whole series of perceptions. This is the reproductive faculty of imagination which is and can be empirical only.

If representations, as they happen to meet with one another, could reproduce each other at haphazard, they would have no definite coherence, but would form irregular agglomerations only, and never produce knowledge. It is necessary therefore that their reproduction should be subject to a rule by which one representation connects itself in imagination with a second and not with a third. It is this subjective and empirical ground of reproduction according to rules, which is called the *association* of representations.

If this unity of association did not possess an objective foundation also, which makes it impossible that phenomena should be apprehended by imagination in any other way but under the condition of a possible synthetical unity of that apprehension, it would be a mere accident that phenomena lend themselves to a certain connection in human knowledge. Though we might have the power of associating perceptions, it would still be a matter of uncertainty and chance whether they themselves are associable; and, in case they should not be so, a number of perceptions, nay, the whole of our sensibility, might possibly contain a great deal of empirical consciousness, but

---

* It has hardly struck any psychologist that this imagination is a necessary ingredient of perception. This was partly owing to their confining this faculty to reproduction, partly to our belief that the senses do not only give us impressions, but compound them also for us, thus producing pictures of objects. This, however, beyond our receptivity of impressions, requires something more, namely, a function for their synthesis.

in a separate state, nay, without belonging to the *one* consciousness of myself, which, however, is impossible. Only by ascribing all perceptions to one consciousness (the original apperception) can I say of all of them that I am conscious of them. It must be therefore an objective ground, that is, one that can be understood as existing *a priori,* and before all empirical laws of imagination, on which alone the possibility, nay, even the necessity of a law can rest, which pervades all phenomena, and which makes us look upon them all, without exception, as data of the senses, associable by themselves, and subject to general rules of a permanent connection in their reproduction. This objective ground of all association of phenomena I call their *affinity,* and this can nowhere be found except in the principle of the unity of apperception applied to all knowledge which is to belong to me. According to it all phenomena, without exception, must so enter into the mind or be apprehended as to agree with the unity of apperception. This, without a synthetical unity in their connection, which is therefore necessary objectively also, would be impossible.

We have thus seen that the objective unity of all (empirical) consciousness in one consciousness (that of the original apperception) is the necessary condition even of all possible perception, while the affinity of all phenomena (near or remote) is a necessary consequence of a synthesis in imagination which is *a priori* founded on rules.

Imagination is therefore likewise the power of a synthesis *a priori* which is the reason why we called it productive imagination, and so far as this aims at nothing but the necessary unity in the synthesis of all the manifold in phenomena, it may be called the transcendental function of imagination. However strange therefore it may appear at first, it must nevertheless have become clear by this time that the affinity of phenomena and with it their association, and through that, lastly, their reproduction also according to laws, that is, the whole of our experience, becomes possible only by means of that transcendental function of imagination, without which no concepts of objects could never come together in one experience.

It is the permanent and unchanging Ego (or pure apperception) which forms the correlative of all our representations, if we are to become conscious of them, and all consciousness belongs quite as much to such an all-embracing pure apperception as all sensuous intuition belongs, as a representation, to a pure internal intuition, namely, time. This apperception it is which must be added to pure imagination, in order to render its function intellectual. For by itself, the synthesis of imagination, though carried out *a priori,* is always sensuous, and only connects the manifold as it appears in intuition, for instance, the shape of a triangle. But when the manifold is brought into relation with the unity of apperception, concepts which belong to the understanding become possible, but only as related to sensuous intuition through imagination.

We have therefore a pure imagination as one of the fundamental faculties of the human soul, on which all knowledge *a priori* depends. Through it we bring the manifold of intuition on one side in connection with the condition of the necessary unity of pure apperception on the other. These two extreme ends, sense and understanding, must be brought into contact with each other by means of the transcendental function of imagination, because, without it, the senses might give us phenomena, but no objects of empirical knowledge, therefore no experience. Real experience, which is made up of apprehension, association (reproduction), and lastly recognition of phenomena, contains in this last and highest (among the purely empirical elements of experience) concepts, which render possible the formal unity of experience, and with it, all objective validity (truth) of empirical knowledge. These grounds for the recognition of the manifold, so far as they concern the form only of experience in general, are our categories. On them is founded the whole formal unity in the synthesis of imagination and, through it, of[14] the whole empirical use of them (in recognition, reproduction, association, and apprehension) down to the very phenomena, because it is only by means of those elements of knowledge that the phenomena can belong to our consciousness and therefore to ourselves.

It is we therefore who carry into the phenomena which we *call nature,* order and regularity, nay, we should never find them in nature, if we ourselves, or the nature of our mind, had not originally placed them there. For the unity of nature is meant to be a necessary and *a priori* certain unity in the connection of all phenomena. And how should we *a priori* have arrived at such a synthetical unity, if the subjective grounds of such unity were not contained *a priori* in the original sources of our knowledge, and if those subjective conditions did not at the same time possess objective validity, as being the grounds on which alone an object becomes possible in our experience?

We have before given various definitions of the understanding, by calling it the spontaneity of knowledge (as opposed to the receptivity of the senses), or the faculty of thinking, or the

---

[14] *Of* may be omitted, if we read *aller empirischer Gebrauch.*

faculty of concepts or of judgments; all of these explanations, if more closely examined, coming to the same. We may now characterise it as *the faculty of rules*. This characteristic is more significant, and approaches nearer to the essence of the understanding. The senses give us forms (of intuition), the understanding rules, being always busy to examine phenomena, in order to discover in them some kind of rule. Rules, so far as they are objective (therefore necessarily inherent in our knowledge of an object), are called laws. Although experience teaches us many laws, yet these are only particular determinations of higher laws, the highest of them, to which all others are subject, springing *a priori* from the understanding; not being derived from experience, but, on the contrary, imparting to the phenomena their regularity, and thus making experience possible. The understanding therefore is not only a power of making rules by a comparison of phenomena, it is itself the lawgiver of nature, and without the understanding nature, that is, a synthetical unity of the manifold of phenomena, according to rules, would be nowhere to be found, because phenomena, as such, cannot exist without us, but exist in our sensibility only. This sensibility, as an object of our knowledge in any experience, with everything it may contain, is possible only in the unity of apperception, which unity of apperception is transcendental ground of the necessary order of all phenomena in an experience. The same unity of apperception with reference to the manifold of representations (so as to determine it out of one)[15] forms what we call the rule, and the faculty of these rules I call the understanding. As possible experience therefore, all phenomena depend in the same way *a priori* on the understanding, and receive their formal possibility from it as, when looked upon as mere intuitions, they depend on sensibility, and become possible through it, so far as their form is concerned.

However exaggerated therefore and absurd it may sound, that the understanding is itself the source of the laws of nature, and of its formal unity, such a statement is nevertheless correct and in accordance with experience. It is quite true, no doubt, that empirical laws, as such, cannot derive their origin from the pure understanding, as little as the infinite manifoldness of phenomena could be sufficiently comprehended through the pure form of sensuous intuition. But all empirical laws are only particular determinations of the pure laws of the understanding, under which and according to which the former become possible, and phenomena assume

---

[15] That is, out of one, or out of the unity of apperception.

a regular form, quite as much as all phenomena, in spite of the variety of their empirical form, must always submit to the conditions of the pure form of sensibility.

The pure understanding is therefore in the categories the law of the synthetical unity of all phenomena, and thus makes experience, so far as its form is concerned, for the first time possible. This, and no more than this, we were called upon to prove in the transcendental deduction of the categories, namely, to make the relation of the understanding to our sensibility, and through it to all objects of experience, that is the objective validity of the pure concepts *a priori* of the understanding, conceivable, and thus to establish their origin and their truth.

SUMMARY REPRESENTATION OF THE CORRECTNESS AND OF THE ONLY POSSIBILITY OF THIS DEDUCTION OF THE PURE CONCEPTS OF THE UNDERSTANDING

If the objects with which our knowledge has to deal were things by themselves, we could have no concepts *a priori* of them. For where should we take them? If we took them from the object (without asking even the question, how that object could be known to us) our concepts would be empirical only, not concepts *a priori*. If we took them from within ourselves, then that which is within us only, could not determine the nature of an object different from our representations, that is, supply a ground why there should be a thing to which something like what we have in our thoughts really belongs, and why all this representation should not rather be altogether empty. But if on the contrary, we have to deal with phenomena only, then it becomes not only possible, but necessary, that certain concepts *a priori* should precede our empirical knowledge of objects. For being phenomena, they form an object that is within us only, because a mere modification of our sensibility can never exist outside us. The very idea that all these phenomena, and therefore all objects with which we have to deal, are altogether within me, or determinations of my own identical self, implies by itself the necessity of a permanent unity of them in one and the same apperception.

In that unity of a possible consciousness consists also the form of all knowledge of objects, by which the manifold is thought as belonging to *one* object. The manner therefore in which the manifold of sensuous representation (intuition) belongs to our consciousness, precedes all knowledge of an object, as its intellectual form, and constitutes a kind of formal *a priori* knowledge of all objects in general, if they are to be thought (categories). Their synthesis by means of pure imagination, and the unity of all representations with reference to the original apperception, precede all empirical knowledge. Pure concepts of the understanding are therefore *a priori* possible, nay, with regard to experience, necessary, for this simple reason, because our knowledge has to deal with nothing but phenomena, the possibility of which depends on ourselves, and the connection and unity of which (in the representation of an object) can be found in ourselves only, as antecedent to all experience, nay, as first rendering all experience possible, so far as its form is concerned. On this ground, as the only possible one, our deduction of the categories has been carried out.]

Transcendental Analytic

Book II
Analytic of Principles

General logic is built up on a plan that coincides accurately with the division of the higher faculties of knowledge. These are, *Understanding, Judgment,* and *Reason.* Logic therefore treats in its analytical portion of *concepts, judgments,* and *syllogisms* corresponding with the functions and the order of the above-named faculties of the mind, which are generally comprehended under the vague name of the understanding.

As formal logic takes no account of the contents of our knowledge (pure or empirical), but treats of the form of thought only (discursive knowledge), it may well contain in its analytical portion the canon of reason also, reason being, according to its form, subject to definite rules which, without reference to the particular nature of the knowledge to which they are applied, can be found out *a priori* by a mere analysis of the acts of reasoning into their component parts.

Transcendental logic, being limited to a certain content, namely, to pure knowledge *a priori,* cannot follow general logic in this division; for it is clear that the *transcendental use of reason* cannot be objectively valid, and cannot therefore belong to the *logic of truth,* that is, to Analytic, but must be allowed to form a separate part of our scholastic system, as a *logic of illusion,* under the name of *transcendental Dialectic.*

Understanding and judgment have therefore a canon of their objectively valid, and therefore true use in transcendental logic, and belong to its analytical portion. But reason, in its attempts to determine anything *a priori* with reference to objects, and to extend knowledge beyond the limits of possible experience, is altogether dialectical, and its illusory assertions have no place in a canon such as Analytic demands.

Our Analytic of principles therefore will be merely a canon of the faculty of judgment, teaching it how to apply to phenomena the concepts of the understanding, which contain the condition of rules *a priori.* For this reason, and in order to indicate my purpose more clearly, I shall use the name of *doctrine of the faculty of judgment,* while treating of the real *principles of the understanding.*

INTRODUCTION
OF THE TRANSCENDENTAL FACULTY OF
JUDGMENT IN GENERAL

If the understanding is explained as the faculty of rules, the faculty of judgment consists in performing the subsumption under these rules, that is, in determining whether anything falls under a given rule (*casus datae legis*) or not. General logic contains no precepts for the faculty of judgment and cannot contain them. For as it takes no account of the contents of our knowledge, it has only to explain analytically the mere form of knowledge in concepts, judgments, and syllogisms, and thus to establish formal rules for the proper employment of the understanding. If it were to attempt to show in general how anything should be arranged under these rules, and how we should determine whether something falls under them or not, this could only take place by means of a new rule. This, because it is a new rule, requires a new precept for the faculty of judgment, and we thus learn that, though the understanding is capable of being improved and instructed by means of rules, the faculty of judgment is a special talent which cannot be taught, but must be practised. This is what constitutes our so-called mother-wit, the absence of which cannot be remedied by any schooling. For although the teacher may offer, and as it were graft into a narrow understanding, plenty of rules borrowed from the experience of others, the faculty of using them rightly must belong to the pupil himself, and without that talent no precept that may be given is safe from abuse.* A physician, therefore, a judge, or a politician, may carry in his head many beautiful pathological, juridical, or political rules, nay, he may even become an accurate teacher of them, and he may yet in the application of these rules commit many a blunder, either because he is deficient in judgment, though not in understanding, knowing the general in the abstract, but unable to determine whether a concrete case falls under it; or, it may be, because his judgment has not been sufficiently trained by examples and practical experience. It is the one great advantage of examples that they sharpen the faculty of judgment, but they are apt to impair the accuracy and precision of the understanding, because they fulfil but rarely the conditions of the rule quite adequately (as *casus in terminis*). Nay, they often weaken the effort of the understanding in comprehending rules according to their general adequacy, and independent of the special circumstances of experience, and accustom us to use those rules in the end as formulas rather than as principles. Examples may thus be called the go-cart of the judgment, which those who are deficient in that natural talent[16] can never do without.

But although general logic can give no precepts to the faculty of judgment, the case is quite different with transcendental logic, so that it even seems as if it were the proper business of the latter to correct and to establish by definite rules the

---

* Deficiency in the faculty of judgment is really what we call stupidity, and there is no remedy for that. An obtuse and narrow mind, deficient in nothing but a proper degree of understanding and correct concepts, may be improved by study, so far as to become even learned. But as even then there is often a deficiency of judgment (*secunda Petri*) we often meet with very learned men, who in handling their learning betray that original deficiency which can never be mended.

[16] *Desselben* has been changed into *derselben* in later editions. *Desselben*, however, may be meant to refer to *Urtheil*, as contained in *Urtheilskraft*. The Second Edition has *desselben*.

faculty of the judgment in the use of the pure understanding. For as a doctrine and a means of enlarging the field of pure knowledge *a priori* for the benefit of the understanding, philosophy does not seem necessary, but rather hurtful, because, in spite of all attempts that have been hitherto made, hardly a single inch of ground has been gained by it. For critical purposes, however, and in order to guard the faculty of judgment against mistakes (*lapsus judicii*) in its use of the few pure concepts of the understanding which we possess, philosophy (though its benefits may be negative only) has to employ all the acuteness and penetration at its command.

What distinguishes transcendental philosophy is, that besides giving the rules (or rather the general condition of rules) which are contained in the pure concept of the understanding, it can at the same time indicate *a priori* the case to which each rule may be applied. The superiority which it enjoys in this respect over all other sciences, except mathematics, is due to this, that it treats of concepts which are meant to refer to their objects *a priori*, so that their objective validity cannot be proved *a posteriori*, because this would not affect their own peculiar dignity. It must show, on the contrary, by means of general but sufficient marks, the conditions under which objects can be given corresponding to those concepts; otherwise these would be without any contents, mere logical forms, and not pure concepts of the understanding.

Our transcendental doctrine of the faculty of judgment will consist of two chapters. The first will treat of the sensuous condition under which alone pure concepts of the understanding can be used. This is what I call the *schematism* of the pure understanding. The second will treat of the synthetical judgments, which can be derived *a priori* under these conditions from pure concepts of the understanding, and on which all knowledge *a priori* depends. It will treat, therefore, of the principles of the pure understanding.

The Transcendental Doctrine of the Faculty of Judgment or Analytic of Principles
Chapter 1
Of the Schematism of the Pure Concepts of the Understanding

In comprehending any object under a concept, the representation of the former must be homogeneous with the latter,[17] that is, the concept must contain that which is represented in the object to be comprehended under it, for this is the only meaning of the expression that an object is comprehended under a concept. Thus, for instance, the empirical concept of a plate is homogeneous with the pure geometrical concept of a circle, the roundness which is conceived in the first forming an object of intuition in the latter.

Now it is clear that pure concepts of the understanding, as compared with empirical or sensuous impressions in general, are entirely heterogeneous, and can never be met with in any intuition. How then can the latter be comprehended under the former, or how can the categories be applied to phenomena, as no one is likely to say that causality, for instance, could be seen through the senses, and was contained in the phenomenon? It is really this very natural and important question which renders a transcendental doctrine of the faculty of judgment necessary, in order to show how it is possible that any of the pure concepts of the understanding can be applied to phenomena. In all other sciences in which the concepts by which the object is thought in general are not so heterogeneous or different from those which represent it *in concreto,* and as it is given, there is no necessity to enter into any discussions as to the applicability of the former to the latter.

In our case there must be some third thing homogeneous on the one side with the category, and on the other with the phenomenon, to render the application of the former to the latter possible. This intermediate representation must be pure (free from all that is empirical) and yet intelligible on the one side, and sensuous on the other. Such a representation is the *transcendental schema.*

The concept of the understanding contains pure synthetical

[17] Read *dem letzteren,* as corrected by Rosenkranz, for *der letzteren.*

unity of the manifold in general. Time, as the formal condition of the manifold in the internal sense, consequently of the conjunction of all representations, contains a manifold *a priori* in pure intuition. A transcendental determination of time is so far homogeneous with the category (which constitutes its unity) that it is general and founded on a rule *a priori;* and it is on the other hand so far homogeneous with the phenomenon, that time must be contained in every empirical representation of the manifold. The application of the category to phenomena becomes possible therefore by means of the transcendental determination of time, which, as a *schema* of the concepts of the understanding, allows the phenomena to be comprehended under the category.

After what has been said in the deduction of the categories, we hope that nobody will hesitate in answering the question whether these pure concepts of the understanding allow only of an empirical or also of a transcendental application, that is, whether, as conditions of a possible experience, they refer *a priori* to phenomena only, or whether, as conditions of the possibility of things in general, they may be extended to objects by themselves (without restriction to our sensibility). For there we saw that concepts are quite impossible, and cannot have any meaning unless there be an object given either to them or, at least, to some of the elements of which they consist, and that they can never refer to things by themselves (without regard as to whether and how things may be given to us). We likewise saw that the only way in which objects can be given to us, consists in a modification of our sensibility, and lastly, that pure concepts *a priori* must contain, besides the function of the understanding in the category itself, formal conditions *a priori* of sensibility (particularly of the internal sense) which form the general condition under which alone the category may be applied to any object. We shall call this formal and pure condition of sensibility, to which the concept of the understanding is restricted in its application, its *schema;* and the function of the understanding in these schemata, the *schematism of the pure understanding.*

The schema by itself is no doubt a product of the imagination only, but as the synthesis of the imagination does not aim at a single intuition, but at some kind of unity alone in the determination of sensibility, the schema ought to be distinguished from the image. Thus, if I place five points, one after the other . . . . . , this is an image of the number five. If, on the contrary, I think of a number in general, whether it be five or a hundred, this thinking is rather the representation of a method of representing in one image a certain quantity (for instance a thousand) according to a certain concept, than the image itself, which, in the case of a thousand, I could hardly take in and compare with the concept. This representation of a general procedure of the imagination by which a concept receives its image, I call the schema of such concept.

The fact is that our pure sensuous concepts do not depend on images of objects, but on schemata. No image of a triangle in general could ever be adequate to its concept. It would never attain to that generality of the concept, which makes it applicable to all triangles, whether right-angled, or acute-angled, or anything else, but would always be restricted to one portion only of the sphere of the concept. The schema of the triangle can exist nowhere but in thought, and is in fact a rule for the synthesis of imagination with respect to pure forms in space. Still less does an object of experience or its image ever cover the empirical concept, which always refers directly to the schema of imagination as a rule for the determination of our intuitions, according to a certain general concept. The concept of dog means a rule according to which my imagination can always draw a general outline of the figure of a four-footed animal, without being restricted to any particular figure supplied by experience or to any possible image which I may draw in the concrete. This schematism of our understanding applied to phenomena and their mere form is an art hidden in the depth of the human soul, the true secrets of which we shall hardly ever be able to guess and reveal. So much only we can say, that the *image* is a product of the empirical faculty of the productive imagination, while the *schema* of sensuous concepts (such as of figures in space) is a product and so to say a monogram of the pure imagination *a priori,* through which and according to which images themselves become possible, though they are never fully adequate to the concept, and can be connected with it by means of their schema only. The schema of a pure concept of the understanding, on the contrary, is something which can never be made into an image; for it is nothing but the pure synthesis determined by a rule of unity, according to concepts, a synthesis as expressed by the category, and represents a transcendental product of the imagination, a product which concerns the determination of the internal sense in general, under the conditions of its form (time), with reference to all representations, so far as these are meant to be joined *a priori* in one concept, according to the unity of apperception.

Without dwelling any longer on a dry and tedious determination of all that is required for the transcendental schemata of the pure concepts of the understanding in general, we shall proceed at once to represent them according to the order of the categories, and in connection with them.

The pure image of all quantities (*quanta*) before the external sense, is space; that of all objects of the senses in general, time. The pure schema of quantity (*quantitas*), however, as a concept of the understanding, is *number*, a representation which comprehends the successive addition of one to one (homogeneous). Number therefore is nothing but the unity of the synthesis of the manifold (repetition) of a homogeneous intuition in general, I myself producing the time in the apprehension of the intuition.

Reality is, in the pure concept of the understanding, that which corresponds to a sensation in general: that, therefore, the concept of which indicates by itself being (in time), while negation is that the concept of which represents not-being (in time). The opposition of the two takes place therefore by a distinction of one and the same time, as either filled or empty. As time is only the form of intuition, that is, of objects as phenomena, that which in the phenomena corresponds to sensation, constitutes the transcendental matter of all objects, as things by themselves (reality, *Sachheit*). Every sensation, however, has a degree of quantity by which it can fill the same time (that is, the internal sense, with reference to the same representation of an object), more or less, till it vanishes into nothing (equal to nought or negation). There exists, therefore, a relation and connection, or rather a transition from reality to negation, which makes every reality representable as a quantum; and the schema of a reality, as the quantity of something which fills time, is this very continuous and uniform production of reality in time; while we either descend from the sensation which has a certain degree, to its vanishing in time, or ascend from the negation of sensation to some quantity of it.

The schema of substance is the permanence of the real in time, that is, the representation of it as a substratum for the empirical determination of time in general, which therefore remains while everything else changes. (It is not time that passes, but the existence of the changeable passes in time. What corresponds therefore in the phenomena to time, which in itself is unchangeable and permanent, is the unchangeable in existence, that is, substance; and it is only in it that the succession and the coexistence of phenomena can be determined according to time.)

The schema of cause and of the causality of a thing in general is the real which, when once supposed to exist, is always followed by something else. It consists therefore in the succession of the manifold, in so far as that succession is subject to a rule.

The schema of community (reciprocal action) or of the reciprocal causality of substances, in respect to their accidents, is the coexistence, according to a general rule, of the determinations of the one with those of the other.

The schema of possibility is the agreement of the synthesis of different representations with the conditions of time in general, as, for instance, when opposites cannot exist at the same time in the same thing, but only one after the other. It is therefore the determination of the representation of a thing at any time whatsoever.

The schema of reality is existence at a given time.

The schema of necessity is the existence of an object at all times.

It is clear, therefore, if we examine all the categories, that the schema of quantity contains and represents the production (synthesis) of time itself in the successive apprehension of an object; the schema of quality, the synthesis of sensation (perception) with the representation of time or the filling-up of time; the schema of relation, the relation of perceptions to each other at all times (that is, according to a rule which determines time); lastly, the schema of modality and its categories, time itself as the correlative of the determination of an object as to whether and how it belongs to time. The schemata therefore are nothing but determinations of time *a priori* according to rules, and these, as applied to all possible objects, refer in the order of the categories to the *series of time*, the *contents of time*, the *order of time*, and lastly, the *comprehension of time*.

We have thus seen that the schematism of the understanding, by means of a transcendental synthesis of imagination, amounts to nothing else but to the unity of the manifold in the intuition of the internal sense, and therefore indirectly to the unity of apperception, as an active function corresponding to the internal sense (as receptive). These schemata therefore of the pure concepts of the understanding are the true and only conditions by which these concepts can gain a relation to objects, that is, a *significance*, and the categories are thus in the end of no other but a possible empirical use, serving only, on account of an *a priori* necessary unity (the necessary connection of all consciousness in one original apperception) to subject all phenomena to general rules of synthesis, and thus to render them capable of a general connection in experience.

All our knowledge is contained within this whole of possible experience, and transcendental truth, which precedes all empirical truth and renders it possible, consists in general relation of it to that experience.

But although the schemata of sensibility serve thus to realise the categories, it must strike everybody that they at the same time restrict them, that is, limit them by conditions foreign to the understanding and belonging to sensibility. Hence the schema is really the phenomenon, or the sensuous concept of an object in agreement with the category (numerus *est quantitas phaenomenon,* sensatio *realitas phaenomenon,* constans et perdurabile rerum *substantia phaenomenon*—aeternitas *necessitas phaenomenon,* etc.). If we omit a restrictive condition, it would seem that we amplify a formerly limited concept, and that therefore the categories in their pure meaning, free from all conditions of sensibility, should be valid of things in general, *as they are,* while their schemata represent them only *as they appear,* so that these categories might claim a far more extended power, independent of all schemata. And in truth we must allow to these pure concepts of the understanding, apart from all sensuous conditions, a certain significance, though a logical one only, with regard to the mere unity of representations produced by them, although these representations have no object and therefore no meaning that could give us a concept of an object. Thus substance, if we leave out the sensuous condition of permanence, would mean nothing but a something that may be conceived as a subject, without being the predicate of anything else. Of such a representation we can make nothing, because it does not teach us how that thing is determined which is thus to be considered as the first subject. Categories, therefore, without schemata are functions only of the understanding necessary for concepts, but do not themselves represent any object. This character is given to them by sensibility only, which realizes the understanding by, at the same time, restricting it. . . .

III. [THE ANALOGIES OF EXPERIENCE

The general principle of them is: All phenomena, as far as their existence is concerned, are subject *a priori* to rules, determining their mutual relation in one and the same time]

Analogies of Experience

Their principle is: Experience is possible only through the representation of a necessary connection of perceptions.

Proof

Experience is empirical knowledge, that is, knowledge which determines an object by means of perceptions. It is, therefore, a synthesis of perceptions, which synthesis itself is not contained in the perception, but contains the synthetical unity of the manifold of the perceptions in a consciousness, that unity constituting the essential of our knowledge of the objects of the senses, i.e. of experience (not only of intuition or of sensation of the senses). In experience perceptions come together contingently only, so that no necessity of their connection could be discovered in the perceptions themselves, apprehension being only a composition of the manifold of empirical intuition, but containing no representation of the necessity of the connected existence, in space and time, of the phenomena which it places together. Experience, on the contrary, is a knowledge of objects by perceptions, in which therefore the relation in the existence of the manifold is to be represented, not as it is put together in time, but as it is in time, objectively. Now, as time itself cannot be perceived, the determination of the existence of objects in time can take place only by their connection in time in general, that is, through concepts connecting them a priori. As these concepts always imply necessity, we are justified in saying that experience is possible only through a representation of the necessary connection of perceptions.

The three modi of time are *permanence, succession,* and *coexistence.* There will therefore be three rules of all relations of phenomena in time, by which the existence of every phenomenon with regard to the unity of time is determined, and these rules will precede all experience, nay, render experience possible.

The general principle of the three analogies depends on the necessary unity of apperception with reference to every possible empirical consciousness (perception) *at every time,* and, consequently, as that unity forms an *a priori* ground, on the synthetical unity of all phenomena, according to their relation in time. For the original apperception refers to the internal sense (comprehending all representations), and it does so *a priori* to its form, that is, to the relation of the manifold of the empirical consciousness in time. The original apperception is intended to combine all this manifold according to its relations in time, for this is what is meant by its transcendental unity *a priori*, to which all is subject which is to belong to my own and my uniform knowledge, and thus to become an object for me. This synthetical unity in the time relations of all perceptions, which is determined *a priori*, is expressed therefore in the law, that all empirical determinations of time must be subject to rules of the general determination of time; and the analogies of experience, of which we are now going to treat, are exactly rules of this kind.

These principles have this peculiarity, that they do not refer to phenomena and the synthesis of their empirical intuition, but only to the *existence* of phenomena and their mutual *relation* with regard to their existence. The manner in which something is apprehended as a phenomenon may be so determined *a priori* that the rule of its synthesis may give at the same time this intuition *a priori* in any empirical case, nay, may really render it possible. But the existence of phenomena can never be known *a priori*, and though we might be led in this way to infer some kind of existence, we should never be able to know it definitely, or to anticipate that by which the empirical intuition of one differs from that of others.

The principles which we considered before and which, as they enable us to apply mathematics to phenomena, I called mathematical, refer to phenomena so far only as they are possible, and showed how, with regard both to their intuition and to the real in their perception, they can be produced according to the rules of a mathematical synthesis, so that, in the one as well as in the other, we may use numerical quantities, and with them a determination of all phenomena as quantities. Thus I might, for example, compound the degree of sensations of the sunlight out of, say, 200,000 illuminations by the moon, and thus determine it *a priori* or construct it. Those former principles might therefore be called *constitutive*.

The case is totally different with those principles which are meant to bring the existence of phenomena under rules *a priori*, for as existence cannot be constructed, they can only refer to the relations of existence and become merely *regulative* principles. Here therefore we could not think of either axioms or anticipations, and whenever a perception is given us as related in time to some others (although undetermined), we could not say *a priori* what other perception or how great a perception is necessarily connected with it, but only how, if existing, it is necessarily connected with the other in a certain mode of time.

In philosophy analogy means something very different to what it does in mathematics. In the latter they are formulas which state the equality of two quantitative relations, and they are always constitutive so that when three[18] terms of a proposition are given, the fourth also is given by it, that is, can be constructed out of it. In philosophy, on the contrary, analogy does not consist in the equality of two quantitative, but of two qualitative relations, so that when three terms are given I may learn from them *a priori* the relation to a fourth only, but not that fourth term itself. All I can thus gain is a rule according to which I may look in experience for the fourth term, or a characteristic mark by which I may find it. An analogy of experience can therefore be no more than a rule according to which a certain unity of experience may arise from perceptions (but not how perception itself, as an empirical intuition, may arise); it may serve as a principle for objects (as phenomena[19]) not in a constitutive, but only in a regulative capacity.

Exactly the same applies to the postulates of empirical thought in general, which relate to the synthesis of mere intuition (the form of phenomena), the synthesis of perception (the matter of them), and the synthesis of experience (the relation of these perceptions). They too are regulative principles only, and differ from the mathematical, which are constitutive, not in their certainty, which is established in both *a priori*, but in the character of their evidence, that is, in that which is intuitive in it, and therefore in their demonstration also.

What has been remarked of all synthetical principles and must be enjoined here more particularly is this, that these analogies have their meaning and validity, not as principles of the transcendent, but only as principles of the empirical use of the understanding. They can be established in this character only, nor can phenomena ever be comprehended under the categories directly, but only under their schemata. If the objects to which these principles refer were things by themselves, it would be perfectly impossible to know anything of them *a priori* and synthetically. But they are nothing but phenomena, and our whole knowledge of them, to which, after all, all principles *a priori* must relate, is only our possible experience of them. Those principles therefore can aim at nothing but the conditions of the unity of empirical knowledge in the synthesis of phenomena, which synthesis is represented only in the schema of the pure concepts of the understanding, while the category contains the function, restricted by no sensuous condition, of

[18] The First and Second Editions read 'When two terms of a proposition are given, the third also.'
[19] Read *den Erscheinungen.*

the unity of that synthesis as synthesis in general. Those principles will therefore authorise us only to connect phenomena, according to analogy, with the logical and universal unity of concepts, so that, though in using the principle we use the category, yet in practice (in the application to phenomena) we put the schema of the category, as a practical key, in its[20] place, or rather put it by the side of the category as a restrictive condition, or, as what may be called, a formula of the category.

A

FIRST ANALOGY

[PRINCIPLE OF PERMANENCE

All phenomena contain the permanent (substance) as the object itself, and the changeable as its determination only, that is, as a mode in which the object exists

Proof of the First Analogy

All phenomena take place in time. Time can determine in two ways the relation in the existence of phenomena, so far as they are either successive or coexistent. In the first case time is considered as a series, in the second as a whole.]

Principle of the Permanence of Substance

In all changes of phenomena the substance is permanent, and its quantum is neither increased nor diminished in nature.

Proof

All phenomena exist in time, and in it alone, as the substratum (as permanent form of the internal intuition), can simultaneousness as well as succession be represented. Time, therefore, in which all change of phenomena is to be thought, does not change, for it is that in which simultaneousness and

---

[20] I read *deren,* and afterwards *der ersteren,* though even then the whole passage is very involved. Professor Noiré thinks that *dessen* may be referred to *Gebrauch,* and *des ersteren* to *Grundsatz.*

succession can be represented only as determinations of it. As time by itself cannot be perceived, it follows that the substratum which represents time in general, and in which all change or simultaneousness can be perceived in apprehension, through the relation of phenomena to it, must exist in the objects of perception, that is, in the phenomena. Now the substratum of all that is real, that is, of all that belongs to the existence of things, is the substance, *and all that belongs to existence can be conceived only as a determination of it. Consequently the permanent, in reference to which alone all temporal relations of phenomena can be determined, is the substance in phenomena, that is, what is real in them, and, as the substratum of all change, remains always the same. As therefore substance cannot change in existence, we were justified in saying that its quantum can neither be increased nor diminished in nature.*

Our apprehension of the manifold of phenomena is always successive, and therefore always changing. By it alone therefore we can never determine whether the manifold, as an object of experience, is coexistent or successive, unless there is something in it which exists always, that is, something constant and permanent, while change and succession are nothing but so many kinds (*modi*) of time in which the permanent exists. Relations of time are therefore possible in the permanent only (coexistence and succession being the only relations of time) so that the permanent is the substratum of the empirical representation of time itself, and in it alone all determination of time is possible. Permanence expresses time as the constant correlative of all existence of phenomena, of all change and concomitancy. For change does not affect time itself, but only phenomena in time (nor is coexistence a mode of time itself, because in it no parts can be coexistent, but successive only). If we were to ascribe a succession to time itself, it would be necessary to admit another time in which such succession should be possible. Only through the permanent does *existence* in different parts of a series of time assume a *quantity* which we call *duration.* For in mere succession existence always comes and goes, and never assumes the slightest quantity. Without something permanent therefore no relation of time is possible. Time by itself, however, cannot be perceived, and it is therefore the permanent in phenomena that forms the substratum for all determination of time, and at the same time the condition of the possibility of all synthetical unity of perceptions, that is, of experience; while with regard to that permanent all existence and all change in time can only be taken as a mode of existence of what is permanent. In all phenomena therefore the permanent is the object itself, that is, the substance (phenomenon), while all that changes or can change belongs only to the mode in which substance or substances exist, therefore to their determinations.

I find that in all ages not only the philosopher, but also the man of common understanding has admitted this permanence as a substratum of all change of phenomena. It will be the same in future, only that a philosopher generally expresses himself somewhat more definitely by saying that in all changes in the world the substance remains, and only the accidents change. But I nowhere find even the attempt at a proof of this very synthetical proposition, and it occupies but seldom that place which it ought to occupy at the head of the pure and entirely *a priori* existing laws of nature. In fact the proposition that substance is permanent is tautological, because that permanence is the only ground why we apply the category of substance to a phenomenon, and it ought first to have been proved that there is in all phenomena something permanent, while the changeable is only a determination of its existence. But as such a proof can never be given dogmatically and as deduced from concepts, because it refers to a synthetical proposition *a priori*, and as no one ever thought that such propositions could be valid only in reference to possible experience, and could therefore be proved only by a deduction of the possibility of experience, we need not wonder that, though it served as the foundation of all experience (being felt to be indispensable for every kind of empirical knowledge), it has never been established by proof.

A philosopher was asked, What is the weight of smoke? He replied, Deduct from the weight of the wood burnt the weight of the remaining ashes, and you have the weight of the smoke. He was therefore convinced that even in fire matter (substance) does not perish but that its form only suffers a change. The proposition also, from nothing comes nothing, was only another conclusion from the same principle of permanence, or rather of the constant presence of the real subject in phenomena. For if that which people call substance in a phenomenon is to be the true substratum for all determination in time, then all existence in the past as well as the future must be determined in it, and in it only. Thus we can only give to a phenomenon the name of substance because we admit its existence at all times, which is not even fully expressed by the word *permanence,* because it refers rather to future time only. The internal necessity however of permanence is inseparably connected with the necessity to have been always, and the expression may therefore stand. *Gigni de nihilo nihil, in nihilum nil posse reverti,* were two propositions which the ancients never separated, but which at present are sometimes parted, because people imagine that they refer to things by themselves, and that the former might contradict the dependence of the world on a Supreme Cause (even with regard to its substance), an apprehension entirely needless, as we are only speaking here of phenomena in the sphere of experience, the unity of which would never be possible, if we allowed that new things (new in substance) could ever arise. For in that case we should lose that which alone can represent the unity of time, namely, the identity of the substratum, in which alone all change retains complete unity. This permanence, however, is nothing but the manner in which we represent the existence of things (as phenomenal).

The different determinations of a substance, which are nothing but particular modes in which it exists, are called accidents. They are always real, because they concern the existence of a substance (negations are nothing but determinations which express the non-existence of something in the substance). If we want to ascribe a particular kind of existence to these real determinations of the substance, as, for instance, to motion, as an accident of matter, we call it *inherence,* in order to distinguish it from the existence of substance, which[21] we call *subsistence.* This, however, has given rise to many misunderstandings, and we shall express ourselves better and more correctly, if we define the accident through the manner only in which the existence of a substance is positively determined. It is inevitable, however, according to the conditions of the logical use of our understanding, to separate, as it were, whatever can change in the existence of a substance, while the substance itself remains unchanged, and to consider it in its relation to that which is radical and truly permanent. Hence a place has been assigned to this category under the title of relations, not so much because it contains itself a relation, as because it contains their condition.

On this permanence depends also the right understanding of the concept of *change.* To arise and to perish are not changes of that which arises or perishes. Change is a mode of existence, which follows another mode of existence of the same object. Hence whatever changes is permanent, and its condition only changes. As this alteration refers only to determinations which may have an end or a beginning, we may use an expression that seems somewhat paradoxical and say: the permanent only (substance) is changed, the changing itself suffers no change,

---

[21] Read *das man.*

but only an alteration, certain determinations ceasing to exist, while others begin.

It is therefore in substances only that change can be perceived. Arising or perishing absolutely, and not referring merely to a determination of the permanent can never become a possible perception, because it is the permanent only which renders the representations of a transition from one state to another, from not being to being, possible, which (changes) consequently can only be known empirically, as alternating determinations of what is permanent. If you suppose that something has an absolute beginning, you must have a moment of time in which it was not. But with what can you connect that moment, if not with that which already exists? An empty antecedent time cannot be an object of perception. But if you connect this beginning with things which existed already and continue to exist till the beginning of something new, then the latter is only a determination of the former, as of the permanent. The same holds good with regard to perishing, for this would presuppose the empirical representation of a time in which a phenomenon exists no longer.

Substances therefore (as phenomena) are the true substrata of all determinations of time. If some substances could arise and others perish, the only condition of the empirical unity of time would be removed, and phenomena would then be referred to two different times, in which existence would pass side by side, which is absurd. For there is but one time in which all different times must be placed, not as simultaneous, but as successive.

Permanence, therefore, is a necessary condition under which alone phenomena, as things or objects, can be determined in a possible experience. What the empirical criterion of this necessary permanence, or of the substantiality of phenomena may be, we shall have to explain in the sequel.

B

SECOND ANALOGY

[PRINCIPLE OF PRODUCTION

    Everything that happens (begins to be), presupposes
    something on which it follows according to a rule]

*Principle of the Succession of Time, according to the Law
of Causalty*

*All changes take place according to the law of
connection between cause and effect.*

Proof

(*It has been shown by the preceding principle, that all phenomena in the succession of time are* changes *only, i.e. a successive being and not-being of the determinations of the substance,
which is permanent, and consequently that the being of the
substance itself, which follows upon its not-being, and its not-
being, which follows on its being—in other words, that an
arising or perishing of the substance itself is inadmissible. The
same principle might also have been expressed thus:* all change
(succession) *of phenomena consists in modification only, for
arising and perishing are no modifications of the substance,
because the concept of modification presupposes the same subject as existing with two opposite determinations, and therefore
as permanent. After this preliminary remark, we shall proceed
to the proof.*)

I perceive that phenomena succeed each other, that is, that
there is a state of things at one time the opposite of which
existed at a previous time. I am therefore really connecting
two perceptions in time. That connection is not a work of the
senses only and of intuition, but is here the product of a synthetical power of the faculty of imagination, which determines
the internal sense with reference to relation in time. Imagination, however, can connect those two states in two ways, so
that either the one or the other precedes in time: for time cannot be perceived by itself, nor can we determine in the object
empirically and with reference to time, what precedes and what
follows. I am, therefore, conscious only that my imagination
places the one before, the other after, and not, that in the
object the one state comes before the other. In other words,
the objective relation of phenomena following upon each other
remains undetermined by mere perception. In order that this
may be known as determined, it is necessary to conceive the
relation between the two states in such a way that it should be
determined thereby with necessity, which of the two should
be taken as coming first, and which as second, and not conversely. Such a concept, involving a necessity of synthetical
unity, can be a pure concept of the understanding only, which
is not supplied by experience, and this is, in this case, the concept of the relation of cause and effect, *the former determining
the latter in time as the consequence,* the cause not being something that might be antecedent in imagination only, or might
not be perceived at all. Experience itself, therefore, that is, an

empirical knowledge of phenomena, is possible only by our subjecting the succession of phenomena, and with it all change, to the law of causality, and phenomena themselves, as objects of experience, are consequently possible according to the same law only.

The apprehension of the manifold of phenomena is always successive. The representations of the parts follow one upon another. Whether they also follow one upon the other in the object is a second point for reflection, not contained in the former. We may indeed call everything, even every representation, so far as we are conscious of it, an object; but it requires a more profound investigation to discover what this word may mean with regard to phenomena, not in so far as they (as representations) are objects, but in so far as they only signify an object. So far as they, as representations only, are at the same time objects of consciousness, they cannot be distinguished from our apprehension, that is from their being received in the synthesis of our imagination, and we must therefore say, that the manifold of phenomena is always produced in the mind successively. If phenomena were things by themselves, the succession of the representations of their manifold would never enable us to judge how that manifold is connected in the object. We have always to deal with our representations only; how things may be by themselves (without reference to the representations by which they affect us) is completely beyond the sphere of our knowledge. Since, therefore, phenomena are not things by themselves, and are yet the only thing that can be given to us to know, I am asked to say what kind of connection in time belongs to the manifold of the phenomena itself, when the representation of it in our apprehension is always successive. Thus, for instance, the apprehension of the manifold in the phenomenal appearance of a house that stands before me, is successive. The question then arises, whether the manifold of the house itself be successive by itself, which of course no one would admit. Whenever I ask for the transcendental meaning of my concepts of an object, I find that a house is not a thing by itself, but a phenomenon only, that is, a representation the transcendental object of which is unknown. What then can be the meaning of the question, how the manifold in the phenomenon itself (which is not a thing by itself) may be connected? Here that which is contained in our successive apprehension is considered as representation, and the given phenomenon, though it is nothing but the whole of those representations, as their object, with which my concept, drawn from the representations of my apprehension, is to accord. As the accord between knowledge and its object is truth, it is easily seen, that we can ask here only for the formal conditions of empirical truth, and that the phenomenon, in contradistinction to the representations of our apprehension, can only be represented as the object different from them, if it is subject to a rule distinguishing it from every other apprehension, and necessitating a certain kind of conjunction of the manifold. That which in the phenomenon contains the condition of this necessary rule of apprehension is *the object*.

Let us now proceed to our task. That something takes place, that is, that something, or some state, which did not exist before, begins to exist, cannot be perceived empirically, unless there exists antecedently a phenomenon which does not contain that state; for a reality, following on empty time, that is a beginning of existence, preceded by no state of things, can be apprehended as little as empty time itself. Every apprehension of an event is therefore a perception following on another perception. But as this applies to all synthesis of apprehension, as I showed before in the phenomenal appearance of a house, that apprehension would not thereby be different from any other. But I observe at the same time, that if in a phenomenon which contains an event I call the antecedent state of perception A, and the subsequent B, B can only follow A in my apprehension, while the perception A can never follow B, but can only precede it. I see, for instance, a ship gliding down a stream. My perception of its place below follows my perception of its place higher up in the course of the stream, and it is impossible in the apprehension of this phenomenon that the ship should be perceived first below and then higher up. We see therefore that the order in the succession of perceptions in our apprehension is here determined, and our apprehension regulated by that order. In the former example of a house my perceptions could begin in the apprehension at the roof and end in the basement, or begin below and end above: they could apprehend the manifold of the empirical intuition from right to left or from left to right. There was therefore no determined order in the succession of these perceptions, determining the point where I had to begin in apprehension, in order to connect the manifold empirically; while in the apprehension of an event there is always a rule, which makes the order of the successive perceptions (in the apprehension of this phenomenon) necessary.

In our case, therefore, we shall have to derive the subjective succession in our apprehension from the objective succession of the phenomena, because otherwise the former would be entirely undetermined, and unable to distinguish one phenomenon from another. The former alone proves nothing as to the connection of the manifold in the object, because it is quite arbitrary. The latter must therefore consist in the order of the manifold in a phenomenon, according to which the apprehension of what is happening follows upon the apprehension of what has happened, in conformity with a rule. Thus only can I be justified in saying, not only of my apprehension, but of the phenomenon itself, that there exists in it a succession, which is the same as to say that I cannot arrange the apprehension otherwise than in that very succession.

In conformity with this, there must exist in that which always precedes an event the condition of a rule, by which this event follows at all times, and necessarily; but I cannot go back from the event and determine by apprehension that which precedes. For no phenomenon goes back from the succeeding to the preceding point of time, though it is related to some preceding point of time, while the progress from a given time to a determined following time is necessary. Therefore, as there certainly is something that follows, I must necessarily refer it to something else which precedes, and upon which it follows by rule, that is, by necessity. So that the event, as being conditional, affords a safe indication of some kind of condition, while that condition itself determines the event.

If we supposed that nothing precedes an event upon which such event must follow according to rule, all succession of perception would then exist in apprehension only, that is, subjectively; but it would not thereby be determined objectively, what ought properly to be the antecedent and what the subsequent in perception. We should thus have a mere play of representations unconnected with any object, that is, no phenomenon would, by our perception, be distinguished in time from any other phenomenon, because the succession in apprehension would always be uniform, and there would be nothing in the phenomena to determine the succession, so as to render a certain sequence objectively necessary. I could not say therefore that two states follow each other in a phenomenon, but only that one apprehension follows another, which is purely subjective, and does not determine any object, and cannot be considered therefore as knowledge of anything (even of something purely phenomenal).

If therefore experience teaches us that something happens, we always presuppose that something precedes on which it follows by rule. Otherwise I could not say of the object that it followed, because its following in my apprehension only, without being determined by rule in reference to what precedes, would not justify us in admitting an objective following.[22] It is therefore always with reference to a rule by which phenomena as they follow, that is as they happen, are determined by an antecedent state, that I can give an objective character to my subjective synthesis (of apprehension); nay, it is under this supposition only that an experience of anything that happens becomes possible.

It might seem indeed as if this were in contradiction to all that has always been said on the progress of the human understanding, it having been supposed that only by a perception and comparison of many events, following in the same manner on preceding phenomena, we were led to the discovery of a rule according to which certain events always follow on certain phenomena, and that thus only we were enabled to form to ourselves the concept of a cause. If this were so, that concept would be empirical only, and the rule which it supplies, that everything which happens must have a cause, would be as accidental as experience itself. The universality and necessity of that rule would then be fictitious only, and devoid of any true and general validity, because not being *a priori*, but founded on induction only. The case is the same as with other pure representations *a priori* (for instance space and time), which we are only able to draw out as pure concepts from experience, because we have put them first into experience, nay, have rendered experience possible only by them. It is true, no doubt, that the logical clearness of this representation of a rule, determining the succession of events, as a concept of cause, becomes possible only when we have used it in experience, but, as the condition of the synthetical unity of phenomena in time, it was nevertheless the foundation of all experience, and consequently preceded it *a priori*.

It is necessary therefore to show by examples that we never, even in experience, ascribe the sequence or consequence (of an event or something happening that did not exist before) to the object, and distinguish it from the subjective sequence of our apprehension, except when there is a rule which forces us to observe a certain order of perceptions, and no other; nay, that it is this force which from the first renders the representation of a succession in the object possible.

We have representations within us, and can become conscious of them; but however far that consciousness may extend, and however accurate and minute it may be, yet the representations are always representations only, that is, internal determinations of our mind in this or that relation of time.

[22] Read *anzunehmen berechtigt*.

What right have we then to add to these representations an object, or to ascribe to these modifications, beyond their subjective reality, another objective one? Their objective character cannot consist in their relation to another representation (of that which one wished to predicate of the object), for thus the question would only arise again, how that representation could again go beyond itself, and receive an objective character in addition to the subjective one, which belongs to it, as a determination of our mind. If we try to find out what new quality or dignity is imparted to our representations by their relation to an *object*, we find that it consists in nothing but the rendering necessary the connection of representations in a certain way, and subjecting them to a rule; and that on the other hand they receive their objective character only because a certain order is necessary in the time relations of our representations.

In the synthesis of phenomena the manifold of our representations is always successive. No object can thus be represented, because through the succession which is common to all apprehensions, nothing can be distinguished from anything else. But as soon as I perceive or anticipate that there is in this succession a relation to an antecedent state from which the representation follows by rule, then something is represented as an event, or as something that happens: that is to say, I know an object to which I must assign a certain position in time, which, after the preceding state, cannot be different from what it is. If therefore I perceive that something happens, this representation involves that something preceded, because the phenomenon receives its position in time with reference to what preceded, that is, it exists after a time in which it did not exist. Its definite position in time can only be assigned to it, if in the antecedent state something is presupposed on which it always follows by rule. It thus follows that, first of all, I cannot invert the order, and place that which happens before that on which it follows; secondly, that whenever the antecedent state is there, the other event must follow inevitably and necessarily. Thus it happens that there arises an order among our representations, in which the present state (as having come to be), points to an antecedent state, as a correlative of the event that is given; a correlative which, though as yet indefinite, refers as determining to the event, as its result, and connects that event with itself by necessity, in the succession of time.

If then it is a necessary law of our sensibility, and therefore a *formal* condition of all perception, that a preceding necessarily determines a suceeding time (because I cannot arrive at the succeeding time except through the preceding), it is also an indispensable *law of the empirical representation* of the series of time that the phenomena of past time determine every existence in suceeding times, nay, that these, as events, cannot take place except so far as the former determine their existence in time, that is, determine it by rule. *For it is of course in phenomena only that we can know empirically this continuity in the coherence of times.*

What is required for all experience and renders it possible is the understanding, and the first that is added by it is not that it renders the representation of objects clear, but that it really renders the representation of any object for the first time possible. This takes place by the understanding transferring the order of time to the phenomena and their existence, and by assigning to each of them as to a consequence a certain *a priori* determined place in time, with reference to antecedent phenomena, without which place phenomena would not be in accord with time, which determines *a priori* their places to all its parts. This determination of place cannot be derived from the relation in which phenomena stand to absolute time (for that can never be an object of perception); but, on the contrary, phenomena must themselves determine to each other their places in time, and render them necessary in the series of time. In other words, what happens or follows must follow according to a general rule on that which was contained in a previous state. We thus get a series of phenomena which, by means of the understanding, produces and makes necessary in the series of possible perceptions the same order and continuous coherence which exists *a priori* in the form of internal intuition (time), in which all perceptions must have their place.

That something happens is therefore a perception which belongs to a possible experience, and this experience becomes real when I consider the phenomenon as determined with regard to its place in time, that is to say, as an object which can always be found, according to a rule, in the connection of perceptions. This rule, by which we determine everything according to the succession of time, is this: the condition under which an event follows at all times (necessarily) is to be found in what precedes. All possible experience therefore, that is, all objective knowledge of phenomena with regard to their relation in the succession of time, depends on 'the principle of sufficient reason.'

The proof of this principle rests entirely on the following considerations. All empirical knowledge requires synthesis of the manifold by imagination, which is always successive, one representation following upon the other. That succession, however, in the imagination is not at all determined with regard to the order in which something precedes and something follows, and the series of successive representations may be taken as retrogressive as well as progressive. If that synthesis, however, is a synthesis of apperception (of the manifold in a given phenomenon), then the order is determined in the object, or, to speak more accurately, there is then in it an order of successive synthesis which determines the object, and according to which something must necessarily precede, and, when it is once there, something else must necessarily follow. If therefore my perception is to contain the knowledge of an event, or something that really happens, it must consist of an empirical judgment, by which the succession is supposed to be determined, so that the event presupposes another phenomenon in time on which it follows necessarily and according to a rule. If it were different, if the antecedent phenomenon were there, and the event did not follow on it necessarily, it would become to me a mere play of my subjective imaginations, or if I thought it to be objective, I should call it a dream. It is therefore the relation of phenomena (as possible perceptions) according to which the existence of the subsequent (what happens) is determined in time by something antecedent necessarily and by rule, or, in other words, the relation of cause and effect, which forms the condition of the objective validity of our empirical judgments with regard to the series of perceptions, and therefore also the condition of the empirical truth of them, and of experience. The principle of the causal relation in the succession of phenomena is valid therefore for all objects of experience, also (under the conditions of succession), because that principle is itself the ground of the possibility of such experience.

Here, however, we meet with a difficulty that must first be removed. The principle of the causal connection of phenomena is restricted in our formula to their succession, while in practice we find that it applies also to their coexistence, because cause and effect may exist at the same time. There may be, for instance, inside a room heat which is not found in the open air. If I look for its cause, I find a heated stove. But that stove, as cause, exists at the same time with its effect, the heat of the room, and there is therefore no succession in time between cause and effect, but they are coexistent, and yet the law applies. The fact is, that the greater portion of the active causes[23] in nature is coexistent with its effects, and the succession of these effects in time is due only to this, that a cause cannot produce its whole effect in one moment. But at the moment in which an effect first arises it is always coexistent with the

[23] The reading of the First Edition is *Ursache; Ursachen* is a conjecture made by Rosenkranz and approved by others.

causality of its cause, because if that had ceased one moment before, the effect would never have happened. Here we must well consider that what is thought of is the *order,* not the *lapse* of time, and that the relation remains, even if no time had lapsed. The time between the causality of the cause and its immediate effect can be *vanishing* (they may be simultaneous), but the relation of the one to the other remains for all that determinable in time. If I look upon a ball that rests on a soft cushion, and makes a depression in it, as a cause, it is simultaneous with its effect. But I nevertheless distinguish the two through the temporal relation of dynamical connection. For if I place the ball on a cushion, its smooth surface is followed by a depression, while, if there is a depression in the cushion (I know not whence), a leaden ball does by no means follow from it.

The succession in time is therefore the only empirical criterion of an effect with regard to the causality of the cause which precedes it. The glass is the cause of the rising of the water above its horizontal surface, although both phenomena are simultaneous. For as soon as I draw water in a glass from a larger vessel, something follows, namely, the change of the horizontal state which it had before into a concave state which it assumes in the glass.

This causality leads to the concept of action, that to the concept of force, and lastly, to the concept of substance. As I do not mean to burden my critical task, which only concerns the sources of synthetical knowledge *a priori,* with analytical processes which aim at the explanation, and not at the expansion of our concepts, I leave a fuller treatment of these to a future system of pure reason; nay, I may refer to many well-known manuals in which such an analysis may be found. I cannot pass, however, over the empirical criterion of a substance, so far as it seems to manifest itself, not so much through the permanence of the phenomenon as through action.

Wherever there is action, therefore activity and force, there must be substance, and in this alone the seat of that fertile source of phenomena can be sought. This sounds very well, but if people are asked to explain what they mean by substance, they find it by no means easy to answer without reasoning in a circle. How can we conclude immediately from the action to the *permanence* of the agent, which nevertheless is an essential and peculiar characteristic of substance (*phaenomenon*)? After what we have explained before, however, the answer to this question is not so difficult, though it would be impossible, according to the ordinary way of proceeding analytically only with our concepts. Action itself implies the relation of the subject of the causality to the effect. As all effect consists in that which happens, that is, in the changeable, indicating time in succession, the last subject of it is the *permanent,* as the substratum of all that changes, that is substance. For, according to the principle of causality, actions are always the first ground of all change of phenomena, and cannot exist therefore in a subject that itself changes, because in that case other actions and another subject would be required to determine that change. Action, therefore, is a sufficient empirical criterion to prove substantiality, nor is it necessary that I should first establish its permanency by means of compared perceptions, which indeed would hardly be possible in this way, at least with that completeness which is required by the magnitude and strict universality of the concept. That the first subject of the causality of all arising and perishing cannot itself (in the field of phenomena) arise and perish, is a safe conclusion, pointing in the end to empirical necessity and permanency in existence, that is, the concept of a substance as a phenomenon.

If anything happens, the mere fact of something arising, without any reference to what it is, is in itself a matter for enquiry. The transition from the not-being of a state into that state, even though it contained no quality whatever as a phenomenon, must itself be investigated. This arising, as we have shown in No. A, does not concern the substance (because a substance never arises), but its state only. It is therefore mere change, and not an arising out of nothing. When such an arising is looked upon as the effect of a foreign cause, it is called creation. This can never be admitted as an event among phenomena, because its very possibility would destroy the unity of experience. If, however, we consider all things, not as phenomena, but as things by themselves and objects of the understanding only, then, though they are substances, they may be considered as dependent in their existence on a foreign cause. Our words would then assume quite a different meaning, and no longer be applicable to phenomena, as possible objects of experience.

How anything can be changed at all, how it is possible that one state in a given time is followed by another at another time, of that we have not the slightest conception *a priori.* We want for that a knowledge of real powers, which can be given empirically only: for instance, a knowledge of motive powers, or what is the same, a knowledge of certain successive phenomena (as movements) which indicate the presence of such forces. What can be considered *a priori,* according to the law of causality and the conditions of time, are the form of every change, the condition under which alone, as an arising of another state, it can take place (its contents, that is, the state, which is changed, being what it may), and therefore the succession itself of the states (that which has happened).*

When a substance passes from one state a into another b, the moment of the latter is different from the moment of the former state, and follows it. Again, that second state, as a reality (in phenomena), differs from the first in which that reality did not exist, as b from zero; that is, even if the state b differed from the state a in quantity only, that change is an arising of $b - a$, which in the former state was non-existent, and in relation to which that state is $= 0$.

The question therefore arises how a thing can pass from a state $= a$ to another $= b$? Between two moments there is always a certain time, and between two states in these two moments there is always a difference which must have a certain quantity, because all parts of phenomena are always themselves quantities. Every transition therefore from one state into another takes place in a certain time between two moments, the first of which determines the state from which a thing arises, the second that at which it arrives. Both therefore are the temporal limits of a change or of an intermediate state between two states, and belong as such to the whole of the change. Every change, however, has a cause which proves its causality during the whole of the time in which the change takes place. The cause therefore does not produce the change suddenly (in one moment), but during a certain time; so that, as the time grows from the initiatory moment a to its completion in b, the quantity of reality also $(b - a)$ is produced through all the smaller degrees between the first and the last. All change therefore is possible only through a continuous action of causality which, so far as it is uniform, is called a momentum. A change does not consist of such momenta, but is produced by them as their effect.

This is the law of continuity in all change, founded on this, that neither time nor a phenomenon in time consists of parts which are the smallest possible, and that nevertheless the state of a thing which is being changed passes through all these parts, as elements, to its new state. No difference of the real in phenomena and no difference in the quantity of times is ever the smallest; and thus the new state of reality grows from the first state in which that reality did not exist through all

* It should be remarked that I am not speaking here of the change of certain relations, but of the change of a state. Therefore when a body moves in a uniform way, it does not change its state of movement, but it does so when its motion increases or decreases.

the infinite degrees thereof, the differences of which from one another are smaller than that between zero and *a*.

It does not concern us at present of what utility this principle may be in physical science. But how such a principle, which seems to enlarge our knowledge of nature so much, can be possible *a priori*, that requires a careful investigation, although we can see that it is real and true, and might thus imagine that the question how it was possible is unnecessary. For there are so many unfounded pretensions to enlarge our knowledge by pure reason that we must accept it as a general principle, to be always distrustful, and never to believe or accept anything of this kind without documents capable of a thorough deduction, however clear the dogmatical proof of it may appear.

All addition to our empirical knowledge and every advance in perception is nothing but an enlargement of the determinations of our internal sense, that is, a progression in time, whatever the objects may be, whether phenomena or pure intuitions. This progression in time determines everything, and is itself determined by nothing else, that is, the parts of that progression are only given in time, and through the synthesis of time, but not time before this synthesis. For this reason every transition in our perception to something that follows in time is really a determination of time through the production of that perception, and as time is always and in all its parts a quantity, the production of a perception as a quantity, through all degrees (none of them being the smallest), from zero up to its determined degree. This shows how it is possible to know *a priori* a law of changes, as far as their form is concerned. We are only anticipating our own apprehension, the formal condition of which, as it dwells in us before all given phenomena, may well be known *a priori*.

In the same manner therefore in which time contains the sensuous condition *a priori* of the possibility of a continuous progression of that which exists to that which follows, the understanding, by means of the unity of apperception, is a condition *a priori* of the possibility of a continuous determination of the position of all phenomena in that time, and this through a series of causes and effects, the former producing inevitably the existence of the latter, and thus rendering the empirical knowledge of the relations of time valid for all times (universally) and therefore objectively valid.

C

THIRD ANALOGY

[PRINCIPLE OF COMMUNITY

All substances, in so far as they are coexistent, stand in complete community, that is, reciprocity one to another]

Principle of Coexistence, according to the Law of Reciprocity or Community

All substances, so far as they can be perceived as coexistent in space, are always affecting each other reciprocally.

Proof

Things are coexistent when, in empirical intuition, the perception of the one can follow upon the perception of the other, and vice versa, *which, as was shown in the second principle, is impossible in the temporal succession of phenomena. Thus I may first observe the moon and afterwards the earth, or, conversely also, first the earth and afterwards the moon, and because the perceptions of these objects can follow each other in both ways, I say that they are coexistent. Now coexistence is the existence of the manifold in the same time. Time itself, however, cannot be perceived, so that we might learn from the fact that things exist in the same time that their perceptions can follow each other reciprocally. The synthesis of imagination in apprehension would, therefore, give us each of these perceptions as existing in the subject, when the other is absent, and* vice versa: *it would never tell us that the objects are coexistent, that is, that if the one is there, the other also must be there in the same time, and this by necessity, so that the perceptions may follow each other reciprocally. Hence we require a concept of understanding of the reciprocal sequence of determinations of things existing at the same time, but outside each other, in order to be able to say, that the reciprocal sequence of the perceptions is founded in the object, and thus to represent their coexistence as objective. The relation of substances, however, of which the first has determinations the ground of which is contained in the other, is the relation of influence, and if, conversely also, the first contains the ground of determinations in the latter, the relation is that of community or reciprocity. Hence the coexistence of substances in space cannot be known in experience otherwise but under the supposition of reciprocal action: and this is therefore the condition also of the possibility of things themselves as objects of experience.*

Things are coexistent in so far as they exist at one and the same time. But how can we know that they exist at one and the same time? Only if the order in the synthesis of apprehension of the manifold is indifferent, that is, if I may advance from A through B, C, D, to E, or contrariwise from E to A. For, if the synthesis were successive in time (in the order beginning with A and ending with E), it would be impossible to begin the apprehension with the perception of E and to go backwards to A, because A belongs to past time, and can no longer be an object of apprehension.

If we supposed it possible that in a number of substances, as phenomena, each were perfectly isolated, so that none influenced another or received influences from another, then the coexistence of them could never become an object of possible perception, nor could the existence of the one through any process of empirical synthesis lead us on to the existence of another. For if we imagined that they were separated by a perfectly empty space, a perception, proceeding from the one in time to the other might no doubt determine the existence of it by means of a subsequent perception, but would never be able to determine whether that phenomenon followed objectively on the other or was coexistent with it.

There must therefore be something besides their mere existence by which *A* determines its place in time for *B*, and *B* for *A*, because thus only can these two substances be represented empirically as coexistent. Nothing, however, can determine the place of anything else in time, except that which is its cause or the cause of its determinations. Therefore every substance (since it can be effect with regard to its determinations only) must contain in itself the causality of certain determinations in another substance, and, at the same time, the effects of the causality of that other substance, that is, substances must stand in dynamical communion, immediately or mediately, with each other, if their coexistence is to be known in any possible experience. Now, everything without which the experience of any objects would be impossible, may be said to be necessary with reference to such objects of experience; from which it follows that it is necessary for all substances, so far as they are coexistent as phenomena, to stand in a complete communion of reciprocity with each other.

The word *communion* (*Gemeinschaft*) may be used in two senses, meaning either *communio* or *commercium*. We use it here in the latter sense: as a dynamical communion without which even the local *communio spatii* could never be known empirically. We can easily perceive in our experience, that continuous influences only can lead our senses in all parts of space from one object to another; that the light which plays between our eyes and celestial bodies produces a mediate communion between us and them, and proves the coexistence of the latter; that we cannot change any place empirically (perceive such a change) unless matter itself renders the perception of our own place possible to us, and that by means of its reciprocal influence only matter can evince its simultaneous existence, and thus (though mediately only) its coexistence, even to the most distant objects. Without this communion every perception (of any phenomenon in space) is separated from the others, and the chain of empirical representations, that is, experience itself, would have to begin *de novo* with every new object, without the former experience being in the least connected with it, or standing to it in any temporal relation. I do not want to say anything here against empty space. Empty space may exist where perception cannot reach, and where therefore no empirical knowledge of coexistence takes place, but, in that case, it is no object for any possible experience.

The following remarks may elucidate this. It is necessary that in our mind all phenomena, as being contained in a possible experience, must share a communion of apperception, and if the objects are to be represented as connected in coexistence, they must reciprocally determine their place in time, and thus constitute a whole. If this subjective communion is to rest on an objective ground, or is to refer to phenomena as substances, then the perception of the one as cause must render possible the perception of the other, and *vice versa:* so that the succession which always exists in perceptions, as apprehensions, may not be attributed to the objects, but that the objects should be represented as existing simultaneously. This is a reciprocal influence, that is a real *commercium* of substances, without which the empirical relation of coexistence would be impossible in our experience. Through this *commercium,* phenomena as being apart from each other and yet connected, constitute a compound (*compositum reale*), and such compounds become possible in many ways. The three dynamical relations, therefore, from which all others are derived, are *inherence, consequence,* and *composition.*

*   *   *

These are the three analogies of experience. They are nothing but principles for determining the existence of phenomena in time, according to its three modes. First, the relation of time itself, as to a quantity (quantity of existence, that is duration).

Secondly, the relation in time, as in a series (successively). And thirdly, likewise in time, as the whole of all existence (simultaneously). This unity in the determination of time is dynamical only, that is, time is not looked upon as that in which experience assigns immediately its place to every existence, for this would be impossible; because absolute time is no object of perception by which phenomena could be held together; but the rule of the understanding through which alone the existence of phenomena can receive synthetical unity in time determines the place of each of them in time, therefore *a priori* and as valid for all time.

By nature (in the empirical sense of the word) we mean the coherence of phenomena in their existence, according to necessary rules, that is, laws. There are therefore certain laws, and they exist *a priori,* which themselves make nature possible, while the empirical laws exist and are discovered through experience, but in accordance with those original laws which first render experience possible. Our analogies therefore represent the unity of nature in the coherence of all phenomena, under certain exponents, which express the relation of time (as comprehending all existence) to the unity of apperception, which apperception can only take place in the synthesis according to rules. The three analogies, therefore, simply say, that all phenomena exist in one nature, and must so exist because, without such unity *a priori* no unity of experience, and therefore no determination of objects in experience, would be possible.

With regard to the mode of proof, by which we have arrived at these transcendental laws of nature and its peculiar character, a remark must be made which will become important as a rule for any other attempt to prove intelligible, and at the same time synthetical propositions *a priori.* If we had attempted to prove these analogies dogmatically, that is from concepts, showing that all which exists is found only in that which is permanent, that every event presupposes something in a previous state on which it follows by rule, and lastly, that in the manifold which is coexistent, states coexist in relation to each other by rule, all our labour would have been in vain. For we may analyse as much as we like, we shall never arrive from one object and its existence at the existence of another, or at its mode of existence by means of the concepts of these things only. What else then remained? There remained the possibility of experience, as that knowledge in which all objects must in the end be capable of being given to us, if their representation is to have any objective reality for us. In this, namely in the synthetical unity of apperception of all phenomena, we discovered the conditions *a priori* of an absolute and necessary determination in time of all phenomenal existence. Without this even the empirical determinations in time would be impossible, and we thus established the rules of the synthetical unity *a priori*, by which we might anticipate experience. It was because people were ignorant of this method, and imagined that they could prove dogmatically synthetical propositions which the empirical use of the understanding follows as its principles, that so many and always unsuccessful attempts have been made to prove the proposition of the 'sufficient reason.' The other two analogies have not even been thought of, though everybody followed them unconsciously,* because the method of the categories was wanting, by which alone every gap in the understanding, both with regard to concepts and principles, can be discovered and pointed out. . . .

The Transcendental Doctrine of the Faculty of Judgment or Analytic of Principles
Chapter 3
On the Ground of Distinction of All Subjects into Phenomena and Noumena

We have now not only traversed the whole domain of the pure understanding, and carefully examined each part of it, but we have also measured its extent, and assigned to everything in it its proper place. This domain, however, is an island and enclosed by nature itself within limits that can never be changed. It is the country of truth (a very attractive name), but surrounded by a wide and stormy ocean, the true home of illusion, where many a fog bank and ice that soon melts away tempt us to believe in new lands, while constantly deceiving

---

* The unity of the universe, in which all phenomena are supposed to be connected, is evidently a mere deduction of the quietly adopted principle of the communion of all substances as coexistent; for if they were isolated, they would not form parts of a whole, and if their connection (the reciprocity of the manifold) were not necessary for the sake of their coexistence, it would be impossible to use the latter, which is a purely ideal relation, as a proof of the former, which is real. We have shown, however, that communion is really the ground of the possibility of an empirical knowledge of coexistence, and that really we can only conclude from this the existence of the former, as its condition.

the adventurous mariner with vain hopes, and involving him in adventures which he can never leave, and yet can never bring to an end. Before we venture ourselves on this sea, in order to explore it on every side, and to find out whether anything is to be hoped for there, it will be useful to glance once more at the map of that country which we are about to leave, and to ask ourselves, first, whether we might not be content with what it contains, nay, whether we must not be content with it, supposing that there is no solid ground anywhere else on which we could settle; secondly, by what title we possess even that domain, and may consider ourselves safe against all hostile claims. Although we have sufficiently answered these questions in the course of the analytic, a summary recapitulation of their solutions may help to strengthen our conviction, by uniting all arguments in one point.

We have seen that the understanding possesses everything which it draws from itself, without borrowing from experience, for no other purpose but for experience. The principles of the pure understanding, whether constitutive *a priori* (as the mathematical) or simply relative (as the dynamical), contain nothing but, as it were, the pure schema of possible experience; for that experience derives its unity from that synthetical unity alone which the understanding originally and spontaneously imparts to the synthesis of imagination, with reference to apperception, and to which all phenomena, as data of a possible knowledge, must conform *a priori*. But although these rules of the understanding are not only true *a priori*, but the very source of all truth, that is, of the agreement of our knowledge with objects, because containing the conditions of the possibility of experience, as the complete sphere of all knowledge in which objects can be given to us, nevertheless we do not seem to be content with hearing only what is true, but want to know a great deal more. If therefore this critical investigation does not teach us any more than what, even without such subtle researches, we should have practised ourselves in the purely empirical use of the understanding, it would seem as if the advantages derived from it were hardly worth the labour. One might reply that nothing would be more prejudicial to the enlargement of our knowledge than that curiosity which, before entering upon any researches, wishes to know beforehand the advantages likely to accrue from them, though quite unable as yet to form the least conception of such advantages, even though they were placed before our eyes. There is, however, one advantage in this transcendental investigation which can be rendered intelligible, nay, even attractive to the most troublesome and reluctant apprentice, namely this, that the understanding confined to its empirical use only and unconcerned with regard to the sources of its own knowledge, may no doubt fare very well in other respects, but can never determine for itself the limits of its own use and know what is inside or outside its own sphere. It is for that purpose that such profound investigations are required as we have just instituted. If the understanding cannot decide whether certain questions lie within its own horizon or not, it can never feel certain with regard to its claims and possessions, but must be prepared for many humiliating corrections, when constantly transgressing, as it certainly will, the limits of its own domain, and losing itself in follies and fancies.

That the understanding cannot make any but an empirical, and never a transcendental, use of all its principles *a priori*, nay, of all its concepts, is a proposition which, if thoroughly understood, leads indeed to most important consequences. What we call the transcendental use of a concept in any proposition is its being referred to things in general and to things by themselves, while its empirical use refers to phenomena only, that is, to objects of a possible experience. That the latter use alone is admissible will be clear from the following considerations. What is required for every concept is, first, the logical form of a concept (of thought) in general; and, secondly, the possibility of an object to which it refers. Without the latter, it has no sense, and is entirely empty, though it may still contain the logical function by which a concept can be formed out of any data. The only way in which an object can be given to a concept is in intuition, and though a pure intuition is possible *a priori* and before the object, yet even that pure intuition can receive its object, and with it its objective validity, by an empirical intuition only, of which it is itself nothing but the form. All concepts, therefore, and with them all principles, though they may be possible *a priori*, refer nevertheless to empirical intuitions, that is, to data of a possible experience. Without this, they can claim no objective validity, but are a mere play, whether of the imagination or of the understanding with their respective representations. Let us take the concepts of mathematics as an example, and, first, with regard to pure intuitions. Although such principles as 'space has three dimensions,' 'between two points there can be only one straight line,' as well as the representation of the object with which that science is occupied, may be produced in the mind *a priori*, they would have no meaning, if we were not able at all times to show their meaning as applied to phenomena (empirical objects). It is for this reason that an abstract concept is required to be made *sensuous*, that is, that its corresponding object is required to be shown in intuition, because, without this, the concept (as people say) is without *sense,* that is, without meaning. Mathematics fulfil this requirement by the construction of the figure, which is a phenomenon present to the senses (although constructed *a priori*). In the same science the concept of quantity finds its support and sense in number; and this in turn in the fingers, the beads of the abacus, or in strokes and points which can be presented to the eyes. The concept itself was produced *a priori,* together with all the synthetical principles or formulas which can be derived from such concepts; but their use and their relation to objects can nowhere be found except in experience, of which those concepts contain *a priori* the (formal) possibility only.

That this is the case with all categories and with all the principles drawn from them, becomes evident from the fact that we could not define any one of them (really, that is, make conceivable the possibility of their object),[24] without at once having recourse to the conditions of sensibility or the form of phenomena, to which, as their only possible objects, these categories must necessarily be restricted, it being impossible, if we take away these conditions, to assign to them any meaning, that is, any relation to an object, or to make it intelligible to ourselves by an example what kind of thing could be intended by such concepts.

[When representing the table of the categories, we dispensed with the definition of every one of them, because at that time it seemed unnecessary for our purpose, which concerned their synthetical use only, and because entailing responsibilities which we were not bound to incur. This was not a mere excuse, but a very important prudential rule, viz. not to rush into definitions, and to attempt or pretend completeness or precision in the definition of a concept, when one or other of its characteristic marks is sufficient without a complete enumeration of all that constitute the whole concept. Now, however, we can perceive that this caution had even a deeper ground, namely, that we could not have defined them, even if we had wished;* for, if we remove all conditions of sensibility, which distinguish them as the concepts of a possible empirical

---

[24] Additions of the Second Edition.

* I am treating here of the real definition, which not only puts in place of the name of a thing other and more intelligible words, but that which contains a clear mark by which the object (*definitum*) can at all times be safely recognised, and by which the defined concept becomes fit for practical use. A real definition (*Realerklärung*) must therefore render clear the concept itself, and its objective reality also. Of this kind are the mathematical explanations which represent an object in intuition, according to its concept.

use, and treat them as concepts of things in general (therefore as of transcendental use), nothing remains but to regard the logical function in judgments as the condition of the possibility of the things themselves, without the slightest indication as to where they could have their application and their object, or how they could have any meaning or objective validity in the pure understanding, apart from sensibility.][25]

No one can explain the concept of quantity in general, except, it may be, by saying that it is the determination of an object, by which we may know how many times the one is supposed to exist in it. But this 'how many times' is based on successive repetition, that is on time, and on the synthesis in it of the homogeneous.

Reality, again, can only be explained in opposition to a negation, if we think of time (as containing all being) being either filled or empty.

Were I to leave out permanence (which means existence at all times), nothing would remain of my concept of substance but the logical representation of a subject which I think I can realise by imagining something which is a subject only, without being a predicate of anything. But in this case we should not only be ignorant of all conditions under which this logical distinction could belong to anything, but we should be unable to make any use of it or draw any conclusions from it, because no object is thus determined for the use of this concept, and no one can tell whether such a concept has any meaning at all.

Of the concept of cause also (if I leave out time, in which something follows on something else by rule) I should find no more in the pure category than that it is something which enables us to conclude the existence of something else, so that it would not only be impossible to distinguish cause and effect from each other, but the concept of cause would possess no indication as to how it can be applied to any object, because, in order to form any such conclusion, certain conditions require to be known of which the concept itself tells us nothing. The so-called principle that everything contingent has a cause, comes no doubt before us with great solemnity and self-assumed dignity. But, if I ask what you understand by contingent and you answer, something of which the non-existence is possible, I should be glad to know how you can recognise this possibility of non-existence, if you do not represent to yourselves, in the series of phenomena, some kind of succession, and in it an existence that follows upon non-existence (or *vice versa*), and consequently a change? To say that the

[25] Read *nimmt* instead of *nehmen,* and *können* instead of *könne.*

non-existence of a thing is not self-contradictory is but a lame appeal to a logical condition which, though it is necessary for the concept, yet is by no means sufficient for its real possibility. I can perfectly well remove in thought every existing substance, without contradicting myself, but I can by no means conclude from this as to its objective contingency in its existence, that is, the possibility of its non-existence in itself.

As regards the concept of community, it is easy to see that, as the pure categories of substance and causality admit of no explanation that would determine their object, neither could such an explanation apply to the reciprocal causality in the relation of substances to each other (*commercium*).

As to possibility, existence, and necessity, no one has yet been able to explain them, except by a manifest tautology, so long as their definition is to be exclusively drawn from the pure understanding. To substitute the transcendental possibility of things (when an object corresponds to a concept) for the logical possibility of the concept (when the concept does not contradict itself) is a quibble such as could deceive and satisfy the inexperienced only.*

[It seems to be something strange and even illogical that there should be a concept which must have a meaning, and yet is incapable of any explanation. But the case of these categories is peculiar, because it is only by means of the general sensuous condition that they can acquire a definite meaning, and a reference to any objects. That condition being left out in the pure category, it follows that it can contain nothing but the logical function by which the manifold is brought into a concept. By means of this function, that is, the pure form of the concept, nothing can be known nor distinguished as to the object belonging to it, because the sensuous condition, under which alone objects can belong to it, has been removed. Thus we see that the categories require, besides the pure concept of the understanding, certain determinations of their application to sensibility in general (schemata). Without them, they would not be concepts by which an object can be known and distinguished from other objects, but only so many ways of thinking an object for possible intuitions, and giving to it, according to one of the functions of the understanding, its meaning (certain requisite conditions being given). They are

---

* *In one word, none of these concepts admit of being* authenticated, *nor can their real possibility be proved, if all sensuous intuition (the only one which we possess) is removed, and there remains in that case a* logical *possibility only, that is, that a concept (a thought) is possible. This, however, does not concern us here, but only whether the concept refers to an object and does therefore signify anything.*

needed to define an object, and cannot therefore be defined themselves. The logical functions of judgments in general, namely, unity and plurality, assertion and negation, subject and predicate, cannot be defined without arguing in a circle, because the definition would itself be a judgment and contain these very functions. The pure categories are nothing but representations of things in general, so far as the manifold in intuition must be thought by one or the other of these functions. Thus, magnitude is the determination which can only be thought by a judgment possessing quantity (*judicium commune*); reality, the determination which can only be thought by an affirmative judgment; while substance is that which, in regard to intuition, must be the last subject of all other determinations. With all this it remains perfectly undetermined, what kind of things they may be with regard to which we have to use one rather than another of these functions, so that, without the condition of sensuous intuition, for which they supply the synthesis, the categories have no relation to any definite object, cannot define any object, and consequently have not in themselves the validity of objective concepts.]

From this it follows incontestably, that the pure concepts of the understanding never admit of a transcendental, but only of an empirical use, and that the principles of the pure understanding can only be referred, as general conditions of a possible experience, to objects of the senses, never to things by themselves (without regard to the manner in which we have to look at them).

Transcendental Analytic has therefore yielded us this important result, that the understanding *a priori* can never do more than anticipate the form of a possible experience; and as nothing can be an object of experience except the phenomenon, it follows that the understanding can never go beyond the limits of sensibility, within which alone objects are given to us. Its principles are principles for the exhibition of phenomena only; and the proud name of Ontology, which presumes to supply in a systematic form different kinds of synthetical knowledge *a priori* of things by themselves (for instance the principle of causality), must be replaced by the more modest name of a mere Analytic of the pure understanding.

Thought is the act of referring a given intuition to an object. If the mode of such intuition is not given, the object is called transcendental, and the concept of the understanding admits then of a transcendental use only, in producing a unity in the thought of the manifold in general. A pure category therefore, in which every condition of sensuous intuition, the only one that is possible for us, is left out, cannot determine an object, but only the thought of an object in general, according to different modes. Now, if we want to use a concept, we require in addition some function of the faculty of judgment, by which an object is subsumed under a concept, consequently the at least formal condition under which something can be given in intuition. If this condition of the faculty of judgment (schema) is wanting, all subsumption is impossible, because nothing is given that could be subsumed under the concept. The purely transcendental use of categories therefore is in reality of no use at all, and has no definite or even, with regard to its form only, definable object. Hence it follows that a pure category is not fit for any synthetical *a priori* principle, and that the principles of the pure understanding admit of empirical only, never of transcendental application, nay, that no synthetical principles *a priori* are possible beyond the field of possible experience.

It might therefore be advisable to express ourselves in the following way: the pure categories, without the formal conditions of sensibility, have a transcendental character only, but do not admit of any transcendental use, because such use in itself is impossible, as the categories are deprived of all the conditions of being used in judgments, that is, of the formal conditions of the subsumption of any possible object under these concepts. As therefore (as pure categories) they are not meant to be used empirically, and cannot be used transcendentally, they admit, if separated from sensibility, of no use at all; that is, they cannot be applied to any possible object, and are nothing but the pure form of the use of the understanding with reference to objects in general, and of thought, without ever enabling us to think or determine any object by their means alone.

[Appearances, so far as they are thought as objects under the unity of the categories, are called *phenomena*. But if I admit things which are objects of the understanding only, and nevertheless can be given as objects of an intuition, though not of sensuous intuition (as *coram intuitu intellectuali*), such things would be called *Noumena* (*intelligibilia*).

One might feel inclined to think that the concept of *Phenomena*, as limited by the transcendental aesthetic, suggested by itself the objective reality of the *Noumena*, and justified a division of objects into phenomena and noumena, and consequently of the world into a *sensible* and *intelligible* world (*mundus sensibilis et intelligibilis*); and this in such a way that the distinction between the two should not refer to the logical form only of a more or less clear knowledge of one and the same object, but to a difference in their original presentation to our knowledge, which makes them to differ in themselves from each other in kind. For if the senses only represent to us something as it appears, that something must by itself also be a thing, and an object of a non-sensuous intuition, i.e. of the understanding. That is, there must be a kind of knowledge in which there is no sensibility, and which alone possesses absolute objective reality, representing objects as they are, while through the empirical use of our understanding we know things only as they appear. Hence it would seem to follow that, beside the empirical use of the categories (limited by sensuous conditions), there was another one, pure and yet objectively valid, and that we could not say, as we have hitherto done, that our knowledge of the pure understanding contained nothing but principles for the exhibition of phenomena, which, even *a priori*, could not apply to anything but the formal possibility of experience. Here, in fact, quite a new field would seem to be open, a world, as it were, realised in thought (nay, according to some, even in intuition), which would be a more, and not a less, worthy object for the pure understanding.

All our representations are no doubt referred by the understanding to some sort of object, and as phenomena are nothing but representations, the understanding refers them to a *something*, as the object of our sensuous intuition, this something being however the transcendental object only. This means a something equal to *x*, of which we do not, nay, with the present constitution of our understanding, cannot know anything, but which[26] can only serve, as a correlatum of the unity of apperception, for the unity of the manifold in sensuous intuition, by means of which the understanding unites the manifold into the concept of an object. This transcendental object cannot be separated from the sensuous data, because in that case nothing would remain by which it could be thought. It is not therefore an object of knowledge in itself, but only the representation of phenomena, under the concept of an object in general, which can be defined by the manifold of sensuous intuition.

For this very reason the categories do not represent a peculiar object, given to the understanding only, but serve only to define the transcendental object (the concept of something in general) by that which is given us through the senses, in order thus to know empirically phenomena under the concepts of objects.

What then is the cause why people, not satisfied with the

[26] Read *welches* instead of *welcher*.

substratum of sensibility, have added to the phenomena the noumena, which the understanding only is supposed to be able to realise? It is this, that sensibility and its sphere, that is the sphere of phenomena, is so limited by the understanding itself that it should not refer to things by themselves, but only to the mode in which things appear to us, in accordance with our own subjective qualification. This was the result of the whole transcendental aesthetic, and it really follows quite naturally from the concept of a phenomenon in general, that something must correspond to it, which in itself is not a phenomenon, because a phenomenon cannot be anything by itself, apart from our mode of representation. Unless therefore we are to move in a constant circle, we must admit that the very word *phenomenon* indicates a relation to something the immediate representation of which is no doubt sensuous, but which nevertheless, even without this qualification of our sensibility (on which the form of our intuition is founded) must be something by itself, that is an object independent of our sensibility.

Hence arises the concept of a noumenon, which however is not positive, nor a definite knowledge of anything, but which implies only the thinking of something, without taking any account of the form of sensuous intuition. But in order that a noumenon may signify a real object that can be distinguished from all phenomena, it is not enough that I should free my thought of all conditions of sensuous intuition, but I must besides have some reason for admitting another kind of intuition besides the sensuous, in which such an object can be given; otherwise my thought would be empty, however free it may be from contradictions. It is true that we were not able to prove that the sensuous is the only possible intuition, though it is so for us: but neither could we prove that another kind of intuition was possible; and although our thought may take no account of any sensibility, the question always remains whether, after that, it is not a mere form of a concept, and whether any real object would thus be left.

The object to which I refer the phenomenon in general is the transcendental object, that is, the entirely indefinite thought of something in general. This cannot be called the noumenon, for I know nothing of what it is by itself, and have no conception of it, except as the object of sensuous intuition in general, which is therefore the same for all phenomena. I cannot lay hold of it by any of the categories, for these are valid for empirical intuitions only, in order to bring them under the concept of an object in general. A pure use of the categories is no doubt possible, that is, not self-contradictory, but it has no kind of objective validity, because it refers to no intuition to which it is meant to impart the unity of an object. The categories remain for ever mere functions of thought by which no object can be given to me, but by which I can only think whatever may be given to me in intuition.]

We are met here by an illusion which is difficult to avoid. The categories do not depend in their origin on sensibility, like the forms of intuition, *space, and time, and seem, therefore, to admit of an application extending beyond the objects of the senses. But, on the other side, they are nothing but* forms of thought, *containing the logical faculty only of comprehending a priori in one consciousness the manifold that is given in intuition, and they would therefore, if we take away the only intuition which is possible to us, have still less significance than those pure sensuous forms by which at least an object is given, while a peculiar mode of our understanding of connecting the manifold* (unless that intuition, in which the manifold alone can be given, is added), *signifies nothing at all.*

Nevertheless, it seems to follow from our very concept, if we call certain objects, as phenomena, beings of the senses, by distinguishing between the mode of our intuition and the nature of those objects by themselves, that we may take either the same objects in that latter capacity, though they cannot as such come before our intuition, or other possible things, which are not objects of our senses at all, and place them, as objects thought only by the understanding, in opposition to the former, calling them beings of the understanding (noumena). *The question then arises, whether our pure concepts of the understanding do not possess some significance with regard to these so-called beings of the understanding, and constitute a mode of knowing them?*

At the very outset, however, we meet with an ambiguity which may cause great misapprehension. The understanding, by calling an object in one aspect a phenomenon only, makes to itself, apart from that aspect, another representation of an object by itself, *and imagines itself able to form* concepts *of such an object. As, then, the understanding yields no other concepts but the categories, it supposes that the object in the latter aspect can be thought at least by those pure concepts of the understanding, and is thus induced to take the entirely indefinite concept of a being of the understanding, as of a something in general outside our sensibility, as a* definite *concept of a being which we might know to a certain extent through the understanding.*

If by noumenon we mean a thing so far as it is not an object of our sensuous intuition, *and make abstraction of our mode of intuition, it may be called a noumenon in a* negative *sense. If, however, we mean by it an* object *of a* non-sensuous *intuition, we admit thereby a peculiar mode of intuition, namely, the intellectual, which, however, is not our own, nor one of which we can understand even the possibility. This would be the noumenon in a* positive *sense.*

The doctrine of sensibility is at the same time the doctrine of noumena in their negative sense; that is, of things which the understanding must think without reference to our mode of intuition, and therefore, not as phenomena only, but as things by themselves, but to which, after it has thus separated them, the understanding knows that it must not, in this new aspect, apply its categories; because these categories have significance only with reference to the unity of intuitions in space and time, and can therefore a priori *determine that unity, on account of the mere ideality of space and time only, by means of general connecting concepts. Where that unity in time cannot be found, i.e. in the noumenon, the whole use, nay, the whole significance of categories comes to an end: because even the possibility of things that should correspond to the categories, would be unintelligible. On this point I may refer the reader to what I have said at the very beginning of the general note to the previous chapter. The possibility of a thing can never be proved from the fact that its concept is not self-contradictory, but only by being authenticated by an intuition corresponding to it. If, therefore, we attempted to apply the categories to objects which are not considered as phenomena, we should have to admit an intuition other than the sensuous, and thus the object would become a noumenon in a* positive *sense. As, however, such an intuition, namely, an intellectual one, is entirely beyond our faculty of knowledge, the use of the categories also can never reach beyond the limits of the objects of experience. Beings of the understanding correspond no doubt to beings of the senses, and there may be beings of the understanding to which our faculty of sensuous intuition has no relation at all; but our concepts of the understanding, being forms of thought for our sensuous intuition only, do not reach so far, and what is called by us a noumenon must be understood as such in a* negative sense *only.*

If all thought (by means of categories) is taken away from empirical knowledge, no knowledge of any object remains, because nothing can be thought by mere intuition, and the mere fact that there is within me an affection of my sensibility, establishes in no way any relation of such a representation to any object. If, on the contrary, all intuition is taken away, there always remains the form of thought, that is, the mode of determining an object for the manifold of a possible intuition. In this sense the categories may be said to extend further than sensuous intuition, because they can think objects in general without any regard to the special mode of sensibility in which they may be given; but they do not thus prove a larger sphere of objects, because we cannot admit that such objects can be given, without admitting the possibility of some other but sensuous intuition, for which we have no right whatever.

I call a concept problematic, if it is not self-contradictory, and if, as limiting other concepts, it is connected with other kinds of knowledge, while its objective reality cannot be known in any way. Now the concept of a noumenon, that is of a thing which can never be thought as an object of the senses, but only as a thing by itself (by the pure understanding), is not self-contradictory, because we cannot maintain that sensibility is the only form of intuition. That concept is also necessary, to prevent sensuous intuition from extending to things by themselves; that is, in order to limit the objective validity of sensuous knowledge (for all the rest to which sensuous intuition does not extend is called noumenon, for the very purpose of showing that sensuous knowledge cannot extend its domain over everything that can be thought by the understanding). But, after all, we cannot understand the possibility of such noumena, and whatever lies beyond the sphere of phenomena is (to us) empty; that is, we have an understanding which *problematically* extends beyond that sphere, but no intuition, nay not even the conception of a possible intuition, by which, outside the field of sensibility, objects could be given to us, and our understanding could extend beyond that sensibility in its assertory use. The concept of a noumenon is therefore merely *limitative,* and intended to keep the claims of sensibility within proper bounds, therefore of negative use only. But it is not a mere arbitrary fiction, but closely connected with the limitation of sensibility, though incapable of adding anything positive to the sphere of the senses.

A real division of objects into phenomena and noumena, and of the world into a sensible and intelligible world *in a positive sense,* is therefore quite inadmissible, although concepts may very well be divided into sensuous and intellectual. For no objects can be assigned to these intellectual concepts, nor can they be represented as objectively valid. If we drop the senses, how are we to make it conceivable that our categories (which would be the only remaining concepts for noumena) have any meaning at all, considering that, in order to refer them to any object, something more must be given than the mere unity of thought, namely, a possible intuition, to which the categories could be applied? With all this the concept of a noumenon, if taken as problematical only, remains not only admissible, but, as a concept to limit the sphere of sensibility, indispensable. In this case, however, it is not a particular *intelligible object* for *our* understanding, but an understanding to which it could belong is itself a problem, if we ask how it could know an object, not discursively by means of categories, but intuitively, and yet in a non-sensuous intuition, a process of which we could not understand even the bare possibility. Our understanding thus acquires a kind of negative extension, that is, it does not become itself limited by sensibility, but, on the contrary, limits it, by calling things by themselves (not considered as phenomena) noumena. In doing this, it immediately proceeds to prescribe limits to itself, by admitting that it cannot know these noumena by means of the categories, but can only think of them under the name of something unknown.

In the writings of modern philosophers, however, I meet with a totally different use of the terms of *mundus sensibilis* and *intelligibilis*,* totally different from the meaning assigned to these terms by the ancients. Here all difficulty seems to disappear. But the fact is, that there remains nothing but mere word-mongery. In accordance with this, some people have been pleased to call the whole of phenomena, so far as they are seen, the world of sense; but so far as their connection, according to general laws of the understanding, is taken into account, the world of the understanding. Theoretical astronomy, which only teaches the actual observation of the starry heavens, would represent the former; contemplative astronomy, on the contrary (taught according to the Copernican system, or, it may be, according to Newton's laws of gravitation), the latter, namely, a purely intelligible world. But this twisting of words is a mere sophistical excuse, in order to avoid a troublesome question, by changing its meaning according to one's own convenience. Understanding and reason may be applied to phenomena, but it is very questionable whether they can be applied at all to an object which is not a phenomenon, but a noumenon; and it is this, when the object is represented as purely intelligible, that is, as given to the understanding only, and not to the senses. The question therefore is whether, besides the empirical use of the understanding

* We must not speak, as is often done, of an intellectual *world, for intellectual and sensitive apply to* knowledge only. *That, however, to which the one or the other mode of intuition applies, that is, the* objects *themselves, must, however harsh it may sound, be called intelligible or sensible.* [Note in 2nd Edition.]

(even in the Newtonian view of the world), a transcendental use is possible, referring to the noumenon, as its object; and that question we have answered decidedly in the negative.

When *we* therefore say that the senses represent objects to us as they *appear,* and the understanding as they *are,* the latter is not to be taken in a transcendental, but in a purely empirical meaning, namely, as to how they, as objects of experience, must be represented, according to the regular connection of phenomena, and not according to what they may be, as objects of the pure understanding, apart from their relation to possible experience, and therefore to our senses. This will always remain unknown to us; nay, we shall never know whether such a transcendental and exceptional knowledge is possible at all, at least as comprehended under our ordinary categories. With us understanding and sensibility cannot determine objects, unless they are joined together. If we separate them, we have intuitions without concepts, or concepts without intuitions, in both cases representations which we cannot refer to any definite object.

If, after all these arguments, anybody should still hesitate to abandon the purely transcendental use of the categories, let him try an experiment with them for framing any synthetical proposition. An analytical proposition does not in the least advance the understanding, which, as in such a proposition it is only concerned with what is already thought in the concept, does not ask whether the concept in itself has any reference to objects, or expresses only the unity of thought in general (this completely ignoring the manner in which an object may be given). The understanding in fact is satisfied if it knows what is contained in the concept of an object; it is indifferent as to the object to which the concept may refer. But let him try the experiment with any synthetical and so-called transcendental proposition, as for instance, 'Everything that exists, exists as a substance, or as a determination inherent in it,' or 'Everything contingent exists as an effect of some other thing, namely, its cause,' etc. Now I ask, whence can the understanding take these synthetical propositions, as the concepts are to apply, not to some possible experience, but to things by themselves (noumena)? Where is that third term to be found which is always required for a synthetical proposition, in order thus to join concepts which have no logical (analytical) relation with each other? It will be impossible to prove such a proposition, nay even to justify the possibility of any such pure assertion, without appealing to the empirical use of the understanding, and thus renouncing entirely the so-called pure and non-sensuous judgment. There are no principles therefore according to which the concepts of pure and merely intelligible objects could ever be applied, because we cannot imagine any way in which they could be given, and the problematic thought, which leaves a place open to them, serves only, like empty space, to limit the sphere of empirical principles, without containing or indicating any other object of knowledge, lying beyond that sphere. . . .

Transcendental Logic

SECOND DIVISION
TRANSCENDENTAL DIALECTIC

INTRODUCTION

1. OF TRANSCENDENTAL APPEARANCE (ILLUSION)

We call Dialectic in general a logic of *illusion* (*eine Logik des Scheins*). This does not mean that it is a doctrine of *probability* (*Wahrscheinlichkeit*), for probability is a kind of truth, known through insufficient causes, the knowledge of which is therefore deficient, but not deceitful, and cannot properly be separated from the analytical part of logic. Still less can *phenomenon* (*Erscheinung*) and *illusion* (*Schein*) be taken as identical. For truth or illusion is not to be found in the objects of intuition, but in the judgments upon them, so far as they are thought. It is therefore quite right to say, that the senses never err, not because they always judge rightly, but because they do not judge at all. Truth therefore and error, and consequently illusory appearance also, as the cause of error, exist in our judgments only, that is, in the relation of an object to our understanding. No error exists in our knowledge, if it completely agrees with the laws of our understanding, nor can there be an error in a representation of the senses, because they involve no judgment, and no power of nature can, of its own accord, deviate from its own laws. Therefore neither the understanding by itself (without the influence of another cause), nor the senses by themselves could ever err. The understanding could not err, because as long as it acts according to its own laws, the effect (the judgment) must necessarily agree with those laws, and the formal test of all truth consists in this agreement with the laws of the understanding. The senses cannot err, because there is in them no judgment at all, whether true or false. Now as we have no other sources of knowledge but these two, it follows that error can only arise through the unperceived influence of the sensibility on the understanding, whereby it happens that subjective grounds of judgment are mixed up with the objective, and cause them to deviate from their destination;* just as a body in motion would, if left to itself, always follow a straight line in the same direction, which is changed however into a curvilinear motion, as soon as another force influences it at the same time in a different direction. In order to distinguish the proper action of the understanding from that other force which is mixed up with it, it will be necessary to look on an erroneous judgment as the diagonal between two forces, which determine the judgment in two different directions, forming as it were an angle, and to dissolve that composite effect into the simple ones of the understanding and of the sensibility, which must be effected in pure judgments *a priori* by transcendental reflection, whereby, as we tried to show, the right place is assigned to each representation in the faculty of knowledge corresponding to it, and the influence of either faculty upon such representation is determined.

It is not at present our business to treat of empirical, for instance, optical appearance or illusion, which occurs in the empirical use of the otherwise correct rules of the understanding, and by which, owing to the influence of imagination, the faculty of judgment is misled. We have to deal here with nothing but the *transcendental illusion*, which touches principles never even intended to be applied to experience, which might give us a test of their correctness, an illusion which, in spite of all the warnings of criticism, tempts us far beyond the empirical use of the categories, and deludes us with the mere dream of an extension of the pure understanding. All principles the application of which is entirely confined within the limits of possible experience, we shall call *immanent;* those, on the contrary, which tend to transgress those limits, *transcendent.* I do not mean by this the transcen-

---

* Sensibility, if subjected to the understanding as the object on which it exercises its function, is the source of real knowledge, but sensibility, if it influences the action of the understanding itself and leads it on to a judgment, is the cause of error.

dental use or abuse of the categories, which is a mere fault of the faculty of the judgment, not being as yet sufficiently subdued by criticism nor sufficiently attentive to the limits of the sphere within which alone the pure understanding has full play, but real principles which call upon us to break down all those barriers, and to claim a perfectly new territory, which nowhere recognises any demarcation at all. Here *transcendental* and *transcendent* do not mean the same thing. The principles of the pure understanding, which we explained before, are meant to be only of empirical, and not of transcendental application, that is, they cannot transcend the limits of experience. A principle, on the contrary, which removes these landmarks, nay, insists on our transcending them, is called *transcendent*. If our critique succeeds in laying bare the illusion of those pretended principles, the other principles of a purely empirical use may, in opposition to the former, be called *immanent*.

Logical illusion, which consists in a mere imitation of the forms of reason (the illusion of sophistic syllogisms), arises entirely from want of attention to logical rules. It disappears at once, when our attention is roused. Transcendental illusion, on the contrary, does not disappear, although it has been shown up, and its worthlessness rendered clear by means of transcendental criticism, as, for instance, the illusion inherent in the proposition that the world must have a beginning in time. The cause of this is that there exists in our reason (considered subjectively as a faculty of human knowledge) principles and maxims of its use, which have the appearance of objective principles, and lead us to mistake the subjective necessity of a certain connection of our concepts in favour of the understanding for an objective necessity in the determination of things by themselves. This illusion is as impossible to avoid as it is to prevent the sea from appearing to us higher at a distance than on the shore, because we see it by higher rays of light; or to prevent the moon from appearing, even to an astronomer, larger at its rising, although he is not deceived by that illusion.

Transcendental Dialectic must, therefore, be content to lay bare the illusion of transcendental judgments and guarding against its deceptions—but it will never succeed in removing the transcendental illusion (like the logical), and putting an end to it altogether. For we have here to deal with a natural and inevitable illusion, which itself rests on subjective principles, representing them to us as objective, while logical Dialectic, in removing sophisms, has to deal merely with a mistake in applying the principles, or with an artificial illusion produced by an imitation of them. There exists, therefore, a natural and inevitable Dialectic of pure reason, not one in which a mere bungler might get entangled from want of knowledge, or which a sophist might artificially devise to confuse rational people, but one that is inherent in, and inseparable from human reason, and which, even after its illusion has been exposed, will never cease to fascinate our reason, and to precipitate it into momentary errors, such as require to be removed again and again.

2. OF PURE REASON, AS THE SEAT OF TRANSCENDENTAL ILLUSION

A. Of Reason in General

All our knowledge begins with the senses, proceeds thence to the understanding, and ends with reason. There is nothing higher than reason, for working up the material of intuition, and comprehending it under the highest unity of thought. As it here becomes necessary to give a definition of that highest faculty of knowledge, I begin to feel considerable misgivings. There is of reason, as there is of the understanding, a purely formal, that is logical use, in which no account is taken of the contents of knowledge; but there is also a real use, in so far as reason itself contains the origin of certain concepts and principles, which it has not borrowed either from the senses or from the understanding. The former faculty has been long defined by logicians as the faculty of mediate conclusions, in contradistinction to immediate ones (*consequentiae immediatae*); but this does not help us to understand the latter, which itself produces concepts. As this brings us face to face with the division of reason into a logical and a transcendental faculty, we must look for a higher concept for this source of knowledge, to comprehend both concepts: though, according to the analogy of the concepts of the understanding, we may expect that the logical concept will give us the key to the transcendental, and that the table of the functions of the former will give us the genealogical outline of the concepts of reason.

In the first part of our transcendental logic we defined the understanding as the *faculty of rules*, and we now distinguish reason from it, by calling it the *faculty of principles*.

The term *principle* is ambiguous, and signifies commonly some kind of knowledge only that may be used as a principle, though in itself, and according to its origin, it is no principle at all. Every general proposition, even though it may have been derived from experience (by induction), may serve as a major in a syllogism of reason; but it is not on that account a principle. Mathematical axioms, as, for instance, that between two points there can be only one straight line, constitute even general knowledge *a priori*, and may therefore, with reference to the cases which can be brought under them, rightly be called principles. Nevertheless it would be wrong to say, that this property of a straight line, in general and by itself, is known to us from principles, for it is known from pure intuition only.

I shall therefore call it knowledge from principles, whenever we know the particular in the general, by means of concepts. Thus every syllogism of reason is a form of deducing some kind of knowledge from a principle, because the major always contains a concept which enables us to know, according to a principle, everything that can be comprehended under the conditions of that concept. As every general knowledge may serve as a major in such a syllogism, and as the understanding supplies such general propositions *a priori,* these no doubt may, with reference to their possible use, be called principles.

But, if we consider these principles of the pure understanding in themselves, and according to their origin, we find that they are anything rather than knowledge from concepts. They would not even be possible *a priori*, unless we relied on pure intuition (in mathematics) or on conditions of a possible experience in general. That everything which happens has a cause, can by no means be concluded from the concept of that which happens; on the contrary, that very principle shows in what manner alone we can form a definite empirical concept of that which happens.

It is impossible therefore for the understanding to supply us with synthetical knowledge from concepts, and it is really that kind of knowledge which I call principles absolutely; while all general propositions may be called principles relatively.

It is an old desideratum, which at some time, however distant, may be realised, that, instead of the endless variety of civil laws, their principles might be discovered, for thus alone the secret might be found of what is called simplifying legislation. Such laws, however, are only limitations of our freedom under conditions by which it always agrees with itself; they refer to something which is entirely our own work, and of which we ourselves can be the cause, by means of these concepts. But that objects in themselves, as for instance material nature, should be subject to principles, and be determined according to mere concepts, is something, if not impossible, at all events extremely contradictory. But be that as it may (for on this point we have still all investigations before us), so much at least is clear, that knowledge from principles (by itself) is something totally different from mere knowledge of the understanding, which, in the form of a principle, may no doubt precede other knowledge, but which by itself (in so far as it is synthetical) is not based on mere thought, nor contains anything general, according to concepts.

If the understanding is a faculty for producing unity among phenomena, according to rules, reason is the faculty for producing unity among the rules of the understanding, according to principles. Reason therefore never looks directly to experience, or to any object, but to the understanding, in order to impart *a priori* through concepts to its manifold kinds of knowledge a unity that may be called the unity of reason, and is very different from the unity which can be produced by the understanding.

This is a general definition of the faculty of reason, so far as it was possible to make it intelligible without the help of illustrations, which are to be given hereafter.

B.   Of the Logical Use of Reason

A distinction is commonly made between what is immediately known and what is only inferred. That in a figure bounded by three straight lines there are three angles, is known immediately, but that these angles together are equal to two right angles, is only inferred. As we are constantly obliged to infer, we grow so accustomed to it, that in the end we no longer perceive this difference, and as in the case of the so-called deceptions of the senses, often mistake what we have only inferred for something perceived immediately. In every syllogism there is first a fundamental proposition; secondly, another deduced from it; and lastly, the conclusion (consequence), according to which the truth of the latter is indissolubly connected with the truth of the former. If the judgment or the conclusion is so clearly contained in the first that it can be inferred from it without the mediation or intervention of a third representation, the conclusion is called immediate (*consequentia immediata*): though I should prefer to call it a conclusion of the understanding. But if, besides the fundamental knowledge, another judgment is required to bring out the consequence, then the conclusion is called a conclusion of reason. In the proposition 'all men are mortal,' the following propositions are contained: some men are mortal; or some mortals are men; or nothing that is immortal is a man. These are therefore immediate inferences from the first. The proposition, on the contrary, all the learned are mortal, is not contained in the fundamental judgment, because the concept of learned does not occur in it, and can only be deduced from it by means of an intervening judgment.

In every syllogism I first think a rule (the major) by means of the understanding. I then bring some special knowledge under the condition of the rule (the minor) by means of the faculty of judgment, and I finally determine my knowledge through the predicate of the rule (*conclusio*), that is, *a priori*, by means of reason. It is therefore the relation represented by the major proposition, as the rule, between knowledge and its condition, that constitutes the different kinds of syllogism. Syllogisms are therefore threefold, like all judgments, differing from each other in the manner in which they express the relation of knowledge in the understanding, namely, categorical, hypothetical, and disjunctive.

If, as often happens, the conclusion is put forward as a judgment, in order to see whether it does not follow from other judgments by which a perfectly different object is conceived, I try to find in the understanding the assertion of that conclusion, in order to see whether it does not exist in it, under certain conditions, according to a general rule. If I find such a condition, and if the object of the conclusion can be brought under the given condition, then that conclusion follows from the rule *which is valid for other objects of knowledge also*. Thus we see that reason, in forming conclusions, tries to reduce the great variety of the knowledge of the understanding to the smallest number of principles (general conditions), and thereby to produce in it the highest unity.

C. Of the Pure Use of Reason

The question to which we have at present to give an answer, though a preliminary one only, is this, whether reason can be isolated and thus constitute by itself an independent source of concepts and judgments, which spring from it alone, and through which it has reference to objects, or whether it is only a subordinate faculty for imparting a certain form to any given knowledge, namely, a logical form, a faculty whereby the cognitions of the understanding are arranged among themselves only, and lower rules placed under higher ones (the condition of the latter comprehending in its sphere the condition of the former) so far as all this can be done by their comparison. Variety of rules with unity of principles is a requirement of reason for the purpose of bringing the understanding into perfect agreement with itself, just as the understanding brings the variety of intuition under concepts, and thus imparts to intuition a connected form. Such a principle however prescribes no law to the objects themselves, nor does it contain the ground on which the possibility of knowing and determining objects depends. It is merely a subjective law of economy, applied to the stores of our understanding; having for its purpose, by means of a comparison of concepts, to reduce the general use of them to the smallest possible number, but without giving us a right to demand of the objects themselves such a uniformity as might conduce to the comfort and the extension of our understanding, or to ascribe to that maxim any objective validity. In one word, the question is, whether reason in itself, that is pure reason, contains synthetical principles and rules *a priori,* and what those principles are?

The merely formal and logical procedure of reason in syllogisms gives us sufficient hints as to the ground on which the transcendental principle of synthetical knowledge, by means of pure reason, is likely to rest.

First, a syllogism, as a function of reason, does not refer to intuitions in order to bring them under rules (as the understanding does with its categories), but to concepts and judgments. Although pure reason refers in the end to objects, it has no immediate relation to them and their intuition, but only to the understanding and its judgments, these having a direct relation to the senses and their intuition, and determining their objects. Unity of reason is therefore never the unity of a possible experience, but essentially different from it, as the unity of the understanding. That everything which happens has a cause, is not a principle discovered or prescribed by reason, it only makes the unity of experience possible, and borrows nothing from reason, which without this relation to possible experience could never, from mere concepts, have prescribed such a synthetical unity.

Secondly. Reason, in its logical employment, looks for the general condition of its judgment (the conclusion), and the syllogism produced by reason is itself nothing but a judgment by means of bringing its condition under a general rule (the major). But as this rule is again liable to the same experiment, reason having to seek, as long as possible, the condition of a condition (by means of a prosyllogism), it is easy to see that it is the peculiar principle of reason (in its logical use) to find for every conditioned knowledge of the understanding the unconditioned, whereby the unity of that knowledge may be completed.

This logical maxim, however, cannot become a principle of *pure reason,* unless we admit that, whenever the condition is given, the whole series of conditions, subordinated to one another, a series, which consequently is itself unconditioned, is likewise given (that is, is contained in the object and its connection).

Such a principle of pure reason, however, is evidently synthetical; for analytically the conditioned refers no doubt to some condition, but not to the unconditioned. From this principle several other synthetical propositions also must arise of which the pure understanding knows nothing; because it has to deal with objects of a possible experience only, the knowledge and synthesis of which are always conditioned. The unconditioned, if it is really to be admitted, has to be especially considered with regard to all the determinations which distinguish it from whatever is conditioned, and will thus supply material for many a synthetical proposition *a priori*.

The principles resulting from this highest principle of pure reason will however be *transcendent,* with regard to all phenomena; that is to say, it will be impossible ever to make any adequate empirical use of such a principle. It will thus be completely different from all principles of the understanding, the use of which is entirely *immanent* and directed to the possibility of experience only. The task that is now before us in the transcendental Dialectic which has to be developed from sources deeply hidden in the human reason, is this: to discover the correctness or otherwise the falsehood of the principle that the series of conditions (in the synthesis of phenomena, or of objective thought in general) extends to the unconditioned, and what consequences result therefrom with regard to the empirical use of the understanding: to find out whether there is really such an objectively valid principle of reason, and not only, in place of it, a logical rule which requires us, by ascending to ever higher conditions, to approach their completeness, and thus to bring the highest unity of reason, which is possible to us, into our knowledge: to find out, I say, whether, by some misconception, a mere tendency of reason has not been mistaken for a transcendental principle of pure reason, postulating, without sufficient reflection, absolute completeness in the series of conditions in the objects themselves, and what kind of misconceptions and illusions may in that case have crept into the syllogisms of reason, the major proposition of which has been taken over from pure reason (being perhaps a *petitio* rather than a *postulatum*), and which ascend from experience to its conditions. We shall divide it into two parts, of which the first will treat of the *transcendent concepts* of pure reason, the second of *transcendent and dialectical syllogisms.*

Transcendental Dialectic

Book I
Of the Concepts of Pure Reason

Whatever may be thought of the possibility of concepts of pure reason, it is certain that they are not simply obtained by reflection, but by inference. Concepts of the understanding exist *a priori*, before experience, and for the sake of it, but they contain nothing but the unity of reflection applied to phenomena, so far as they are necessarily intended for a possible empirical consciousness. It is through them alone that knowledge and determination of an object become possible. They are the first to give material for conclusions, and they are not preceded by any concepts *a priori* of objects from which they could themselves be deduced. Their objective reality however depends on this, that because they constitute the intellectual form of all experience, it is necessary that their application should always admit of being exhibited in experience.

The very name, however, of a *concept of reason* gives a kind of intimation that it is not intended to be limited to experience, because it refers to a kind of knowledge of which every empirical knowledge is a part only (it may be, the whole of possible experience or of its empirical synthesis): and to which all real experience belongs, though it can never fully attain to it. Concepts of reason serve for conceiving or comprehending; concepts of the understanding for understanding (perceptions). If they contain the unconditioned, they refer to something to which all experience may belong, but which itself can never become an object of experience; something to which reason in its conclusions from experience leads up, and by which it estimates and measures the degree of its own empirical use, but which never forms part of empirical synthesis. If such concepts possess, notwithstanding, objective validity, they may be called *conceptus ratiocinati* (concepts legitimately formed); if they have only been surreptitiously obtained, by a kind of illusory conclusion, they may be called *conceptus ratiocinantes* (sophistical concepts). But as this subject can only be fully treated in the chapter on the dialectical conclusions of pure reason, we shall say no more of it now, but shall only, as we gave the name of categories to the pure concepts of the understanding, give a new name to the concepts of pure reason, and call them *tran-scendental ideas*, a name that has now to be explained and justified.

Transcendental Dialectic

Book I

FIRST SECTION

OF IDEAS IN GENERAL

In spite of the great wealth of our languages, a thoughtful mind is often at a loss for an expression that should square exactly with its concept; and for want of which he cannot make himself altogether intelligible, either to others or to himself. To coin new words is to arrogate to oneself legislative power in matters of language, a proceeding which seldom succeeds, so that, before taking so desperate a step, it is always advisable to look about, in dead and learned languages, whether they do not contain such a concept and its adequate expression. Even if it should happen that the original meaning of the word had become somewhat uncertain, through carelessness on the part of its authors, it is better nevertheless to determine and fix the meaning which principally belonged to it (even if it should remain doubtful whether it was originally used exactly in that meaning), than to spoil our labour by becoming unintelligible.

Whenever therefore there exists one single word only for a certain concept, which, in its received meaning, exactly covers that concept, and when it is of great consequence to keep that concept distinct from other related concepts, we ought not to be lavish in using it nor employ it, for the sake of variety only, as a synonym in the place of others, but carefully preserve its own peculiar meaning, as otherwise it may easily happen that the expression ceases to attract special attention, and loses itself in a crowd of other words of very different import, so that the thought, which that expression alone could have preserved, is lost with it.

From the way in which Plato uses the term *idea*, it is easy to see that he meant by it something which not only was never borrowed from the senses, but which even far transcends the concepts of the understanding, with which Aristotle occupied himself, there being nothing in experience corresponding to the ideas. With him the ideas are archetypes of things themselves, not only, like the categories, keys to possible experiences. According to his opinion they flowed out from the highest reason, which however exists no longer in its original state, but has to recall, with difficulty, the old but now very obscure ideas, which it does by means of reminiscence, commonly called philosophy. I shall not enter here on any literary discussions in order to determine the exact meaning which the sublime philosopher himself connected with that expression. I shall only remark, that it is by no means unusual, in ordinary conversations, as well as in written works, that by carefully comparing the thoughts uttered by an author on his own subject, we succeed in understanding him better than he understood himself, because he did not sufficiently define his concept, and thus not only spoke, but sometimes even thought, in opposition to his own intentions.

Plato knew very well that our faculty of knowledge was filled with a much higher craving than merely to spell out phenomena according to a synthetical unity, and thus to read and understand them as experience. He knew that our reason, if left to itself, tries to soar up to knowledge to which no object that experience may give can ever correspond; but which nevertheless is real, and by no means a mere cobweb of the brain.

Plato discovered his ideas principally in what is practical,* that is, in what depends on freedom, which again belongs to a class of knowledge which is a peculiar product of reason. He who would derive the concept of virtue from experience, and would change what at best could only serve as an example or an imperfect illustration, into a type and a source of knowledge (as many have really done), would indeed transform virtue into an equivocal phantom, changing according to times and

---

* It is true, however, that he extended his concept of ideas to speculative knowledge also, if only it was pure, and given entirely *a priori*. He extended it even to mathematics, although they can have their object nowhere but in possible experience. In this I cannot follow him, nor in the mystical deduction of his ideas, and in the exaggerations which led him, as it were, to hypostasise them, although the high-flown language which he used, when treating of this subject, may well admit of a milder interpretation, and one more in accordance with the nature of things.

circumstances, and utterly useless to serve as a rule. Everybody can surely perceive that, when a person is held up to us as a model of virtue, we have always in our own mind the true original with which we compare this so-called model, and estimate it accordingly. The true original is the idea of virtue, in regard to which all possible objects of experience may serve as examples (proofs of the practicability, in a certain degree, of that which is required by the concept of reason), but never as archetypes. That no man can ever act up to the pure idea of virtue does not in the least prove the chimerical nature of that concept; for every judgment as to the moral worth or unworth of actions is possible by means of that idea only, which forms, therefore, the necessary foundation for every approach to moral perfection, however far the impediments inherent in human nature, the extent of which it is difficult to determine, may keep us removed from it.

The Platonic Republic has been supposed to be a striking example of purely imaginary perfection. It has become a byword, as something that could exist in the brain of an idle thinker only, and Brucker thinks it ridiculous that Plato could have said that no prince could ever govern well, unless he participated in the ideas. We should do better, however, to follow up this thought and endeavour (where that excellent philosopher leaves us without his guidance) to place it in a clearer light by our own efforts, rather than to throw it aside as useless, under the miserable and very dangerous pretext of its impracticability. A constitution founded on the greatest possible human freedom, according to laws which enable the freedom of each individual to exist by the side of the freedom of others (without any regard to the highest possible human happiness, because that must necessarily follow by itself), is, to say the least, a necessary idea, on which not only the first plan of a constitution or a state, but all laws must be based, it being by no means necessary to take account from the beginning of existing impediments, which may owe their origin not so much to human nature itself as to the actual neglect of true ideas in legislation. For nothing can be more mischievous and more unworthy a philosopher than the vulgar appeal to what is called adverse experience, which possibly might never have existed, if at the proper time institutions had been framed according to those ideas, and not according to crude concepts, which, because they were derived from experience only, have marred all good intentions. The more legislation and government are in harmony with that idea, the rarer, no doubt, punishments would become; and it is therefore quite rational to say (as Plato did), that in a perfect state no punishments would be necessary. And though this can never be realised, yet the idea is quite correct which sets up this maximum as an archetype, in order thus to bring our legislative constitutions nearer and nearer to the greatest possible perfection. Which may be the highest degree where human nature must stop, and how wide the chasm may be between the idea and its realisation, no one can or ought to determine, because it is this very freedom that may be able to transcend any limits hitherto assigned to it.

It is not only, however, where human reason asserts its free causality and ideas become operative agents (with regard to actions and their objects), that is to say, in the sphere of ethics, but also in nature itself, that Plato rightly discovered clear proofs of its origin from ideas. A plant, an animal, the regular plan of the cosmos (most likely therefore the whole order of nature), show clearly that they are possible according to ideas only; and that though no single creature, under the singular conditions of its existence, can fully correspond with the idea of what is most perfect of its kind (as little as any individual man with the idea of humanity, which, for all that, he carries in his mind as the archetype of all his actions), those ideas are nevertheless determined throughout in the highest understanding each by itself as unchangeable, and are in fact the original causes of things, although it can only be said of the whole of them, connected together in the universe, that it is perfectly adequate to the idea. If we make allowance for the exaggerated expression, the effort of the philosopher to ascend from the mere observing and copying of the physical side of nature to an architectonic system of it, teleologically, that is according to ideas, deserves respect and imitation, while with regard to the principles of morality, legislation, and religion, where it is the ideas themselves that make experience of the good possible, though they can never be fully realised in experience, such efforts are of very eminent merit, which those only fail to recognise who attempt to judge it according to empirical rules, the very validity of which, as principles, was meant to be denied by Plato. With regard to nature, it is experience no doubt which supplies us with rules, and is the foundation of all truth: with regard to moral laws, on the contrary, experience is, alas! but the source of illusion; and it is altogether reprehensible to derive or limit the laws of what we ought to do according to our experience of what has been done.

Instead of considering these subjects, the full development of which constitutes in reality the peculiar character and dignity of philosophy, we have to occupy ourselves at present with a task less brilliant, though not less useful, of building and strengthening the foundation of that majestic edifice of morality, which at present is undermined by all sorts of moletracks, the work of our reason, which thus vainly, but always with the same confidence, is searching for buried treasures. It is our duty at present to acquire an accurate knowledge of the transcendental use of the pure reason, its principles and ideas, in order to be able to determine and estimate correctly their influence and value. But before I leave this preliminary introduction, I beg those who really care for philosophy (which means more than is commonly supposed) if they are convinced by what I have said and shall still have to say, to take the term *idea,* in its original meaning, under their special protection, so that it should no longer be lost among other expressions, by which all sorts of representations are loosely designated, to the great detriment of philosophy. There is no lack of names adequate to express every kind of representation, without our having to encroach on the property of others. I shall give a graduated list of them. The whole class may be called *representation* (*repraesentatio*). Under it stands conscious representation, *perception* (*perceptio*). A *perception* referring to the subject only, as a modification of his state, is *sensation* (*sensatio*), while an objective sensation is called *knowledge, cognition* (*cognitio*). Cognition is either *intuition* or *concept* (*intuitus vel conceptus*). The former refers immediately to an object and is singular, the latter refers to it mediately, that is, by means of a characteristic mark that can be shared by several things in common. A concept is either *empirical* or *pure,* and the pure concept, so far as it has its origin in the understanding only (not in the pure image of sensibility) is called *notion* (*notio*). A concept formed of notions and transcending all possible experience is an *idea,* or a concept of reason. To any one who has once accustomed himself to these distinctions, it must be extremely irksome to hear the representation of red colour called an idea, though it could not even be rightly called a notion (a concept of the understanding).

Transcendental Dialectic

Book I

SECOND SECTION

OF TRANSCENDENTAL IDEAS

We had an instance in our transcendental Analytic, how the mere logical form of our knowledge could contain the origin of pure concepts *a priori*, which represent objects antecedently to all experience, or rather indicate a synthetical unity by which alone an empirical knowledge of objects becomes possible. The form of judgments (changed into a concept of the synthesis of intuitions) gave us the categories that guide and determine the use of the understanding in every experience. We may expect, therefore, that the form of the syllogisms, if referred to the synthetical unity of intuitions, according to the manner of the categories, will contain the origin of certain concepts *a priori*, to be called concepts of pure reason, or *transcendental ideas*, which ought to determine the use of the understanding within the whole realm of experience, according to principles.

The function of reason in its syllogisms consists in the universality of cognition, according to concepts, and the syllogism itself is in reality a judgment, determined *a priori* in the whole extent of its condition. The proposition 'Caius is mortal,' might be taken from experience, by means of the understanding only. But what we want is a concept, containing the condition under which the predicate (assertion in general) of that judgment is given (here the concept of man), and after I have arranged it under this condition, taken in its whole extent (all men are mortal), I proceed to determine accordingly the knowledge of my object (Caius is mortal).

What we are doing therefore in the conclusion of a syllogism is to restrict the predicate to a certain object, after we have used it first in the major, in its whole extent, under a certain condition. This completeness of its extent, in reference to such a condition, is called universality (*universalitas*); and to this corresponds, in the synthesis of intuitions, the totality (*universitas*) of conditions. The transcendental concept of reason is, therefore, nothing but the concept of the totality of the conditions of anything given as conditioned. As therefore the unconditioned alone renders a totality of conditions possible, and as conversely the totality of conditions must always be unconditioned, it follows that a pure concept of reason in general may be explained as a concept of the unconditioned, so far as it contains a basis for the synthesis of the conditioned.

As many kinds of relations as there are, which the understanding represents to itself by means of the categories, so many pure concepts of the reason we shall find, that is, first, the *unconditioned* of the *categorical* synthesis in a subject; secondly, the *unconditioned* of the *hypothetical* synthesis of the members of a series; thirdly, the *unconditioned* of the *disjunctive* synthesis of the parts of a system.

There are exactly as many kinds of syllogisms, each of which tries to advance by means of prosyllogisms to the unconditioned: the first to the subject, which itself is no longer a predicate; the second to the presupposition, which presupposes nothing else; and the third to an aggregate of the members of a division, which requires nothing else, in order to render the division of the concept complete. Hence the pure concepts of reason implying totality in the synthesis of the conditions are necessary, at least as problems, in order to carry the unity of the understanding to the unconditioned, if that is possible, and they are founded in the nature of human reason, even though these transcendental concepts may be without any proper application *in concreto,* and thus have no utility beyond bringing the understanding into a direction where its application, being extended as far as possible, is brought throughout in harmony with itself.

Whilst speaking here of the totality of conditions, and of the unconditioned, as the common title of all the concepts of reason, we again meet with a term which we cannot do without, but which, by long abuse, has become so equivocal that we cannot employ it with safety. The term *absolute* is one of those few words which, in their original meaning, were fitted to a concept, which afterwards could not be exactly fitted with any other word of the same language, and the loss of which, or what is the same, the loose employment of which, entails the loss of the concept itself, and that of a concept with which reason is constantly occupied, and cannot dispense with without real damage to all transcendental investigations. At present the term *absolute* is frequently used simply in order to indicate that something applies to an object, considered in itself, and thus as it were internally. In this way *absolutely possible* would mean that something is possible in itself (*interné*), which in reality is the least that could be said of it. It is sometimes used also to indicate that something is valid in all respects (without limitation), as people speak of absolute sovereignty. In this way *absolutely possible* would mean that which is possible in all respects, and this is again the utmost that could be said of the possibility of a thing. It is true that these two significations sometimes coincide, because something that is internally impossible is impossible also in every respect, and therefore absolutely impossible. But in most cases they are far apart, and I am by no means justified in concluding that, because something is possible in itself, it is possible also in every respect, that is, absolutely possible. Nay, with regard to absolute necessity, I shall be able to show hereafter that it by no means always depends on internal necessity, and that the two cannot therefore be considered synonymous. No doubt, if the opposite of a thing is intrinsically impossible, that opposite is also impossible in every respect, and the thing itself therefore absolutely necessary. But I cannot conclude conversely, that the opposite of what is absolutely necessary is internally impossible, or that the absolute necessity of things is the same as an internal necessity. For in certain cases that internal necessity is an entirely empty expression, with which we cannot connect the least concept, while that of the necessity of a thing in every respect (with regard to all that is possible) implies very peculiar determinations. As therefore the loss of a concept which has acted a great part in speculative philosophy can never be indifferent to philosophers, I hope they will also take some interest in the definition and careful preservation of the term with which that concept is connected.

I shall therefore use the term *absolute* in this enlarged meaning only, in opposition to that which is valid relatively and in particular respects only, the latter being restricted to conditions, the former free from any restrictions whatsoever.

It is then the absolute totality in the synthesis of conditions at which the transcendental concept of reason aims, nor does it rest satisfied till it has reached that which is unconditioned absolutely and in every respect. Pure reason leaves everything to the understanding, which has primarily to do with the objects of intuition, or rather their synthesis in imagination. It is only the absolute totality in the use of the concepts of the understanding, which reason reserves for itself, while trying to carry the synthetical unity, which is realised in the category, to the absolutely unconditioned. We might therefore call the latter the unity of the phenomena in reason, the former, which is expressed by the category, the unity in the understanding. Hence reason is only concerned with the use of the understanding, not so far as it contains the basis of possible experience (for the absolute totality of conditions is not a concept that can be used in experience, because no experience is unconditioned), but in order to impart to it a direction towards a certain unity of which the understanding knows nothing, and which is meant to comprehend all acts of the understanding, with regard to any object, into an absolute whole. On this account the objective use of the pure concepts of reason must always be *transcendent:* while that of the pure concepts of the understanding must always be *immanent,* being by its very nature restricted to possible experience.

By idea I understand the necessary concept of reason, to which the senses can supply no corresponding object. The concepts of reason, therefore, of which we have been speaking, are *transcendental ideas.* They are concepts of pure reason, so far as they regard all empirical knowledge as determined by an absolute totality of conditions. They are not mere fancies, but supplied to us by the very nature of reason, and referring by necessity to the whole use of the understanding. They are, lastly, transcendent, as overstepping the limits of all experience which can never supply an object adequate to the transcendental idea. If we speak of an idea, we say a great deal with respect to the object (as the object of the pure understanding) but very little with respect to the subject, that is, with respect to its reality under empirical conditions, because an idea, being the concept of a maximum, can never be adequately given *in concreto.* As the latter is really the whole aim in the merely speculative use of reason, and as the mere approaching a concept, which in reality can never be reached, is the same as if the concept were missed altogether, people, when speaking of such a concept, are wont to say, it is an idea only. Thus one might say, that the absolute whole of all phenomena is an idea only, for as we can never form a representation of such a whole, it remains a problem without a solution. In the practical use of the understanding, on the contrary, where we are only concerned with practice, according to rules, the idea of practical reason can always be realised *in concreto,* although partially only; nay, it is the indispensable condition of all practical use of reason. The practical realisation of the idea is here always limited and deficient, but these limits cannot be defined, and it always remains under the influence of a concept, implying absolute completeness and perfection. The practical idea is therefore in this case truly fruitful, and, with regard to practical conduct, indispensable and necessary. In it pure reason becomes a cause and active power, capable of realising what is contained in its concept. Hence we cannot say of wisdom, as if contemptuously, that it is an idea only, but for the very reason that it contains the idea of the necessary unity of all possible aims, it must determine all practical acts, as an original and, at least, limitative condition.

Although we must say that all transcendental concepts of reason are ideas only, they are not therefore to be considered as superfluous and useless. For although we cannot by them determine any object, they may nevertheless, even unobserved, supply the understanding with a canon or rule of its extended and consistent use, by which, though no object can be better known than it is according to its concepts, yet the understanding may be better guided onwards in its knowledge, not to mention that they may possibly render practicable a transition from physical to practical concepts, and thus impart to moral ideas a certain strength and connection with the speculative knowledge of reason. On all this more light will be thrown in the sequel.

For our present purposes we are obliged to set aside a consideration of these practical ideas, and to treat of reason in its speculative, or rather, in a still more limited sense, its purely transcendental use. Here we must follow the same road which we took before in the deduction of the categories; that is, we must consider the logical form of all knowledge of reason, and see whether, perhaps, by this logical form, reason may become a source of concepts also, which enable us to regard objects in themselves, as determined synthetically *a priori* in relation to one or other of the functions of reason.

Reason, if considered as a faculty of a certain logical form of knowledge, is the faculty of concluding, that is, of judging mediately, by bringing the condition of a possible under the condition of a given judgment. The given judgment is the general rule (*major*). Bringing the condition of another possible judgment under the condition of the rule, which may be called subsumption, is the *minor*, and the actual judgment, which contains the assertion of the rule in the subsumed case, is the conclusion. We know that the rule asserts something as general under a certain condition. The condition of the rule is then found to exist in a given case. Then that which, under that condition, was asserted as generally valid, has to be considered as valid in that given case also, which complies with that condition. It is easy to see therefore that reason arrives at knowledge by acts of the understanding, which constitute a series of conditions. If I arrive at the proposition that all bodies are changeable, only by starting from a more remote knowledge (which does not yet contain the concept of body, but a condition of such a concept only), namely, that all which is composite is changeable; and then proceed to something less remotely known, and depending on the former, namely, that bodies are composite; and, lastly, only advance to a third proposition, connecting the more remote knowledge (changeable) with the given case, and conclude that bodies therefore are changeable, we see that we have passed through a series of conditions (premisses) before we arrived at knowledge (conclusion). Every series, the exponent of which (whether of a categorical or hypothetical judgment) is given, can be continued, so that this procedure of reason leads to *ratiocinatio polysyllogistica,* a series of conclusions which, either on the side of the conditions (*per prosyllogismos*) or of the conditioned (*per episyllogismos*), may be continued indefinitely.

It is soon perceived, however, that the chain or series of prosyllogisms, that is, of knowledge deduced on the side of reasons or conditions of a given knowledge, in other words, the *ascending series* of syllogisms, must stand in a very different relation to the faculty of reason from that of the *descending series,* that is, of the progress of reason on the side of the conditioned, by means of episyllogisms. For, as in the former case the knowledge embodied in the conclusion is given as conditioned only, it is impossible to arrive at it by means of reason in any other way except under the supposition at least that all the members of the series on the side of the conditions are given (totality in the series of premisses), because it is under that supposition only that the contemplated judgment *a priori* is possible; while on the side of the conditioned, or of the inferences, we can only think of a growing series, not of one presupposed as complete or given, that is, of a potential progression only. Hence, when our knowledge is considered as conditioned, reason is constrained to look upon the series of conditions in the ascending line as complete, and given in their totality. But if the same knowledge is looked upon at the same time as a condition of other kinds of knowledge, which constitute among themselves a series of inferences in a descending line, it is indifferent to reason how far that progression may go *a parte posteriori,* or whether a totality of the series is possible at all, because such a series is not required for the conclusion in hand, which is sufficiently determined and secured on grounds *a parte priori.* Whether the series of premisses on the side of the conditions have a something that stands first as the highest condition, or whether it be without limits *a parte priori,* it must at all events contain a totality of conditions, even though we should never succeed in comprehending it; and the whole series must be unconditionally true, if the conditioned, which is considered as a consequence resulting from it, is to be accepted as true. This is a demand of reason which pronounces its knowledge as determined *a priori* and as necessary, either in itself, and in that case it requires no reasons, or, if derivative, as a member of a series of reasons, which itself is unconditionally true.

Transcendental Dialectic

Book I

THIRD SECTION

SYSTEM OF TRANSCENDENTAL IDEAS

We are not at present concerned with logical Dialectic, which takes no account of the contents of knowledge, and has only to lay bare the illusions in the form of syllogisms, but with transcendental Dialectic, which is supposed to contain entirely *a priori* the origin of certain kinds of knowledge, arising from pure reason, and of certain deduced concepts, the object of which can never be given empirically, and which therefore lie entirely outside the domain of the pure understanding. We gathered from the natural relation which must exist between the transcendental and the logical use of our knowledge, in syllogisms as well as in judgments, that there must be three kinds of dialectic syllogisms, and no more, corresponding to the three kinds of conclusion by which reason may from principles arrive at knowledge, and that in all of these it is the object of reason to ascend from the conditioned synthesis, to which the understanding is always restricted, to an unconditioned synthesis, which the understanding can never reach.

The relations which all our representations share in common are, 1st, relation to the subject; 2ndly, the relation to objects, either as phenomena, or as objects of thought in general. If we connect this subdivision with the former division, we see that the relation of the representations of which we can form a concept or an idea can only be threefold: 1st, the relation to the subject; 2ndly, the relation to the manifold of the phenomenal object; 3rdly, the relation to all things in general.

All pure concepts in general aim at a synthetical unity of representations, while concepts of pure reason (transcendental ideas) aim at unconditioned synthetical unity of all conditions. All transcendental ideas therefore can be arranged in three classes: the *first* containing the absolute (unconditioned) *unity of the thinking subject;* the *second* the absolute *unity of the series of conditions of phenomena;* the *third* the absolute *unity of the condition of all objects of thought in general.*

The thinking subject is the object-matter of *psychology,* the system of all phenomena (the world) the object-matter of *cosmology,* and the being which contains the highest condition of the possibility of all that can be thought (the Being of all beings), the object-matter of *theology.* Thus it is pure reason which supplies the idea of a transcendental science of the soul (*psychologia rationalis*), of a transcendental science of the world (*cosmologia rationalis*), and, lastly, of a transcendental science of God (*theologia transcendentalis*). Even the mere plan of any one of these three sciences does not come from the understanding, even if connected with the highest logical use of reason, that is, with all possible conclusions, leading from one of its objects (phenomenon) to all others, and on to the most remote parts of any possible empirical synthesis, but is altogether a pure and genuine product or rather problem of pure reason.

What kinds of pure concepts of reason are comprehended under these three titles of all transcendental ideas will be fully explained in the following chapter. They follow the thread of the categories, for pure reason never refers direct to objects, but to the concepts of objects framed by the understanding. Nor can it be rendered clear, except hereafter in a detailed explanation, how first, reason simply by the synthetical use of the same function which it employs for categorical syllogisms is necessarily led on to the concept of the absolute unity of the thinking subject; secondly, how the logical procedure in hypothetical syllogisms leads to the idea of something absolutely unconditioned, in a series of given conditions, and how, thirdly, the mere form of the disjunctive syllogism produces necessarily the highest concept of reason, that of a Being of all beings; a thought which, at first sight, seems extremely paradoxical.

No objective deduction, like that given of the categories, is possible with regard to these transcendental ideas; they are ideas only, and for that very reason they have no relation to any object corresponding to them in experience. What we could undertake to give was a subjective deduction[27] of them from the nature of reason, and this has been given in the present chapter.

[27] Instead of *Anleitung* read *Ableitung.*

We can easily perceive that pure reason has no other aim but the absolute totality of synthesis *on the side of conditions* (whether of inherence, dependence, or concurrence), and that it has nothing to do with the absolute completeness *on the part of the conditioned*. It is the former only which is required for presupposing the whole series of conditions, and thus presenting it *a priori* to the understanding. If once we have a given condition, complete and unconditioned itself, no concept of reason is required to continue the series, because the understanding takes by itself every step downward from the condition to the conditioned. The transcendental ideas therefore serve only for *ascending* in the series of conditions till they reach the unconditioned, that is, the principles. With regard to *descending* to the conditioned, there is no doubt a widely extended logical use which our reason may make of the rules of the understanding, but no transcendental one; and if we form an idea of the absolute totality of such a synthesis (by *progressus*), as, for instance, of the whole series of all future changes in the world, this is only a thought (*ens rationis*) that may be thought if we like, but is not presupposed as necessary by reason. For the possibility of the conditioned, the totality of its conditions only, but not of its consequences, is presupposed. Such a concept therefore is not one of the transcendental ideas, with which alone we have to deal.

Finally, we can perceive, that there is among the transcendental ideas themselves a certain connection and unity by which pure reason brings all its knowledge into one system. There is in the progression from our knowledge of ourselves (the soul) to a knowledge of the world, and through it to a knowledge of the Supreme Being, something so natural that it looks like the logical progression of reason from premises to a conclusion.* Whether there exists here a real though hidden relation-

---

* *Metaphysic has for the real object of its investigations three ideas only, God, Freedom, and Immortality; the second concept connected with the first leading by necessity to the third as conclusion. Everything else treated by that science is a means only in order to establish those ideas and their reality. Metaphysic does not require these ideas for the sake of natural science; but in order to go beyond nature. A right insight into them would make theology, morality, and, by the union of both, religion also, therefore the highest objects of our existence, dependent on the speculative faculty of reason only, and on nothing else. In a systematical arrangement of those ideas the above order, being synthetical, would be the most appropriate; but in their elaboration, which must necessarily come first, the analytical or inverse order is more practical, enabling us, by starting from what is given us by experience, namely, the study of the soul (psychology), and a proceeding thence to the study of the world (cosmology), and lastly, to a knowledge of God (theology), to carry out the whole of our great plan in its entirety.*

ship, such as we saw before between the logical and transcendental use of reason, is also one of the questions the answer to which can only be given in the progress of these investigations. For the present we have achieved what we wished to achieve, by removing the transcendental concepts of reason, which in the systems of other philosophers are generally mixed up with other concepts, without being distinguished even from the concepts of the understanding, out of so equivocal a position; by being able to determine their origin and thereby at the same time their number, which can never be exceeded, and by thus bringing them into a systematic connection, marking out and enclosing thereby a separate field for pure reason.

Transcendental Dialectic

Book II
Of the Dialectical Conclusions of Pure Reason

One may say that the object of a purely transcendental idea is something of which we have no concept, although the idea is produced with necessity according to the original laws of reason. Nor is it possible indeed to form of an object that should be adequate to the demands of reason, a concept of the understanding, that is, a concept which could be shown in any possible experience, and rendered intuitive. It would be better, however, and less liable to misunderstandings, to say that we can have no knowledge of an object corresponding to an idea, but a problematic concept only.

The transcendental (subjective) reality, at least of pure concepts of reason, depends on our being led to such ideas by a necessary syllogism of reason. There will be syllogisms therefore which have no empirical premisses, and by means of which we conclude from something which we know to something else of which we have no concept, and to which, constrained by an inevitable illusion, we nevertheless attribute objective reality. As regards their result, such syllogisms are rather to be called sophistical than rational, although, as regards their origin, they may claim the latter name, because they are not purely fictitious or accidental, but products of the very nature of reason. They are sophistications, not of men, but of pure reason itself, from which even the wisest of men cannot escape. All he can do is, with great effort, to guard against error, though never able to rid himself completely of an illusion which constantly torments and mocks him.

Of these dialectical syllogisms of reason there are therefore three classes only, that is as many as the ideas to which their conclusions lead. In the syllogism of the *first* class, I conclude from the transcendental concept of the subject, which contains nothing manifold, the absolute unity of the subject itself, of which however I have no concept in this regard. This dialectical syllogism I shall call the transcendental *paralogism*.

The *second* class of the so-called sophistical syllogisms aims at the transcendental concept of an absolute totality in the series of conditions to any given phenomenon; and I conclude from the fact that my concept of the unconditioned synthetical unity of the series is always self-contradictory on one side, the correctness of the opposite unity, of which nevertheless I have no concept either. The state of reason in this class of dialectical syllogisms, I shall call the *antinomy* of pure reason.

Lastly, according to the *third* class of sophistical syllogisms, I conclude from the totality of conditions, under which objects in general, so far as they can be given to me, must be thought, the absolute synthetical unity of all conditions of the possibility of things in general; that is to say, I conclude from things which I do not know according to their mere transcendental[28] concept, a Being of all beings, which I know still less through a transcendental concept, and of the unconditioned necessity of which I can form no concept whatever. This dialectical syllogism of reason I shall call the *ideal* of pure reason.

[28] *Transcendent* is a misprint.

Transcendental Dialectic

Book II

CHAPTER I

OF THE PARALOGISMS OF PURE REASON

The logical paralogism consists in the formal faultiness of a conclusion, without any reference to its contents. But a transcendental paralogism arises from a transcendental cause, which drives us to a formally false conclusion. Such a paralogism, therefore, depends most likely on the very nature of human reason, and produces an illusion which is inevitable, though not insoluble.

We now come to a concept which was not inserted in our general list of transcendental concepts, and yet must be reckoned with them, without however changing that table in the least, or proving it to be deficient. This is the concept, or, if the term is preferred, the judgment, *I think*. It is easily seen, however, that this concept is the vehicle of all concepts in general, therefore of transcendental concepts also, being always comprehended among them, and being itself transcendental also, though without any claim to a special title, inasmuch as it serves only to introduce all thought, as belonging to consciousness. However free that concept may be from all that is empirical (impressions of the senses), it serves nevertheless to distinguish two objects within the nature of our faculty of representation. *I*, as thinking, am an object of the internal sense, and am called soul. That which is an object of the external senses is called body. The term *I*, as a thinking being, signifies the object of psychology, which may be called the rational science of the soul, supposing that we want to know nothing about the soul except what, independent of all experience (which determines the I more especially and *in concreto*), can be deduced from the concept of I, so far as it is present in every act of thought.

Now the rational science of the soul is really such an undertaking; for if the smallest empirical element of my thought or any particular perception of my internal state were mixed up with the sources from which that science derives its materials, it would be an empirical, and no longer a purely rational science of the soul. There is therefore a pretended science, founded on the single proposition of *I think,* and the soundness or unsoundness of which may well be examined in this place, according to the principles of transcendental philosophy. It should not be objected that even in that proposition, which expresses the perception of oneself, I have an internal experience, and that therefore the rational science of the soul, which is founded on it, can never be quite pure, but rests, to a certain extent, on an empirical principle. For this inner perception is nothing more than the mere apperception, *I think,* without which even all transcendental concepts would be impossible, in which we really say, I think the substance, I think the cause, etc. This internal experience in general and its possibility, or perception in general and its relation to other perceptions, there being no special distinction or empirical determination of it, cannot be regarded as empirical knowledge, but must be regarded as knowledge of the empirical in general, and falls therefore under the investigation of the possibility of all experience, which investigation is certainly transcendental. The smallest object of perception (even pleasure and pain), if added to the general representation of self-consciousness, would at once change rational into empirical psychology.

I think is, therefore, the only text of rational psychology, out of which it must evolve all its wisdom. It is easily seen that this thought, if it is to be applied to any object (my self), cannot contain any but transcendental predicates, because the smallest empirical predicate would spoil the rational purity of the science, and its independence of all experience.

We shall therefore follow the thread of the categories, with this difference, however, that as here the first thing which is given is a thing, the I, a thinking being, we must begin with the category of substance, by which a thing in itself is represented, and then proceed backwards, though without changing the respective order of the categories, as given before in our table. The topic of the rational science of the soul, from which has to be derived whatever else that science may contain, is therefore the following.

I
The Soul is *substance.*

II	III
As regards its quality, *simple.*	As regards the different times in which it exists, numerically identical, that is *unity* (not plurality).

IV

It is in relation to
possible objects in space.*

All concepts of pure psychology arise from these elements, simply by way of combination, and without the admixture of any other principle. This substance, taken simply as the object of the internal sense, gives us the concept of *immateriality;* and as simple substance, that of *incorruptibility;* its identity, as that of an intellectual substance, gives us *personality;* and all these three together, *spirituality;* its relation to objects in space gives us the concept of *commercium* (intercourse) with *bodies;* the pure psychology thus representing the thinking substance as the principle of life in matter, that is, as soul (*anima*), and as the ground of *animality;* which again, as restricted by spirituality, gives us the concept of *immortality.*

To these concepts refer four paralogisms of a transcendental psychology, which is falsely supposed to be a science of pure reason, concerning the nature of our thinking being. We can, however, use as the foundation of such a science nothing but the single, and in itself perfectly empty, representation of the *I*, of which we cannot even say that it is a concept, but merely a consciousness that accompanies all concepts. By this *I*, or *he*, or *it* (the thing), which thinks, nothing is represented beyond a transcendental subject of thoughts = *x*, which is known only through the thoughts that are its predicates, and of which, apart from them, we can never have the slightest concept, so that we are really turning round it in a perpetual circle, having already to use its representation, before we can form any judgment about it. And this inconvenience is really inevitable, because consciousness in itself is not so much a representation, distinguishing a particular object, but really a form of representation in general, in so far as it is to be called knowledge, of which alone I can say that I think something by it.

It must seem strange, however, from the very beginning, that the condition under which I think, and which therefore is a property of my own subject only, should be valid at the same

* The reader, who may not guess at once the psychological purport of these transcendental and abstract terms, or understand why the latter attribute of the soul belongs to the category of existence, will find their full explanation and justification in the sequel. Moreover, I have to apologise for the many Latin expressions which, contrary to good taste, have crept in instead of their native equivalents, not only here, but throughout the whole of the work. My only excuse is, that I thought it better to sacrifice something of the elegance of language, rather than to throw any impediments in the way of real students, by the use of inaccurate and obscure expressions.

time for everything which thinks, and that, depending on a proposition which seems to be empirical, we should venture to found the apodictical and general judgment, namely, that everything which thinks is such as the voice of my own consciousness declares it to be within me. The reason of it is, that we are constrained to attribute *a priori* to things all the qualities which form the conditions, under which alone we are able to think them. Now it is impossible for me to form the smallest representation of a thinking being by any external experience, but I can do it through self-consciousness only. Such objects therefore are nothing but a transference of my own consciousness to other things, which thus, and thus only, can be represented as thinking beings. The proposition *I think* is used in this case, however, as problematical only; not so far as it may contain the perception of an existence (the Cartesian, *cogito, ergo sum*), but with regard to its mere possibility, in order to see what properties may be deduced from such a simple proposition with regard to its subject, whether such subject exists or not.

If our knowledge of thinking beings in general, so far as it is derived from pure reason, were founded on more than the *cogito*, and if we made use at the same time of observations on the play of our thoughts and the natural laws of the thinking self, derived from them, we should have before us an empirical psychology, which would form a kind of physiology of the internal sense, and perhaps explain its manifestations, but would never help us to understand such properties as do not fall under any possible experience (as, for instance, simplicity), or to teach apodictically anything touching the nature of thinking beings in general. It would not therefore be a rational psychology.

As the proposition *I think* (taken problematically) contains the form of every possible judgment of the understanding, and accompanies all categories as their vehicle, it must be clear that the conclusions to be drawn from it can only contain a transcendental use of the understanding, which declines all admixture of experience, and of the achievements of which, after what has been said before, we cannot form any very favourable anticipations. We shall therefore follow it, with a critical eye, through all the predicaments of pure psychology.

[The First Paralogism of Substantiality

That the representation of which is the absolute subject of our judgments, and cannot be used therefore as the determination of any other thing, is the *substance*.

I, as a thinking being, am the absolute subject of all my possible judgments, and this representation of myself can never be used as the predicate of any other thing.

Therefore I, as a thinking being (Soul), am *Substance*.

Criticism of the First Parologism of Pure[29] Psychology

We showed in the analytical portion of transcendental logic, that pure categories, and among them that of substance, have in themselves no objective meaning, unless they rest on some intuition, and are applied to the manifold of such intuitions as functions of synthetical unity. Without this they are merely functions of a judgment without contents. I may say of everything, that it is a substance, so far as I distinguish it from what are mere predicates and determinations. Now in all our thinking the I is the subject, in which thoughts are inherent as determinations only; nor can that I ever be used as a determination of any other thing. Thus everybody is constrained to look upon himself as the substance, and on thinking as the accidents only of his being, and determinations of his state.

But what use are we to make of such a concept of a substance? That I, as a thinking being, *continue* for myself, and naturally neither *arise* nor *perish,* is no legitimate deduction from it; and yet this conclusion would be the only advantage that could be gained from the concept of the substantiality of my own thinking subject, and, but for that, I could do very well without it.

So far from being able to deduce these properties from the pure category of substance, we have on the contrary to observe the permanency of an object in our experience and then lay hold of this permanency, if we wish to apply to it the empirically useful concept of substance. In this case, however, we had no experience to lay hold of, but have only formed a deduction from the concept of the relation which all thinking has to the I, as the common subject to which it belongs. Nor should we, whatever we did, succeed by any certain observation in proving such permanency. For though the I exists in all thoughts, not the slightest intuition is connected with that representation, by which it might be distinguished from other objects of intuition. We may very well perceive therefore that this representation appears again and again in every act of thought, but not that it is a constant and permanent intuition, in which thoughts, as being changeable, come and go.

Hence it follows that in the first syllogism of transcendental psychology reason imposes upon us an apparent knowledge

---

[29] Afterwards *transcendental* instead of *pure.*

only, by representing the constant logical subject of thought as the knowledge of the real subject in which that knowledge inheres. Of that subject, however, we have not and cannot have the slightest knowledge, because consciousness is that which alone changes representations into thoughts, and in which therefore, as the transcendental subject, all our perceptions must be found. Beside this logical meaning of the I, we have no knowledge of the subject in itself, which forms the substratum and foundation of it and of all our thoughts. In spite of this, the proposition that the soul is a substance may well be allowed to stand, if only we see that this concept cannot help us on in the least or teach us any of the ordinary conclusions of rationalising psychology, as, for instance, the everlasting continuance of the soul amid all changes and even in death, and that it therefore signifies a substance in idea only, and not in reality.

The Second Paralogism of Simplicity

Everything, the action of which can never be considered as the concurrence of several acting things, is simple.

Now the Soul, or the thinking I, is such a thing:

Therefore, etc.

Criticism of the Second Paralogism of Transcendental Psychology

This is the strong (yet not invulnerable) syllogism among all dialectical syllogisms of pure psychology, not a mere sophism contrived by a dogmatist in order to impart a certain plausibility to his assertions, but a syllogism which seems able to stand the sharpest examination and the gravest doubts of the philosopher. It is this:

Every composite substance is an aggregate of many substances, and the action of something composite, or that which is inherent in it as such, is an aggregate of many actions or accidents distributed among many substances. An effect due to the concurrence of many acting substances is no doubt possible, if that effect is external only (as, for instance, the motion of a body is the combined motion of all its parts). The case is different however with thoughts, if considered as accidents belonging to a thinking being within. For suppose it is the composite which thinks, then every part of it would contain a part of the thought, and all together only the whole of it. This however is self-contradictory. For as representations, distributed among different beings (like the single words of a verse), never make a whole thought (a verse), it is impossible that a thought should be inherent in something composite, as such. Thought therefore is possible only in a substance which is not an aggregate of many, and therefore absolutely simple.*

What is called the *nervus probandi* in this argument lies in the proposition that, in order to constitute a thought, the many representations must be comprehended under the absolute unity of the thinking subject. Nobody however can prove this proposition from concepts. For how would he undertake to do it? The proposition that a thought can only be the effect of the absolute unity of a thinking being, cannot be considered as analytical. For the unity of thought, consisting of many representations, is collective, and may, so far as mere concepts are concerned, refer to the collective unity of all co-operating substances (as the movement of a body is the compound movement of all its parts) quite as well as to the absolute unity of the subject. According to the rule of identity it would be impossible therefore to establish the necessity of the presupposition of a simple substance, the thought being composite. That, on the other hand, such a proposition might be established synthetically and entirely *a priori* from mere concepts, no one will venture to affirm who has once understood the grounds on which the possibility of synthetical propositions *a priori* rests, as explained by us before.

It is likewise impossible, however, to derive this necessary unity of the subject, as the condition of the possibility of the unity of every thought, from experience. For experience never supplies any necessity of thought, much less the concept of absolute unity. Whence then do we take that proposition on which the whole psychological syllogism of reason rests?

It is manifest that if we wish to represent to ourselves a thinking being, we must put ourselves in its place, and supplant as it were the object which has to be considered by our own subject (which never happens in any other kind of investigation). The reason why we postulate for every thought absolute unity of the subject is because otherwise we could not say of it, I think (the manifold in one representation). For although the whole of a thought may be divided and distributed under many subjects, the subjective I can never thus be divided and distributed, and it is this I which we presuppose in every thought.

As in the former paralogism therefore, so here also, the formal proposition of apperception, I think, remains the sole

* It would be very easy to give to this argument the ordinary scholastic dress. But for my purposes it is sufficient to have clearly exhibited, even in a popular form, the ground on which it rests.

ground on which rational psychology ventures to undertake the extension of its knowledge. That proposition, however, is no experience, but only the form of apperception inherent in, and antecedent to, every experience, that is a *purely subjective condition*, having reference to a possible experience only, but by no means the condition of the possibility of the knowledge of objects, and by no means necessary to the concept of a thinking being in general; although it must be admitted that we cannot represent to ourselves another intelligent being without putting ourselves in its place with that formula of our consciousness.

Nor is it true that the simplicity of my self (as a soul) is really deduced from the proposition, I think, for it is already involved in every thought itself. The proposition *I am simple* must be considered as the immediate expression of apperception, and the so-called syllogism of Cartesius, *cogito, ergo sum*, is in reality tautological, because *cogito* (*sum cogitans*) predicates reality immediately. *I am simple* means no more than that this representation of I does not contain the smallest trace of manifoldness, but is absolute (although merely logical) unity.

Thus we see that the famous psychological argument is founded merely on the indivisible unity of a representation, which only determines the verb with reference to a person; and it is clear that the subject of inherence is designated transcendentally only by the I, which accompanies the thought, without our perceiving the smallest quality of it, in fact, without our knowing anything about it. It signifies a something in general (a transcendental subject) the representation of which must no doubt be simple, because nothing is determined in it, and nothing can be represented more simple than by the concept of a mere something. The simplicity however of the representation of a subject is not therefore a knowledge of the simplicity of the subject, because no account whatever is taken of its qualities when it is designated by the entirely empty expression I, an expression that can be applied to every thinking subject.

So much is certain therefore that though I always represent by the I an absolute, but only logical unity of the subject (simplicity), I never know thereby the real simplicity of my subject. We saw that the proposition, I am a substance, signified nothing but the mere category of which I must not make any use (empirically) *in concreto*. In the same manner, I may well say, I am a simple substance, that is, a substance the representation of which contains no synthesis of the manifold; but that concept, or that proposition also, teaches us nothing at all with reference to myself, as an object of experience, because the concept of substance itself is used as a function of synthesis only, without any intuition to rest on, and therefore without any object, valid with reference to the condition of our knowledge only, but not with reference to any object of it. We shall test the usefulness of this proposition by an experiment.

Everybody must admit that the assertion of the simple nature of the soul can only be of any value in so far as it enables me to distinguish the soul from all matter, and thus to except it from that decay to which matter is at all times subject. It is for that use that our proposition is really intended, and it is therefore often expressed by, the soul is not corporeal. If then I can show that, although we allow to this cardinal proposition of rational psychology (as a mere judgment of reason from pure categories) all objective validity (everything that thinks is simple substance), we cannot make the least use of it, in order to establish the homogeneousness or non-homogeneousness of soul and matter, this will be the same as if I had relegated this supposed psychological truth to the field of mere ideas, without any real or objective use.

We have irrefutably proved in the transcendental Aesthetic that bodies are mere phenomena of our external sense, not things by themselves. We are justified therefore in saying that our thinking subject is not a body, i.e. that, because it is represented by us as an object of the internal sense, it is, so far as it thinks, no object of our external senses, and no phenomenon in space. This means the same as that among external phenomena we can never have thinking beings as such, or ever see their thoughts, their consciousness, their desires, etc., externally. All this belongs to the internal sense. This argument seems indeed so natural and popular that even the commonest understanding has always been led to it, the distinction between souls and bodies being of very early date.

But although extension, impermeability, cohesion, and motion, in fact everything that the external senses can give us, cannot be thoughts, feeling, inclination, and determination, or contain anything like them, being never objects of external intuition, it might be possible, nevertheless, that that something which forms the foundation of external phenomena, and which so affects our sense as to produce in it the representations of space, matter, form, etc., if considered as a noumenon (or better as a transcendental object) might be, at the same time, the subject of thinking, although by the manner in which it affects our external sense it produces in us no intuitions of representations, will, etc., but only of space and its determinations. This something, however, is not extended, not impermeable, not composite, because such predicates concern sensibility only and its intuition, whenever we are affected by these (to use otherwise unknown) objects. These expressions, however, do not give us any information as to what kind of object it is, but only that, if considered by itself, without reference to the external senses, it has no right to these predicates, peculiar to external appearance. The predicates of the internal sense, on the contrary, such as representation, thinking, etc., are by no means contradictory to it, so that really, even if we admit the simplicity of its nature, the human soul is by no means sufficiently distinguished from matter, so far as its substratum is concerned, if (as it ought to be) matter is considered as a phenomenon only.

If matter were a thing by itself, it would, as a composite being, be totally different from the soul, as a simple being. But what we call matter is an external phenomenon only, the substratum of which cannot possibly be known by any possible predicates. I can therefore very well suppose that that substratum is simple, although in the manner in which it affects our senses it produces in us the intuition of something extended, and therefore composite, so that the substance which, with reference to our external sense, possesses extension, might very well by itself possess thoughts which can be represented consciously by its own internal sense. In such wise the same thing which in one respect is called corporeal, would in another respect be at the same time a thinking being, of which though we cannot see its thoughts, we can yet see the signs of them phenomenally. Thus the expression that souls only (as a particular class of substances) think, would have to be dropped, and we should return to the common expression that men think, that is, that the same thing which, as an external phenomenon, is extended, is internally, by itself, a subject, not composite, but simple and intelligent.

But without indulging in such hypotheses, we may make this general remark, that if I understand by soul a being by itself, the very question would be absurd, whether the soul be homogeneous or not with matter which is not a thing by itself, but only a class of representations within us; for so much at all events must be clear, that a thing by itself is of a different nature from the determinations which constitute its state only.

If, on the contrary, we compare the thinking I, not with matter, but with that object of the intellect that forms the foundation of the external phenomena which we call matter, then it follows, as we know nothing whatever of the matter, that we have no right to say that the soul by itself is different from it in any respect.

The simple consciousness is not therefore a knowledge of

the simple nature of our subject, so that we might thus distinguish the soul from matter, as a composite being.

If therefore, in the only case where that concept might be useful, namely, in comparing myself with objects of external experience, it is impossible to determine the peculiar and distinguishing characteristics of its nature, what is the use, if we pretend to know that the thinking I, or the soul (a name for the transcendental object of the internal sense), is simple? Such a proposition admits of no application to any real object, and cannot therefore enlarge our knowledge in the least.

Thus collapses the whole of rational psychology, with its fundamental support, and neither here nor elsewhere can we hope by means of mere concepts (still less through the mere subjective form of all our concepts, that is, through our consciousness) and without referring these concepts to a possible experience, to extend our knowledge, particularly as even the fundamental concept of a *simple nature* is such that it can never be met with in experience, so that no chance remains of arriving at it as a concept of objective validity.

The Third Paralogism of Personality

Whatever is conscious of the numerical identity of its own self at different times, is in so far a person.

Now the Soul, etc.

Therefore the Soul is a person.

Criticism of the Third Paralogism of Transcendental Psychology

Whenever I want to know by experience the numerical identity of an external object, I shall have to attend to what is permanent in that phenomenon to which, as the subject, everything else refers as determination, and observe the identity of the former during the time that the latter is changing. I myself, however, am an object of the internal sense, and all time is but the form of the internal sense. I therefore refer each and all of my successive determinations to the numerically identical self; and this in all time, that is, in the form of the inner intuition of myself. From this point of view, the personality of the soul should not even be considered as inferred, but as an entirely identical proposition of self-consciousness in time, and that is indeed the reason why it is valid *a priori*. For it really says no more than this: that during the whole time, while I am conscious of myself, I am conscious of that time as belonging to the unity of myself; and it comes to the same thing whether I say that this whole time is within me as an individual unity, or that I with numerical identity am present in all that time.

In my own consciousness, therefore, the identity of person is inevitably present. But if I consider myself from the point of view of another person (as an object of his external intuition), then that external observer considers me, first of all, in time, for in the apperception time is really represented in *me* only. Though he admits, therefore, the I, which at all times accompanies all representations in *my* consciousness, and with entire identity, he will not yet infer from it the objective permanence of myself. For as in that case the time in which the observer places me is not the time of my own, but of his sensibility, it follows that the identity which is connected with my consciousness is not therefore connected with his, that is, with the external intuition of my subject.

The identity of my consciousness at different times is therefore a formal condition only of my thoughts and their coherence, and proves in no way the numerical identity of my subject, in which, in spite of the logical identity of the I, such a change may have passed as to make it impossible to retain its identity, though we may still attribute to it the same name of I, which in every other state, and even in the change of the subject, might yet retain the thought of the preceding and hand it over to the subsequent subject.*

Although the teaching of some old schools that everything is in a flux, and nothing in the world permanent, cannot be admitted, if we admit substances, yet it must not be supposed that it can be refuted by the unity of self-consciousness. For we ourselves cannot judge from our own consciousness whether, as souls, we are permanent or not, because we reckon as belonging to our own identical self that only of which we are conscious, and therefore are constrained to admit that, during the whole time of which we are conscious, we are one and the same. From the point of view of a stranger, however, such a judgment would not be valid, because, perceiving in the soul

* An elastic ball, which impinges on another in a straight line, communicates to it its whole motion, and therefore (if we only consider the places in space) its whole state. If then, in analogy with such bodies, we admit substances of which the one communicates to the other representations with consciousness, we could imagine a whole series of them, in which the first communicates its state and its consciousness to the second, the second its own state with that of the first substance to a third, and this again all the states of the former, together with its own, and a consciousness of them, to another. That last substance would be conscious of all the states of the previously changed substances, as of its own, because all of them had been transferred to it with the consciousness of them; but for all that it would not have been the same person in all those states.

no permanent phenomena, except the representation of the I, which accompanies and connects them all, we cannot determine whether that I (being a mere thought) be not in the same state of flux as the other thoughts which are chained together by the I.

It is curious, however, that the personality and what is presupposed by it, namely, the permanence and substantiality of the soul, has now to be proved first. For if we could presuppose these, there would follow, if not the permanence of consciousness, yet the possibility of a permanent consciousness in one and the same subject, and this is sufficient to establish personality which does not cease at once, because its effect is interrupted at the time. This permanence, however, is by no means given us before the numerical identity of ourself, which we infer from identical apperception, but is itself inferred from it, so that, according to rule, the concept of substance, which alone is empirically useful, would have to follow first upon it. But as the identity of person follows by no means from the identity of the I, in the consciousness of all time in which I perceive myself, it follows that we could not have founded upon it the substantiality of the soul.

Like the concept of substance and of the simple, however, the concept of personality also may remain, so long as it is used as transcendental only, that is, as a concept of the unity of the subject which is otherwise unknown to us, but in the determinations of which there is an uninterrupted connection by apperception. In this sense such a concept is necessary for practical purposes and sufficient, but we can never pride ourselves on it as helping to expand our knowledge of our self by means of pure reason, which only deceives us if we imagine that we can conclude an uninterrupted continuance of the subject from the mere concept of the identical self. That concept is only constantly turning round itself in a circle, and does not help us as with respect to any question which aims at synthetical knowledge. What matter may be as a thing by itself (a transcendental object) is entirely unknown to us; though we may observe its permanence as a phenomenon, since it is represented as something external. When however I wish to observe the mere I during the change of all representations, I have no other correlative for my comparisons but again the I itself, with the general conditions of my consciousness. I cannot therefore give any but tautological answers to all questions, because I put my concept and its unity in the place of the qualities that belong to me as an object, and thus really take for granted what was wished to be known.

The Fourth Paralogism of Ideality (with Regard to External Relations)

That, the existence of which can only be inferred as a cause of given perceptions, has a doubtful existence only:

All external phenomena are such that their existence cannot be perceived immediately, but that we can only infer them as the cause of given perceptions:

Therefore the existence of all objects of the external senses is doubtful. This uncertainty I call the ideality of external phenomena, and the doctrine of that ideality is called *idealism;* in comparison with which the other doctrine, which maintains a possible certainty of the objects of the external senses, is called *dualism.*

Criticism of the Fourth Paralogism of Transcendental Psychology

We shall first have to examine the premisses. We are perfectly justified in maintaining that that only which is within ourselves can be perceived immediately, and that my own existence only can be the object of a mere perception. The existence of a real object therefore outside me (taking this word in its intellectual meaning) can never be given directly in perception, but can only be added in thought to the perception, which is a modification of the internal sense, and thus inferred as its external cause. Hence Cartesius was quite right in limiting all perception, in the narrowest sense, to the proposition, I (as a thinking being) am. For it must be clear that, as what is without is not within me, I cannot find it in my apperception; nor hence in any perception which is in reality a determination of appreciation only.

In the true sense of the word, therefore, I can never perceive external things, but only from my own internal perception infer their existence, taking the perception as an effect of which something external must be the proximate cause. An inference, however, from a given effect to a definite cause is always uncertain, because the effect may be due to more than one cause. Therefore in referring a perception to its cause, it always remains doubtful whether that cause be internal or external; whether in fact all so-called external perceptions are not a mere play of our external sense, or point to real external objects as their cause. At all events the existence of the latter is inferential only, and liable to all the dangers of inferences, while the object of the internal sense (I myself with all my representations) is perceived immediately, and its existence cannot be questioned.

It must not be supposed, therefore, that an idealist is he who denies the existence of external objects of the senses; all he does is to deny that it is known by immediate perception, and to infer that we can never become perfectly certain of their reality by any experience whatsoever.

Before I expose the deceptive illusion of our paralogism, let me remark that we must necessarily distinguish two kinds of idealism, the transcendental and the empirical. *Transcendental idealism* teaches that all phenomena are representations only, not things by themselves, and that space and time therefore are only sensuous forms of our intuition, not determinations given independently by themselves or conditions of objects, as things by themselves. Opposed to this transcendental idealism, is a *transcendental realism,* which considers space and time as something in itself (independent of our sensibility). Thus the transcendental realist represents all external phenomena (admitting their reality) as things by themselves, existing independently of us and our sensibility, and therefore existing outside us also, if regarded according to pure concepts of the understanding. It is this transcendental realist who afterwards acts the empirical idealist, and who, after wrongly supposing that the objects of the senses, if they are to be external, must have an existence by themselves, and without our senses, yet from this point of view considers all our sensuous representations insufficient to render certain the reality of their objects.

The transcendental idealist, on the contrary, may well be an empirical realist, or, as he is called, a dualist; that is, he may admit the existence of matter, without taking a step beyond mere self-consciousness, or admitting more than the certainty of representations within me, that is the *cogito, ergo sum.* For as he considers matter, and even its internal possibility, as a phenomenon only, which, if separated from our sensibility, is nothing, matter with him is only a class of representations (intuition) which are called external, not as if they referred to objects external by themselves, but because they refer perceptions to space, in which everything is outside everything else, while space itself is inside us.

We have declared ourselves from the very beginning in favour of this transcendental idealism. In our system, therefore, we need not hesitate to admit the existence of matter on the testimony of mere self-consciousness, and to consider it as established by it (i.e. the testimony), in the same manner as the existence of myself, as a thinking being. I am conscious of my representations, and hence they exist as well as I myself, who has these representations. External objects, however (bodies), are phenomena only, therefore nothing but a class of my representations, the objects of which are something by means of these representations only, and apart from them nothing. External things, therefore, exist by the same right as I myself, both on the immediate testimony of my self-consciousness, with this difference only, that the representation of myself, as a thinking subject, is referred to the internal sense only, while the representations which indicate extended beings are referred to the external sense also. With reference to the reality of external objects, I need as little trust to inference, as with reference to the reality of the object of my internal sense (my thoughts), both being nothing but representations, the immediate perception (consciousness) of which is at the same time a sufficient proof of their reality.

The transcendental idealist is, therefore, an empirical realist, and allows to matter, as a phenomenon, a reality which need not be inferred, but may be immediately perceived. The transcendental realism, on the contrary, is necessarily left in doubt, and obliged to give way to empirical idealism, because it considers the objects of the external senses as something different from the senses themselves, taking mere phenomena as independent beings, existing outside us. And while with the very best consciousness of our representation of these things, it is far from certain that, if a representation exists, its corresponding object must exist also, it is clear that in our system external things, that is, matter in all its shapes and changes, are nothing but mere phenomena, that is, representations within us, of the reality of which we are immediately conscious.

As, so far as I know, all psychologists who believe in empirical idealism are transcendental realists, they have acted no doubt quite consistently, in ascribing great importance to empirical idealism, as one of the problems from which human reason could hardly extricate itself. For indeed, if we consider external phenomena as representations produced inside us by their objects, as existing as things by themselves outside us, it is difficult to see how their existence could be known otherwise but through a syllogism from effect to cause, where it must always remain doubtful, whether the cause be within or without us. Now we may well admit that something which, taken transcendentally, is outside us, may be the cause of our external intuitions, but this can never be the object which we mean by the representations of matter and material things; for these are phenomena only, that is, certain kinds of representations existing always within us, and the reality of which depends on our immediate consciousness, quite as much as the consciousness of my own thoughts. The transcendental object is unknown equally in regard to internal and external intuition.

Of this, however, we are not speaking at present, but only of the empirical object, which is called external, if represented in space, and internal, when represented in temporal relations only, both space and time being to be met with nowhere except in ourselves.

The expression, *outside us*, involves however an inevitable ambiguity, because it may signify either, something which, as a thing by itself, exists apart from us, or what belongs to outward appearance only. In order, therefore, to remove all uncertainty from that concept, taken in the latter meaning (which alone affects the psychological question as to the reality of our external intuition) we shall distinguish *empirically external* objects from those that may be called so in a transcendental sense, by calling the former simply *things occurring in space*.

Space and time are no doubt representations *a priori*, which dwell in us as forms of our sensuous intuition, before any real object has determined our senses by means of sensation, enabling them to represent the object under those sensuous conditions. But this something, material or real, that is to be seen in space, presupposes necessarily perception, and cannot be fancied or produced by means of imagination without that perception, which indicates the reality of something in space. It is sensation, therefore, that indicates reality in space and time, according as it is related to the one or the other mode of sensuous intuition. If sensation is once given (which, if referring to an object in general, and not specialising it, is called perception), many an object may be put together in imagination from the manifold materials of perception, which has no empirical place in space or time, but in imagination only. This admits of no doubt, whether we take the sensations of pain and pleasure, or the external ones of colour, heat, etc.; it is always perception by which the material for thinking of any objects of external intuition must be first supplied. This perception, therefore (to speak at present of external intuitions only), represents something real in space. For, first, perception is the representation of a reality, while space is the representation of a mere possibility of coexistence. Secondly, this reality is represented before the external sense, that is, in space. Thirdly, space itself is nothing but mere representation, so that nothing in it can be taken as real, except what is represented in it;* or, *vice versa*, whatever is given in it, that

* We must well master this paradoxical, but quite correct proposition, that nothing can be in space, except what is represented in it. For space itself is nothing but representation, and whatever is in it must therefore be contained in that representation. There is nothing whatever in space, except so far as it is really represented in it. That a thing can exist only

is, whatever is represented in it by perception, is also real in it, because, if it were not real in it, that is, given immediately by empirical intuition, it could not be created by fancy, the real of intuition being unimaginable *a priori*.

Thus we see that all external perception proves immediately something real in space, or rather is that real itself. Empirical realism is therefore perfectly true, that is, something real in space always corresponds to our external intuitions. Space itself, it is true, with all its phenomena, as representations, exists within me only, but the real or the material of all objects of intuition is nevertheless given in that space, independent of all fancy or imagination; nay, it is impossible that *in that space anything outside us* (in a transcendental sense) could be given, because space itself is nothing outside our sensibility. The strictest idealist, therefore, can never require that we should prove that the object without us (in its true meaning) corresponds to our perception. For granted there are such objects, they could never be represented and seen, as outside us, because this presupposes space, and the reality in space, as a mere representation, is nothing but the perception itself. It thus follows, that what is real in external phenomena, is real in perception only, and cannot be given in any other way.

From such perceptions, whether by mere play of fancy or by experience, knowledge of objects can be produced, and here no doubt deceptive representations may arise, without truly corresponding objects, the deception being due, either to illusions of imagination (in dreams), or to a fault of judgment (the so-called deceptions of the senses). In order to escape from these false appearances, one has to follow the rule that, *whatever is connected according to empirical laws with a perception, is real.* This kind of illusion, however, and its prevention, concerns idealism as well as dualism, since it affects the form of experience only. In order to refute empirical idealism and its unfounded misgivings as to the objective reality of our external perceptions, it is sufficient to consider (1) that external perception proves immediately a reality in space, which space, though in itself a mere form of representations, possesses nevertheless objective reality with respect to all external phenomena (which themselves are mere representations only); (2) that without perception, even the creations of fancy and dreams would not be possible, so that our external senses, with

---

in the representation of it, may no doubt sound strange; but will lose its strangeness if we consider that the things with which we have to deal, are not things by themselves, but phenomena only, that is, representations.

reference to the data from which experience can spring, must have real objects corresponding to them in space.

There are two kinds of idealists, the *dogmatic,* who denies the existence of matter, and the *sceptical,* who doubts it, because he thinks it impossible to prove it. At present we have nothing to do with the former, who is an idealist, because he imagines he finds contradictions in the possibility of matter in general. This is a difficulty which we shall have to deal with in the following section on dialectical syllogisms, treating of reason in its internal struggle with reference to the concepts of the possibility of all that belongs to the connection of experience. The sceptical idealist, on the contrary, who attacks only the ground of our assertion, and declares our conviction of the existence of matter, which we founded on immediate perception, as insufficient, is in reality a benefactor of human reason, because he obliges us, even in the smallest matter of common experience, to keep our eyes well open, and not to consider as a well-earned possession what may have come to us by mistake only. We now shall learn to understand the great advantage of these idealistic objections. They drive us by main force, unless we mean to contradict ourselves in our most ordinary propositions, to consider all perceptions, whether we call them internal or external, as a consciousness only of what affects our sensibility, and to look on the external objects of them, not as things by themselves, but only as representations of which, as of every other representation, we can become immediately conscious, and which are called external, because they depend on what we call the external sense with its intuition of space, space being itself nothing but an internal kind of representation in which certain perceptions become associated.

If we were to admit external objects to be things by themselves, it would be simply impossible to understand how we can arrive at a knowledge of their reality outside us, considering that we always depend on representations which are inside us. It is surely impossible that we should feel outside us, and not inside us, and the whole of our self-consciousness cannot give us anything but our own determinations. Thus sceptical idealism forces us to take refuge in the only place that is left to us, namely, in the ideality of all phenomena: the very ideality which, though as yet unprepared for its consequences, we established in our own transcendental Aesthetic. If then we ask whether, consequently, dualism only must be admitted in psychology, we answer, certainly, but only in its empirical acceptation. In the connection of experience matter, as the substance of phenomena, is really given to the external sense in the same manner as the thinking I, likewise as the substance of phenomena, is given to the internal sense; and it is according to the rules which this category introduces into the empirical connection of our external as well as internal perceptions, that phenomena on both sides must be connected among themselves. If, on the contrary, as often happens, we were to extend the concept of dualism and take it in its transcendental acceptation, then neither it, nor on one side the *pneumatism,* or on the other side the *materialism,* which are opposed to dualism, would have the smallest foundation; we should have missed the determination of our concepts, and have mistaken the difference in our mode of representing objects, which, with regard to what they are in themselves, remain always unknown to us, for a difference of the things themselves. No doubt I, as represented by the internal sense in time, and objects in space outside me, are two specifically different phenomena, but they are not therefore conceived as different things. The transcendental object, which forms the foundation of external phenomena, and the other, which forms the foundation of our internal intuition, is therefore neither matter, nor a thinking being by itself, but simply an unknown cause of phenomena which supply to us the empirical concept of both.

If therefore, as evidently forced to do by this very criticism, we remain faithful to the old rule, never to push questions beyond where possible experience can supply us with an object, we shall never dream of going beyond the objects of our senses and asking what they may be by themselves, that is, without any reference to our senses. But if the psychologist likes to take phenomena for things by themselves, then, whether he admit into his system, as a materialist, matter only, or, as a spiritualist, thinking beings only (according to the form of our own internal sense), or, as a dualist, both, as things existing in themselves, he will always be driven by his mistake to invent theories as to how that which is not a thing by itself, but a phenomenon only, could exist by itself.

CONSIDERATION

On the Whole of Pure Psychology, as affected by these Paralogisms

If we compare the science of the soul, as the physiology of the internal sense, with the science of the body, as a physiology of the objects of external senses, we find, besides many things which in both must be known empirically, this important difference, that in the latter many things can be known *a priori* from the mere concept of an extended and impermeable being, while in the former nothing can be known *a priori* and synthetically from the concept of a thinking being. The cause is this. Though both are phenomena, yet the phenomena of the external sense have something permanent, which suggests a substratum of varying determinations, and consequently a synthetical concept, namely, that of space, and of a phenomenon in space; while time, the only form of our internal intuition, has nothing permanent, and makes us to know the change of determinations only, but not the determinable object. For in what we call soul there is a continuous flux, and nothing permanent, except it may be (if people will so have it) the simple *I*, so simple because this representation has no contents, consequently nothing manifold, so that it seems to represent, or more accurately to indicate, a simple object. This I or Ego would have to be an intuition, which, being presupposed in all thought (before all experience), might as an intuition *a priori* supply synthetical propositions, if it should be possible to get any knowledge by pure reason of the nature of a thinking being in general. But this I is neither an intuition nor a concept of any object, but the mere form of consciousness which can accompany both classes of representations, and impart to them the character of knowledge, provided something else be given in intuition which supplies matter for a representation of an object. Thus we see that the whole of rational psychology is impossible as transcending the powers of human reason, and nothing remains to us but to study our soul under the guidance of experience, and to keep ourselves within the limits of questions which do not go beyond the line where the material can be supplied by possible internal experience.

But although rational psychology is of no use in extending our knowledge, but as such is made up of paralogisms only, we cannot deny to it an important negative utility, if it does not pretend to be more than a critical investigation of our dialectical syllogisms, as framed by our common and natural reason.

What purpose can be served by psychology founded on pure principles of reason? Its chief purpose is meant to be to guard our thinking self against the danger of materialism. This purpose however is answered, as we have shown, by the concept which reason gives of our thinking self. For, so far from there being any fear lest, if matter be taken away, all thought, and even the existence of thinking beings might vanish, it has been on the contrary clearly shown that, if we take away the thinking subject, the whole material world would vanish, because it is nothing but a phenomenon in the sensibility of our own subject, and a certain class of its representations.

It is true that I do not know thus this thinking self any better according to its qualities, nor can I perceive its permanence, or even the independence of its existence from the problematical transcendental substratum of external phenomena, both being necessarily unknown to us. But as it is nevertheless possible that I may find reason, from other than purely speculative causes, to hope for an independent, and, during every possible change of my states, permanently abiding existence of my thinking nature, much is gained if, though I freely confess my own ignorance, I can nevertheless repel the dogmatical attacks of a speculative opponent, showing to him that he can never know more of the nature of the subject, in order to deny the possibility of my expectations, than I can know, in order to cling to them.

Three dialectical questions, which form the real object of all rational psychology, are founded on this transcendental illusion of our psychological concepts, and cannot be answered except by means of the considerations in which we have just been engaged, namely; (1) the question of the possibility of the association of the soul with an organic body, that is, of animality and the state of the soul in the life of man; (2) the question of the beginning of that association of the soul at the time and before the time of our birth; (3) the question of the end of that association of the soul at and after the time of death (immortality).

What I maintain is, that all the difficulties which we imagine to exist in those questions, and with which, as dogmatical objections, people wish to give themselves an air of deeper insight into the nature of things than the common understanding can ever claim, rest on a mere illusion, which leads us to hypostatize what exists in thought only, and to accept it in the same quality in which it is thought as a real object, outside the thinking subject, taking in fact extension, which is phenomenal only, for a quality of external things, existing without our sensibility also, and movement as their effect, taking place by itself also, and independently of our senses. For matter, the association of which with the soul causes so much misgiving, is nothing but a mere orm, or a certain mode of representing an unknown object by that intuition which we call the external sense. There may, therefore, well be something outside us to which the phenomenon which we call matter corresponds; though in its quality of phenomenon it cannot be outside us, but merely as a thought within us, although that thought represents it through the external sense as existing outside us. Matter, therefore, does not signify a class of substances totally heterogeneous and different from the object of the internal sense (the soul), but only the different nature of the phenomenal appearance of objects (in themselves unknown to us), the representations of which we call external, as compared with those which we assign to the internal sense, although, like other thoughts, those external representations also belong to the thinking subject only. They possess however this illusion that, as they represent objects in space, they seem to separate themselves from the soul and to move outside it, although even the space, in which they are seen, is nothing but a representation of which no homogeneous original can ever be found outside the soul. The question therefore is no longer as to the possibility of an association of the soul with other known and foreign substances outside us, but only as to the connection of the representations of the internal sense with the modifications of our external sensibility, and how these can be connected with each other according to constant laws, and acquire cohesion in experience.

So long as we connect internal and external phenomena with each other as mere representations in our experience, there is nothing irrational, nor anything to make the association of both senses to appear strange. As soon however as we hypostatize the external phenomena, looking upon them no longer as representations, but *as things existing by themselves and outside us, with the same quality in which they exist inside us,* and referring to our own thinking subject their acts which they, as phenomena, show in their mutual relation, the effective causes outside us assume a character which will not harmonise with their effects within us, because that character refers to the external senses only, but the effects to the internal sense, both being entirely unhomogeneous, though united in the same subject. We then have no other external effects but changes of place, and no forces but tendencies, which have for their effects relations in space only. Within us, on the contrary, those effects are mere thoughts, without any relations of space, movement, shape, or local determination between them; and we entirely lose the thread of the causes in the effects which ought to show themselves in the internal sense. We ought to consider therefore that bodies are not objects by themselves which are present to us, but a mere appearance of we do not know what unknown object, and that movement likewise is not the effect of that unknown cause, but only the appearance of its influence on our senses. Both are not something outside us, but only representation within us, and consequently it is not the movement of matter which produces representations within us, but that motion itself (and matter also, which makes itself known through it) is representation only. Our whole self-created difficulty turns on this, how and why the representations of our sensibility are so connected with each other that those which we call external intuitions can, according to empirical laws, be represented as objects outside us; a question which is entirely free from the imagined difficulty of explaining the origin of our representations from totally heterogeneous efficient causes, existing outside us, the confusion arising from our mistaking the phenomenal appearance of an unknown cause for the very cause outside us. In judgments in which there is a misapprehension confirmed by long habit, it is impossible to bring its correction at once to that clearness which can be produced in other cases, where no inevitable illusion confuses our concept. Our attempt therefore at freeing reason from these sophistical theories can hardly claim as yet that perspicuity which would render it perfectly satisfactory. I hope however to arrive at greater lucidity in the following manner.

All *objections* may be divided into *dogmatical, critical,* and *sceptical.* The dogmatical attacks the *proposition,* the critical the *proof* of a proposition. The former presupposes an insight into the peculiar nature of the object in order to be able to assert the contrary of what the proposition asserts. It is therefore itself dogmatical, and pretends to know the peculiar nature of the object in question better than the opponent. The critical objection, as it says nothing about the worth or worthlessness of the proposition, and attacks the proof only, need not know the object itself better, or claim a better knowledge of it. All it wants to show is, that a proposition is not well grounded, not that it is false. The sceptical objection, lastly, places assertion and denial side by side, as of equal value, taking one or the other now as dogma, and now as denial; and being thus in appearance dogmatical on both sides, it renders every judgment on the object impossible. Both the dogmatical and sceptical objections must pretend to so much knowledge of their object as is necessary in order to assert or deny anything about it. The critical objection, on the contrary, wishes only to show that something purely futile and fanciful has been used in support of a proposition, and thus upsets a theory by depriving it of its pretended foundation, without wishing to establish itself anything else about the nature of the object.

According to the ordinary concepts of our reason with regard to the association between our thinking subject and the things outside us, we are dogmatical, and look upon them as real objects, existing independently of ourselves, in accordance with a certain transcendental dualism which does not reckon external phenomena as representations belonging to the subject, but places them, as they are given us in sensuous intuition, as objects outside us and entirely separated from the thinking subject. This mere assumption is the foundation of all theories on the association between soul and body. It is never asked whether this objective reality of phenomena is absolutely true, but it is taken for granted, and the only question seems to be, how it is to be explained and understood. The three systems which are commonly suggested, and which in fact are alone possible, are those, 1st, of *physical influence,* 2nd, of *pre-established harmony,* and 3rd, of *supernatural assistance.*

The second and third explanations of the association between soul and matter arise from objections to the first, which is that of the ordinary understanding, the objection being, that what appears as matter cannot by its immediate influence be the cause of representations, these being a totally heterogeneous class of effects. Those who start this objection cannot understand by the objects of the external senses matter, conceived as phenomenon only, and therefore itself a mere representation produced by whatever external objects. For in that case they would really say that the representations of external objects (phenomena) cannot be the external causes of the representations in our mind, which would be a meaningless objection, because nobody would think of taking for an external cause what he knows to be a mere representation. According to our principles the object of their theory can only be, that that which is the true (transcendental) object of our external senses cannot be the cause of those representations (phenomena) which we mean by the name of matter. As no one has any right to say that he knows anything of the transcendental cause of the representations of our external senses, their assertion is entirely groundless. And if the pretended reformers of the doctrine of physical influence represent, according to the ordinary views of transcendental dualism, matter, as such, as a thing by itself (not simply as a mere phenomenal appearance of an unknown thing), and then proceed in their objections to show that such an external object, which shows no causality but that of movements, can never be the efficient cause of representations, but that a third being must intervene in order to produce, if not reciprocal action, at least correspondence and harmony between the two, they would really begin their refutation by admitting in their dualism the πρῶτον ψεῦδος of a physical influence, and thus refute by their objection, not so much the physical influence as their own dualistic premisses. For all the difficulties with regard to a possible connection between a thinking nature and matter arise, without exception, from that too readily admitted dualistic representation, namely, that matter, as such, is not phenomenal, that is, a mere representation of the mind to which an unknown object corresponds, but the object itself, such as it exists outside us, and independent of all sensibility.

It is impossible, therefore, to start a dogmatical objection against the commonly received theory of a physical influence. For if the opponent were to say that matter and its movements are purely phenomenal and therefore mere representations, the only difficulty remaining to him would be that the unknown object of our senses could not be the cause of our representations, and this he has no right to say, because no one is able to determine what an unknown object may or may not be able to effect; and, according to our former arguments, he must necessarily admit this transcendental idealism, unless he wishes to hypostatize mere representations and place them outside himself as real things.

What is quite possible, however, is to raise a well-founded *critical objection* to the commonly received opinion of a physical influence. For the pretended association between two kinds of substances, the one thinking, the other extended, rests on a coarse dualism, and changes the latter, though they are nothing but representations of the thinking subject, into things existing by themselves. Thus the misunderstood physical influence may be entirely upset by showing that the proof which was to establish it, was surreptitiously obtained, and therefore, valueless.

The notorious problem, therefore, as to a possible association between the thinking and the extended, would, when all that is purely imaginative is deducted, come to this, *how external intuition,* namely, that of space (or what fills space, namely, form and movement), *is possible in any thinking subject?* To this question, however, no human being can return an answer, and instead of attempting to fill this gap in our knowledge, all we can do is to indicate it by ascribing external phenomena to a transcendental object as the cause of this class of representations, but which we shall never know, nor be able to form any concept of. In all practical questions we treat phenomena as objects by themselves, without troubling ourselves about the first cause of their possibility (as phenomena). But as soon as we go beyond, the concept of a transcendental object becomes inevitable.

The decision of all the discussions on the state of a thinking being, before this association with matter (life) or after the ceasing of such association (death), depends on the remarks which we have just made on the association between the thinking and the extended. The opinion that the thinking subject was able to think before any association with bodies, would assume the following form, that before the beginning of that kind of sensibility through which something appears to us in space, the same transcendental objects, which in our present state appear as bodies, could have been seen in a totally different way. The other opinion that, after the cessation of its association with the material world, the soul could continue to think, would be expressed as follows: that, if that kind of sensibility through which transcendental and, for the present, entirely unknown objects appear to us as a material world, should cease, it would not follow that thereby all intuition of them would be removed: it being quite possible that the same unknown objects should continue to be known by the thinking subject, although no longer in the quality of bodies.

Now it is quite true that no one can produce from speculative principles the smallest ground for such an assertion, or do more than presuppose its possibility, but neither can any valid dogmatical objection be raised against it. For whoever would attempt to do so, would know neither more nor less than I myself, or anybody else, about the absolute and internal cause of external and material phenomena. As he cannot pretend to know on what the reality of external phenomena in our present state (in life) really rests, neither can he know that the condition of all external intuition, or the thinking subject itself, will cease after this state (in death).

We thus see that all the wrangling about the nature of a thinking being, and its association with the material world, arises simply from our filling the gap, due to our ignorance, with paralogisms of reason, and by changing thoughts into things and hypostatizing them. On this an imaginary science is built up, both by those who assert and by those who deny, some pretending to know about objects of which no human being has any conception, while others make their own representations to be objects, all turning round in a constant circle of ambiguities and contradictions. Nothing but a sober, strict, and just criticism can free us of this dogmatical illusion, which, through theories and systems, deceives so many by an imaginary happiness. It alone can limit our speculative pretensions to the sphere of possible experience, and this not by a shallow scoffing at repeated failures or by pious sighs over the limits of our reason, but by a demarcation made according to well-established principles, writing the *nihil ulterius* with perfect assurance on those Herculean columns which Nature herself has erected, in order that the voyage of our reason should be continued so far only as the continuous shores of experience extend—shores which we can never forsake without being driven upon a boundless ocean, which, after deceiving us again and again, makes us in the end cease all our laborious and tedious endeavours as perfectly hopeless.

* * *

We have yet to give a general and clear investigation of the transcendental, and yet natural illusion, produced by the paralogisms of pure reason, and the justification of our systematical arrangement of them, which ran parallel with the table of the categories. We could not have done this at the beginning of this section, without running the risk of becoming obscure, or inconveniently anticipating our arguments. We shall now try to fulfil our duty.

All illusion may be explained as mistaking the subjective condition of thought for the knowledge of the object. In the introduction to the transcendental Dialectic, we showed that pure reason is occupied exclusively with the totality of the synthesis of conditions belonging to anything conditioned. Now as the dialectical illusion of pure reason cannot be an empirical illusion, such as occurs in certain empirical kinds of knowledge, it can refer only to the conditions of thought in general, so that there can only be three cases of the dialectical use of pure reason:

1. The synthesis of the conditions of a thought in general.
2. The synthesis of the conditions of empirical thought.
3. The synthesis of the conditions of pure thought.

In every one of these three cases pure reason is occupied only with the absolute totality of that synthesis, that is, with that condition, which is itself unconditioned. It is on this division also that the threefold transcendental illusion is founded which leads to three subdivisions of the Dialectic, and to as many pretended sciences flowing from pure reason, namely, transcendental psychology, cosmology, and theology. We are at present concerned with the first only.

As, in thinking in general, we take no account of the relation of our thoughts to any object (whether of the senses or of the pure understanding), what is called (1) the synthesis of the conditions of a thought in general, is not objective at all, but only a synthesis of thought with the subject, which synthesis is wrongly taken for the synthetical representation of an object.

It follows from this that the dialectical conclusion as to the condition of all thought in general, which condition itself is unconditioned, does not involve a fault in its contents (for it ignores all contents or objects), but only a fault in form, and must therefore be called a paralogism.

As, moreover, the only condition which accompanies all

thought is the *I*, in the general proposition *I think*, reason has really to deal with this condition, so far as that condition is itself unconditioned. It is however a formal condition only, namely, the logical unity of every thought, no account being taken of any object; but it is represented nevertheless as an object which I think, namely, as the I itself and its unconditioned unity.

If I were asked what is the nature of a thing which thinks, I could not give any answer *a priori*, for the answer ought to be synthetical, as an analytical answer might explain perhaps the meaning of the term "thought," but could never add any real knowledge of that on which the possibility of thought depends. For a synthetical solution, however, we should require intuition, and this has been entirely left out of account in the general form given to our problem. It is equally impossible to answer the general question, what is the nature of a thing which is moveable, because in that case the impermeable extension (matter) is not given. But although I have no answer to return to that question in general, it might seem that I could answer it in a special case, namely, in the proposition which expresses the self-consciousness, I think. For this I is the first subject, i.e. substance, it is simple, etc. These, however, ought then to be propositions of experience, which nevertheless, without a general rule containing the conditions of the possibility of thought in general and *a priori*, could not contain such predicates (which are not empirical). This consideration makes our knowledge of the nature of a thinking being derived from pure concepts, which seemed at first so plausible, extremely suspicious, though we have not yet discovered the place where the fault really lies.

A further investigation, however, of the origin of the attributes which I predicate of myself as a thinking being in general, may help us to discover the fault. They are no more than pure categories by which I can never think a definite object, but only the unity of the representations which is requisite in order to determine an object. Without a previous intuition, no category by itself can give me a concept of an object, for by intuition alone the object is given, which afterwards is thought in accordance with a category. In order to declare a thing to be a substance in phenomenal appearance, predicates of its intuition must first be given to me, in which I may distinguish the permanent from the changeable, and the substratum (the thing in itself) from that which is merely inherent in it. If I call a thing simple as a phenomenon, what I mean is that its intuition is a part of phenomenal appearance, but cannot itself be divided into parts, etc. But if I know something to be simple by a concept only, and not by phenomenal appearance, I have really no knowledge whatever of the object, but only of my concept which I make to myself of something in general, that is incapable of any real intuition. I only say that I think something is perfectly simple, because I have really nothing to say of it except that it is something.

Now the mere apperception (the I) is substance in concept, simple in concept, etc., and so far all the psychological propositions of which we spoke before are incontestably true. Nevertheless what we really wish to know of the soul becomes by no means known to us in that way, because all those predicates are with regard to intuition non-valid, entailing no consequences with regard to objects of experience, and therefore entirely empty. For that concept of substance does not teach me that the soul continues by itself, or that it is a part of external intuitions, which itself cannot be resolved into parts, and cannot therefore arise or perish by any changes of nature. These are qualities which would make the soul known to us in its connection with experience, and might give us an insight into its origin and future state. But if I say, by means of the category only, that the soul is a simple substance, it is clear that the bare rational concept of substance contains nothing beyond the thought that a thing should be represented as a subject in itself, without becoming in turn a predicate of anything else. Nothing can be deduced from this, with regard to the permanence (of the I), nor can the attribute of simplicity add that of permanence, nor can we thus learn anything whatsoever as to the fate of the soul in the revolutions of the world. If anybody could tell us that the soul is a *simple part of matter,* we might, with the help of experience, deduce from this the permanence and, on account of its simple nature, the indestructibility of the soul. But of all this, the concept of the I, in the psychological proposition of *I think,* tells us nothing.

The reason why that being which thinks within us imagines that it knows itself by means of pure categories, and especially by that which expresses absolute unity under each head, is this. The apperception itself is the ground of the possibility of the categories, and these represent nothing but the synthesis of the manifold in intuition, so far as it has unity in apperception. Self-consciousness therefore is the representation of that which forms the condition of all unity, and is itself unconditioned. One may therefore say of the thinking I (the soul), which represents itself as substance, simple, numerically identical in all time, and as the correlative of all existence, from which in fact all other existence must be concluded, that it *does not know itself through the categories,* but knows the *categories* only, and through them all objects, in the absolute unity of apperception, *that is, through itself*. It may seem no doubt self-evident that I cannot know as an object that which is presupposed in order to enable me to know an object, and that the determining self (thought) differs from the self that is to be determined (the thinking subject), like knowledge from its object. Nevertheless nothing is more natural or at least more tempting than the illusion which makes us look upon the unity in the synthesis of thoughts as a perceived unity in the subject of thoughts. One might call it the surreptitious admission of an hypostatized consciousness (*apperceptionis substantiatae*).

If we want to have a logical term for the paralogism in the dialectical syllogisms of rational psychology, based on perfectly correct premises, it might be called a *sophisma figurae dictionis*. In the major we use the category, with reference to its condition, transcendentally only; in the minor and in the conclusion, we use the same category, with reference to the soul which is to be comprehended under that condition, empirically. Thus, in the paralogism of substantiality,[30] the concept of substance is a purely intellectual concept which, without the conditions of sensuous intuition, admits of a transcendental use only, that is, of no use at all. In the minor, however, we refer the same concept to the object of all internal experience, though without having previously established the condition of its application *in concreto*, namely, its permanence. We thus are making an empirical, and therefore entirely inadmissible use of it.

Lastly, in order to show the systematical connection of all these dialectical propositions of a rationalising psychology, according to their connection in pure reason, and thus to establish their completeness, it should be remarked that the apperception is carried through all the classes of the categories, but only with reference to those concepts of the understanding, which in each of them formed a foundation of unity for the others in a possible perception, namely subsistence, reality, unity (not plurality), and existence, all of which are here represented by reason, as conditions (themselves unconditioned) of the possibility of a thinking being. Thus the soul knows in itself:

I

The unconditioned unity
of the relation,
that is,
itself, not as inherent,
but as
subsisting.

[30] *Simplicität* was a misprint for *substantialität*.

II

The unconditioned unity
of quality,
that is;
not as a real whole,
but as
simple.*

III

The unconditioned unity
in the manifoldness of time,
that is,
not as at different times
numerically different,
but as
one and the same subject.

IV

The unconditioned unity
of existence in space,
that is,
not as the consciousness of many things outside it,
but as the consciousness of the existence of itself only,
and of other things, merely
as its representations.

Reason is the faculty of principles. The statements of pure psychology do not contain empirical predicates of the soul, but such as, if they exist, are meant to determine the object by itself, independent of all experience, and therefore by a pure reason only. They ought therefore to rest on principles and on general concepts of thinking beings. Instead of this we find that a single representation, I think,[31] governs them all, a representation which, for the very reason that it expresses the pure formula of all my experience (indefinitely), claims to be a general proposition, applicable to all thinking beings, and, though single in all respects, has the appearance of an absolute unity of the conditions of thought in general, thus stretching far beyond the limits of possible experience.]

We shall therefore follow it with a critical eye through all the predicaments of pure psychology; but we shall, for the sake of brevity, let their examination proceed uninterruptedly.

The following general remark may at the very outset make us more attentive to this mode of syllogism. I do not know any object by merely thinking, but only by determining a given intuition with respect to that unity of consciousness in which all thought consists; therefore, I do not know myself by being conscious of myself, as thinking, but only if I am conscious of

---

* How the simple can again correspond to the category of reality cannot yet be explained here; but will be shown in the following chapter, when another use has to be discussed which reason makes of the same concept.

[31] *Ich bin* was a mistake, it can only be meant for *Ich denke.*

the intuition of myself as determined with respect to the func-
tion of thought. All modes of self-consciousness in thought are
therefore by themselves not yet concepts of understanding of
objects (categories), but mere logical functions, which present
no object to our thought to be known, and therefore do not
present myself either as an object. It is not a consciousness of
the determining, but only that of the determinable self, that is,
of my internal intuition (so far as the manifold in it can be
connected in accordance with the general condition of the unity
of apperception in thought) which forms the object.

1. In all judgments I am always the determining subject
only of the relation which constitutes the judgment. That I,
who think, can be considered in thinking as subject only, and
as something not simply inherent in the thinking, as predicate,
is an apodictical and even identical proposition; but it does not
mean that, as an object, I am a self-dependent being or a sub-
stance. The latter would be saying a great deal, and requires
for its support data which are not found in the thinking, per-
haps (so far as I consider only the thinking subject as such)
more than I shall ever find in it.

2. That the Ego of apperception, and therefore the Ego in
every act of thought, is a singular which cannot be dissolved
into a plurality of subjects, and that it therefore signifies a logi-
cally simple subject, follows from the very concept of thinking,
and is consequently an analytical proposition. But this does not
mean that a thinking Ego is a simple substance, which would
indeed be a synthetical proposition. The concept of substance
always relates to intuitions which, with me, cannot be other
but sensuous, and which therefore lie completely outside the
field of the understanding and its thinking, which alone is in-
tended here, when we say that the Ego, in thinking, is simple.
It would indeed be strange, if what elsewhere requires so great
an effort, namely, to distinguish in what is given by intuition
what is substance, and still more, whether that substance can
be simple (as in the case of the component parts of matter),
should in our case be given to us so readily in what is really
the poorest of all representations, and, as it were, by an act of
revelation.

3. The proposition of the identity of myself amidst the mani-
fold of which I am conscious, likewise follows from the con-
cepts themselves, and is therefore analytical; but the identity of
the subject of which, in all its representations, I may become
conscious, does not refer to the intuition by which it is given
as an object, and cannot therefore signify the identity of the
person, by which is understood the consciousness of the iden-

tity of one's own substance, as a thinking being, in all the changes of circumstances. In order to prove this, the mere analysis of the proposition, I think, would avail nothing: but different synthetical judgments would be required, which are based on the given intuition.

4. *To say that I distinguish my own existence, as that of a thinking being, from other things outside me (one of them being my body) is likewise an analytical proposition; for other things are things which I conceive as different from myself. But, whether such a consciousness of myself is even possible without things outside me, whereby representations are given to me, and whether I could exist merely as a thinking being (without being a man), I do not know at all by that proposition.*

Nothing therefore is gained by the analysis of the consciousness of myself, in thought in general, towards the knowledge of myself as an object. The logical analysis of thinking in general is simply mistaken for a metaphysical determination of the object.

It would be a great, nay, even the only objection to the whole of our critique, if there were a possibility of proving a priori that all thinking beings are by themselves simple substances, that as such (as a consequence of the same argument) personality is inseparable from them, and that they are conscious of their existence as distinct from all matter. For we should thus have made a step beyond the world of sense and entered into the field of noumena, and after that no one could dare to question our right of advancing further, of settling in it, and, as each of us is favoured by luck, taking possession of it. The proposition that every thinking being is, as such, a simple substance, is synthetical a priori, because, first, it goes beyond the concept on which it rests, and adds to the act of thinking in general the mode of existence; and secondly, because it adds to that concept a predicate (simplicity) which cannot be given in any experience. Hence synthetical propositions a priori would be not only admissible, as we maintained, in reference to objects of possible experience, and then only as principles of the possibility of that experience, but could be extended to things in general and to things by themselves, a result which would put an end to the whole of our critique, and bid us to leave everything as we found it. However, the danger is not so great, if only we look more closely into the matter.

In this process of rational psychology, there lurks a paralogism, which may be represented by the following syllogism.

That which cannot be conceived otherwise than as a subject, does not exist otherwise than as a subject, and is therefore a substance.

A thinking being, considered as such, cannot be conceived otherwise than as a subject.

Therefore it exists also as such only, that is, as a substance.

In the major they speak of a being that can be thought in every respect, and therefore also as it may be given in intuition. In the minor, however, they speak of it only so far as it considers itself, as subject, with respect to the thinking and the unity of consciousness only, but not at the same time in respect to the intuition whereby this unity is given as an object of thinking. The conclusion, therefore, has been drawn by a sophism, and more especially by sophisma figurae dictionis.*

That we are perfectly right in thus resolving that famous argument into a paralogism, will be clearly seen by referring to the general note on the systematical representation of the principles, and to the section on the noumena, for it has been proved there that the concept of a thing, which can exist by itself as a subject, and not as a mere predicate, carries as yet no objective reality, that is, that we cannot know whether any object at all belongs to it, it being impossible for us to understand the possibility of such a mode of existence. It yields us therefore no knowledge at all. If such a concept is to indicate, under the name of a substance, an object that can be given, and thus become knowledge, it must be made to rest on a permanent intuition, as the indispensable condition of the objective reality of a concept, that is, as that by which alone the object can be given. In internal intuition, however, we have nothing permanent, for the Ego is only the consciousness of my thinking; and if we do not go beyond this thinking, we are without the necessary condition for applying the concept of substance, that is, of an independent subject, to the self, as a thinking being. Thus the simplicity of the substance entirely disappears with the objective reality of the concept: and is changed into a purely logical qualitative unity of self-consciousness in thinking in general, whether the subject be composite or not.

---

* *The thinking is taken in each of the two premises in a totally different meaning: in the major, as it refers to an object in general (and therefore also as it may be given in intuition), but in the minor, only as it exists in its relation to self-consciousness, where no object is thought of, but where we only represent the relation to the self as the subject (as the form of thought). In the former, things are spoken of that cannot be conceived otherwise than as subjects; while in the second we do not speak of things, but of the thinking (abstraction being made of all objects), wherein the Ego always serves as the subject of consciousness. The conclusion, therefore, ought not to be that I cannot exist otherwise than as a subject, but only, that in thinking my existence I can use myself as the subject of a judgment only. This is an identical proposition, and teaches us nothing whatever as to the mode of our existence.*

Refutation of Mendelssohn's Proof of the Permanence of
the Soul

This acute philosopher perceived very quickly how the ordinary argument that the soul (if it is once admitted to be a simple being) cannot cease to exist by decomposition, was insufficient to prove its necessary continuance, because it might cease to exist by simply vanishing. He therefore tried, in his Phaedon, to prove that the soul was not liable to that kind of perishing which would be a real annihilation, by endeavouring to show that a simple being cannot cease to exist, because as it could not be diminished, and thus gradually lose something of its existence, and be changed, by little and little, into nothing (it having no parts, and therefore no plurality in itself), there could be no time between the one moment in which it exists, and the other in which it exists no longer; and this would be impossible.

He did not consider, however, that, though we might allow to the soul this simple nature, namely, that it contains nothing manifold, nothing by the side of each other, and therefore no extensive quantity, yet we could not deny to it, as little as to any other existing thing, intensive quantity, i.e. a degree of reality with respect to all its faculties, nay, to all which constitutes its existence. Such a degree of reality might diminish by an infinite number of smaller degrees, and thus the supposed substance (the thing, the permanence of which has not yet been established), might be changed into nothing, not indeed through decomposition, but through a gradual remission of its powers, or, if I may say so, through elanguescence. For even consciousness has always a degree, which admits of being diminished,* and therefore also the faculty of being conscious of oneself, as well as all other faculties.

The permanence of the soul, therefore, considered merely as an object of the internal sense, remains undemonstrated and undemonstrable, though its permanence in life, while the thinking being (as man) is at the same time to itself an object of the

* *Clearness is not, as the Logicians maintain, the consciousness of a representation; for a certain degree of consciousness, though insufficient for recollection, must exist, even in many dark representations, because without all consciousness we should make no distinction in the connection of dark representations, which yet we are able to do with the* notae *of many concepts (such as those of right and justice, or as the musician does who in improvising strikes several keys at once). A representation is clear in which the consciousness is sufficient for a consciousness of its* difference *from others. If the consciousness is sufficient for distinguishing, but not for a consciousness of the difference, the representation would still have to be called dark. There is, therefore, an infinite number of degrees of consciousness, down to its complete vanishing.*

external senses, is clear by itself. But this does not satisfy the rational psychologist, who undertakes to prove, from mere concepts, the absolute permanence of the soul, even beyond this life.**

If now we take the above propositions in synthetical *connection, as indeed they must be taken, as valid for all thinking beings, in a system of rational psychology, and proceed from the category of relation, with the proposition, all thinking beings, as such, are substances, backwards through the series till the circle is completed, we arrive in the end at their exist-*

---

* Those who, in establishing the possibility of a new theory, imagine that they have done enough if they can show triumphantly that no one can show a contradiction in their premisses (as do those who believe that they understand the possibility of thinking, of which they have an example in the empirical intuitions of human life only, even after the cessation of life) can be greatly embarrassed by other possible theories, which are not a whit bolder than their own. Such is, for instance, the possibility of a division of simple substance into several, or of the coalition of several substances into one simple substance. For although divisibility presupposes a composite, it does not necessarily require a composite of substances, but of degrees only (of the manifold faculties) of one and the same substance. As, then, we may conceive all powers and faculties of the soul, even that of consciousness, as diminished by one-half, the substance still remaining, we may also represent to ourselves, without any contradiction, that extinguished half as preserved, though not within it, but outside it, so that as the whole of what is real in it and has a degree, and therefore the whole existence of it, without any rest, has been halved, another separate substance would arise apart from it. For the plurality, which has been divided, existed before, though not as a plurality of substances, yet of every reality as a quantum of existence in it, and the unity of substance was only a mode of existence, which by mere division has been changed into a plurality of substantiality. In the same manner several simple substances might coalesce again into one, nothing being lost thereby, but merely the plurality of substantiality; so that one substance would contain in itself the degree of reality of all former substances together. We might suppose that the simple substances which give us matter as a phenomenon (not indeed through a mechanical or chemical influence upon each other, but yet, it may be, by some unknown influence, of which the former is only a manifestation), produce by such a dynamical division of parental souls, taken as intensive quantities, what may be called child-souls, while they themselves repair their loss again through a coalition with new matter of the same kind. I am far from allowing the slightest value of validity to such vague speculations, and I hope that the principles of our Analytic have given a sufficient warning against using the categories (as, for instance, that of substance) for any but empirical purposes. But if the rationalist is bold enough to create an independent being out of the mere faculty of thought, without any permanent intuition, by which an object can be given, simply because the unity of apperception in thought does not allow him to explain it as something composite, instead of simply confessing that he cannot explain the possibility of a thinking nature, why should not a materialist, though he can as little appeal to experience in support of his theories, be entitled to use the same boldness, and use his principle for the opposite purpose, though retaining the formal unity on which his opponent relied?

ence, and this, according to that system, they are not only conscious of, independently of external things, but are supposed to be able to determine it even of themselves (with respect to that permanence which necessarily belongs to the character of substance). Hence it follows, that in this rationalistic system idealism is inevitable, at least problematical idealism, because, if the existence of external things is not required at all for the determination of one's own existence in time, their existence is really a gratuitous assumption of which no proof can ever be given.

If, on the contrary, we proceed analytically, taking the proposition, I think, which involves existence (according to the category of modality) as given, and analyse it, in order to find out whether, and how, the Ego determines its existence in space and time by it alone, the propositions of rational psychology would not start from the concept of a thinking being, in general, but from a reality, and the inference would consist in determining from the manner in which that reality is thought, after everything that is empirical in it has been removed, what belongs to a thinking being in general. This may be shown by the following Table.

1.
I think,

2.   **3.**
as Subject,   *as simple Subject,*

4.
as identical Subject,
in every state of my thought.

As it has not been determined in the second proposition, whether I can exist and be conceived to exist as a subject only, and not also as a predicate of something else, the concept of subject is here taken as logical only, and it remains undetermined whether we are to understand by it a substance or not. In the third proposition, however, the absolute unity of apperception, the simple I, being the representation to which all connection or separation (which constitute thought) relate, assumes its own importance, although nothing is determined as yet with regard to the nature of the subject, or its subsistence. The apperception is something real, and it is only possible, if it is simple. In space, however, there is nothing real that is simple, for points (the only simple in space) are limits only, and not themselves something which, as a part, serves to constitute space. From this follows the impossibility of explaining the nature of myself, as merely a thinking subject, from the materialistic *point of view. As, however, in the first proposition, my existence is taken for granted, for it is not said in it that every thinking being exists (this would predicate too much, namely, absolute necessity of them), but only,* I exist, *as thinking, the proposition itself is empirical, and contains only the determinability of my existence, in reference to my representations in time. But as for that purpose again I require, first of all, something permanent, such as is not given to me at all in internal intuition, so far as I think myself, it is really impossible by that simple self-consciousness to determine the manner in which I exist, whether as a substance or as an accident. Thus, if materialism was inadequate to explain my existence, spiritualism is equally insufficient for that purpose, and the conclusion is, that, in no way whatsoever can we know anything of the nature of our soul, so far as the possibility of its separate existence is concerned.*

And how indeed should it be possible by means of that unity of consciousness which we only know because it is indispensable to us for the very possibility of experience, to get beyond experience (our existence in life), and even to extend our knowledge to the nature of all thinking beings in general, by the empirical, but, with reference to every kind of intuition, undetermined proposition, I think.

There is, therefore, no rational psychology, as a doctrine, *furnishing any addition to our self-knowledge, but only as a* discipline, *fixing unpassable limits to speculative reason in this field, partly to keep us from throwing ourselves into the arms of a soulless materialism, partly to warn us against losing ourselves in a vague, and, with regard to practical life, baseless spiritualism. It reminds us at the same time to look upon this refusal of our reason to give a satisfactory answer to such curious questions, which reach beyond the limits of this life, as a hint to turn our self-knowledge away from fruitless speculations to a fruitful practical use—a use which, though directed always to objects of experience only, derives its principle from a higher source, and so regulates our conduct, as if our destination reached far beyond experience, and therefore far beyond this life.*

We see from all this, that rational psychology owes its origin to a mere misunderstanding. The unity of consciousness, on which the categories are founded, is mistaken for an intuition of the subject as object, and the category of substance applied to it. But that unity is only the unity in thought, *by which alone no object is given, and to which, therefore, the category of substance, which always presupposes a given* intuition, *cannot be* *applied, and therefore the subject cannot be known. The subject of the categories, therefore, cannot, by thinking them, receive a concept of itself, as an object of the categories; for in order to think the categories, it must presuppose its pure self-consciousness, the very thing that had to be explained. In like manner the subject, in which the representation of time has its original source, cannot determine by it its own existence in time; and if the latter is impossible, the former, as a determination of oneself (as of a thinking being in general) by means of the categories, is equally so.**

*   *   *

Thus vanishes, as an idle dream, that knowledge which was to go beyond the limits of possible experience, and was connected no doubt with the highest interests of humanity, so far at least as speculative philosophy was to supply it. Yet no unimportant service has thus been rendered to reason by the severity of our criticism, in proving, at the same time, the impossibility of settling anything dogmatically with reference to an object of experience, beyond the limits of experience, and thus securing it against all possible assertions to the contrary. This can only be done in two ways, either by proving one's own proposition apodictically, or, if that does not succeed, by

* *The 'I think' is, as has been stated, an empirical proposition, and contains within itself the proposition, I exist. I cannot say, however, everything which thinks exists; for in that case the property of thinking would make all beings which possess it necessary beings. Therefore, my existence cannot, as Descartes supposed, be considered as derived from the proposition, I think (for in that case the major, everything that thinks exists, ought to have preceded), but is identical with it. It expresses an indefinite empirical intuition, that is, a perception (and proves, therefore, that this proposition, asserting existence, is itself based on sensation, which belongs to sensibility), but it precedes experience, which is meant to determine the object of perception through the categories in respect to time. Existence, therefore, is here not yet a category, which never refers to an indefinitely given object, but only to one of which we have a concept, and of which we wish to know whether it exists also apart from that conception or no. An indefinite perception signifies here something real only that has been given merely for thinking in general, not therefore as a phenomenon, nor as a thing by itself (noumenon), but as something that really exists and is designated as such in the proposition, I think. For it must be observed, that if I have called the proposition, I think, an empirical proposition, I did not mean to say thereby, that the ego in that proposition is an empirical representation; it is rather purely intellectual, because it belongs to thought in general. Without some empirical representation, however, which supplies the matter for thought, the act, I think, would not take place, and the empirical is only the condition of the application or of the use of the pure intellectual faculty.*

trying to discover the causes of that failure, which, if they lie in the necessary limits of our reason, must force every opponent to submit to exactly the same law of renunciation with reference to any claims to dogmatic assertion.

Nothing is lost, however, by this with regard to the right, nay, the necessity of admitting a future life, according to the principles of practical, as connected with the speculative employment of reason. It is known besides, that a purely speculative proof has never been able to exercise any influence on the ordinary reason of men. It stands so entirely upon the point of a hair, that even the schools can only keep it from falling so long as they keep it constantly spinning round like a top, so that, even in their own eyes, it yields no permanent foundation upon which anything could be built. The proofs which are useful for the world at large retain their value undiminished, nay, they gain in clearness and natural power, by the surrender of those dogmatical pretensions, placing reason in its own peculiar domain, namely, the system of ends, which is, however, at the same time the system of nature; so that reason, as a practical faculty by itself, without being limited by the conditions of nature, becomes justified in extending the system of ends, and with it, our own existence, beyond the limits of experience and of life. According to the analogy with the nature *of living beings in this world, in which reason must necessarily admit the principle that no organ, no faculty, no impulse, can be found, as being either superfluous or disproportionate to its use, and therefore purposeless, but that everything is adequate to its destination in life, man, who alone can contain in himself the highest end of all this, would be the only creature excepted from it. For, his natural dispositions, not only so far as he uses them according to his talents and impulses, but more especially the moral law within him, go so far beyond all that is useful and advantageous in this life, that he is taught thereby, in the absence of all advantages, even of the shadowy hope of posthumous fame, to esteem the mere consciousness of righteousness beyond everything else, feeling an inner call, by his conduct in this world and a surrender of many advantages, to render himself fit to become the citizen of a better world, which exists in his idea only. This powerful and incontrovertible proof, accompanied by our constantly increasing recognition of a design pervading all that we see around us, and by a contemplation of the immensity of creation, and therefore also by the consciousness of an unlimited possibility in the extension of our knowledge, and a desire commensurate therewith, all this remains and always will remain, although we must surrender the hope of ever being able to understand, from the mere theoretical knowledge of ourselves, the necessary continuance of our existence.*

Conclusion of the Solution of the Psychological Paralogism

The dialectical illusion in rational psychology arises from our confounding an idea of reason (that of a pure intelligence) with the altogether indefinite concept of a thinking being in general. What we are doing is, that we conceive ourselves for the sake of a possible experience, taking no account, as yet, of any real experience, and thence conclude that we are able to become conscious of our existence, independently of experience and of its empirical conditions. We are, therefore, confounding the possible abstraction *of our own empirically determined existence with the imagined consciousness of a possible* separate *existence of our thinking self, and we bring ourselves to believe that we know the substantial within us as the transcendental subject, while what we have in our thoughts is only the unity of consciousness, on which, as on the mere form of knowledge, all determination is based.*

The task of explaining the community of the soul with the body does not properly fall within the province of that psychology of which we are here speaking, because that psychology tries to prove the personality of the soul, apart also from that community (after death), being therefore transcendent, *in the proper sense of that word, inasmuch as, though dealing with an object of experience, it deals with it only so far as it has ceased to be an object of experience. According to our doctrine, however, a sufficient answer may be returned to that question also. The difficulty of the task consists, as is well known, in the assumed heterogeneousness of the object of the internal sense (the soul), and the objects of the external senses, the formal condition of the intuition with regard to the former being time only, with regard to the latter, time and space. If we consider, however, that both kinds of objects thus differ from each other, not internally, but so far only as the one appears* externally *to the other, and that possibly what is at the bottom of phenomenal matter, as a thing by itself, may not be so heterogeneous after all as we imagine, that difficulty vanishes, and there remains that one difficulty only, how a community of substances is possible at all; a difficulty which it is not the business of psychology to solve, and which, as the reader will easily understand, after what has been said in the Analytic of fundamental powers and faculties, lies undoubtedly beyond the limits of all human knowledge.*

General Note on the Transition from Rational Psychology to Cosmology

The proposition, I think, or, I exist thinking, is an empirical proposition. Such a proposition is based on an empirical intuition, and its object is phenomenal: so that it might seem as if, according to our theory, the soul was changed altogether, even in thinking, into something phenomenal, and our consciousness itself, as merely phenomenal, would thus indeed refer to nothing.

Thinking, taken by itself, is a logical function only, and therefore pure spontaneity, in connecting the manifold of a merely possible intuition. It does not represent the subject of consciousness, as phenomenal, for the simple reason, that it takes no account whatsoever of the manner of intuition, whether it be sensuous or intellectual. I do not thereby represent myself to myself, either as I am, or as I appear to myself, but I only conceive of myself, as of any other object, without taking account of the manner of intuition. If thereby I represent myself as the subject of my thoughts, or as the ground of thinking, these modes of representation are not the categories of substance or cause, because these are functions of thought (judgment) as applied already to our sensuous intuition, such sensuous intuition being necessary, if I wish to know myself. But I only wish to become conscious of myself as thinking, and as I take no account of what my own self may be as a phenomenon, it is quite possible that it might be a phenomenon only to me, who thinks, but not to me, so far as I am thinking. In the consciousness of myself in mere thinking I am the substance itself, but of that substance nothing is thus given me for thinking.

The proposition I think, if it means I exist thinking, is not merely logical function, but determines the subject (which then is at the same time object) with reference to its existence, and is impossible without the internal sense, the intuition of which always supplies the object, not as a thing by itself, but as phenomenal only. Here, therefore, we have no longer mere spontaneity of thinking, but also receptivity of intuition, that is, the thinking of myself applied to the empirical intuition of the same subject. In that empirical intuition the thinking self would have to look for the conditions under which its logical functions can be employed as categories of substance, cause, etc., in order not only to distinguish itself as an object by itself, through the Ego, but to determine the mode of its existence also, that is, to know itself as a noumenon. This, as we know, is impossible, because the internal empirical intuition is sensuous, and supplies us with phenomenal data only, which furnish nothing to the object of the pure consciousness *for the knowledge of its own separate existence, but can serve the purpose of experience only.*

Supposing, however, that we should hereafter discover, not indeed in experience, but in certain (not only logical rules, but) a priori *established laws of pure reason, concerning our existence, some ground for admitting ourselves, entirely a* priori, *as determining and ruling our own existence, there would then be a spontaneity by which our reality would be determinable without the conditions of empirical intuition, and we should then perceive that in the consciousness of our existing there is contained a* priori *something which may serve to determine with respect to some inner faculty, our existence, which otherwise can be determined sensuously only with reference to an intelligible, though, of course, an ideal world only.*

This, however, would not in the least benefit the attempts of rational psychology. For though through that wonderful faculty, which becomes first revealed to myself by the consciousness of a moral law, I should have a principle, purely intellectual, for a determination of my existence, what would be its determining predicates? No other but those which must be given to me in sensuous intuition; and I should therefore find myself again in the same situation where I was before in rational psychology, requiring sensuous intuitions in order to give significance to the concepts of my understanding, such as substance, cause, etc., by which alone I can gain a knowledge of myself; and these intuitions can never carry me beyond the field of experience. Nevertheless, for practical purposes, which always concern objects of experience, I should be justified in applying these concepts, in analogy with their theoretical employment, to liberty also and to the subject of liberty, by taking them only as logical functions of subject and predicate,[32] of cause and effect. According to them, acts or effects, as following those (moral) laws, would be so determined that they may together with the laws of nature be explained in accordance with the categories of substance and cause; though arising in reality from a totally different principle. All this is only meant to prevent a misunderstanding to which our doctrine, which represents self-intuition as purely phenomenal, might easily be exposed. In what follows we shall have occasion to make good use of it.

[32] It is necessary to put a comma after *Prädicats.*

The Antinomy

Third Conflict of the

THESIS

Causality, according to the laws of nature, is not the only causality from which all the phenomena of the world can be deduced. In order to account for these phenomena it is necessary also to admit another causality, that of freedom.

Proof

Let us assume that there is no other causality but that according to the laws of nature. In that case everything that *takes place*, presupposes an anterior state, on which it follows inevitably according to a rule. But that anterior state must itself be something which has taken place (which has come to be in time, and did not exist before), because, if it had always existed, its effect too would not have only just arisen, but have existed always. The causality, therefore, of a cause, through which something takes place, is itself an *event*, which again, according to the law of nature, presuppose an anterior state and its causality, and this again an anterior state, and so on. If, therefore, everything takes place according to mere laws of nature, there will always be a secondary only, but never a primary beginning, and therefore no completeness of the series, on the side of successive causes. But the law of nature consists in this, that nothing takes place without a cause sufficiently

(Continued on p. 270)

OF PURE REASON

TRANSCENDENTAL IDEAS

ANTITHESIS

There is no freedom, but everything in the world takes place entirely according to the laws of nature.

Proof

If we admit that there is *freedom,* in the transcendental sense, as a particular kind of causality, according to which the events in the world could take place, that is a faculty of absolutely originating a state, and with it a series of consequences, it would follow that not only a series would have its absolute beginning through this spontaneity, but the determination of that spontaneity itself to produce the series, that is, the causality, would have an absolute beginning, nothing preceding it by which this act is determined according to permanent laws. Every beginning of an act, however, presupposes a state in which the cause is not yet active, and a dynamically primary beginning of an act presupposes a state which has no causal connection with the preceding state of that cause, that is, in no wise follows from it. Transcendental freedom is therefore opposed to the law of causality, and represents such a connection of successive states of effective causes, that no unity of experience is possible with it. It is therefore an empty fiction of the mind, and not to be met with in any experience.

(*Continued on p. 271*)

(*Continued from p. 268*)

THESIS

determined *a priori*. Therefore the proposition, that all causality is possible according to the laws of nature only, contradicts itself, if taken in unlimited generality, and it is impossible, therefore, to admit that causality as the only one.

We must therefore admit another causality, through which something takes place, without its cause being further determined according to necessary laws by a preceding cause, that is, an *absolute spontaneity* of causes, by which a series of phenomena, proceeding according to natural laws, begins by itself; we must consequently admit transcendental freedom, without which, even in the course of nature, the series of phenomena on the side of causes, can never be perfect.

OBSERVATIONS OF THE

I. ON THE THESIS

The transcendental idea of freedom is far from forming the whole content of the psychological concept of that name, which is chiefly empirical, but only that of the absolute spontaneity of action, as the real ground of imputability; it is, however, the real stone of offence in the eyes of philosophy, which finds its unsurmountable difficulties in admitting this kind of unconditioned causality. That element in the question of the freedom of the will, which has always so much embarrassed speculative reason, is therefore in reality *transcendental* only, and refers merely to the question whether we must admit a faculty of *spontaneously* originating a series of successive things or states. How such a faculty is possible need not be answered, because, with regard to the causality, according to the laws of nature also, we must be satisfied to know *a priori*

(*Continued on p. 272*)

(*Continued from p. 269*)

ANTITHESIS

We have, therefore, nothing but *nature,* in which we must try to find the connection and order of cosmical events. Freedom (independence) from the laws of nature is no doubt a *deliverance* from restraint, but also from the *guidance* of all rules. For we cannot say that, instead of the laws of nature, laws of freedom may enter into the causality of the course of the world, because, if determined by laws, it would not be freedom, but nothing else but nature. Nature, therefore, and transcendental freedom differ from each other like legality and lawlessness. The former, no doubt, imposes upon the understanding the difficult task of looking higher and higher for the origin of events in the series of causes, because their causality is always conditioned. In return for this, however, it promises a complete and well-ordered unity of experience; while, on the other side, the fiction of freedom promises, no doubt, to the enquiring mind, rest in the chain of causes, leading him up to an unconditioned causality, which begins to act by itself, but which, as it is blind itself, tears the thread of rules by which alone a complete and coherent experience is possible.

THIRD ANTINOMY

II. ON THE ANTITHESIS

He who stands up for the omnipotence of nature (transcendental *physiocracy*), in opposition to the doctrine of freedom, would defend his position against the sophistical conclusions of that doctrine in the following manner. *If you do not admit something mathematically the first in the world with reference to time, there is no necessity why you should look for something dynamically the first with reference to causality.* Who has told you to invent an absolutely first state of the world, and with it an absolute beginning of the gradually progressing series of phenomena, and to set limits to unlimited nature in order to give to your imagination something to rest on? As substances have always existed in the world, or as the unity of experience renders at least such a supposition necessary, there is no difficulty in assuming that a change of their states, that

(*Continued on p. 273*)

(*Continued from p. 270*)

THESIS

that such a causality has to be admitted, though we can in no wise understand the possibility how, through one existence, the existence of another is given, but must for that purpose appeal to experience alone. The necessity of a first beginning of a series of phenomena from freedom has been proved so far only as it is necessary in order to comprehend an origin of the world, while all successive states may be regarded as a result in succession according to mere laws of nature. But as thus the faculty of originating a series in time by itself has been proved, though by no means understood, it is now permitted also to admit, within the course of the world, different series, beginning by themselves, with regard to their causality, and to attribute to their substances a faculty of acting with freedom. But we must not allow ourselves to be troubled by a misapprehension, namely that, as every sucessive series in the world can have only a relatively primary beginning, some other state of things always preceding in the world, therefore no absolutely primary beginning of different series is possible in the course of the world. For we are speaking here of the absolutely first beginning, not according to time, but according to causality. If, for instance, at this moment I rise from my chair with perfect freedom, without the necessary determining influence of natural causes, a new series has its absolute beginning in this event, with all its natural consequences *ad infinitum*, although, with regard to time, this event is only the continuation of a preceding series. For this determination and this act do not belong to the succession of merely natural effects, nor are they a mere continuation of them, but the determining natural causes completely stop before it, so far as this event is concerned, which no doubt follows them, and does not *result* from them, and may therefore be called an absolutely first beginning in a series of phenomena, not with reference to time, but with reference to causality.

This requirement of reason to appeal in the series of natural causes to a first and free beginning is fully confirmed if we see that, with the exception of the Epicurean school, all philosophers of antiquity have felt themselves obliged to admit, for the sake of explaining all cosmical movements, a *prime mover*, that is, a freely acting cause which, first and by itself, started this series of states. They did not attempt to make a first beginning comprehensible by an appeal to nature only. . . .

(*Continued from p. 271*)

ANTITHESIS

is, a series of their changes, has always existed also, so that there is no necessity for looking for a first beginning either mathematically or dynamically. It is true we cannot render the possibility of such an infinite descent comprehensible without the first member to which everything else is subsequent. But, if for this reason you reject this riddle of nature, you will feel yourselves constrained to reject many synthetical fundamental properties (natural forces), which you cannot comprehend any more, nay, the very possibility of change in general would be full of difficulties. For if you did not know from experience that change exists, you would never be able to conceive *a priori* how such a constant succession of being and not being is possible.

And, even if the transcendental faculty of freedom might somehow be conceded to start the changes of the world, such faculty would at all events have to be outside the world (though it would always remain a bold assumption to admit, outside the sum total of all possible intuitions, an object that cannot be given in any possible experience). But to attribute in the world itself a faculty to substances can never be allowed, because in that case the connection of phenomena determining each other by necessity and according to general laws, which we call nature, and with it the test of empirical truth, which distinguishes experience from dreams, would almost entirely disappear. For by the side of such a lawless faculty of freedom, nature could hardly be conceived any longer, because the laws of the latter would be constantly changed through the influence of the former, and the play of phenomena which, according to nature, is regular and uniform, would become confused and incoherent. . . .

III. SOLUTION OF THE COSMOLOGICAL IDEAS WITH REGARD TO THE TOTALITY OF THE DERIVATION OF COSMICAL EVENTS FROM THEIR CAUSES

We can conceive two kinds of causality only with reference to events, causality either of *nature* or of *freedom*. The former is the connection of one state in the world of sense with a preceding state, on which it follows according to a rule. As the *causality* of phenomena depends on conditions of time, and as the preceding state, if it had always existed, could not have produced an effect, which first takes place in time, it follows that the causality of the cause of that which happens or arises must, according to the principle of the understanding, have itself *arisen* and require a cause.

By freedom, on the contrary, in its cosmological meaning, I understand the faculty of beginning a state *spontaneously*. Its causality, therefore, does not depend, according to the law of nature, on another cause, by which it is determined in time. In this sense freedom is a purely transcendental idea, which, first, contains nothing derived from *experience*, and, secondly, the object of which cannot be determined in any *experience*; because it is a general rule, even of the possibility of all *experience*, that everything which happens has a cause, and that therefore the causality also of the cause, which *itself has happened* or arisen, must again have a cause. In this manner the whole field of experience, however far it may extend, has been changed into one great whole of nature. As, however, it is impossible in this way to arrive at an absolute totality of the conditions in causal relations, reason creates for itself the idea of spontaneity, or the power of beginning by itself, without an antecedent cause determining it to action, according to the law of causal connection.

It is extremely remarkable, that the practical concept of freedom is founded on the *transcendental idea of freedom*, which constitutes indeed the real difficulty which at all times has surrounded the question of the possibility of freedom. *Freedom*, in its *practical sense*, is the independence of our (arbitrary) will from the *coercion* through sensuous impulses. Our (arbitrary) will is *sensuous*, so far as it is *affected pathologically* (by sensuous impulses); it is called animal (*arbitrium brutum*), if *necessitated* pathologically. The human will is certainly sensuous, an *arbitrium sensitivum*, but not *brutum*, but *liberum*, because sensuous impulses do not necessitate its action, but there is in man a faculty of determination, independent of the necessitation through sensuous impulses.

It can easily be seen that, if all causality in the world of sense belonged to nature, every event would be determined in time through another, according to necessary laws. As therefore the phenomena, in determining the will, would render every act necessary as their natural effect, the annihilation of transcendental freedom would at the same time destroy all practical freedom. Practical freedom presupposes that, although something has not happened, it *ought* to have happened, and that its cause therefore had not that determining force among phenomena, which could prevent the causality of our will from producing, independently of those natural causes, and even contrary to their force and influence, something determined in the order of time, according to empirical laws, and from originating *entirely by itself* a series of events.

What happens here is what happens generally in the conflict of reason venturing beyond the limits of possible experience, namely, that the problem is not *physiological,* but *transcendental.* Hence the question of the possibility of freedom concerns no doubt psychology; but its solution, as it depends on dialectical arguments of pure reason, belongs entirely to transcendental philosophy. In order to enable that philosophy to give a satisfactory answer, which it cannot decline to do, I must first try to determine more accurately its proper procedure in this task.

If phenomena were things by themselves, and therefore space and time forms of the existence of things by themselves, the conditions together with the conditioned would always belong, as members, to one and the same series, and thus in our case also, the antinomy which is common to all transcendental ideas would arise, namely, that that series is inevitably too large or too small for the understanding. The dynamical concepts of reason, however, which we have to discuss in this and the following section, have this peculiarity that, as they are not concerned with an object, considered as a quantity, but only with its *existence,* we need take no account of the quantity of the series of conditions. All depends here only on the dynamical relation of conditions to the conditioned, so that in the question on nature and freedom we at once meet with the difficulty, whether freedom is indeed possible, and whether, if it is possible, it can exist together with the universality of the natural law of causality. The question in fact arises, whether it is a proper disjunctive proposition to say, that every effect in the world must arise, *either* from nature, *or* from freedom, or whether *both* cannot coexist in the same event in different relations. The correctness of the principle of the unbroken connection of all events in the world of sense, according to unchangeable natural laws, is firmly established by the transcendental Analytic, and admits of no limitation. The question, therefore, can only be whether, in spite of it, freedom also can be found in the same effect which is determined by nature; or whether freedom is entirely excluded by that inviolable rule? Here the common but fallacious supposition of the *absolute reality* of phenomena shows at once its pernicious influence in embarrassing reason. For if phenomena are things by themselves, freedom cannot be saved. Nature in that case is the complete and sufficient cause determining every event, and its condition is always contained in that series of phenomena only which, together with their effect, are necessary under the law of nature. If, on the contrary, phenomena are taken for nothing except what they are in reality, namely, not things by themselves, but representations only, which are connected with each other according to empirical laws, they must themselves have causes, which are not phenomenal. Such an intelligible cause, however, is not determined with reference to its causality by phenomena, although its effects become phenomenal, and can thus be determined by other phenomena. That intelligible cause, therefore, with its causality, is outside the series, though its effects are to be found in the series of empirical conditions. The effect therefore can, with reference to its intelligible cause, be considered as free, and yet at the same time, with reference to phenomena, as resulting from them according to the necessity of nature; a distinction which, if thus represented, in a general and entirely abstract form, may seem extremely subtle and obscure, but will become clear in its practical application. Here I only wished to remark that, as the unbroken *connection* of all phenomena in the context (woof) of nature, is an unalterable law, it would necessarily destroy all freedom, if we were to defend obstinately the reality of phenomena. Those, therefore, who follow the common opinion on this subject, have never been able to reconcile nature and freedom.

Possibility of a Causality through Freedom, in Harmony with the Universal Law of Natural Necessity

Whatever in an object of the senses is not itself phenomenal, I call *intelligible*. If, therefore, what in the world of sense must be considered as phenomenal, possesses in itself a faculty which is not the object of sensuous intuition, but through which it can become the cause of phenomena, the *causality* of that being may be considered from *two sides*, as *intelligible* in its *action*, as the causality of a thing by itself, and as *sensible* in the *effects* of the action, as the causality of a phenomenon in the world of sense. Of the faculty of such a being we should have to form both an *empirical* and an *intellectual concept* of its causality, both of which consist together in one and the same effect. This twofold way of conceiving the faculty of an object of the senses does not contradict any of the concepts which we have to form of phenomena and of a possible experience. For as all phenomena, not being things by themselves, must have for their foundation a transcendental object, determining them as mere representations, there is nothing to prevent us from attributing to that transcendental object, besides the quality through which it becomes phenomenal, a *causality* also which is not phenomenal, although its *effect* appears in the phenomenon. Every efficient cause, however, must have a *character,* that is, a rule according to which it manifests its causality, and without which it would not be a cause. According to this we should have in every subject of the world of sense, first, an *empirical character,* through which its acts, as phenomena, stand with other phenomena in an unbroken connection, according to permanent laws of nature, and could be derived from them as their conditions, and in connection with them form the links of one and the same series in the order of nature. Secondly, we should have to allow to it an *intelligible character* also, by which, it is true, it becomes the cause of the same acts as phenomena, but which itself is not subject to any conditions of sensibility, and never phenomenal. We might call the former the character of such a thing as a phenomenon, in the latter the character of the thing by itself.

According to its intelligible character, this active subject would not depend on conditions of time, for time is only the condition of phenomena, and not of things by themselves. In it no *act* would *arise* or *perish,* neither would it be subject therefore to the law of determination in time and of all that is changeable, namely, that everything *which happens* must have its cause in *the phenomena* (of the previous state). In one word its causality, so far as it is intelligible, would not have a place in the series of empirical conditions by which the event is rendered necessary in the world of sense. It is true that that intelligible character could never be known immediately, because we cannot perceive anything, except so far as it appears, but it would nevertheless have to be conceived, according to the empirical character, as we must always admit in thought a transcendental object, as the foundation of phenomena, though we know nothing of what it is by itself.

In its empirical character, therefore, that subject, as a phenomenon, would submit, according to all determining laws, to a causal nexus, and in that respect it would be nothing but a part of the world of sense, the effects of which, like every other phenomenon, would arise from nature without fail. As soon as external phenomena began to influence it, and as soon as its empirical character, that is the law of its causality, had been known through experience, all its actions ought to admit of explanation, according to the laws of nature, and all that is requisite for its complete and necessary determination would be found in a possible experience.

In its intelligible character, however (though we could only have a general concept of it), the same subject would have to be considered free from all influence of sensibility, and from all determination through phenomena: and as in it, so far as it is a *noumenon*, nothing *happens*, and no change which requires dynamical determination of time, and therefore no connection with phenomena as causes, can exist, that active being would so far be quite independent and free in its acts from all natural necessity, which can exist in the world of sense only. One might say of it with perfect truth that it originates its effects in the world of sense *by itself*, though the act does not begin *in itself*. And this would be perfectly true, though the effects in the world of sense need not therefore originate by themselves, because in it they are always determined previously through empirical conditions in the previous time, though only by means of the empirical character (which is the phenomenal appearance of the intelligible character), and therefore impossible, except as a continuation of the series of natural causes. In this way freedom and nature, each in its complete signification, might exist together and without any conflict in the same action, according as we refer it to its intelligible or to its sensible cause.

Explanation of the Cosmological Idea of Freedom in Connection with the General Necessity of Nature

I thought it best to give first this sketch of the solution of our transcendental problem, so that the course which reason has to adopt in its solution might be more clearly surveyed. We shall now proceed to explain more fully the points on which the decision properly rests, and examine each by itself.

The law of nature, that everything which happens has a cause, that the causality of that cause, that is, its *activity* (as it is anterior in time, and, with regard to an effect which has *arisen*, cannot itself have always existed, but must have *happened* at some time), must have its cause among the phenomena by which it is determined, and that therefore all events in the order of nature are empirically determined, this law, I say, through which alone phenomena become *nature* and objects of experience, is a law of the understanding, which can on no account be surrendered, and from which no single phenomenon can be exempted; because in doing this we should place it outside all possible experience, separate from all objects of possible experience, and change it into a mere fiction of the mind or a cobweb of the brain.

But although this looks merely like a chain of causes, which in the regressus to its conditions admits of no *absolute totality*, this difficulty does not detain us in the least, because it has already been removed in the general criticism of the antinomy of reason when, starting from the series of phenomena, it aims at the unconditioned. Were we to yield to the illusion of transcendental realism, we should have neither nature nor freedom. The question therefore is, whether, if we recognise in the whole series of events nothing but natural necessity, we may yet regard the same event which on one side is an effect of nature only, on the other side, as an effect of freedom; or whether there is a direct contradiction between these two kinds of causality?

There can certainly be nothing among phenomenal causes that could originate a series absolutely and by itself. Every action, as a phenomenon, so far as it produces an event, is itself an event, presupposing another state, in which its cause can be discovered; and thus everything that happens is only a continuation of the series, and no beginning, happening by itself, is possible in it. Actions of natural causes in the succession of time are therefore themselves effects, which likewise presuppose causes in the series of time. A *spontaneous* and original action by which something takes place, which did not exist before, cannot be expected from the causal nexus of phenomena.

But is it really necessary that, if effects are phenomena, the causality of their cause, which cause itself is phenomenal, could be nothing but empirical; or is it not possible, although for every phenomenal effect a connection with its cause, according to the laws of empirical causality, is certainly required, that empirical causality itself could nevertheless, without breaking in the least its connection with the natural causes, represent an effect of a non-empirical and intelligible causality, that is, of a caused action, original in respect to phenomena, and in so far not phenomenal; but, with respect to this faculty, intelligible, although, as a link in the chain of nature, to be regarded as entirely belonging to the world of sense?

We require the principle of the causality of phenomena

among themselves, in order to be able to look for and to produce natural conditions, that is, phenomenal causes of natural events. If this is admitted and not weakened by any exceptions, the understanding, which in its empirical employment recognises in all events nothing but nature, and is quite justified in doing so, has really all that it can demand, and the explanations of physical phenomena may proceed without let or hindrance. The understanding would not be wronged in the least, if we assumed, though it be a mere fiction, that some among the natural causes have a faculty which is intelligible only, and whose determination to activity does not rest on empirical conditions, but on mere grounds of the intellect, if only the *phenomenal activity* of that cause is in accordance with all the laws of empirical causality. For in this way the active subject, as *causa phaenomenon*, would be joined with nature through the indissoluble dependence of all its actions, and the noumenon[33] only of that subject (with all its phenomenal causality) would contain certain conditions which, if we want to ascend from the empirical to the transcendental object, would have to be considered as intelligible only. For, if only we follow the rule of nature in that which may be the cause among phenomena, it is indifferent to us what kind of ground of those phenomena, and of their connection, may be conceived to exist in the transcendental subject, which is empirically unknown to us. This intelligible ground does not touch the empirical questions, but concerns only, as it would seem, the thought in the pure understanding; and although the effects of that thought and action of the pure understanding may be discovered in the phenomena, these have nevertheless to be completely explained from their phenomenal cause, according to the laws of nature, by taking their empirical character as the highest ground of explanation, and passing by the intelligible character, which is the transcendental cause of the other, as entirely unknown, except so far as it is indicated by the empirical, as its sensuous sign. Let us apply this to experience. Man is one among the phenomena of the world of sense, and in so far one of the natural causes the causality of which must be subject to empirical laws. As such he must therefore have an empirical character, like all other objects of nature. We perceive it through the forces and faculties which he shows in his actions and effects. In the lifeless or merely animal nature we see no ground for admitting any faculty, except as sensuously conditioned. Man, however, who knows all the rest of nature through his

[33] It seems better to read *noumenon* instead of *phenomenon*.

senses only, knows himself through mere apperception also, and this in actions and internal determinations, which he cannot ascribe to the impressions of the senses. Man is thus to himself partly a phenomenon, partly, however, namely with reference to certain faculties, a purely intelligible object, because the actions of these faculties cannot be ascribed to the receptivity of sensibility. We call these faculties understanding and reason. It is the latter, in particular, which is entirely distinguished from all empirically conditioned forces or faculties, because it weighs its objects according to ideas, and determines the understanding accordingly, which then makes an empirical use of its (by themselves, however pure) concepts.

That our reason possesses causality, or that we at least represent to ourselves such a causality in it, is clear from the *imperatives* which, in all practical matters, we impose as rules on our executive powers. The *ought* expresses a kind of necessity and connection with causes, which we do not find elsewhere in the whole of nature. The understanding can know in nature only what is present, past, or future. It is impossible that anything in it *ought to be* different from what it is in reality, in all these relations of time. Nay, if we only look at the course of nature, the ought has no meaning whatever. We cannot ask, what ought to be in nature, as little as we can ask, what qualities a circle ought to possess. We can only ask what happens in it, and what qualities that which happens has.

This ought expresses a possible action, the ground of which cannot be anything but a mere concept; while in every merely natural action the ground must always be a phenomenon. Now it is quite true that the action to which the ought applies must be possible under natural conditions, but these natural conditions do not affect the determination of the will itself, but only its effects and results among phenomena. There may be ever so many natural grounds which impel me to *will* and ever so many sensuous temptations, but they can never produce the *ought,* but only a willing which is always conditioned, but by no means necessary, and to which the ought, pronounced by reason, opposes measure, ay, prohibition and authority. Whether it be an object of the senses merely (pleasure), or of pure reason (the good), reason does not yield to the impulse that is given empirically, and does not follow the order of things, as they present themselves as phenomena, but frames for itself, with perfect spontaneity, a new order according to ideas to which it adapts the empirical conditions, and according to which it declares actions to be necessary, even though they *have not taken place,* and, maybe, never will take place. Yet it is presupposed that reason may have causality with respect to them, for otherwise no effects in experience could be expected to result from these ideas.

Now let us take our stand here and admit it at least as possible, that reason really possesses causality with reference to phenomena. In that case, reason though it be, it must show nevertheless an empirical character, because every cause presupposes a rule according to which certain phenomena follow as effects, and every rule requires in the effects a homogeneousness, on which the concept of cause (as a faculty) is founded. This, so far as it is derived from mere phenomena, may be called the empirical character, which is *permanent,* while the effects, according to a diversity of concomitant, and in part, restraining conditions, appear in *changeable* forms.

Every man therefore has an empirical character of his (arbitrary) will, which is nothing but a certain causality of his reason, exhibiting in its phenomenal actions and effects a rule, according to which one may infer the motives of reason and its actions, both in kind and in degree, and judge of the subjective principles of his will. As that empirical character itself must be derived from phenomena, as an effect, and from their rule which is supplied by experience, all the acts of a man, so far as they are phenomena, are determined from his empirical character and from the other concomitant causes, according to the order of nature; and if we could investigate all the manifestations of his will to the very bottom, there would be not a single human action which we could not predict with certainty and recognise from its preceding conditions as necessary. There is no freedom therefore with reference to this empirical character, and yet it is only with reference to it that we can consider man, when we are merely *observing,* and, as is the case in anthropology, trying to investigate the motive causes of his actions physiologically.

If, however, we consider the same actions with reference to reason, not with reference to speculative reason, in order to *explain* their origin, but solely so far as reason is the cause which *produces* them; in one word, if we compare actions with reason, with reference to *practical* purposes, we find a rule and order, totally different from the order of nature. For, from this point of view, everything, it may be, *ought not to have happened,* which according to the course of nature *has happened,* and according to its empirical grounds, was inevitable. And sometimes we find, or believe at least that we find, that the ideas of reason have really proved their causality with reference to human actions as phenomena, and that these actions have taken place, not because they were determined by empirical causes, but by the causes of reason.

Now supposing one could say that reason possesses causality in reference to phenomena, could the action of reason be called free in that case, as it is accurately determined by the empirical character (the disposition) and rendered necessary by it? That character again is determined in the intelligible character (way of thinking). The latter, however, we do not know, but signify only through phenomena, which in reality give us immediately a knowledge of the disposition (empirical character) only.* An action, so far as it is to be attributed to the way of thinking as its cause, does nevertheless not result from it according to empirical laws, that is, it is not *preceded* by the conditions of pure reason, but only by its effects in the phenomenal form of the internal sense. Pure reason, as a simple intelligible faculty, is not subject to the form of time, or to the conditions of the succession of time. The causality of reason in its intelligible character does *not arise* or begin at a certain time in order to produce an effect; for in that case it would be subject to the natural law of phenomena, which determines all causal series in time, and its causality would then be nature and not freedom. What, therefore, we can say is, that if reason can possess causality with reference to phenomena, it is a faculty *through which* the sensuous condition of an empirical series of effects first begins. For the condition that lies in reason is not sensuous, and therefore does itself not begin. Thus we get what we missed in all empirical series, namely, that the *condition* of a successive series of events should itself be empirically unconditioned. For here the condition is really *outside* the series of phenomena (in the intelligible), and therefore not subject to any sensuous condition, nor to any temporal determination through preceding causes.

Nevertheless the same cause belongs also, in another respect, to the series of phenomena. Man himself is a phenomenon. His will has an empirical character, which is the (empirical) cause of all his actions. There is no condition, determining man according to this character, that is not contained in the series of natural effects and subject to their law, according to which there can be no empirically unconditioned causality of any-

---

* The true morality of actions (merit or guilt), even that of our own conduct, remains therefore entirely hidden. Our imputations can refer to the empirical character only. How much of that may be the pure effect of freedom, how much should be ascribed to nature only, and to the faults of temperament, for which man is not responsible, or its happy constitution (*merito fortunae*), no one can discover, and no one can judge with perfect justice.

thing that happens in time. No given action therefore (as it can be perceived as a phenomenon only) can begin absolutely by itself. Of pure reason, however, we cannot say that the state in which it determines the will is preceded by another in which that state itself is determined. For as reason itself is not a phenomenon, and not subject to any of the conditions of sensibility, there exists in it, even in reference to its causality, no succession of time, and the dynamical law of nature, which determines the succession of time according to rules, cannot be applied to it.

Reason is therefore the constant condition of all free actions by which man takes his place in the phenomenal world. Every one of them is determined beforehand in his empirical character, before it becomes actual. With regard to the intelligible character, however, of which the empirical is only the sensuous schema, there is neither *before* nor *after;* and every action, without regard to the temporal relation which connects it with other phenomena, is the immediate effect of the intelligible character of pure reason. That reason therefore acts freely, without being determined dynamically, in the chain of natural causes, by external or internal conditions, anterior in time. That freedom must then not only be regarded negatively, as independence of empirical conditions (for in that case the faculty of reason would cease to be a cause of phenomena), but should be determined positively also, as the faculty of beginning spontaneously a series of events. Hence nothing begins in reason itself, and being itself the unconditioned condition of every free action, reason admits of no condition antecedent in time above itself, while nevertheless its effect takes its beginning in the series of phenomena, though it can never constitute in that series an *absolutely* first beginning.

In order to illustrate the regulative principle of reason by an example of its empirical application, not in order to confirm it (for such arguments are useless for transcendental propositions), let us take a voluntary action, for example, a malicious lie, by which a man has produced a certain confusion in society, and of which we first try to find out the motives, and afterwards try to determine how far it and its consequences may be imputed to the offender. With regard to the first point, one has first to follow up his empirical character to its very sources, which are to be found in wrong education, bad society, in part also in the viciousness of a natural disposition, and a nature insensible to shame, or ascribed to frivolity and heedlessness, not omitting the occasioning causes at the time. In all this the procedure is exactly the same as in the investigation of a series of determining causes of a given natural effect. But although one believes that the act was thus determined, one nevertheless blames the offender, and not on account of his unhappy natural disposition, not on account of influencing circumstances, not even on account of his former course of life, because one supposes one might leave entirely out of account what that course of life may have been, and consider the past series of conditions as having never existed, and the act itself as totally unconditioned by previous states, as if the offender had begun with it a new series of effects, quite by himself. This blame is founded on a law of reason, reason being considered as a cause which, independent of all the before-mentioned empirical conditions, would and should have determined the behaviour of the man otherwise. Nay, we do not regard the causality of reason as a concurrent agency only, but as complete in itself, even though the sensuous motives did not favour, but even oppose it. The action is imputed to a man's intelligible character. At the moment when he tells the lie, the guilt is entirely his; that is, we regard reason, in spite of all empirical conditions of the act, as completely free, and the act has to be imputed entirely to a fault of reason.

Such an imputation clearly shows that we imagine that reason is not affected at all by the influences of the senses, and that it does not change (although its manifestations, that is the mode in which it shows itself by its effects, do change): that in it no state precedes as determining a following state, in fact, that reason does not belong to the series of sensuous conditions which render phenomena necessary, according to laws of nature. Reason, it is supposed, is present in all the actions of man, in all circumstances of time, and always the same; but it is itself never in time, never in a new state in which it was not before; it is *determining,* never *determined.* We cannot ask, therefore, why reason has not determined itself differently, but only why it has not differently determined the *phenomena* by its causality. And here no answer is really possible. For a different intelligible character would have given a different empirical character, and if we say that, in spite of the whole of his previous course of life, the offender could have avoided the lie, this only means that it was in the power of reason, and that reason, in its causality, is subject to no phenomenal and temporal conditions, and lastly, that the difference of time, though it makes a great difference in phenomena and their relation to each other, can, as these are neither things nor causes by themselves, produce no difference of action in reference to reason.

We thus see that, in judging of voluntary actions, we can, so far as their causality is concerned, get only so far as the intelligible cause, but not beyond. We can see that that cause is free, that it determines as independent of sensibility, and therefore is capable of being the sensuously unconditioned condition of phenomena. To explain why that intelligible character should, under present circumstances, give these phenomena and this empirical character, and no other, transcends all the powers of our reason, nay, all its rights of questioning, as if we were to ask why the transcendental object of our external sensuous intuition gives us intuition in *space* only and no other. But the problem which we have to solve does not require us to ask or to answer such questions. Our problem was, whether freedom is contradictory to natural necessity in one and the same action: and this we have sufficiently answered by showing that freedom may have relation to a very different kind of conditions from those of nature, so that the law of the latter does not affect the former, and both may exist independent of, and undisturbed by, each other.

* * *

It should be clearly understood that, in what we have said, we had no intention of establishing the *reality* of freedom, as one of the faculties which contain the cause of the phenomenal appearances in our world of sense. For not only would this have been no transcendental consideration at all, which is concerned with concepts only, but it could never have succeeded, because from experience we can never infer anything but what must be represented in thought according to the laws of experience. It was not even our intention to prove the *possibility* of freedom, for in this also we should not have succeeded, because from mere concepts *a priori* we can never know the possibility of any real ground or any causality. We have here treated freedom as a transcendental idea only, which makes reason imagine that it can absolutely begin the series of phenomenal conditions through what is sensuously unconditioned, but by which reason becomes involved in an antinomy with its own laws, which it had prescribed to the empirical use of the understanding. That this antinomy rests on a mere illusion, and that nature does *not contradict* the causality of freedom, that was the only thing which we could prove, and cared to prove.

There are only three kinds of proofs of the existence of God from speculative reason.

All the paths that can be followed to this end begin either from definite experience and the peculiar nature of the world of sense, known to us through experience, and ascend from it, according to the laws of causality, to the highest cause, existing outside the world; or they rest on indefinite experience only, that is, on any existence which is empirically given; or lastly, they leave all experience out of account, and conclude, entirely *a priori* from mere concepts, the existence of a supreme cause. The first proof is the *physico-theological*, the second the *cosmological*, the third the *ontological* proof. There are no more, and there can be no more.

I shall show that neither on the one path, the empirical, nor on the other, the transcendental, can reason achieve anything, and that it stretches its wings in vain, if it tries to soar beyond the world of sense by the mere power of speculation. With regard to the order in which these three arguments should be examined, it will be the opposite of that, followed by reason in its gradual development, in which we placed them also at first ourselves. For we shall be able to show that, although experience gives the first impulse, it is the transcendental concept only which guides reason in its endeavours, and fixes the last goal which reason wishes to retain. I shall therefore begin with the examination of the transcendental proof, and see afterwards how far it may be strengthened by the addition of empirical elements. . . .

THE IDEAL OF PURE REASON

SECTION IV

OF THE IMPOSSIBILITY OF AN ONTOLOGICAL PROOF OF THE EXISTENCE OF GOD

It is easily perceived, from what has been said before, that the concept of an absolutely necessary Being is a concept of pure reason, that is, a mere idea, the objective reality of which is by no means proved by the fact that reason requires it. That idea does no more than point to a certain but unattainable completeness, and serves rather to limit the understanding, than to extend its sphere. It seems strange and absurd, however, that a conclusion of an absolutely necessary existence from a given existence in general should seem urgent and correct, and that yet all the conditions under which the understanding can form a concept of such a necessity should be entirely against us.

People have at all times been talking of an *absolutely necessary* Being, but they have tried, not so much to understand whether and how a thing of that kind could even be conceived, as rather to prove its existence. No doubt a verbal definition of that concept is quite easy, if we say that it is something the non-existence of which is impossible. This, however, does not make us much wiser with reference to the conditions that make it necessary[34] to consider the non-existence of a thing as absolutely inconceivable. It is these conditions which we want to know, and whether by that concept we are thinking anything or not. For to use the word *unconditioned,* in order to get rid of all the conditions which the understanding always requires, when wishing to conceive something as necessary, does not render it clear to us in the least whether, after that, we are still thinking anything or perhaps nothing, by the concept of the unconditionally necessary.

Nay, more than this, people have imagined that by a number of examples they had explained this concept, at first risked at haphazard, and afterwards become quite familiar, and that therefore all further inquiry regarding its intelligibility were unnecessary. It was said that every proposition of geometry, such as, for instance, that a triangle has three angles, is absolutely necessary, and people began to talk of an object entirely outside the sphere of our understanding, as if they understood perfectly well what, by that concept, they wished to predicate of it.

But all these pretended examples are taken without exception from *judgments* only, not from *things,* and their existence. Now the unconditioned necessity of judgments is not the same thing as an absolute necessity of things. The absolute necessity of a judgment is only a conditioned necessity of the thing, or of the predicate in the judgment. The above proposition did not say that three angles were absolutely necessary, but that under the condition of the existence of a triangle, three angles are given (in it) by necessity. Nevertheless, this pure logical necessity has exerted so powerful an illusion, that, after having formed of a thing a concept *a priori* so constituted that it seemed to include existence in its sphere, people thought they could conclude with certainty that, because existence necessarily belongs to the object of that concept, provided always that I accept the thing as given (existing), its existence also must necessarily be accepted (according to the rule of identity), and that the Being therefore must itself be absolutely necessary, because its existence is implied in a concept, which is accepted voluntarily only,

[34] Read *nothwendig* instead of *unmöglich.* Noiré.

and always under the condition that I accept the object of it as given.

If in an identical judgment I reject the predicate and retain the subject, there arises a contradiction, and hence, I say, that the former belongs to the latter necessarily. But if I reject the subject as well as the predicate, there is no contradiction, because there is nothing left that can be contradicted. To accept a triangle and yet to reject its three angles is contradictory, but there is no contradiction at all in admitting the non-existence of the triangle and of its three angles. The same applies to the concept of an absolutely necessary Being. Remove its existence, and you remove the thing itself, with all its predicates, so that a contradiction becomes impossible. There is nothing external to which the contradiction could apply, because the thing is not meant to be externally necessary; nor is there anything internal that could be contradicted, for in removing the thing out of existence, you have removed at the same time all its internal qualities. If you say, God is almighty, that is a necessary judgment, because almightiness cannot be removed, if you accept a deity, that is, an infinite Being, with the concept of which that other concept is indentical. But if you say, God is not, then neither his almightiness, nor any other of his predicates is given; they are all, together with the subject, removed out of existence, and therefore there is not the slightest contradiction in that sentence.

We have seen therefore that, if I remove the predicate of a judgment together with its subject, there can never be an internal contradiction, whatever the predicate may be. The only way of evading this conclusion would be to say that there are subjects which cannot be removed out of existence, but must always remain. But this would be the same as to say that there exist absolutely necessary subjects, an assumption the correctness of which I have called in question, and the possibility of which you had undertaken to prove. For I cannot form to myself the smallest concept of a thing which, if it had been removed together with all its predicates, should leave behind a contradiction; and except contradiction, I have no other test of impossibility by pure concepts *a priori*. Against all these general arguments (which no one can object to) you challenge me with a case, which you represent as a proof by a fact, namely, that there is one, and this one concept only, in which the non-existence or the removal of its object would be self-contradictory, namely, the concept of the most real Being (*ens realissimum*). You say that it possesses all reality, and you are no doubt justified in accepting such a Being as possible. This for the present I may admit, though the absence of self-contradictoriness in a concept is far from proving the possibility of its object.* Now reality comprehends existence, and therefore existence is contained in the concept of a thing possible. If that thing is removed, the internal possibility of the thing would be removed, and this is self-contradictory.

I answer: Even in introducing into the concept of a thing, which you wish to think in its possibility only, the concept of its existence, under whatever disguise it may be, you have been guilty of a contradiction. If you were allowed to do this, you would apparently have carried your point; but in reality you have achieved nothing, but have only committed a tautology. I simply ask you, whether the proposition, that *this or that thing* (which, whatever it may be, I grant you as possible) *exists,* is an analytical or a synthetical proposition? If the former, then by its existence you add nothing to your thought of the thing; but in that case, either the thought within you would be the thing itself, or you have presupposed existence, as belonging to possibility, and have according to your own showing deduced existence from internal possibility, which is nothing but a miserable tautology. The mere word *reality,* which in the concept of a thing sounds different from existence in the concept of the predicate, can make no difference. For if you call all accepting or positing (without determining what it is) reality, you have placed a thing, with all its predicates, within the concept of the subject, and accepted it as real, and you do nothing but repeat it in the predicate. If, on the contrary, you admit, as every sensible man must do, that every proposition involving existence is synthetical, how can you say that the predicate of existence does not admit of removal without contradiction, a distinguishing property which is peculiar to analytical propositions only, the very character of which depends on it?

I might have hoped to put an end to this subtle argumentation, without many words, and simply by an accurate definition of the concept of existence, if I had not seen that the illusion, in mistaking a logical predicate for a real one (that is the predicate which determines a thing), resists all correction. Everything can become a *logical predicate,* even the subject itself

---

* A concept is always possible, if it is not self-contradictory. This is the logical characteristic of possibility, and by it the object of the concept is distinguished from the *nihil negativum.* But it may nevertheless be an empty concept, unless the objective reality of the synthesis, by which the concept is generated, has been distinctly shown. This, however, as shown above, must always rest on principles of possible experience, and not on the principle of analysis (the principle of contradiction). This is a warning against inferring at once from the possibility of concepts (logical) the possibility of things (real).

may be predicated of itself, because logic takes no account of any contents of concepts. *Determination,* however, is a predicate, added to the concept of the subject, and enlarging it, and it must not therefore be contained in it.

Being is evidently not a real predicate, or a concept of something that can be added to the concept of a thing. It is merely the admission of a thing, and of certain determinations in it. Logically, it is merely the copula of a judgment. The proposition, *God is almighty,* contains two concepts, each having its object, namely, God and almightiness. The small word *is,* is not an additional predicate, but only serves to put the predicate *in relation* to the subject. If, then, I take the subject (God) with all its predicates (including that of almightiness), and say, *God is,* or there is a God, I do not put a new predicate to the concept of God, but I only put the subject by itself, with all its predicates, in relation to my concept, as its object. Both must contain exactly the same kind of thing, and nothing can have been added to the concept, which expresses possibility only, by my thinking its object as simply given and saying, it is. And thus the real does not contain more than the possible. A hundred real dollars do not contain a penny more than a hundred possible dollars. For as the latter signify the concept, the former the object and its position by itself, it is clear that, in case the former contained more than the latter, my concept would not express the whole object, and would not therefore be its adequate concept. In my financial position no doubt there exists more by one hundred real dollars, than by their concept only (that is their possibility), because in reality the object is not only contained analytically in my concept, but is added to my concept (which is a determination of my state), synthetically; but the conceived hundred dollars are not in the least increased through the existence which is outside my concept.

By whatever and by however many predicates I may think a thing (even in completely determining it), nothing is really added to it, if I add that the thing exists. Otherwise, it would not be the same that exists, but something more than was contained in the concept, and I could not say that the exact object of my concept existed. Nay, even if I were to think in a thing all reality, except one, that one missing reality would not be supplied by my saying that so defective a thing exists, but it would exist with the same defect with which I thought it; or what exists would be different from what I thought. If, then, I try to conceive a being, as the highest reality (without any defect), the question still remains, whether it exists or not. For though in my concept there may be wanting nothing of the possible real content of a thing in general, something is wanting in its relation to my whole state of thinking, namely, that the knowledge of that object should be possible *a posteriori* also. And here we perceive the cause of our difficulty. If we were concerned with an object of our senses, I could not mistake the existence of a thing for the mere concept of it; for by the concept the object is thought as only in harmony with the general conditions of a possible empirical knowledge, while by its existence it is thought as contained in the whole content of experience. Through this connection with the content of the whole experience, the concept of an object is not in the least increased; our thought has only received through it one more possible perception. If, however, we are thinking existence through the pure category alone, we need not wonder that we cannot find any characteristic to distinguish it from mere possibility.

Whatever, therefore, our concept of an object may contain, we must always step outside it, in order to attribute to it existence. With objects of the senses, this takes place through their connection with any one of my perceptions, according to empirical laws; with objects of pure thought, however, there is no means of knowing their existence, because it would have to be known entirely *a priori*, while our consciousness of every kind of existence, whether immediately by perception, or by conclusions which connect something with perception, belongs entirely to the unity of experience, and any existence outside that field, though it cannot be declared to be absolutely impossible, is a presupposition that cannot be justified by anything.

The concept of a Supreme Being is, in many respects, a very useful idea, but, being an idea only, it is quite incapable of increasing, by itself alone, our knowledge with regard to what exists. It cannot even do so much as to inform us any further as to its possibility. The analytical characteristic of possibility, which consists in the absence of contradiction in mere positions (realities), cannot be denied to it; but the connection of all real properties in one and the same thing is a synthesis the possibility of which we cannot judge *a priori* because these realities are not given to us as such, and because, even if this were so, no judgment whatever takes place, it being necessary to look for the characteristic of the possibility of synthetical knowledge in experience only, to which the object of an idea can never belong. Thus we see that the celebrated Leibniz is far from having achieved what he thought he had, namely, to understand *a priori* the possibility of so sublime an ideal Being.

Time and labour therefore are lost on the famous ontological (Cartesian) proof of the existence of a Supreme Being from mere concepts; and a man might as well imagine that he could become richer in knowledge by mere ideas, as a merchant in

capital, if, in order to improve his position, he were to add a
few noughts to his cash account. . . .

The highest formal unity, which is based on concepts of reason alone, is the systematical and purposeful unity of things,
and it is the speculative interest of reason which makes it necessary to regard all order in the world as if it had originated in
the purpose of a supreme wisdom. Such a principle opens to
our reason in the field of experience quite new views, how to
connect the things of the world according to teleological laws,
and thus to arrive at their greatest systematical unity. The admission of a highest intelligence, as the only cause of the universe, though in the idea only, can therefore always benefit
reason, and yet never injure it. For if, with regard to the figure
of the earth (which is round, though somewhat flattened*), of
mountains, and seas, etc., we admit at once nothing but wise
intentions of their author, we are enabled to make in this wise
a number of important discoveries. If we keep to this hypothesis as a purely regulative principle, even error cannot hurt us
much; for the worst that could happen would be that, when we
expected a teleological connection (*nexus finalis*), we only find
a mechanical or physical (*nexus effectivus*), in which case we
merely lose an additional unity, but we do not destroy the unity
of reason in its empirical application. And even this failure
could not affect the law itself, in its general and teleological
character. For although an anatomist may be convicted of
error, if referring any member of an animal body to a purpose
of which it can clearly be shown that it does not belong to it,
it is entirely impossible in any given case to *prove* that an arrangement of nature, be it what it may, has no purpose at all.
Medical physiology, therefore, enlarges its very limited empirical knowledge of the purposes of the members of an organic
body by a principle inspired by pure reason only, so far as to
admit confidently, and with the approbation of all intelligent
persons, that everything in an animal has its purpose and advantage. Such a supposition, if used constitutively, goes far beyond where our present observation would justify us in going,
which shows that it is nothing but a regulative principle of reason, leading us on to the highest systematical unity, by the idea

* The advantage which arises from the circular shape of the earth is
well known; but few only know that its flattening, which gives it the
form of a spheroid, alone prevents the elevations of continents, or even
of smaller volcanically raised mountains, from continuously and, within
no very great space of time, considerably altering the axis of the earth.
The protuberance of the earth at the equator forms however so considerable a mountain, that the impetus of every other mountain can
never drive it perceptibly out of its position with reference to the axis of
the earth. And yet people do not hesitate to explain this wise arrangement simply from the equilibrium of the once fluid mass.

of an intelligent causality in the supreme cause of the world, and by the supposition that this, as the highest intelligence, is the cause of everything, according to the wisest design.

But if we remove this restriction of the idea to a merely regulative use, reason is led away in many ways. It leaves the ground of experience, which ought always to show the vestiges of its progress, and ventures beyond it to what is inconceivable and unsearchable, becoming giddy from the very height of it, and from seeing itself on that high standpoint entirely cut off from its proper work in agreement with experience. . . .

Fundamental Principles of the
Metaphysics of Morals

PREFACE

Ancient Greek philosophy was divided into three sciences: Physics, Ethics, and Logic. This division is perfectly suitable to the nature of the thing; and the only improvement that can be made in it is to add the principle on which it is based, so that we may both satisfy ourselves of its completeness, and also be able to determine correctly the necessary subdivisions.

All rational knowledge is either *material* or *formal:* the former considers some object, the latter is concerned only with the form of the understanding and of the reason itself, and with the universal laws of thought in general without distinction of its objects. Formal philosophy is called logic. Material philosophy, however, which has to do with determinate objects and the laws to which they are subject, is again twofold; for these laws are either laws of *nature* or of *freedom*. The science of the former is physics, that of the latter, ethics; they are also called *natural philosophy* and *moral philosophy* respectively.

Logic cannot have any empirical part—that is, a part in which the universal and necessary laws of thought should rest on grounds taken from experience; otherwise it would not be logic, that is, a canon for the understanding or the reason, valid for all thought, and capable of demonstration. Natural and moral philosophy, on the contrary, can each have their empirical part, since the former has to determine the laws of nature as an object of experience, the latter the laws of the human will, so far as it is affected by nature; the former, however, being laws according to which everything does happen, the latter, laws according to which everything ought to happen.[1] Ethics, however, must also consider the conditions under which what ought to happen frequently does not.

We may call all philosophy *empirical*, so far as it is based on grounds of experience; on the other hand, that which delivers its doctrines from *a priori* principles alone we may call *pure* philosophy. When the latter is merely formal, it is *logic;* if it is restricted to definite objects of the understanding, it is *metaphysic*.

---

[1] The word "law" is here used in two different senses, on which see Whately's *Logic*, Appendix, Art. "Law."

In this way there arises the idea of a twofold metaphysic—a *metaphysic of nature* and a *metaphysic of morals*. Physics will thus have an empirical and also a rational part. It is the same with ethics; but here the empirical part might have the special name of *practical anthropology*, the name *morality* being appropriated to the rational part.

All trades, arts, and handiworks have gained by division of labor, namely, when, instead of one man doing everything, each confines himself to a certain kind of work distinct from others in the treatment it requires, so as to be able to perform it with greater facility and in the greatest perfection. Where the different kinds of work are not so distinguished and divided, where everyone is a jack-of-all trades, there manufactures remain still in the greatest barbarism. It might deserve to be considered whether pure philosophy in all its parts does not require a man specially devoted to it, and whether it would not be better for the whole business of science if those who, to please the tastes of the public, are wont to blend the rational and empirical elements together, mixed in all sorts of proportions unknown to themselves, and who call themselves independent thinkers, giving the name of minute philosophers to those who apply themselves to the rational part only—if these, I say, were warned not to carry on two employments together which differ widely in the treatment they demand, for each of which perhaps a special talent is required, and the combination of which in one person only produces bunglers. But I only ask here whether the nature of science does not require that we should always carefully separate the empirical from the rational part, and prefix to physics proper (or empirical physics) a metaphysic of nature, and to practical anthropology a metaphysic of morals, which must be carefully cleared of everything empirical so that we may know how much can be accomplished by pure reason in both cases, and from what sources it draws this, its *a priori* teaching, and that whether the latter inquiry is conducted by all moralists (whose name is legion), or only by some who feel a calling thereto.

As my concern here is with moral philosophy, I limit the question suggested to this: whether it is not of the utmost necessity to construct a pure moral philosophy, perfectly cleared of everything which is only empirical, and which belongs to anthropology? For that such a philosophy must be possible is evident from the common idea of duty and of the moral laws. Everyone must admit that if a law is to have moral force, that is, to be the basis of an obligation, it must carry with it absolute necessity; that, for example, the precept, "Thou shalt not lie," is not valid for men alone, as if other rational beings had no need to observe it; and so with all the other moral laws properly so called; that, therefore, the basis of obligation must not be sought in the nature of man, or in the circumstances in the world in which he is placed, but *a priori* simply in the conceptions of pure reason; and although any other precept which is founded on principles of mere experience may be in certain respects universal, yet in as far as it rests even in the least degree on an empirical basis, perhaps only as to a motive, such a precept, while it may be a practical rule, can never be called a moral law.

Thus not only are moral laws with their principles essentially distinguished from every other kind of practical knowledge in which there is anything empirical, but all moral philosophy rests wholly on its pure part. When applied to man, it does not borrow the least thing from the knowledge of man himself (anthropology), but gives laws *a priori* to him as a rational being. No doubt these laws require a judgment sharpened by experience, in order, on the one hand, to distinguish in what cases they are applicable, and, on the other, to procure for them access to the will of the man, and effectual influence on conduct; since man is acted on by so many inclinations that, though capable of the idea of a practical pure reason, he is not so easily able to make it effective *in concreto* in his life.

A metaphysic of morals is therefore indispensably necessary, not merely for speculative reasons, in order to investigate the sources of the practical principles which are to be found *a priori* in our reason, but also because morals themselves are liable to all sorts of corruption as long as we are without that clue and supreme canon by which to estimate them correctly. For in order that an action should be morally good, it is not enough that it *conform* to the moral law, but it must also be done *for the sake of the law*, otherwise that conformity is only very contingent and uncertain; since a principle which is not moral, although it may now and then produce actions conformable to the law, will also often produce actions which contradict it. Now it is only in a pure philosophy that we can look for the moral law in its purity and genuineness (and, in a practical matter, this is of the utmost consequence): we must, therefore, begin with pure philosophy (metaphysic), and without it there cannot be any moral philosophy at all. That which mingles these pure principles with the empirical does not deserve the name of philosophy (for what distinguishes philosophy from common rational knowledge is that it treats in separate sciences what the latter only comprehends confusedly); much less does it deserve that of moral philosophy, since by this confusion it even spoils the purity of morals themselves and counteracts its own end.

Let it not be thought, however, that what is here demanded is already extant in the propaedeutic prefixed by the celebrated Wolf[2] to his moral philosophy, namely, his so-called *general practical philosophy,* and that, therefore, we have not to strike into an entirely new field. Just because it was to be a general practical philosophy, it has not taken into consideration a will of any particular kind—say, one which should be determined solely from *a priori* principles without any empirical motives, and which we might call a pure will—but volition in general, with all the actions and conditions which belong to it in this general signification. By this it is distinguished from a metaphysic of morals, just as general logic, which treats of the acts and canons of thought *in general,* is distinguished from transcendental philosophy, which treats of the particular acts and canons of *pure* thought, that is, that whose cognitions are altogether *a priori.* For the metaphysic of morals has to examine the idea and the principles of a possible *pure* will, and not the acts and conditions of human volition generally, which for the most part are drawn from psychology. It is true that moral laws and duty are spoken of in the general practical philosophy (contrary indeed to all fitness). But this is no objection, for in this respect also the authors of that science remain true to their idea of it; they do not distinguish the motives which are prescribed as such by reason alone altogether *a priori,* and which are properly moral, from the empirical motives which the understanding raises to general conceptions merely by comparison of experiences; but without noticing the difference of their sources, and looking on them all as homogeneous, they consider only their greater or less amount. It is in this way they frame their notion of *obligation,* which, though anything but moral, is all that can be asked for in a philosophy which passes no judgment at all on the origin of all possible practical concepts, whether they are *a priori* or only *a posteriori.*

Intending to publish hereafter a metaphysic of morals, I issue in the first instance these fundamental principles. Indeed there is properly no other foundation for it than the *critical examination of a pure practical reason;* just as that of metaphysics is the critical examination of the pure speculative reason, already published. But in the first place the former is not so absolutely necessary as the latter, because in moral concerns human reason can easily be brought to a high degree of correctness and completeness, even in the commonest understanding,

---

[2] Johann Christian Von Wolff (1679–1754) was the author of treatises on philosophy, mathematics, etc., which were for a long time the standard textbooks in the German universities. His philosophy was founded on that of Leibniz.

while on the contrary in its theoretic but pure use it is wholly dialectical; and in the second place, if the critique of a pure practical reason is to be complete, it must be possible at the same time to show its identity with the speculative reason in a common principle, for it can ultimately be only one and the same reason which has to be distinguished merely in its application. I could not, however, bring it to such completeness here without introducing considerations of a wholly different kind, which would be perplexing to the reader. On this account I have adopted the title of *Fundamental Principles of the Metaphysics of Morals* [*Grundlegung zur Metaphysik der Sitten*] instead of that of a *critical examination of the pure practical reason*.

But in the third place, since a metaphysic of morals, in spite of the discouraging title, is yet capable of being presented in a popular form, and one adapted to the common understanding, I find it useful to separate from it this preliminary treatise on its fundamental principles, in order that I may not hereafter have need to introduce these necessarily subtle discussions into a book of a more simple character.

The present treatise is, however, nothing more than the investigation and establishment of *the supreme principle of morality*, and this alone constitutes a study complete in itself, and one which ought to be kept apart from every other moral investigation. No doubt, my conclusions on this weighty question, which has hitherto been very unsatisfactorily examined, would receive much light from the application of the same principle to the whole system, and would be greatly confirmed by the adequacy which it exhibits throughout; but I must forego this advantage, which indeed would be after all more gratifying than useful, since the easy applicability of a principle and its apparent adequacy give no very certain proof of its soundness, but rather inspire a certain partiality, which prevents us from examining and estimating it strictly in itself, and without regard to consequences.

I have adopted in this work the method which I think most suitable, proceeding analytically from common knowledge to the determination of its ultimate principle, and again descending synthetically from the examination of this principle and its sources to the common knowledge in which we find it employed. The division will, therefore, be as follows:

1. *First section:* Transition from the common rational knowledge of morality to the philosophical.
2. *Second section:* Transition from popular moral philosophy to the metaphysic of morals.
3. *Third section:* Final step from the metaphysic of morals to the critique of the pure practical reason.

Fundamental Principles of the
Metaphysics of Morals

First Section
Transition from the Common Rational Knowledge of Morality to the Philosophical

Nothing can possibly be conceived in the world, or even out of it, which can be called good without qualification, except a *good will*. Intelligence, wit, judgment, and the other *talents* of the mind, however they may be named, or courage, resolution, perseverance, as qualities of temperament, are undoubtedly good and desirable in many respects; but these gifts of nature may also become extremely bad and mischievous if the will which is to make use of them, and which, therefore, constitutes what is called *character*, is not good. It is the same with the *gifts of fortune*. Power, riches, honor, even health, and the general well-being and contentment with one's condition which is called *happiness*, inspire pride, and often presumption, if there is not a good will to correct the influence of these on the mind, and with this also to rectify the whole principle of acting, and adapt it to its end. The sight of a being who is not adorned with a single feature of a pure and good will, enjoying unbroken prosperity, can never give pleasure to an impartial rational spectator. Thus a good will appears to constitute the indispensable condition even of being worthy of happiness.

There are even some qualities which are of service to this good will itself, and may facilitate its action, yet which have no intrinsic unconditional value, but always presuppose a good will, and this qualifies the esteem that we justly have for them, and does not permit us to regard them as absolutely good. Moderation in the affections and passions, self-control, and calm deliberation are not only good in many respects, but even seem to constitute part of the intrinsic worth of the person; but they are far from deserving to be called good without qualification, although they have been so unconditionally praised by the ancients. For without the principles of a good will, they may become extremely bad; and the coolness of a villain not only makes him far more dangerous, but also directly makes him more abominable in our eyes than he would have been without it.

A good will is good not because of what it performs or effects, not by its aptness for the attainment of some proposed end, but simply by virtue of the volition—that is, it is good in itself, and considered by itself is to be esteemed much higher than all that can be brought about by it in favor of any inclination, nay, even of the sum-total of all inclinations. Even if it should happen that, owing to special disfavor of fortune, or the niggardly provision of a step-motherly nature, this will should wholly lack power to accomplish its purpose, if with its greatest efforts it should yet achieve nothing, and there should remain only the good will (not, to be sure, a mere wish, but the summoning of all means in our power), then, like a jewel, it would still shine by its own light, as a thing which has its whole value in itself. Its usefulness or fruitlessness can neither add to nor take away anything from this value. It would be, as it were, only the setting to enable us to handle it the more conveniently in common commerce, or to attract to it the attention of those who are not yet connoisseurs, but not to recommend it to true connoisseurs, or to determine its value.

There is, however, something so strange in this idea of the absolute value of the mere will, in which no account is taken of its utility, that notwithstanding the thorough assent of even common reason to the idea, yet a suspicion must arise that it may perhaps really be the product of mere high-flown fancy, and that we may have misunderstood the purpose of nature in assigning reason as the governor of our will. Therefore we will examine this idea from this point of view.

In the physical constitution of an organized being, that is, a being adapted suitably to the purposes of life, we assume it as a fundamental principle that no organ for any purpose will be found but what is also the fittest and best adapted for that purpose. Now in a being which has reason and a will, if the proper object of nature were its *conservation*, its *welfare*, in a word, its *happiness,* then nature would have hit upon a very bad arrangement in selecting the reason of the creature to carry out this purpose. For all the actions which the creature has to perform with a view to this purpose, and the whole rule of its conduct, would be far more surely prescribed to it by instinct, and that end would have been attained thereby much more certainly than it ever can be by reason. Should reason have been communicated to this favored creature over and above, it must only have served it to contemplate the happy constitution of its nature, to admire it, to congratulate itself thereon, and to feel thankful for it to the beneficent cause, but not that it should subject its desires to that weak and delusive guidance, and meddle bunglingly with the purpose of nature. In a word, nature would have taken care that reason should not break forth into *practical exercise,* nor have the presumption, with its weak insight, to think out for itself the plan of happiness and of the means of attaining it. Nature would not only have taken on herself the choice of the ends but also of the means, and with wise foresight would have entrusted both to instinct.

And, in fact, we find that the more a cultivated reason applies itself with deliberate purpose to the enjoyment of life and happiness, so much the more does the man fail of true satisfaction. And from this circumstance there arises in many, if they are candid enough to confess it, a certain degree of *misology,* that is, hatred of reason, especially in the case of those who are most experienced in the use of it, because after calculating all the advantages they derive—I do not say from the invention of all the arts of common luxury, but even from the sciences (which seem to them to be after all only a luxury of the understanding)—they find that they have, in fact, only brought more trouble on their shoulders rather than gained in happiness; and they end by envying rather than despising the more common stamp of men who keep closer to the guidance of mere instinct, and do not allow their reason much influence on their conduct. And this we must admit, that the judgment of those who would very much lower the lofty eulogies of the advantages which reason gives us in regard to the happiness and satisfaction of life, or who would even reduce them below zero, is by no means morose or ungrateful to the goodness with which the world is governed, but that there lies at the root of these judgments the idea that our existence has a different and far nobler end, for which, and not for happiness, reason is properly intended, and which must, therefore, be regarded as the supreme condition to which the private ends of man must, for the most part, be postponed.

For as reason is not competent to guide the will with certainty in regard to its objects and the satisfaction of all our wants (which it to some extent even multiplies), this being an end to which an implanted instinct would have led with much greater certainty; and since, nevertheless, reason is imparted to us as a practical faculty, that is, as one which is to have influence on the *will,* therefore, admitting that nature generally in the distribution of her capacities has adapted the means to the end, its true destination must be to produce a *will,* not merely good as a *means* to something else, but *good in itself,* for which reason was absolutely necessary. This will then, though not indeed the sole and complete good, must be the supreme good and the condition of every other, even of the desire of happiness. Under these circumstances, there is nothing inconsistent with the wisdom of nature in the fact that the cultivation of the reason, which is requisite for the first and unconditional purpose, does in many ways interfere, at least in this life, with the attainment of the second, which is always conditional—namely, happiness. Nay, it may even reduce it to nothing, without nature thereby failing of her purpose. For reason recognizes the establishment of a good will as its highest practical destination, and in attaining this purpose is capable only of a satisfaction of its own proper kind, namely, that from the attainment of an end, which end again is determined by reason only, notwithstanding that this may involve many a disappointment to the ends of inclination.

We have then to develop the notion of a will which deserves to be highly esteemed for itself, and is good without a view to anything further, a notion which exists already in the sound natural understanding, requiring rather to be cleared up than to be taught, and which in estimating the value of our actions always takes the first place and constitutes the condition of all the rest. In order to do this, we will take the notion of duty, which includes that of a good will, although implying certain subjective restrictions and hindrances. These, however, far from concealing it or rendering it unrecognizable, rather bring it out by contrast and make it shine forth so much the brighter.

I omit here all actions which are already recognized as inconsistent with duty, although they may be useful for this or that purpose, for with these the question whether they are done *from duty* cannot arise at all, since they even conflict with it. I also set aside those actions which really conform to duty, but to which men have *no* direct *inclination,* performing them because they are impelled thereto by some other inclination. For in this case we can readily distinguish whether the action which agrees with duty is done *from duty* or from a selfish view. It is much harder to make this distinction when the action accords with duty, and the subject has besides a *direct* inclination to it. For example, it is always a matter of duty that a dealer should not overcharge an inexperienced purchaser; and wherever there is much commerce the prudent tradesman does not overcharge, but keeps a fixed price for everyone, so that a child buys of him as well as any other. Men are thus *honestly* served; but this is not enough to make us believe that the tradesman has so acted from duty and from principles of honesty; his own advantage required it; it is out of the question in this case to suppose that he might besides have a direct inclination in favor of the buyers, so that, as it were, from love he should give no advantage to one over another. Accordingly the action was done neither from duty nor from direct inclination, but merely with a selfish view.

On the other hand, it is a duty to maintain one's life; and, in addition, everyone has also a direct inclination to do so. But on this account the often anxious care which most men take for it has no intrinsic worth, and their maxim has no moral import. They preserve their life *as duty requires,* no doubt, but not *because duty requires.* On the other hand, if adversity and hopeless sorrow have completely taken away the relish for life, if the unfortunate one, strong in mind, indignant at his fate rather than desponding or dejected, wishes for death, and yet preserves his life without loving it—not from inclination or fear, but from duty—then his maxim has a moral worth.

To be beneficent when we can is a duty; and besides this, there are many minds so sympathetically constituted that, without any other motive of vanity or self-interest, they find a pleasure in spreading joy around them, and can take delight in the satisfaction of others so far as it is their own work. But I maintain that in such a case an action of this kind, however proper, however amiable it may be, has nevertheless no true moral worth, but is on a level with other inclinations, for example, the inclination to honor, which, if it is happily directed to that which is in fact of public utility and accordant with duty, and consequently honorable, deserves praise and encouragement, but not esteem. For the maxim lacks the moral import, namely, that such actions be done *from duty,* not from inclination. Put the case that the mind of that philanthropist was clouded by sorrow of his own, extinguishing all sympathy with the lot of others, and that while he still has the power to benefit others in distress, he is not touched by their trouble because he is absorbed with his own; and now suppose that he tears himself out of this dead insensibility and performs the action without any inclination to it, but simply from duty, then first has his action its genuine moral worth. Further still, if nature has put little sympathy in the heart of this or that man, if he, supposed to be an upright man, is by temperament cold and indifferent to the sufferings of others, perhaps because in respect of his own he is provided with the special gift of patience and fortitude, and supposes, or even requires, that others should have the same—and such a man would certainly not be the meanest product of nature—but if nature had not specially framed him for a philanthropist, would he not still find in himself a source from whence to give himself a far higher worth than that of a good-natured temperament could be? Unquestionably. It is just in this that the moral worth of the character is brought out which is incomparably the highest of all, namely, that he is beneficent, not from inclination, but from duty.

To secure one's own happiness is a duty, at least indirectly; for discontent with one's condition, under a pressure of many anxieties and amidst unsatisfied wants, might easily become a great *temptation to transgression of duty*. But here again, without looking to duty, all men have already the strongest and most intimate inclination to happiness, because it is just in this idea that all inclinations are combined in one total. But the precept of happiness is often of such a sort that it greatly interferes with some inclinations, and yet a man cannot form any definite and certain conception of the sum of satisfaction of all of them which is called happiness. It is not then to be wondered at that a single inclination, definite both as to what it promises and as to the time within which it can be gratified, is often able to overcome such a fluctuating idea, and that a gouty patient, for instance, can choose to enjoy what he likes, and to suffer what he may, since, according to his calculation, on this occasion at least, he has [only] not sacrificed the enjoyment of the present moment to a possibly mistaken expectation of a happiness which is supposed to be found in health. But even in this case, if the general desire for happiness did not influence his will, and supposing that in his particular case health was not a necessary element in this calculation, there yet remains in this, as in all other cases, this law—namely, that he should promote his happiness not from inclination but from duty, and by this would his conduct first acquire true moral worth.

It is in this manner, undoubtedly, that we are to understand those passages of Scripture also in which we are commanded to love our neighbor, even our enemy. For love, as an affection, cannot be commanded, but beneficence for duty's sake may, even though we are not impelled to it by any inclination—nay, are even repelled by a natural and unconquerable aversion. This is *practical* love, and not *pathological*—a love which is seated in the will, and not in the propensions of sense—in principles of action and not of tender sympathy; and it is this love alone which can be commanded.

The second[3] proposition is: That an action done from duty derives its moral worth, *not from the purpose* which is to be attained by it, but from the maxim by which it is determined, and therefore does not depend on the realization of the object of the action, but merely on the *principle of volition* by which the action has taken place, without regard to any object of desire. It is clear from what precedes that the purposes which we may have in view in our actions, or their effects regarded as ends and springs of the will, cannot give to actions any unconditional or moral worth. In what, then, can their worth lie if it is not to consist in the will and in reference to its expected effect? It cannot lie anywhere but in the *principle of the will* without regard to the ends which can be attained by the action. For the will stands between its *a priori* principle, which is formal, and its *a posteriori* spring, which is material, as between two roads, and as it must be determined by something, it follows that it must be determined by the formal principle of volition when an action is done from duty, in which case every material principle has been withdrawn from it.

The third proposition, which is a consequence of the two preceding, I would express thus: *Duty is the necessity of acting from respect for the law*. I may have *inclination* for an object as the effect of my proposed action, but I cannot have *respect* for it just for this reason that it is an effect and not an energy of will. Similarly, I cannot have respect for inclination, whether my own or another's; I can at most, if my own, approve it; if another's, sometimes even love it, that is, look on it as favorable to my own interest. It is only what is connected with my will as a principle, by no means as an effect—what does not subserve my inclination, but overpowers it, or at least in case of choice excludes it from its calculation—in other words, simply the law of itself, which can be an object of respect, and hence a command. Now an action done from duty must wholly exclude the influence of inclination, and with it every object of the will, so that nothing remains which can determine the will except objectively the *law,* and subjectively *pure respect* for this practical law, and consequently the maxim* that I

---

[3] The first proposition was that to have moral worth an action must be done from duty.

* A *maxim* is the subjective principle of volition. The objective principle (i.e. that which would also serve subjectively as a practical principle to all rational beings if reason had full power over the faculty of desire) is the practical *law*.

should follow this law even to the thwarting of all my inclinations.

Thus the moral worth of an action does not lie in the effect expected from it, nor in any principle of action which requires to borrow its motive from this expected effect. For all these effects—agreeableness of one's condition, and even the promotion of the happiness of others—could have been also brought about by other causes, so that for this there would have been no need of the will of a rational being; whereas it is in this alone that the supreme and unconditional good can be found. The pre-eminent good which we call moral can therefore consist in nothing else than *the conception of law* in itself, *which certainly is only possible in a rational being,* in so far as this conception, and not the expected effect, determines the will. This is a good which is already present in the person who acts accordingly, and we have not to wait for it to appear first in the result.*

But what sort of law can that be the conception of which must determine the will, even without paying any regard to the effect expected from it, in order that this will may be called good absolutely and without qualification? As I have deprived the will of every impulse which could arise to it from obedience to any law, there remains nothing but the universal conformity of its actions to law in general, which alone is to serve the will as a principle, that is, I am never to act otherwise than so *that*

---

* It might be here objected to me that I take refuge behind the word *respect* in an obscure feeling, instead of giving a distinct solution of the question by a concept of the reason. But although respect is a feeling, it is not a feeling *received* through influence, but is *self-wrought* by a rational concept, and, therefore, is specifically distinct from all feelings of the former kind, which may be referred either to inclination or fear. What I recognize immediately as a law for me, I recognize with respect. This merely signifies the consciousness that my will is *subordinate* to a law, without the intervention of other influences on my sense. The immediate determination of the will by the law, and the consciousness of this, is called *respect,* so that this is regarded as an *effect* of the law on the subject, and not as the *cause* of it. Respect is properly the conception of a worth which thwarts my self-love. Accordingly it is something which is considered neither as an object of inclination nor of fear, although it has something analogous to both. The *object* of respect is the *law* only, that is, the law which we impose on *ourselves,* and yet recognize as necessary in itself. As a law, we are subjected to it without consulting self-love; as imposed by us on ourselves, it is a result of our will. In the former aspect it has an analogy to fear, in the latter to inclination. Respect for a person is properly only respect for the law (of honesty, etc.) of which he gives us an example. Since we also look on the improvement of our talents as a duty, we consider that we see in a person of talents, as it were, the *example of a law* (viz. to become like him in this by exercise), and this constitutes our respect. All so-called moral *interest* consists simply in *respect* for the law.

I could also will that my maxim should become a universal law.
Here, now, it is the simple conformity to law in general, without assuming any particular law applicable to certain actions,
that serves the will as its principle, and must so serve it if duty
is not to be a vain delusion and a chimerical notion. The common reason of men in its practical judgments perfectly coincides with this, and always has in view the principle here
suggested. Let the question be, for example: May I when in
distress make a promise with the intention not to keep it? I
readily distinguish here between the two significations which
the question may have: whether it is prudent or whether it is
right to make a false promise? The former may undoubtedly
often be the case. I see clearly indeed that it is not enough to
extricate myself from a present difficulty by means of this subterfuge, but it must be well considered whether there may not
hereafter spring from this lie much greater inconvenience than
that from which I now free myself, and as, with all my supposed *cunning,* the consequences cannot be so easily foreseen
but that credit once lost may be much more injurious to me
than any mischief which I seek to avoid at present, it should be
considered whether it would not be more *prudent* to act herein
according to a universal maxim, and to make it a habit to
promise nothing except with the intention of keeping it. But it
is soon clear to me that such a maxim will still only be based
on the fear of consequences. Now it is a wholly different thing
to be truthful from duty, and to be so from apprehension of
injurious consequences. In the first case, the very notion of the
action already implies a law for me; in the second case, I must
first look about elsewhere to see what results may be combined
with it which would affect myself. For to deviate from the
principle of duty is beyond all doubt wicked; but to be unfaithful to my maxim of prudence may often be very advantageous
to me, although to abide by it is certainly safer. The shortest
way, however, and an unerring one, to discover the answer to
this question whether a lying promise is consistent with duty,
is to ask myself, Should I be content that my maxim (to extricate myself from difficulty by a false promise) should hold
good as a universal law, for myself as well as for others; and
should I be able to say to myself, "Every one may make a deceitful promise when he finds himself in a difficulty from which
he cannot otherwise extricate himself"? Then I presently become aware that, while I can will the lie, I can by no means will
that lying should be a universal law. For with such a law there
would be no promises at all, since it would be in vain to allege
my intention in regard to my future actions to those who
would not believe this allegation, or if they over-hastily did so,

would pay me back in my own coin. Hence my maxim, as soon as it should be made a universal law, would necessarily destroy itself.

I do not, therefore, need any far-reaching penetration to discern what I have to do in order that my will may be morally good. Inexperienced in the course of the world, incapable of being prepared for all its contingencies, I only ask myself: Canst thou also will that thy maxim should be a universal law? If not, then it must be rejected, and that not because of a disadvantage accruing from it to myself or even to others, but because it cannot enter as a principle into a possible universal legislation, and reason extorts from me immediate respect for such legislation. I do not indeed as yet *discern* on what this respect is based (this the philosopher may inquire), but at least I understand this—that it is an estimation of the worth which far outweighs all worth of what is recommended by inclination, and that the necessity of acting from *pure* respect for the practical law is what constitutes duty, to which every other motive must give place because it is the condition of a will being good *in itself,* and the worth of such a will is above everything.

Thus, then, without quitting the moral knowledge of common human reason, we have arrived at its principle. And although, no doubt, common men do not conceive it in such an abstract and universal form, yet they always have it really before their eyes and use it as the standard of their decision. Here it would be easy to show how, with this compass in hand, men are well able to distinguish, in every case that occurs, what is good, what bad, conformable to duty or inconsistent with it, if, without in the least teaching them anything new, we only, like Socrates, direct their attention to the principle they themselves employ; and that, therefore, we do not need science and philosophy to know what we should do to be honest and good, yea, even wise and virtuous. Indeed we might well have conjectured beforehand that the knowledge of what every man is bound to do, and therefore also to know, would be within the reach of every man, even the commonest. Here we cannot forbear admiration when we see how great an advantage the practical judgment has over the theoretical in the common understanding of men. In the latter, if common reason ventures to depart from the laws of experience and from the perceptions of the senses, it falls into mere inconceivabilities and self-contradictions, at least into a chaos of uncertainty, obscurity, and instability. But in the practical sphere it is just when the common understanding excludes all sensible springs from practical laws that its power of judgment begins to show itself to advantage. It then becomes even subtle, whether it be that it chicanes with its own conscience or with other claims respecting what is to be called right, or whether it desires for its own instruction to determine honestly the worth of actions; and, in the latter case, it may even have as good a hope of hitting the mark as any philosopher whatever can promise himself. Nay, it is almost more sure of doing so, because the philosopher cannot have any other principle, while he may easily perplex his judgment by a multitude of considerations foreign to the matter, and so turn aside from the right way. Would it not therefore be wiser in moral concerns to acquiesce in the judgment of common reason, or at most only to call in philosophy for the purpose of rendering the system of morals more complete and intelligible, and its rules more convenient for use (especially for disputation), but not so as to draw off the common understanding from its happy simplicity, or to bring it by means of philosophy into a new path of inquiry and instruction?

Innocence is indeed a glorious thing; only, on the other hand, it is very sad that it cannot well maintain itself, and is easily seduced. On this account even wisdom—which otherwise consists more in conduct than in knowledge—yet has need of science, not in order to learn from it, but to secure for its precepts admission and permanence. Against all the commands of duty which reason represents to man as so deserving of respect, he feels in himself a powerful counterpoise in his wants and inclinations, the entire satisfaction of which he sums up under the name of happiness. Now reason issues its commands unyieldingly, without promising anything to the inclinations, and, as it were, with disregard and contempt for these claims, which are so impetuous and at the same time so plausible, and which will not allow themselves to be suppressed by any command. Hence there arises a natural *dialectic*, that is, a disposition to argue against these strict laws of duty and to question their validity, or at least their purity and strictness; and, if possible, to make them more accordant with our wishes and inclinations, that is to say, to corrupt them at their very source and entirely to destroy their worth—a thing which even common practical reason cannot ultimately call good.

Thus is the *common reason of man* compelled to go out of its sphere and to take a step into the field of a *practical philosophy*, not to satisfy any speculative want (which never occurs to it as long as it is content to be mere sound reason), but even on practical grounds, in order to attain in it information and clear instruction respecting the source of its principle, and the correct determination of it in opposition to the maxims which are based on wants and inclinations, so that it may escape from the perplexity of opposite claims, and not run the risk of losing all genuine moral principles through the equivocation into which it easily falls. Thus, when practical reason cultivates itself, there insensibly arises in it a dialectic which forces it to seek aid in philosophy, just as happens to it in its theoretic use; and in this case, therefore, as well as in the other, it will find rest nowhere but in a thorough critical examination of our reason.

SECOND SECTION
TRANSITION FROM POPULAR MORAL PHILOSOPHY TO THE METAPHYSICS OF MORALS

If we have hitherto drawn our notion of duty from the common use of our practical reason, it is by no means to be inferred that we have treated it as an empirical notion. On the contrary, if we attend to the experience of men's conduct, we meet frequent and, as we ourselves allow, just complaints that one cannot find a single certain example of the disposition to act from pure duty. Although many things are done in *conformity* with what *duty* prescribes, it is nevertheless always doubtful whether they are done strictly *from duty,* so as to have a moral worth. Hence there have at all times been philosophers who have altogether denied that this disposition actually exists at all in human actions, and have ascribed everything to a more or less refined self-love. Not that they have on that account questioned the soundness of the conception of morality; on the contrary, they spoke with sincere regret of the frailty and corruption of human nature, which, though noble enough to take as its rule an idea so worthy of respect, is yet too weak to follow it; and employs reason, which ought to give it the law only for the purpose of providing for the interest of the inclinations, whether singly or at the best in the greatest possible harmony with one another.

In fact, it is absolutely impossible to make out by experience with complete certainty a single case in which the maxim of an action, however right in itself, rested simply on moral grounds and on the conception of duty. Sometimes it happens that with the sharpest self-examination we can find nothing beside the moral principle of duty which could have been powerful enough to move us to this or that action and to so great a sacrifice; yet we cannot from this infer with certainty that it was not really some secret impulse of self-love, under the false appearance of duty, that was the actual determining cause of the will. We like then to flatter ourselves by falsely taking credit for a more noble motive; whereas in fact we can never, even by the strictest examination, get completely behind the secret springs of action, since, when the question is of moral worth, it is not with the actions which we see that we are concerned, but with those inward principles of them which we do not see.

Moreover, we cannot better serve the wishes of those who ridicule all morality as a mere chimera of human imagination overstepping itself from vanity, than by conceding to them that notions of duty must be drawn only from experience (as from indolence, people are ready to think is also the case with all other notions); for this is to prepare for them a certain triumph. I am willing to admit out of love of humanity that even most of our actions are correct, but if we look closer at them we everywhere come upon the dear self which is always prominent, and it is this they have in view, and not the strict command of duty, which would often require self-denial. Without being an enemy of virtue, a cool observer, one that does not mistake the wish for good, however lively, for its reality, may sometimes doubt whether true virtue is actually found anywhere in the world, and this especially as years increase and the judgment is partly made wiser by experience, and partly also more acute in observation. This being so, nothing can secure us from falling away altogether from our ideas of duty, or maintain in the soul a well-grounded respect for its law, but the clear conviction that although there should never have been actions which really sprang from such pure sources, yet whether this or that takes place is not at all the question; but that reason of itself, independent on all experience, ordains what ought to take place, that accordingly actions of which perhaps the world has hitherto never given an example, the feasibility even of which might be very much doubted by one who founds everything on experience, are nevertheless inflexibly commanded by reason; that, for example, even though there might never yet have been a sincere friend, yet not a whit the less is pure sincerity in friendship required of every man, because, prior to all experience, this duty is involved as duty in the idea of a reason determining the will by *a priori* principles.

When we add further that, unless we deny that the notion of morality has any truth or reference to any possible object, we must admit that its law must be valid, not merely for men, but for all *rational creatures generally*, not merely under certain contingent conditions or with exceptions, but *with absolute necessity,* then it is clear that no experience could enable us to infer even the possibility of such apodictic laws. For with what right could we bring into unbounded respect as a universal precept for every rational nature that which perhaps holds only under the contingent conditions of humanity? Or how could laws of the determination of *our* will be regarded as laws of the determination of the will of rational beings generally, and for us only as such, if they were merely empirical and did not take their origin wholly *a priori* from pure but practical reason?

Nor could anything be more fatal to morality than that we should wish to derive it from examples. For every example of it that is set before me must be first itself tested by principles of morality, whether it is worthy to serve as an original example, that is, as a pattern, but by no means can it authoritatively furnish the conception of morality. Even the Holy One of the Gospels must first be compared with our ideal of moral perfection before we can recognize Him as such; and so He says of Himself, "Why call ye Me [whom you see] good; none is good [the model of good] but God only [whom ye do not see]?" But whence have we the conception of God as the supreme good? Simply from the *idea* of moral perfection, which reason frames *a priori* and connects inseparably with the notion of a free will. Imitation finds no place at all in morality, and examples serve only for encouragement, that is, they put beyond doubt the feasibility of what the law commands, they make visible that which the practical rule expresses more generally, but they can never authorize us to set aside the true original which lies in reason, and to guide ourselves by examples.

If then there is no genuine supreme principle of morality but what must rest simply on pure reason, independent on all experience, I think it is not necessary even to put the question whether it is good to exhibit these concepts in their generality (*in abstracto*) as they are established *a priori* along with the principles belonging to them, if our knowledge is to be distinguished from the *vulgar* and to be called philosophical. In our times indeed this might perhaps be necessary; for if we collected votes, whether pure rational knowledge separated from everything empirical, that is to say, metaphysic of morals, or whether popular practical philosophy is to be preferred, it is easy to guess which side would preponderate.

This descending to popular notions is certainly very commendable if the ascent to the principles of pure reason has first taken place and been satisfactorily accomplished. This implies that we first *found* Ethics on Metaphysics, and then, when it is firmly established, procure a *hearing* for it by giving it a popular character. But it is quite absurd to try to be popular in the first inquiry, on which the soundness of the principles depends. It is not only that this proceeding can never lay claim to the very rare merit of a true *philosophical popularity,* since there is no art in being intelligible if one renounces all thoroughness of insight; but also it produces a disgusting medley of compiled observations and half-reasoned principles. Shallow pates enjoy this because it can be used for everyday chat, but the sagacious find in it only confusion, and being unsatisfied and unable to help themselves, they turn away their eyes, while philosophers, who see quite well through this delusion, are little listened to when they call men off for a time from this pretended popularity in order that they might be rightfully popular after they have attained a definite insight.

We need only look at the attempts of moralists in that favorite fashion, and we shall find at one time the special constitution of human nature (including, however, the idea of a rational nature generally), at one time perfection, at another happiness, here moral sense, there fear of God, a little of this and a little of that, in marvellous mixture, without its occurring to them to ask whether the principles of morality are to be sought in the knowledge of human nature at all (which we can have only from experience); and, if this is not so—if these principles are to be found altogether *a priori* free from everything empirical, in pure rational concepts only, and nowhere else, not even in the smallest degree—then rather to adopt the method of making this a separate inquiry, as pure practical philosophy, or (if one may use a name so decried) as metaphysic of morals,* to bring it by itself to completeness, and to require the public, which wishes for popular treatment, to await the issue of this undertaking.

Such a metaphysic of morals, completely isolated, not mixed with any anthropology, theology, physics, or hyperphysics, and still less with occult qualities (which we might call hypophysical), is not only an indispensable substratum of all sound theoretical knowledge of duties, but is at the same time a desideratum of the highest importance to the actual fulfillment of their precepts. For the pure conception of duty, unmixed with any foreign addition of empirical attractions, and, in a

---

* Just as pure mathematics are distinguished from applied, pure logic from applied, so if we choose we may also distinguish pure philosophy of morals (metaphysic) from applied (viz., applied to human nature). By this designation we are also at once reminded that moral principles are not based on properties of human nature, but must subsist *a priori* of themselves, while from such principles practical rules must be capable of being deduced for every rational nature, and accordingly for that of man.

word, the conception of the moral law, exercises on the human heart, by way of reason alone (which first becomes aware with this that it can of itself be practical), an influence so much more powerful than all other springs* which may be derived from the field of experience that in the consciousness of its worth it despises the latter, and can by degrees become their master; whereas a mixed ethics, compounded partly of motives drawn from feelings and inclinations, and partly also of conceptions of reason, must make the mind waver between motives which cannot be brought under any principle, which lead to good only by mere accident, and very often also to evil.

From what has been said, it is clear that all moral conceptions have their seat and origin completely *a priori* in the reason, and that, moreover, in the commonest reason just as truly as in that which is in the highest degree speculative; that they cannot be obtained by abstraction from any empirical, and therefore merely contingent, knowledge; that it is just this purity of their origin that makes them worthy to serve as our supreme practical principle, and that just in proportion as we add anything empirical, we detract from their genuine influence and from the absolute value of actions; that it is not only of the greatest necessity, in a purely speculative point of view, but is also of the greatest practical importance, to derive these notions and laws from pure reason, to present them pure and unmixed, and even to determine the compass of this practical or pure rational knowledge, that is, to determine the whole faculty of pure practical reason; and, in doing so, we must not make its principles dependent on the particular nature of human reason, though in speculative philosophy this may be permitted, or may even at times be necessary; but since moral laws ought to hold good for every rational creature, we must derive them from the general concept of a rational being. In this way, although

* I have a letter from the late excellent Sulzer, in which he asks me what can be the reason that moral instruction, although containing much that is convincing for the reason, yet accomplishes so little? My answer was postponed in order that I might make it complete. But it is simply this, that the teachers themselves have not got their own notions clear, and when they endeavor to make up for this by raking up motives of moral goodness from every quarter, trying to make their physic right strong, they spoil it. For the commonest understanding shows that if we imagine, on the one hand, an act of honesty done with steadfast mind, apart from every view to advantage of any kind in this world or another, and even under the greatest temptations of necessity or allurement, and, on the other hand, a similar act which was affected, in however low a degree, by a foreign motive, the former leaves far behind and eclipses the second; it elevates the soul, and inspires the wish to be able to act in like manner oneself. Even moderately young children feel this impression, and one should never represent duties to them in any other light.

for its *application* to man morality has need of anthropology, yet, in the first instance, we must treat it independently as pure philosophy, that is, as metaphysic, complete in itself (a thing which in such distinct branches of science is easily done); knowing well that, unless we are in possession of this, it would not only be vain to determine the moral element of duty in right actions for purposes of speculative criticism, but it would be impossible to base morals on their genuine principles, even for common practical purposes, especially of moral instruction, so as to produce pure moral dispositions, and to engraft them on men's minds to the promotion of the greatest possible good in the world.

But in order that in this study we may not merely advance by the natural steps from the common moral judgment (in this case very worthy of respect) to the philosophical, as has been already done, but also from a popular philosophy, which goes no further than it can reach by groping with the help of examples, to metaphysic (which does not allow itself to be checked by anything empirical and, as it must measure the whole extent of this kind of rational knowledge, goes as far as ideal conceptions, where even examples fail us), we must follow and clearly describe the practical faculty of reason, from the general rules of its determination to the point where the notion of duty springs from it.

Everything in nature works according to laws. Rational beings alone have the faculty of acting according *to the conception* of laws—that is, according to principles, that is, have a *will*. Since the deduction of actions from principles requires *reason*, the will is nothing but practical reason. If reason infallibly determines the will, then the actions of such a being which are recognized as objectively necessary are subjectively necessary also, that is, the will is a faculty to choose *that only* which reason independent on inclination recognizes as practically necessary, that is, as good. But if reason of itself does not sufficiently determine the will, if the latter is subject also to subjective conditions (particular impulses) which do not always coincide with the objective conditions, in a word, if the will does not *in itself* completely accord with reason (which is actually the case with men), then the actions which objectively are recognized as necessary are subjectively contingent, and the determination of such a will according to objective laws is *obligation*, that is to say, the relation of the objective laws to a will that is not thoroughly good is conceived as the determination of the will of a rational being by principles of reason, but which the will from its nature does not of necessity follow.

The conception of an objective principle, in so far as it is obligatory for a will, is called a command (of reason), and the formula of the command is called an Imperative.

All imperatives are expressed by the word *ought* [or *shall*], and thereby indicate the relation of an objective law of reason to a will which from its subjective constitution is not necessarily determined by it (an obligation). They say that something would be good to do or to forbear, but they say it to a will which does not always do a thing because it is conceived to be good to do it. That is practically *good*, however, which determines the will by means of the conceptions of reason, and consequently not from subjective causes, but objectively, that is, on principles which are valid for every rational being as such. It is distinguished from the *pleasant* as that which influences the will only by means of sensation from merely subjective causes, valid only for the sense of this or that one, and not as a principle of reason which holds for every one.*

A perfectly good will would therefore be equally subject to objective laws (viz., laws of good), but could not be conceived as *obliged* thereby to act lawfully, because of itself from its subjective constitution it can only be determined by the conception of good. Therefore no imperatives hold for the Divine will, or in general for a *holy* will; *ought* is here out of place because the volition is already of itself necessarily in unison with the law. Therefore imperatives are only formulae to express the relation of objective laws of all volition to the subjective imperfection of the will of this or that rational being, for example, the human will.

Now all *imperatives* command either *hypothetically* or *categorically*. The former represent the practical necessity of a possible action as means to something else that is willed (or at least which one might possibly will). The categorical imperative would be that which represented an action as necessary

---

* The dependence of the desires on sensations is called inclination, and this accordingly always indicates a *want*. The dependence of a contingently determinable will on principles of reason is called an *interest*. This, therefore, is found only in the case of a dependent will which does not always of itself conform to reason; in the Divine will we cannot conceive any interest. But the human will can also *take an interest* in a thing without therefore acting *from interest*. The former signifies the *practical* interest in the action, the latter the *pathological* in the object of the action. The former indicates only dependence of the will on principles of reason in themselves; the second, dependence on principles of reason for the sake of inclination, reason supplying only the practical rules how the requirement of the inclination may be satisfied. In the first case the action interests me; in the second the object of the action (because it is pleasant to me). We have seen in the first section that in an action done from duty we must look not to the interest in the object, but only to that in the action itself, and in its rational principle (viz., the law).

of itself without reference to another end, that is, as objectively necessary.

Since every practical law represents a possible action as good, and on this account, for a subject who is practically determinable by reason as necessary, all imperatives are formulae determining an action which is necessary according to the principle of a will good in some respects. If now the action is good only as a means *to something else,* then the imperative is *hypothetical;* if it is conceived as good *in itself* and consequently as being necessarily the principle of a will which of itself conforms to reason, then it is *categorical.*

Thus the imperative declares what action possible by me would be good, and presents the practical rule in relation to a will which does not forthwith perform an action simply because it is good, whether because the subject does not always know that it is good, or because, even if it know this, yet its maxims might be opposed to the objective principles of practical reason.

Accordingly the hypothetical imperative only says that the action is good for some purpose, *possible* or *actual.* In the first case it is a *problematical,* in the second an *assertorial* practical principle. The categorical imperative which declares an action to be objectively necessary in itself without reference to any purpose, that is, without any other end, is valid as an *apodictic* (practical) principle.

Whatever is possible only by the power of some rational being may also be conceived as a possible purpose of some will; and therefore the principles of action as regards the means necessary to attain some possible purpose are in fact infinitely numerous. All sciences have a practical part consisting of problems expressing that some end is possible for us, and of imperatives directing how it may be attained. These may, therefore, be called in general imperatives of *skill.* Here there is no question whether the end is rational and good, but only what one must do in order to attain it. The precepts for the physician to make his patient thoroughly healthy, and for a poisoner to ensure certain death, are of equal value in this respect, that each serves to effect its purpose perfectly. Since in early youth it cannot be known what ends are likely to occur to us in the course of life, parents seek to have their children taught a *great many things,* and provide for their *skill* in the use of means for all sorts of arbitrary ends, of none of which can they determine whether it may not perhaps hereafter be an object to their pupil, but which it is at all events *possible* that he might aim at; and this anxiety is so great that they commonly neglect to form and correct their judgment on the value of the things which may be chosen as ends.

There is *one* end, however, which may be assumed to be actually such to all rational beings (so far as imperatives apply to them, viz., as dependent beings), and, therefore, one purpose which they not merely *may* have, but which we may with certainty assume that they all actually *have* by a natural necessity, and this is *happiness.* The hypothetical imperative which expresses the practical necessity of an action as means to the advancement of happiness is *assertorial.* We are not to present it as necessary for an uncertain and merely possible purpose, but for a purpose which we may presuppose with certainty and *a priori* in every man, because it belongs to his being. Now skill in the choice of means to his own greatest well-being may be called *prudence,** in the narrowest sense. And thus the imperative which refers to the choice of means to one's own happiness, that is, the precept of prudence, is still always *hypothetical;* the action is not commanded absolutely, but only as means to another purpose.

Finally, there is an imperative which commands a certain conduct immediately, without having as its condition any other purpose to be attained by it. This imperative is *categorical.* It concerns not the matter of the action, or its intended result, but its form and the principle of which it is itself a result; and what is essentially good in it consists in the mental disposition, let the consequence be what it may. This imperative may be called that of *morality.*

There is a marked distinction also between the volitions on these three sorts of principles in the *dissimilarity* of the obligation of the will. In order to mark this difference more clearly, I think they would be most suitably named in their order if we said they are either *rules* of skill, or *counsels* of prudence, or *commands* (*laws*) of morality. For it is *law* only that involves the conception of an *unconditional* and objective necessity, which is consequently universally valid; and commands are laws which must be obeyed, that is, must be followed, even in

---

* The word *prudence* is taken in two senses: in the one it may bear the name of knowledge of the world, in the other that of private prudence. The former is a man's ability to influence others so as to use them for his own purposes. The latter is the sagacity to combine all these purposes for his own lasting benefit. This latter is properly that to which the value even of the former is reduced, and when a man is prudent in the former sense, but not in the latter, we might better say of him that he is clever and cunning, but, on the whole, imprudent. [Compare the difference between *klug* and *gescheut* here alluded to, Kant's *Anthropologie,* § 45.

opposition to inclination. *Counsels,* indeed, involve necessity, but one which can only hold under a contingent subjective condition, viz., they depend on whether this or that man reckons this or that as part of his happiness; the categorical imperative, on the contrary, is not limited by any condition, and as being absolutely, although practically, necessary may be quite properly called a command. We might also call the first kind of imperatives *technical* (belonging to art), the second *pragmatic** (belonging to welfare), the third *moral* (belonging to free conduct generally, that is, to morals).

Now arises the question, how are all these imperatives possible? This question does not seek to know how we can conceive the accomplishment of the action which the imperative ordains, but merely how we can conceive the obligation of the will which the imperative expresses. No special explanation is needed to show how an imperative of skill is possible. Whoever wills the end wills also (so far as reason decides his conduct) the means in his power which are indispensably necessary thereto. This proposition is, as regards the volition, analytical; for in willing an object as my effect there is already thought the causality of myself as an acting cause, that is to say, the use of the means; and the imperative educes from the conception of volition of an end the conception of actions necessary to this end. Synthetical propositions must no doubt be employed in defining the means to a proposed end; but they do not concern the principle, the act of the will, but the object and its realization. For example, that in order to bisect a line on an unerring principle I must draw from its extremities two intersecting arcs; this no doubt is taught by mathematics only in synthetical propositions; but if I know that it is only by this process that the intended operation can be performed, then to say that if I fully will the operation, I also will the action required for it, is an analytical proposition; for it is one and the same thing to conceive something as an effect which I can produce in a certain way, and to conceive myself as acting in this way.

If it were only equally easy to give a definite conception of happiness, the imperatives of prudence would correspond

---

* It seems to me that the proper significance of the word *pragmatic* may be most accurately defined in this way. For *sanctions* are called pragmatic which flow properly, not from the law of the states as necessary enactments, but from *precaution* for the general welfare. A history is composed pragmatically when it teaches *prudence,* that is, instructs the world how it can provide for its interests better, or at least as well as the men of former time.

exactly with those of skill, and would likewise be analytical. For in this case as in that, it could be said whoever wills the end wills also (according to the dictate of reason necessarily) the indispensable means thereto which are in his power. But, unfortunately, the notion of happiness is so indefinite that although every man wishes to attain it, yet he never can say definitely and consistently what it is that he really wishes and wills. The reason of this is that all the elements which belong to the notion of happiness are altogether empirical, that is, they must be borrowed from experience, and nevertheless the idea of happiness requires an absolute whole, a maximum of welfare in my present and all future circumstances. Now it is impossible that the most clear-sighted and at the same time most powerful being (supposed finite) should frame to himself a definite conception of what he really wills in this. Does he will riches, how much anxiety, envy, and snares might he not thereby draw upon his shoulders? Does he will knowledge and discernment, perhaps it might prove to be only an eye so much the sharper to show him so much the more fearfully the evils that are now concealed from him and that cannot be avoided, or to impose more wants on his desires, which already give him concern enough. Would he have long life? Who guarantees to him that it would not be a long misery? Would he at least have health? How often has uneasiness of the body restrained from excesses into which perfect health would have allowed one to fall, and so on? In short, he is unable, on any principle, to determine with certainty what would make him truly happy; because to do so he would need to be omniscient. We cannot therefore act on any definite principles to secure happiness, but only on empirical counsels, for example, of regimen, frugality, courtesy, reserve, etc., which experience teaches do, on the average, most promote well-being. Hence it follows that the imperatives of prudence do not, strictly speaking, command at all, that is, they cannot present actions objectively as practically *necessary;* that they are rather to be regarded as counsels (*consilia*) than precepts (*praecepta*) of reason, that the problem to determine certainly and universally what action would promote the happiness of a rational being is completely insoluble, and consequently no imperative respecting it is possible which should, in the strict sense, command to do what makes happy; because happiness is not an ideal of reason but of imagination, resting solely on empirical grounds, and it is vain to expect that these should define an action by which one could attain the totality of a series of consequences which is really endless. This imperative of prudence would, however, be an analytical proposition if we assume that the means to happiness could be certainly assigned; for it is distinguished from the imperative of skill only by this that in the latter the end is merely *possible*, in the former it is *given;* as, however, both only ordain the means to that which we suppose to be willed as an end, it follows that the imperative which ordains the willing of the means to him who wills the end is in both cases analytical. Thus there is no difficulty in regard to the possibility of an imperative of this kind either.

On the other hand, the question, how the imperative of *morality* is possible, is undoubtedly one, the only one, demanding a solution, as this is not at all hypothetical, and the objective necessity which it presents cannot rest on any hypothesis, as is the case with the hypothetical imperatives. Only here we must never leave out of consideration that we *cannot* make out *by any example,* in other words, empirically, whether there is such an imperative at all; but it is rather to be feared that all those which seem to be categorical may yet be at bottom hypothetical. For instance, when the precept is: Thou shalt not promise deceitfully; and it is assumed that the necessity of this is not a mere counsel to avoid some other evil, so that it should mean: Thou shalt not make a lying promise, lest if it become known thou shouldst destroy thy credit, but that an action of this kind must be regarded as evil in itself, so that the imperative of the prohibition is categorical; then we cannot show with certainty in any example that the will was determined merely by the law, without any other spring of action, although it may appear to be so. For it is always possible that fear of disgrace, perhaps also obscure dread of other dangers, may have a secret influence on the will. Who can prove by experience the non-existence of a cause when all that experience tells us is that we do not perceive it? But in such a case the so-called moral imperative, which as such appears to be categorical and unconditional, would in reality be only a pragmatic precept, drawing our attention to our own interests, and merely teaching us to take these into consideration.

We shall therefore have to investigate *a priori* the possibility of a categorical imperative, as we have not in this case the advantage of its reality being given in experience, so that [the elucidation of] its possibility should be requisite only for its explanation, not for its establishment. In the meantime it may be discerned beforehand that the categorical imperative alone has the purport of a practical law; all the rest may indeed be called *principles* of the will but not laws, since whatever is only necessary for the attainment of some arbitrary purpose may be considered as in itself contingent, and we can at any time be free from the precept if we give up the purpose; on the contrary, the unconditional command leaves the will no liberty to choose the opposite, consequently it alone carries with it that necessity which we require in a law.

Secondly, in the case of this categorical imperative or law of morality, the difficulty (of discerning its possibility) is a very profound one. It is an *a priori* synthetical practical proposition;* and as there is so much difficulty in discerning the possibility of speculative propositions of this kind, it may readily be supposed that the difficulty will be no less with the practical.

In this problem we will first inquire whether the mere conception of a categorical imperative may not perhaps supply us also with the formula of it, containing the proposition which alone can be a categorical imperative; for even if we know the tenor of such an absolute command, yet how it is possible will require further special and laborious study, which we postpone to the last section.

When I conceive a hypothetical imperative, in general I do not know beforehand what it will contain until I am given the condition. But when I conceive a categorical imperative, I know at once what it contains. For as the imperative contains besides the law only the necessity that the maxims† shall conform to this law, while the law contains no conditions restricting it, there remains nothing but the general statement that the maxim of the action should conform to a universal law, and it is this conformity alone that the imperative properly represents as necessary.[4]

---

* I connect the act with the will without presupposing any condition resulting from any inclination, but *a priori*, and therefore necessarily (though only objectively, that is, assuming the idea of a reason possessing full power over all subjective motives). This is accordingly a practical proposition which does not deduce the willing of an action by mere analysis from another already presupposed (for we have not such a perfect will), but connects it immediately with the conception of the will of a rational being, as something not contained in it.

† A "maxim" is a subjective principle of action, and must be distinguished from the *objective principle*, namely, practical law. The former contains the practical rule set by reason according to the conditions of the subject (often its ignorance or its inclinations), so that it is the principle on which the subject *acts;* but the law is the objective principle valid for every rational being, and is the principle on which it *ought to act*—that is an imperative.

[4] I have no doubt that "den" in the original before "Imperativ" is a misprint for "der," and have translated accordingly. Mr. Semple has done the same. The editions that I have seen agree in reading "den," and Mr. Barni so translates. With this reading, it is the conformity that presents the imperative as necessary.

There is therefore but one categorical imperative, namely, this: *Act only on that maxim whereby thou canst at the same time will that it should become a universal law.*

Now if all imperatives of duty can be deduced from this one imperative as from their principle, then, although it should remain undecided whether what is called duty is not merely a vain notion, yet at least we shall be able to show what we understand by it and what this notion means.

Since the universality of the law according to which effects are produced constitutes what is properly called *nature* in the most general sense (as to form)—that is, the existence of things so far as it is determined by general laws—the imperative of duty may be expressed thus: *Act as if the maxim of thy action were to become by thy will a universal law of nature.*

We will now enumerate a few duties, adopting the usual division of them into duties to ourselves and to others, and into perfect and imperfect duties.*

1. A man reduced to despair by a series of misfortunes feels wearied of life, but is still so far in possession of his reason that he can ask himself whether it would not be contrary to his duty to himself to take his own life. Now he inquires whether the maxim of his action could become a universal law of nature. His maxim is: From self-love I adopt it as a principle to shorten my life when its longer duration is likely to bring more evil than satisfaction. It is asked then simply whether this principle founded on self-love can become a universal law of nature. Now we see at once that a system of nature of which it should be a law to destroy life by means of the very feeling whose special nature it is to impel to the improvement of life would contradict itself, and therefore could not exist as a system of nature; hence that maxim cannot possibly exist as a universal law of nature, and consequently would be wholly inconsistent with the supreme principle of all duty.[5]

2. Another finds himself forced by necessity to borrow money. He knows that he will not be able to repay it, but sees

---

* It must be noted here that I reserve the division of duties for a future *metaphysic of morals;* so that I give it here only as an arbitrary one (in order to arrange my examples). For the rest, I understand by a perfect duty one that admits no exception in favor of inclination, and then I have not merely external but also internal perfect duties. This is contrary to the use of the word adopted in the schools; but I do not intend to justify it here, as it is all one for my purpose whether it is admitted or not. [*Perfect* duties are usually understood to be those which can be enforced by external law; *imperfect*, those which cannot be enforced. They are also called respectively *determinate* and *indeterminate*, *officia juris* and *officia virtutis*.]

[5] On suicide cf. further *Metaphysik der Sitten.*

also that nothing will be lent to him unless he promises stoutly to repay it in a definite time. He desires to make this promise, but he has still so much conscience as to ask himself: Is it not unlawful and inconsistent with duty to get out of a difficulty in this way? Suppose, however, that he resolves to do so, then the maxim of his action would be expressed thus: When I think myself in want of money, I will borrow money and promise to repay it, although I know that I never can do so. Now this principle of self-love or of one's own advantage may perhaps be consistent with my whole future welfare; but the question now is, Is it right? I change then the suggestion of self-love into a universal law, and state the question thus: How would it be if my maxim were a universal law? Then I see at once that it could never hold as a universal law of nature, but would necessarily contradict itself. For supposing it to be a universal law that everyone when he thinks himself in a difficulty should be able to promise whatever he pleases, with the purpose of not keeping his promise, the promise itself would become impossible, as well as the end that one might have in view in it, since no one would consider that anything was promised to him, but would ridicule all such statements as vain pretenses.

3. A third finds in himself a talent which with the help of some culture might make him a useful man in many respects. But he finds himself in comfortable circumstances and prefers to indulge in pleasure rather than to take pains in enlarging and improving his happy natural capacities. He asks, however, whether his maxim of neglect of his natural gifts, besides agreeing with his inclination to indulgence, agrees also with what is called duty. He sees then that a system of nature could indeed subsist with such a universal law, although men (like the South Sea islanders) should let their talents rest and resolve to devote their lives merely to idleness, amusement, and propagation of their species—in a word, to enjoyment; but he cannot possibly *will* that this should be a universal law of nature, or be implanted in us as such by a natural instinct. For, as a rational being, he necessarily wills that his faculties be developed, since they serve him, and have been given him, for all sorts of possible purposes.

4. A fourth, who is in prosperity, while he sees that others have to contend with great wretchedness and that he could help them, thinks: What concern is it of mine? Let everyone be as happy as Heaven pleases, or as he can make himself; I will take nothing from him nor even envy him, only I do not wish to contribute anything to his welfare or to his assistance in distress! Now no doubt, if such a mode of thinking were a

universal law, the human race might very well subsist, and doubtless even better than in a state in which everyone talks of sympathy and good-will, or even takes care occasionally to put it into practice, but, on the other side, also cheats when he can, betrays the rights of men, or otherwise violates them. But although it is possible that a universal law of nature might exist in accordance with that maxim, it is impossible to *will* that such a principle should have the universal validity of a law of nature. For a will which resolved this would contradict itself, inasmuch as many cases might occur in which one would have need of the love and sympathy of others, and in which, by such a law of nature, sprung from his own will, he would deprive himself of all hope of the aid he desires.

These are a few of the many actual duties, or at least what we regard as such, which obviously fall into two classes on the one principle that we have laid down. We must be *able to will* that a maxim of our action should be a universal law. This is the canon of the moral appreciation of the action generally. Some actions are of such a character that their maxim cannot without contradiction be even *conceived* as a universal law of nature, far from it being possible that we should *will* that it *should* be so. In others, this intrinsic impossibility is not found, but still it is impossible to *will* that their maxim should be raised to the universality of a law of nature, since such a will would contradict itself. It is easily seen that the former violate strict or rigorous (inflexible) duty; the latter only laxer (meritorious) duty. Thus it has been completely shown by these examples how all duties depend as regards the nature of the obligation (not the object of the action) on the same principle.

If now we attend to ourselves on occasion of any transgression of duty, we shall find that we in fact do not will that our maxim should be a universal law, for that is impossible for us; on the contrary, we will that the opposite should remain a universal law, only we assume the liberty of making an *exception* in our own favor or (just for this time only) in favor of our inclination. Consequently, if we considered all cases from one and the same point of view, namely, that of reason, we should find a contradiction in our own will, namely, that a certain principle should be objectively necessary as a universal law, and yet subjectively should not be universal, but admit of exceptions. As, however, we at one moment regard our action from the point of view of a will wholly conformed to reason, and then again look at the same action from the point of view of a will affected by inclination, there is not really any contradiction, but an antagonism of inclination to the precept of reason, whereby the universality of the principle is changed into a mere generality, so that the practical principle of reason shall meet the maxim half way. Now, although this cannot be justified in our own impartial judgment, yet it proves that we do really recognize the validity of the categorical imperative and (with all respect for it) only allow ourselves a few exceptions which we think unimportant and forced from us.

We have thus established at least this much—that if duty is a conception which is to have any import and real legislative authority for our actions, it can only be expressed in categorical, and not at all in hypothetical, imperatives. We have also, which is of great importance, exhibited clearly and definitely for every practical application the content of the categorical imperative, which must contain the principle of all duty if there is such a thing at all. We have not yet, however, advanced so far as to prove *a priori* that there actually is such an imperative, that there is a practical law which commands absolutely of itself and without any other impulse, and that the following of this law is duty.

With the view of attaining to this it is of extreme importance to remember that we must not allow ourselves to think of deducing the reality of this principle from the *particular attributes of human nature.* For duty is to be a practical, unconditional necessity of action; it must therefore hold for all rational beings (to whom an imperative can apply at all), and *for this reason only* be also a law for all human wills. On the contrary, whatever is deduced from the particular natural characteristics of humanity, from certain feelings and propensions,[6] nay, even, if possible, from any particular tendency proper to human reason, and which need not necessarily hold for the will of every rational being—this may indeed supply us with a maxim but not with a law; with a subjective principle on which we may have a propension and inclination to act, but not with an objective principle on which we should be *enjoined* to act, even though all our propensions, inclinations, and natural dispositions were opposed to it. In fact, the sublimity and intrinsic dignity of the command in duty are so much the more evident, the less the subjective impulses favor it and the more they

[6] Kant distinguishes "Hang (*propensio*)" from "Neigung (*inclinatio*)" as follows: "Hang" is a predisposition to the desire of some enjoyment; in other words, it is the subjective possibility of excitement of a certain desire which precedes the conception of its object. When the enjoyment has been experienced, it produces a "Neigung" (inclination) to it, which accordingly is defined "habitual sensible desire."—*Anthropologie*, §§ 72, 79.

oppose it, without being able in the slightest degree to weaken the obligation of the law or to diminish its validity.

Here then we see philosophy brought to a critical position, since it has to be firmly fixed, notwithstanding that it has nothing to support it in heaven or earth. Here it must show its purity as absolute director of its own laws, not the herald of those which are whispered to it by an implanted sense or who knows what tutelary nature. Although these may be better than nothing, yet they can never afford principles dictated by reason, which must have their source wholly *a priori* and thence their commanding authority, expecting everything from the supremacy of the law and the due respect for it, nothing from inclination, or else condemning the man to self-contempt and inward abhorrence.

Thus every empirical element is not only quite incapable of being an aid to the principle of morality, but is even highly prejudicial to the purity of morals; for the proper and inestimable worth of an absolutely good will consists just in this that the principle of action is free from all influence of contingent grounds, which alone experience can furnish. We cannot too much or too often repeat our warning against this lax and even mean habit of thought which seeks for its principle among empirical motives and laws; for human reason in its weariness is glad to rest on this pillow, and in a dream of sweet illusions (in which, instead of Juno, it embraces a cloud) it substitutes for morality a bastard patched up from limbs of various derivation, which looks like anything one chooses to see in it; only not like virtue to one who has once beheld her in her true form.*

The question then is this: Is it a necessary law *for all rational beings* that they should always judge of their actions by maxims of which they can themselves will that they should serve as universal laws? If it is so, then it must be connected (altogether *a priori*) with the very conception of the will of a rational being generally. But in order to discover this connection we must, however reluctantly, take a step into metaphysic, although into a domain of it which is distinct from speculative philosophy—namely, the metaphysic of morals. In a practical philosophy, where it is not the reasons of what *happens* that we have to ascertain, but the laws of what *ought to happen*,

* To behold virtue in her proper form is nothing else but to contemplate morality stripped of all admixture of sensible things and of every spurious ornament of reward or self-love. How much she then eclipses everything else that appears charming to the affections, everyone may readily perceive with the least exertion of his reason, if it be not wholly spoiled for abstraction.

even although it never does, that is, objective practical laws, there it is not necessary to inquire into the reasons why anything pleases or displeases, how the pleasure of mere sensation differs from taste, and whether the latter is distinct from a general satisfaction of reason; on what the feeling of pleasure or pain rests, and how from it desires and inclinations arise, and from these again maxims by the cooperation of reason; for all this belongs to an empirical psychology, which would constitute the second part of physics, if we regard physics as the *philosophy* of nature, so far as it is based on *empirical laws.* But here we are concerned with objective practical laws, and consequently with the relation of the will to itself so far as it is determined by reason alone, in which case whatever has reference to anything empirical is necessarily excluded; since if *reason of itself alone* determines the conduct (and it is the possibility of this that we are now investigating), it must necessarily do so *a priori.*

The will is conceived as a faculty of determining oneself to action *in accordance with the conception of certain laws.* And such a faculty can be found only in rational beings. Now that which serves the will as the objective ground of its self-determination is the *end,* and if this is assigned by reason alone, it must hold for all rational beings. On the other hand, that which merely contains the ground of possibility of the action of which the effect is the end, this is called the *means.* The subjective ground of the desire is the *spring,* the objective ground of the volition is the *motive;* hence the distinction between subjective ends which rest on springs, and objective ends which depend on motives valid for every rational being. Practical principles are *formal* when they abstract from all subjective ends; they are *material* when they assume these, and therefore particular, springs of action. The ends which a rational being proposes to himself at pleasure as *effects* of his actions (material ends) are all only relative, for it is only their relation to the particular desires of the subject that gives them their worth, which therefore cannot furnish principles universal and necessary for all rational beings and for every volition, that is to say, practical laws. Hence all these relative ends can give rise only to hypothetical imperatives.

Supposing, however, that there were something *whose existence* has *in itself* an absolute worth, something which, being *an end in itself,* could be a source of definite laws, then in this and this alone would lie the source of a possible categorical imperative, that is, a practical law.

Now I say: man and generally any rational being *exists* as

an end in himself, *not merely as a means* to be arbitrarily used by this or that will, but in all his actions, whether they concern himself or other rational beings, must be always regarded at the same time as an end. All objects of the inclinations have only a conditional worth; for if the inclinations and the wants founded on them did not exist, then their object would be without value. But the inclinations themselves, being sources of want, are so far from having an absolute worth for which they should be desired that, on the contrary, it must be the universal wish of every rational being to be wholly free from them. Thus the worth of any object which is *to be acquired* by our action is always conditional. Beings whose existence depends not on our will but on nature's, have nevertheless, if they are nonrational beings, only a relative value as means, and are therefore called *things;* rational beings, on the contrary, are called *persons,* because their very nature points them out as ends in themselves, that is, as something which must not be used merely as means, and so far therefore restricts freedom of action (and is an object of respect). These, therefore, are not merely subjective ends whose existence has a worth *for us* as an effect of our action, but *objective ends,* that is, things whose existence is an end in itself—an end, moreover, for which no other can be substituted, which they should subserve *merely* as means, for otherwise nothing whatever would possess *absolute worth;* but if all worth were conditioned and therefore contingent, then there would be no supreme practical principle of reason whatever.

If then there is a supreme practical principle or, in respect of the human will, a categorical imperative, it must be one which, being drawn from the conception of that which is necessarily an end for everyone because it is *an end in itself,* constitutes an *objective* principle of will, and can therefore serve as a universal practical law. The foundation of this principle is: *rational nature exists as an end in itself.* Man necessarily conceives his own existence as being so; so far then this is a *subjective* principle of human actions. But every other rational being regards its existence similarly, just on the same rational principle that holds for me;* so that it is at the same time an objective principle from which as a supreme practical law all laws of the will must be capable of being deduced. Accordingly the practical imperative will be as follows: *So act as to treat humanity, whether in thine own person or in that of any other, in every case as an end withal, never as means only.*

* This proposition is here stated as a postulate. The ground of it will be found in the concluding section.

We will now inquire whether this can be practically carried out.

To abide by the previous examples:

First, under the head of necessary duty to oneself: He who contemplates suicide should ask himself whether his action can be consistent with the idea of humanity *as an end in itself.* If he destroys himself in order to escape from painful circumstances, he uses a person merely as *a mean* to maintain a tolerable condition up to the end of life. But a man is not a thing, that is to say, something which can be used merely as means, but must in all his actions be always considered as an end in himself. I cannot, therefore, dispose in any way of a man in my own person so as to mutilate him, to damage or kill him. (It belongs to ethics proper to define this principle more precisely, so as to avoid all misunderstanding, for example, as to the amputation of the limbs in order to preserve myself; as to exposing my life to danger with a view to preserve it, etc. This question is therefore omitted here.)

Secondly, as regards necessary duties, or those of strict obligation, towards others: He who is thinking of making a lying promise to others will see at once that he would be using another man *merely as a mean,* without the latter containing at the same time the end in himself. For he whom I propose by such a promise to use for my own purposes cannot possibly assent to my mode of acting towards him, and therefore cannot himself contain the end of this action. This violation of the principle of humanity in other men is more obvious if we take in examples of attacks on the freedom and property of others. For then it is clear that he who transgresses the rights of men intends to use the person of others merely as means, without considering that as rational beings they ought always to be esteemed also as ends, that is, as beings who must be capable of containing in themselves the end of the very same action.*

Thirdly, as regards contingent (meritorious) duties to oneself: It is not enough that the action does not violate humanity in our own person as an end in itself, it must also *harmonize with it.* Now there are in humanity capacities of greater perfection which belong to the end that nature has in view in

---

* Let it not be thought that the common: *quod tibi non vis fieri, etc.,* could serve here as the rule or principle. For it is only a deduction from the former, though with several limitations; it cannot be a universal law, for it does not contain the principle of duties to oneself, nor of the duties of benevolence to others (for many a one would gladly consent that others should not benefit him, provided only that he might be excused from showing benevolence to them), nor finally that of duties of strict obligation to one another, for on this principle the criminal might argue against the judge who punishes him, and so on.

regard to humanity in ourselves as the subject; to neglect these might perhaps be consistent with the *maintenance* of humanity as an end in itself, but not with the *advancement* of this end.

Fourthly, as regards meritorious duties towards others: The natural end which all men have is their own happiness. Now humanity might indeed subsist although no one should contribute anything to the happiness of others, provided he did not intentionally withdraw anything from it; but after all, this would only harmonize negatively, not positively, with *humanity as an end in itself,* if everyone does not also endeavor, as far as in him lies, to forward the ends of others. For the ends of any subject which is an end in himself ought as far as possible to be *my* ends also, if that conception is to have its *full* effect with me.

This principle that humanity and generally every rational nature is *an end in itself* (which is the supreme limiting condition of every man's freedom of action), is not borrowed from experience, *first,* because it is universal, applying as it does to all rational beings whatever, and experience is not capable of determining anything about them; *secondly,* because it does not present humanity as an end to men (subjectively), that is, as an object which men do of themselves actually adopt as an end; but as an objective end which must as a law constitute the supreme limiting condition of all our subjective ends, let them be what we will; it must therefore spring from pure reason. In fact the objective principle of all practical legislation lies (according to the first principle) in *the rule* and its form of universality which makes it capable of being a law (say, for example, a law of nature); but the *subjective* principle is in the *end;* now by the second principle, the subject of all ends is each rational being inasmuch as it is an end in itself. Hence follows the third practical principle of the will, which is the ultimate condition of its harmony with the universal practical reason, viz., the idea of *the will of every rational being as a universally legislative will.*

On this principle all maxims are rejected which are inconsistent with the will being itself universal legislator. Thus the will is not subject to the law, but so subject that it must be regarded *as itself giving the law,* and on this ground only subject to the law (of which it can regard itself as the author).

In the previous imperatives, namely, that based on the conception of the conformity of actions to general laws, as in a *physical system of nature,* and that based on the universal *prerogative* of rational beings as *ends* in themselves—these imperatives just because they were conceived as categorical excluded from any share in their authority all admixture of any interest as a spring of action; they were, however, only *assumed* to be categorical, because such an assumption was necessary to explain the conception of duty. But we could not prove independently that there are practical propositions which command categorically, nor can it be proved in this section; one thing, however, could be done, namely, to indicate in the imperative itself, by some determinate expression, that in the case of volition from duty all interest is renounced, which is the specific criterion of categorical as distinguished from hypothetical imperatives. This is done in the present (third) formula of the principle, namely, in the idea of the will of every rational being as a *universally legislating will*.

For although a will *which is subject to laws* may be attached to this law by means of an interest, yet a will which is itself a supreme lawgiver, so far as it is such, cannot possibly depend on any interest, since a will so dependent would itself still need another law restricting the interest of its self-love by the condition that it should be valid as universal law.

Thus the *principle* that every human will is *a will which in all its maxims gives universal laws,** provided it be otherwise justified, would be very *well adapted* to be the categorical imperative, in this respect, namely, that just because of the idea of universal legislation it is *not based on any interest*, and therefore it alone among all possible imperatives can be *unconditional*. Or still better, converting the proposition, if there is a categorical imperative (that is, a law for the will of every rational being), it can only command that everything be done from maxims of one's will regarded as a will which could at the same time will that it should itself give universal laws, for in that case only the practical principle and the imperative which it obeys are unconditional, since they cannot be based on any interest.

Looking back now on all previous attempts to discover the principle of morality, we need not wonder why they all failed. It was seen that man was bound to laws by duty, but it was not observed that the laws to which he is subject are *only those of his own giving*, though at the same time they are *universal*, and that he is only bound to act in conformity with his own will—a will, however, which is designed by nature to give universal laws. For when one has conceived man only as subject to a law (no matter what), then this law required some interest, either by way of attraction or constraint, since it did not origi-

---

* I may be excused from adducing examples to elucidate this principle, as those which have already been used to elucidate the categorical imperative and its formula would all serve for the like purpose here.

nate as a law from *his own* will, but this will was according to a law obliged by *something else* to act in a certain manner. Now by this necessary consequence all the labor spent in finding a supreme principle of *duty* was irrevocably lost. For men never elicited duty, but only a necessity of acting from a certain interest. Whether this interest was private or otherwise, in any case the imperative must be conditional, and could not by any means be capable of being a moral command. I will therefore call this the principle of *Autonomy* of the will, in contrast with every other which I accordingly reckon as *Heteronomy*.

The conception of every rational being as one which must consider itself as giving in all the maxims of its will universal laws, so as to judge itself and its actions from this point of view—this conception leads to another which depends on it and is very fruitful, namely, that of a *kingdom of ends*.

By a "kingdom" I understand the union of different rational beings in a system by common laws. Now since it is by laws that ends are determined as regards their universal validity, hence, if we abstract from the personal differences of rational beings, and likewise from all the content of their private ends, we shall be able to conceive all ends combined in a systematic whole (including both rational beings as ends in themselves, and also the special ends which each may propose to himself), that is to say, we can conceive a kingdom of ends, which on the preceding principles is possible.

For all rational beings come under the *law* that each of them must treat itself and all others *never merely as means*, but in every case *at the same time as ends in themselves*. Hence results a systematic union of rational beings by common objective laws, that is, a kingdom which may be called a kingdom of ends, since what these laws have in view is just the relation of these beings to one another as ends and means. It is certainly only an ideal.

A rational being belongs as a *member* to the kingdom of ends when, although giving universal laws in it, he is also himself subject to these laws. He belongs to it *as sovereign* when, while giving laws, he is not subject to the will of any other.

A rational being must always regard himself as giving laws either as member or as soverign in a kingdom of ends which is rendered possible by the freedom of will. He cannot, however, maintain the latter position merely by the maxims of his will, but only in case he is a completely independent being without wants and with unrestricted power adequate to his will.

Morality consists then in the reference of all action to the legislation which alone can render a kingdom of ends possible.

This legislation must be capable of existing in every rational being, and of emanating from his will, so that the principle of this will is never to act on any maxim which could not without contradiction be also a universal law, and accordingly always so to act *that the will could at the same time regard itself as giving in its maxims universal laws*. If now the maxims of rational beings are not by their own nature coincident with this objective principle, then the necessity of acting on it is called practical necessitation, that is, *duty*. Duty does not apply to the sovereign in the kingdom of ends, but it does to every member of it and to all in the same degree.

The practical necessity of acting on this principle, that is, duty, does not rest at all on feelings, impulses, or inclinations, but solely on the relation of rational beings to one another, a relation in which the will of a rational being must always be regarded as *legislative*, since otherwise it could not be conceived as *an end in itself*. Reason then refers every maxim of the will, regarding it as legislating universally, to every other will and also to every action towards oneself; and this not on account of any other practical motive or any future advantage, but from the idea of the *dignity* of a rational being, obeying no law but that which he himself also gives.

In the kingdom of ends everything has either *value* or *dignity*. Whatever has a value can be replaced by something else which is *equivalent;* whatever, on the other hand, is above all value, and therefore admits of no equivalent, has a dignity.

Whatever has reference to the general inclinations and wants of mankind has a *market value;* whatever, without presupposing a want, corresponds to a certain taste, that is, to a satisfaction in the mere purposeless play of our faculties, has a *fancy value;* but that which constitutes the condition under which alone anything can be an end in itself, this has not merely a relative worth, that is, value, but an intrinsic worth, that is, *dignity*.

Now morality is the condition under which alone a rational being can be an end in himself, since by this alone it is possible that he should be a legislating member in the kingdom of ends. Thus morality, and humanity as capable of it, is that which alone has dignity. Skill and diligence in labor have a market value; wit, lively imagination, and humor have fancy value; on the other hand, fidelity to promises, benevolence from principle (not from instinct), have an intrinsic worth. Neither nature nor art contains anything which in default of these it could put in their place, for their worth consists not in the effects which spring from them, not in the use and advantage which they secure, but in the disposition of mind, that is, the maxims of the will which are ready to manifest themselves in such actions, even though they should not have the desired effect. These actions also need no recommendation from any subjective taste or sentiment, that they may be looked on with immediate favor and satisfaction; they need no immediate propension or feeling for them; they exhibit the will that performs them as an object of an immediate respect, and nothing but reason is required to *impose* them on the will; not to *flatter* it into them, which, in the case of duties, would be a contradiction. This estimation therefore shows that the worth of such a disposition is dignity, and places it infinitely above all value, with which it cannot for a moment be brought into comparison or competition without as it were violating its sanctity.

What then is it which justifies virtue or the morally good disposition, in making such lofty claims? It is nothing less than the privilege it secures to the rational being of participating in the giving of universal laws, by which it qualifies him to be a member of a possible kingdom of ends, a privilege to which he was already destined by his own nature as being an end in himself, and on that account legislating in the kingdom of ends; free as regards all laws of physical nature, and obeying those only which he himself gives, and by which his maxims can belong to a system of universal law to which at the same time he submits himself. For nothing has any worth except what the law assigns it. Now the legislation itself which assigns the

worth of everything must for that very reason possess dignity, that is, an unconditional incomparable worth; and the word *respect* alone supplies a becoming expression for the esteem which a rational being must have for it. *Autonomy* then is the basis of the dignity of human and of every rational nature.

The three modes of presenting the principle of morality that have been adduced are at bottom only so many formulae of the very same law, and each of itself involves the other two. There is, however, a difference in them, but it is rather subjectively than objectively practical, intended, namely, to bring an idea of the reason nearer to intuition (by means of a certain analogy), and thereby nearer to feeling. All maxims, in fact, have—

1. A *form,* consisting in universality; and in this view the formula of the moral imperative is expressed thus, that the maxims must be so chosen as if they were to serve as universal laws of nature.

2. A *matter,*[7] namely, an end, and here the formula says

[7] The reading "Maxime," which is that both of Rosenkranz and Hartenstein, is obviously an error for "Materie."

that the rational being, as it is an end by its own nature and therefore an end in itself, must in every maxim serve as the condition limiting all merely relative and arbitrary ends.

3. A *complete characterization* of all maxims by means of that formula, namely, that all maxims ought, by their own legislation, to harmonize with a possible kingdom of ends as with a kingdom of nature.* There is a progress here in the order of the categories of *unity* of the form of the will (its universality), *plurality* of the matter (the objects, that is, the ends), and *totality* of the system of these. In forming our moral *judgment* of actions it is better to proceed always on the strict method, and start from the general formula of the categorical imperative: *Act according to a maxim which can at the same time make itself a universal law.* If, however, we wish to gain an *entrance* for the moral law, it is very useful to bring one and the same action under the three specified conceptions, and thereby as far as possible to bring it nearer to intuition.

We can now end where we started at the beginning, namely, with the conception of a will unconditionally good. *That will* is *absolutely good* which cannot be evil—in other words, whose maxim, if made a universal law, could never contradict itself. This principle, then, is its supreme law: *Act always on such a maxim as thou canst at the same time will to be a universal law;* this is the sole condition under which a will can never contradict itself; and such an imperative is categorical. Since the validity of the will as a universal law for possible actions is analogous to the universal connection of the existence of things by general laws, which is the formal notion of nature in general, the categorical imperative can also be expressed thus: *Act on maxims which can at the same time have for their object themselves as universal laws of nature.* Such then is the formula of an absolutely good will.

Rational nature is distinguished from the rest of nature by this that it sets before itself an end. This end would be the matter of every good will. But since in the idea of a will that is absolutely good without being limited by any condition (of attaining this or that end) we must abstract wholly from every end *to be effected* (since this would make every will only relatively good), it follows that in this case the end must be conceived, not as an end to be effected, but as an *independently*

---

* Teleology considers nature as a kingdom of ends; ethics regards a possible kingdom of ends as a kingdom of nature. In the first case, the kingdom of ends is a theoretical idea, adopted to explain what actually is. In the latter it is a practical idea, adopted to bring about that which is not yet, but which can be realized by our conduct, namely, if it conforms to this idea.

existing end. Consequently it is conceived only negatively, that is, as that which we must never act against, and which, therefore, must never be regarded merely as means, but must in every volition be esteemed as an end likewise. Now this end can be nothing but the subject of all possible ends, since this is also the subject of a possible absolutely good will; for such a will cannot without contradiction be postponed to any other object. This principle: So act in regard to every rational being (thyself and others) that he may always have place in thy maxim as an end in himself, is accordingly essentially identical with this other: Act upon a maxim which, at the same time, involves its own universal validity for every rational being. For that in using means for every end I should limit my maxim by the condition of its holding good as a law for every subject, this comes to the same thing as that the fundamental principle of all maxims of action must be that the subject of all ends, that is, the rational being himself, be never employed merely as means, but as the supreme condition restricting the use of all means— that is, in every case as an end likewise.

If follows incontestably that, to whatever laws any rational being may be subject, he being an end in himself must be able to regard himself as also legislating universally in respect of these same laws, since it is just this fitness of his maxims for universal legislation that distinguishes him as an end in himself; also it follows that this implies his dignity (prerogative) above all mere physical beings, that he must always take his maxims from the point of view which regards himself, and likewise every other rational being, as lawgiving beings (on which account they are called persons). In this way a world of rational beings (*mundus intelligibilis*) is possible as a kingdom of ends, and this by virtue of the legislation proper to all persons as members. Therefore, every rational being must so act as if he were by his maxims in every case a legislating member in the universal kingdom of ends. The formal principle of these maxims is: So act as if thy maxim were to serve likewise as the universal law (of all rational beings). A kingdom of ends is thus only possible on the analogy of a kingdom of nature, the former, however, only by maxims—that is, self-imposed rules —the latter only by the laws of efficient causes acting under necessitation from without. Nevertheless, although the system of nature is looked upon as a machine, yet so far as it has reference to rational beings as its ends, it is given on this account the name of a kingdom of nature. Now such a kingdom of ends would be actually realized by means of maxims conforming to the canon which the categorical imperative prescribes to all rational beings, *if they were universally followed.* But although a rational being, even if he punctually follows this maxim himself, cannot reckon upon all others being therefore true to the same, nor expect that the kingdom of nature and its orderly arrangements shall be in harmony with him as a fitting member, so as to form a kingdom of ends to which he himself contributes, that is to say, that it shall favor his expectation of happiness, still that law: Act according to the maxims of a member of a merely possible kingdom of ends legislating in it universally, remains in its full force inasmuch as it commands categorically. And it is just in this that the paradox lies; that the mere dignity of man as a rational creature, without any other end or advantage to be attained thereby, in other words, respect for a mere idea, should yet serve as an inflexible precept of the will, and that it is precisely in this independence of the maxim on all such springs of action that its sublimity consists; and it is this that makes every rational subject worthy to be a legislative member in the kingdom of ends, for otherwise he would have to be conceived only as subject to the physical law of his wants. And although we should suppose the kingdom of nature and the kingdom of ends to be united under one sovereign, so that the latter kingdom thereby ceased to be a mere idea and acquired true reality, then it would no doubt gain the accession of a strong spring, but by no means any increase of its intrinsic worth. For this sole absolute lawgiver must, notwithstanding this, be always conceived as estimating the worth of rational beings only by their disinterested behavior, as prescribed to themselves from that idea [the dignity of man] alone. The essence of things is not altered by their external relations, and that which, abstracting from these, alone constitutes the absolute worth of man is also that by which he must be judged, whoever the judge may be, and even by the Supreme Being. *Morality,* then, is the relation of actions to the autonomy of the will, that is, to the potential universal legislation by its maxims. An action that is consistent with the autonomy of the will is *permitted;* one that does not agree therewith is *forbidden.* A will whose maxims necessarily coincide with the laws of autonomy is a *holy* will, good absolutely. The dependence of a will not absolutely good on the principle of autonomy (moral necessitation) is obligation. This, then, cannot be applied to a holy being. The objective necessity of actions from obligation is called *duty.*

From what has just been said, it is easy to see how it happens that, although the conception of duty implies subjection to the law, we yet ascribe a certain *dignity* and sublimity to the person who fulfills all his duties. There is not, indeed, any sublimity in him, so far as he is *subject* to the moral law; but inasmuch as in regard to that very law he is likewise a *legislator,* and on that account alone subject to it, he has sublimity. We have also shown above that neither fear nor inclination, but simply respect for the law, is the spring which can give actions a moral worth. Our own will, so far as we suppose it to act only under the condition that its maxims are potentially universal laws, this ideal will which is possible to us is the proper object of respect; and the dignity of humanity consists just in this capacity of being universally legislative, though with the condition that it is itself subject to this same legislation.

THE AUTONOMY OF THE WILL AS THE SUPREME PRINCIPLE OF MORALITY

Autonomy of the will is that property of it by which it is a law to itself (independently on any property of the objects of volition). The principle of autonomy then is: Always so to choose that the same volition shall comprehend the maxims of our choice as a universal law. We cannot prove that this practical rule is an imperative, that is, that the will of every rational being is necessarily bound to it as a condition, by a mere analysis of the conceptions which occur in it, since it is a synthetical proposition; we must advance beyond the cognition of the objects to a critical examination of the subject, that is, of the pure practical reason, for this synthetic proposition which commands apodictically must be capable of being cognized wholly *a priori*. This matter, however, does not belong to the present section. But that the principle of autonomy in question is the sole principle of morals can be readily shown by mere analysis of the conceptions of morality. For by this analysis we find that its principle must be a categorical imperative, and that what this commands is neither more nor less than this very autonomy.

HETERONOMY OF THE WILL AS THE SOURCE OF ALL SPURIOUS PRINCIPLES OF MORALITY

If the will seeks the law which is to determine it *anywhere else* than in the fitness of its maxims to be universal laws of its own dictation, consequently if it goes out of itself and seeks this law in the character of any of its objects, there always results *heteronomy.* The will in that case does not give itself the law, but it is given by the object through its relation to the will. This relation, whether it rests on inclination or on conceptions of reason, only admits of hypothetical imperatives: I ought to do something *because I wish for something else.* On the contrary, the moral, and therefore categorical, imperative says: I ought to do so and so, even though I should not wish for anything else. For example, the former says: I ought not to lie if I would retain my reputation; the latter says: I ought not to lie although it should not bring me the least discredit. The latter therefore must so far abstract from all objects that they shall have no *influence* on the will, in order that practical reason (will) may not be restricted to administering an interest not belonging to it, but may simply show its own commanding authority as the supreme legislation. Thus, for example, I ought to endeavor to promote the happiness of others, not as if its realization involved any concern of mine (whether by immediate inclination or by any satisfaction indirectly gained through reason), but simply because a maxim which excludes it cannot be comprehended as a universal law[8] in one and the same volition.

CLASSIFICATION

OF ALL PRINCIPLES OF MORALITY WHICH CAN BE FOUNDED

ON THE CONCEPTION OF HETERONOMY

Here as elsewhere human reason in its pure use, so long as it was not critically examined, has first tried all possible wrong ways before it succeeded in finding the one true way.

All principles which can be taken from this point of view are either *empirical* or *rational.* The *former,* drawn from the principle of *happiness,* are built on physical or moral feelings; the *latter,* drawn from the principle of *perfection,* are built either on the rational conception of perfection as a possible effect, or on that of an independent perfection (the will of God) as the determining cause of our will.

Empirical principles are wholly incapable of serving as a foundation for moral laws. For the universality with which these should hold for all rational beings without distinction, the unconditional practical necessity which is thereby imposed on them is lost when their foundation is taken from the *particu-*

[8] I read *allgemeines* instead of *allgemeinem.*

lar constitution of human nature or the accidental circumstances in which it is placed. The principle of *private happiness,* however, is the most objectionable, not merely because it is false, and experience contradicts the supposition that prosperity is always proportioned to good conduct, nor yet merely because it contributes nothing to the establishment of morality—since it is quite a different thing to make a prosperous man and a good man, or to make one prudent and sharp-sighted for his own interests, and to make him virtuous—but because the springs it provides for morality are such as rather undermine it and destroy its sublimity, since they put the motives to virtue and to vice in the same class, and only teach us to make a better calculation, the specific difference between virtue and vice being entirely extinguished. On the other hand, as to moral feeling, this supposed special sense,* the appeal to it is indeed superficial when those who cannot *think* believe that *feeling* will help them out, even in what concerns general laws; and besides, feelings which naturally differ infinitely in degree cannot furnish a uniform standard of good and evil, nor has anyone a right to form judgments for others by his own feelings; nevertheless this moral feeling is nearer to morality and its dignity in this respect that it pays virtue the honor of ascribing to her *immediately* the satisfaction and esteem we have for her, and does not, as it were, tell her to her face that we are not attached to her by her beauty but by profit.

Among the *rational* principles of morality, the ontological conception of *perfection,* notwithstanding its defects, is better than the theological conception which derives morality from a Divine absolutely perfect will. The former is, no doubt, empty and indefinite, and consequently useless for finding in the boundless field of possible reality the greatest amount suitable for us; moreover, in attempting to distinguish specifically the reality of which we are now speaking from every other, it inevitably tends to turn in a circle and cannot avoid tacitly presupposing the morality which it is to explain; it is nevertheless preferable to the theological view, first, because we have no intuition of the Divine perfection, and can only deduce it from our own conceptions the most important of which is that of morality, and our explanation would thus be involved in a gross circle; and, in the next place, if we avoid this, the only

* I class the principle of moral feeling under that of happiness, because every empirical interest promises to contribute to our well-being by the agreeableness that a thing affords, whether it be immediately and without a view to profit, or whether profit be regarded. We must likewise, with Hutcheson, class the principle of sympathy with the happiness of others under his assumed moral sense.

notion of the Divine will remaining to us is a conception made up of the attributes of desire of glory and dominion, combined with the awful conceptions of might and vengeance, and any system of morals erected on this foundation would be directly opposed to morality.

However, if I had to choose between the notion of the moral sense and that of perfection in general (two systems which at least do not weaken morality, although they are totally incapable of serving as its foundation), then I should decide for the latter, because it at least withdraws the decision of the question from the sensibility and brings it to the court of pure reason; and although even here it decides nothing, it at all events preserves the indefinite idea (of a will good in itself) free from corruption, until it shall be more precisely defined.

For the rest I think I may be excused here from a detailed refutation of all these doctrines; that would only be superfluous labor, since it is so easy, and is probably so well seen even by those whose office requires them to decide for one of those theories (because their hearers would not tolerate suspension of judgment). But what interests us more here is to know that the prime foundation of morality laid down by all these principles is nothing but heteronomy of the will, and for this reason they must necessarily miss their aim.

In every case where an object of the will has to be supposed, in order that the rule may be prescribed which is to determine the will, there the rule is simply heteronomy; the imperative is conditional, namely, *if* or *because* one wishes for this object, one should act so and so; hence it can never command morally, that is, categorically. Whether the object determines the will by means of inclination, as in the principle of private happiness, or by means of reason directed to objects of our possible volition generally, as in the principle of perfection, in either case the will never determines itself *immediately* by the conception of the action, but only by the influence which the foreseen effect of the action has on the will; *I ought to do something, on this account, because 1 wish for something else;* and here there must be yet another law assumed in me as its subject, by which I necessarily will this other thing, and this law again requires an imperative to restrict this maxim. For the influence which the conception of an object within the reach of our faculties can exercise on the will of the subject in consequence of its natural properties, depends on the nature of the subject, either the sensibility (inclination and taste) or the understanding and reason, the employment of which is by the peculiar constitution of their nature attended with satisfaction. It follows that the law would be, properly speaking, given by nature, and as such it must be known and proved by experience, and would consequently be contingent, and therefore incapable of being an apodictic practical rule, such as the moral rule must be. Not only so, but it is *inevitably only heteronomy;* the will does not give itself the law, but it is given by a foreign impulse by means of a particular natural constitution of the subject adapted to receive it. An absolutely good will, then, the principle of which must be a categorical imperative, will be indeterminate as regards all objects, and will contain merely the *form of volition* generally, and that as autonomy, that is to say, the capability of the maxims of every good will to make themselves a universal law, is itself the only law which the will of every rational being imposes on itself, without needing to assume any spring or interest as a foundation.

How such a synthetical practical a priori *proposition is possible,* and why it is necessary, is a problem whose solution does not lie within the bounds of the metaphysic of morals; and we have not here affirmed its truth, much less professed to have a proof of it in our power. We simply showed by the development of the universally received notion of morality that an autonomy of the will is inevitably connected with it, or rather is its foundation. Whoever then holds morality to be anything real, and not a chimerical idea without any truth, must likewise admit the principle of it that is here assigned. This section, then, like the first, was merely analytical. Now to prove that morality is no creation of the brain, which it cannot be if the categorical imperative and with it the autonomy of the will is true, and as an *a priori* principle absolutely necessary, this supposes the *possibility of a synthetic use of pure practical reason,* which, however, we cannot venture on without first giving a critical examination of this faculty of reason. In the concluding section we shall give the principal outlines of this critical examination as far as is sufficient for our purpose.

THIRD SECTION
TRANSITION FROM THE METAPHYSICS OF MORALS TO THE CRITIQUE OF PURE PRACTICAL REASON

THE CONCEPT OF FREEDOM IS THE KEY THAT EXPLAINS THE AUTONOMY OF THE WILL

The *will* is a kind of causality belonging to living beings in so far as they are rational, and *freedom* would be this property of such causality that it can be efficient, independently on foreign causes *determining* it; just as *physical necessity* is the property that the causality of all irrational beings has of being determined to activity by the influence of foreign causes.

The preceding definition of freedom is *negative,* and therefore unfruitful for the discovery of its essence; but it leads to a *positive* conception which is so much the more full and fruitful. Since the conception of causality involves that of laws, according to which, by something that we call cause, something else, namely, the effect, must be produced [laid down];[9] hence, although freedom is not a property of the will depending on physical laws, yet it is not for that reason lawless; on the contrary, it must be a causality acting according to immutable laws, but of a peculiar kind; otherwise a free will would be an absurdity. Physical necessity is a heteronomy of the efficient causes, for every effect is possible only according to this law— that something else determines the efficient cause to exert its causality. What else then can freedom of the will be but autonomy, that is, the property of the will to be a law to itself? But the proposition: The will is in every action a law to itself, only expresses the principle to act on no other maxim than that which can also have as an object itself as a universal law. Now this is precisely the formula of the categorical imperative and is the principle of morality, so that a free will and a will subject to moral laws are one and the same.

On the hypothesis, then, of freedom of the will, morality together with its principle follows from it by mere analysis of the conception. However, the latter is a synthetic proposition, viz., an absolutely good will is that whose maxim can always

---

[9] *Gesetz*—there is in the original a play on the etymology of *Gesetz,* which does not admit of reproduction in English. It must be confessed that without it the statement is not self-evident.

include itself regarded as a universal law; for this property of its maxim can never be discovered by analyzing the conception of an absolutely good will. Now such synthetic propositions are only possible in this way—that the two cognitions are connected together by their union with a third in which they are both to be found. The *positive* concept of freedom furnishes this third cognition, which cannot, as with physical causes, be the nature of the sensible world (in the concept of which we find conjoined the concept of something in relation as cause to *something else* as effect). We cannot now at once show what this third is to which freedom points us, and of which we have an idea *a priori*, nor can we make intelligible how the concept of freedom is shown to be legitimate from principles of pure practical reason, and with it the possibility of a categorical imperative; but some further preparation is required.

FREEDOM

MUST BE PRESUPPOSED AS A PROPERTY OF THE

WILL OF ALL RATIONAL BEINGS

It is not enough to predicate freedom of our own will, from whatever reason, if we have not sufficient grounds for predicating the same of all rational beings. For as morality serves as a law for us only because we are *rational beings,* it must also hold for all rational beings; and as it must be deduced simply from the property of freedom, it must be shown that freedom also is a property of all rational beings. It is not enough, then, to prove it from certain supposed experiences of human nature (which indeed is quite impossible, and it can only be shown *a priori*), but we must show that it belongs to the activity of all rational beings endowed with a will. Now I say every being that cannot act except *under the idea of freedom* is just for that reason in a practical point of view really free, that is to say, all laws which are inseparably connected with freedom have the same force for him as if his will had been shown to be free in itself by a proof theoretically conclusive.* Now I affirm that we

* I adopt this method of assuming freedom merely *as an idea* which rational beings suppose in their actions, in order to avoid the necessity of proving it in its theoretical aspect also. The former is sufficient for my purpose; for even though the speculative proof should not be made out, yet a being that cannot act except with the idea of freedom is bound by the same laws that would oblige a being who was actually free. Thus we can escape here from the onus which presses on the theory. [Compare Butler's treatment of the question of liberty in his *Analogy*, part I., ch. vi.]

must attribute to every rational being which has a will that it has also the idea of freedom and acts entirely under this idea. For in such a being we conceive a reason that is practical, that is, has causality in reference to its objects. Now we cannot possibly conceive a reason consciously receiving a bias from any other quarter with respect to its judgments, for then the subject would ascribe the determination of its judgment not to its own reason, but to an impulse. It must regard itself as the author of its principles independent on foreign influences. Consequently, as practical reason or as the will of a rational being it must regard itself as free, that is to say, the will of such a being cannot be a will of its own except under the idea of freedom. This idea must therefore in a practical point of view be ascribed to every rational being.

OF THE INTEREST ATTACHING TO THE IDEAS OF MORALITY

We have finally reduced the definite conception of morality to the idea of freedom. This latter, however, we could not prove to be actually a property of ourselves or of human nature; only we saw that it must be presupposed if we would conceive a being as rational and conscious of its causality in respect of its actions, that is, as endowed with a will; and so we find that on just the same grounds we must ascribe to every being endowed with reason and will this attribute of determining itself to action under the idea of its freedom.

Now it resulted also from the presupposition of this idea that we became aware of a law that the subjective principles of action, that is, maxims, must also be so assumed that they can also hold as objective, that is, universal principles, and so serve as universal laws of our own dictation. But why, then, should I subject myself to this principle and that simply as a rational being, thus also subjecting to it all other beings endowed with reason? I will allow that no interest *urges* me to this, for that would not give a categorical imperative, but I must *take* an interest in it and discern how this comes to pass; for this "I ought" is properly an "I would," valid for every rational being, provided only that reason determined his actions without any hindrance. But for beings that are in addition affected as we are by springs of a different kind, namely, sensibility, and in whose case that is not always done which reason alone would do, for these that necessity is expressed only as an "ought," and the subjective necessity is different from the objective.

It seems, then, as if the moral law, that is, the principle of autonomy of the will, were properly speaking only presupposed in the idea of freedom, and as if we could not prove its reality and objective necessity independently. In that case we should still have gained something considerable by at least determining the true principle more exactly than had previously been done; but as regards its validity and the practical necessity of subjecting oneself to it, we should not have advanced a step. For if we were asked why the universal validity of our maxim as a law must be the condition restricting our actions, and on what we ground the worth which we assign to this manner of acting—a worth so great that there cannot be any higher interest—and if we were asked further how it happens that it is by this alone a man believes he feels his own personal worth, in comparison with which that of an agreeable or disagreeable condition is to be regarded as nothing, to these questions we could give no satisfactory answer.

We find indeed sometimes that we can take an interest in a personal quality which does not involve any interest of external condition,[10] provided this quality makes us capable of participating in the condition in case reason were to effect the allotment; that is to say, the mere being worthy of happiness can interest of itself even without the motive of participating in this happiness. This judgment, however, is in fact only the effect of the importance of the moral law which we before presupposed (when by the idea of freedom we detach ourselves from every empirical interest); but that we ought to detach ourselves from these interests, that is, to consider ourselves as free in action and yet as subject to certain laws, so as to find a worth simply in our own person which can compensate us for the loss of everything that gives worth to our condition, this we are not yet able to discern in this way, nor do we see how it is possible so to act—in other words, *whence the moral law derives its obligation.*

It must be freely admitted that there is a sort of circle here from which it seems impossible to escape. In the order of efficient causes we assume ourselves free, in order that in the order of ends we may conceive ourselves as subject to moral laws; and we afterwards conceive ourselves as subject to these laws because we have attributed to ourselves freedom of will; for freedom and self-legislation of will are both autonomy, and therefore are reciprocal conceptions, and for this very reason one must not be used to explain the other or give the reason of it, but at most only for logical purposes to reduce apparently different notions of the same object to one single concept (as we reduce different fractions of the same value to the lowest terms).

[10] "Interest" means a spring of the will, in so far as this spring is presented by Reason. See note, p. 357.

One resource remains to us, namely, to inquire whether we do not occupy different points of view when by means of freedom we think ourselves as causes efficient *a priori,* and when we form our conception of ourselves from our actions as effects which we see before our eyes.

It is a remark which needs no subtle reflection to make, but which we may assume that even the commonest understanding can make, although it be after its fashion by an obscure discernment of judgment which it calls feeling, that all the "ideas"[11] that come to us involuntarily (as those of the senses) do not enable us to know objects otherwise than as they affect us; so that what they may be in themselves remains unknown to us, and consequently that as regards "ideas" of this kind even with the closest attention and clearness that the understanding can apply to them, we can by them only attain to the knowledge of *appearances,* never to that of *things in themselves.* As soon as this distinction has once been made (perhaps merely in consequence of the difference observed between the ideas given us from without, and in which we are passive, and those that we produce simply from ourselves, and in which we show our own activity), then it follows of itself that we must admit and assume behind the appearance something else that is not an appearance, namely, the things in themselves; although we must admit that, as they can never be known to us except as they affect us, we can come no nearer to them, nor can we ever know what they are in themselves. This must furnish a distinction, however crude, between a *world of sense* and the *world of understanding,* of which the former may be different according to the difference of the sensuous impressions in various observers, while the second which is its basis always remains the same. Even as to himself, a man cannot pretend to know what he is in himself from the knowledge he has by internal sensation. For as he does not as it were create himself, and does not come by the conception of himself *a priori* but empirically, it naturally follows that he can obtain his knowledge even of himself only by the inner sense, and consequently only through the appearances of his nature and the way in which his consciousness is affected. At the same time, beyond these characteristics of his own subject, made up of mere appearances, he must necessarily suppose something else as their basis, namely, his *ego,* whatever its characteristics in itself may be. Thus in respect to mere perception and receptivity of sensations he must reckon himself as belonging to the *world of sense;* but in

[11] The common understanding being here spoken of, I use the word "idea" in its popular sense.

respect of whatever there may be of pure activity in him (that which reaches consciousness immediately and not through affecting the senses), he must reckon himself as belonging to the *intellectual world*, of which, however, he has no further knowledge. To such a conclusion the reflecting man must come with respect to all the things which can be presented to him; it is probably to be met with even in persons of the commonest understanding, who, as is well known, are very much inclined to suppose behind the objects of the senses something else invisible and acting of itself. They spoil it, however, by presently sensualizing this invisible again, that is to say, wanting to make it an object of intuition, so that they do not become a whit the wiser.

Now man really finds in himself a faculty by which he distinguishes himself from everything else, even from himself as affected by objects, and that is *reason*. This being pure spontaneity is even elevated above the *understanding*. For although the latter is a spontaneity and does not, like sense, merely contain intuitions that arise when we are affected by things (and are therefore passive), yet it cannot produce from its activity any other conceptions than those which merely serve *to bring the intuitions of sense under rules*, and thereby to unite them in one consciousness, and without this use of the sensibility it could not think at all; whereas, on the contrary, reason shows so pure a spontaneity in the case of what I call "ideas" [Ideal Conceptions] that it thereby far transcends everything that the sensibility can give it, and exhibits its most important function in distinguishing the world of sense from that of understanding, and thereby prescribing the limits of the understanding itself.

For this reason a rational being must regard himself *qua* intelligence (not from the side of his lower faculties) as belonging not to the world of sense, but to that of understanding; hence he has two points of view from which he can regard himself, and recognize laws of the exercise of his faculties, and consequently of all his actions; *first*, so far as he belongs to the world of sense, he finds himself subject to laws of nature (heteronomy); *secondly*, as belonging to the intelligible world, under laws which, being independent on nature, have their foundation not in experience but in reason alone.

As a reasonable being, and consequently belonging to the intelligible world, man can never conceive the causality of his own will otherwise than on condition of the idea of freedom, for independence on the determining causes of the sensible world (an independence which reason must always ascribe to itself) is freedom. Now the idea of freedom is inseparably connected with the conception of *autonomy,* and this again with the universal principle of morality which is ideally the foundation of all actions of *rational* beings, just as the law of nature is of all phenomena.

Now the suspicion is removed which we raised above, that there was a latent circle involved in our reasoning from freedom to autonomy, and from this to the moral law, viz., that we laid down the idea of freedom because of the moral law only that we might afterwards in turn infer the latter from freedom, and that consequently we could assign no reason at all for this law, but could only [present][12] it as a *petitio principii* which well-disposed minds would gladly concede to us, but which we could never put forward as a provable proposition. For now we see that when we conceive ourselves as free we transfer ourselves into the world of understanding as members of it, and recognize the autonomy of the will with its consequence, morality; whereas, if we conceive ourselves as under obligation, we consider ourselves as belonging to the world of sense, and at the same time to the world of understanding.

HOW IS A CATEGORICAL IMPERATIVE POSSIBLE?

Every rational being reckons himself *qua* intelligence as belonging to the world of understanding, and it is simply as an efficient cause belonging to that world that he calls his causality a *will.* On the other side, he is also conscious of himself as a part of the world of sense in which his actions, which are mere appearances [phenomena] of that causality, are displayed; we cannot, however, discern how they are possible from this causality which we do not know; but instead of that, these actions as belonging to the sensible world must be viewed as determined by other phenomena, namely, desires and inclinations. If therefore I were only a member of the world of understanding, then all my actions would perfectly conform to the principle of autonomy of the pure will; if I were only a part of the world of sense, they would necessarily be assumed to conform wholly to the natural law of desires and inclinations, in other words, to the heteronomy of nature. (The former would rest on morality as the supreme principle, the latter on happiness.) Since, however, *the world of understanding contains the foundation of the world of sense, and consequently of its laws also,* and accordingly gives the law to my will (which belongs wholly to the world of understanding) directly, and must be conceived

[12] The verb is wanting in the original.

as doing so, it follows that, although on the one side I must regard myself as a being belonging to the world of sense, yet, on the other side, I must recognize myself, as an intelligence, as subject to the law of the world of understanding, that is, to reason, which contains this law in the idea of freedom, and therefore as subject to the autonomy of the will; consequently I must regard the laws of the world of understanding as imperatives for me, and the actions which conform to them as duties.

And thus what makes categorical imperatives possible is this —that the idea of freedom makes me a member of an intelligible world, in consequence of which, if I were nothing else, all my actions *would* always conform to the autonomy of the will; but as I at the same time intuit myself as a member of the world of sense, they *ought* so to conform, and this *categorical* "ought" implies a synthetic *a priori* proposition, inasmuch as besides my will as affected by sensible desires there is added further the idea of the same will, but as belonging to the world of the understanding, pure and practical of itself, which contains the supreme condition according to reason of the former will; precisely as to the intuitions of sense there are added concepts of the understanding which of themselves signify nothing but regular form in general, and in this way synthetic *a priori* propositions become possible, on which all knowledge of physical nature rests.

The practical use of common human reason confirms this reasoning. There is no one, not even the most consummate villain, provided only that he is otherwise accustomed to the use of reason, who, when we set before him examples of honesty of purpose, of steadfastness in following good maxims, of sympathy and general benevolence (even combined with great sacrifices of advantages and comfort), does not wish that he might also possess these qualities. Only on account of his inclinations and impulses he cannot attain this in himself, but at the same time he wishes to be free from such inclinations which are burdensome to himself. He proves by this that he transfers himself in thought with a will free from the impulses of the sensibility into an order of things wholly different from that of his desires in the field of the sensibility; since he cannot expect to obtain by that wish any gratification of his desires, nor any position which would satisfy any of his actual or supposable inclinations (for this would destroy the preeminence of the very idea which wrests that wish from him), he can only expect a greater intrinsic worth of his own person. This better person, however, he imagines himself to be when he transfers himself to the point of view of a member of the world of the understanding, to which he is involuntarily forced by the idea of freedom, that is, of independence on *determining* causes of the world of sense; and from this point of view he is conscious of a good will, which by his own confession constitutes the law for the bad will that he possesses as a member of the world of sense—a law whose authority he recognizes while transgressing it. What he morally "ought" is then what he necessarily "would" as a member of the world of the understanding, and is conceived by him as an "ought" only inasmuch as he likewise considers himself as a member of the world of sense.

ON THE EXTREME LIMITS OF ALL PRACTICAL PHILOSOPHY

All men attribute to themselves freedom of will. Hence come all judgments upon actions as being such as *ought to have been done,* although they *have not been* done. However, this freedom is not a conception of experience, nor can it be so, since it still remains, even though experience shows the contrary of what on supposition of freedom are conceived as its necessary consequences. On the other side, it is equally necessary that everything that takes place should be fixedly determined according to laws of nature. This necessity of nature is likewise not an empirical conception, just for this reason that it involves the notion of necessity and consquently of *a priori* cognition. But this conception of a system of nature is confirmed by experience; and it must even be inevitably presupposed if experience itself is to be possible, that is, a connected knowledge of the objects of sense resting on general laws. Therefore freedom is only an *idea* [Ideal Conception] of *reason,* and its objective reality in itself is doubtful; while nature is a *concept* of the *understanding* which proves, and must necessarily prove, its reality in examples of experience.

There arises from this a dialectic of reason, since the freedom attributed to the will appears to contradict the necessity of nature, and, placed between these two ways, reason for *speculative purposes* finds the road of physical necessity much more beaten and more appropriate than that of freedom; yet for *practical purposes* the narrow footpath of freedom is the only one on which it is possible to make use of reason in our conduct; hence it is just as impossible for the subtlest philosophy as for the commonest reason of men to argue away freedom. Philosophy must then assume that no real contradiction will be found between freedom and physical necessity of the same human actions, for it cannot give up the conception of nature any more than that of freedom.

Nevertheless, even though we should never be able to comprehend how freedom is possible, we must at least remove this apparent contradiction in a convincing manner. For if the thought of freedom contradicts either itself or nature, which is equally necessary, it must in competition with physical necessity be entirely given up.

It would, however, be impossible to escape this contradiction if the thinking subject, which seems to itself free, conceived itself *in the same sense* or in *the very same relation* when it calls itself free as when in respect of the same action it assumes itself to be subject to the law of nature. Hence it is an indispensable problem of speculative philosophy to show that its illusion respecting the contradiction rests on this that we think of man in a different sense and relation when we call him free, and when we regard him as subject to the laws of nature as being part and parcel of nature. It must therefore show that not only *can* both these very well coexist, but that both must be thought *as necessarily united* in the same subject, since otherwise no reason could be given why we should burden reason with an idea which, though it may possibly *without contradiction* be reconciled with another that is sufficiently established, yet entangles us in a perplexity which sorely embarrasses reason in its theoretic employment. This duty, however, belongs only to speculative philosophy, in order that it may clear the way for practical philosophy. The philosopher, then, has no option whether he will remove the apparent contradiction or leave it untouched; for in the latter case the theory respecting this would be *bonum vacans* into the possession of which the fatalist would have a right to enter, and chase all morality out of its supposed domain as occupying it without title.

We cannot, however, as yet say that we are touching the bounds of practical philosophy. For the settlement of that controversy does not belong to it; it only demands from speculative reason that it should put an end to the discord in which it entangles itself in theoretical questions, so that practical reason may have rest and security from external attacks which might make the ground debatable on which it desires to build.

The claims to freedom of will made even by common reason are founded on the consciousness and the admitted supposition that reason is independent on merely subjectively determined causes which together constitute what belongs to sensation only, and which consequently come under the general designation of sensibility. Man considering himself in this way as an intelligence places himself thereby in a different order of things and in a relation to determining grounds of a wholly different kind when on the one hand he thinks of himself as an intelligence endowed with a will, and consequently with causality, and when on the other he perceives himself as a phenomenon in the world of sense (as he really is also), and affirms that his causality is subject to external determination according to laws of nature.[13] Now he soon becomes aware that both can hold good, nay, must hold good at the same time. For there is not the smallest contradiction in saying that a *thing in appearance* (belonging to the world of sense) is subject to certain laws on which the very same *as a thing* or being *in itself* is independent; and that he must conceive and think of himself in this two-fold way, rests as to the first on the consciousness of himself as an object affected through the senses, and as to the second on the consciousness of himself as an intelligence, that is, as independent on sensible impressions in the employment of his reason (in other words as belonging to the world of understanding).

Hence it comes to pass that man claims the possession of a will which takes no account of anything that comes under the head of desires and inclinations, and on the contrary conceives actions as possible to him, nay, even as necessary, which can only be done by disregarding all desires and sensible inclinations. The causality of such actions[14] lies in him as an intelligence and in the laws of effects and actions [which depend] on the principles of an intelligible world, of which indeed he knows nothing more than that in it pure reason alone independent on sensibility gives the law; moreover, since it is only in that world, as an intelligence, that he is his proper self (being as man only the appearance of himself), those laws apply to him directly and categorically, so that the incitements of inclinations and appetites (in other words, the whole nature of the world of sense) cannot impair the laws of his volition as an intelligence. Nay, he does not even hold himself responsible for the former or ascribe them to his proper self, that is, his will; he only ascribes to his will any indulgence which he might yield them if he allowed them to influence his maxims to the prejudice of the rational laws of the will.

When practical reason *thinks* itself into a world of understanding, it does not thereby transcend its own limits, as it

---

[13] The punctuation of the original gives the following sense: "Submits his causality, as regards its external determination, to laws of nature." I have ventured to make what appears to be a necessary correction, by simply removing a comma.

[14] M. Barni translates as if he read *desselben* instead of *derselben,* "the causality of this will." So also Mr. Semple.

would if it tried to enter it by *intuition* or *sensation*. The former is only a negative thought in respect of the world of sense, which does not give any laws to reason in determining the will, and is positive only in this single point that this freedom as a negative characteristic is at the same time conjoined with a (positive) faculty and even with a causality of reason, which we designate a will, namely, a faculty of so acting that the principle of the actions shall conform to the essential character of a rational motive, that is, the condition that the maxim have universal validity as a law. But were it to borrow an *object of will*, that is, a motive, from the world of understanding, then it would overstep its bounds and pretend to be acquainted with something of which it knows nothing. The conception of a world of the understanding is then only a *point of view* which reason finds itself compelled to take outside the appearances in order to *conceive itself as practical*, which would not be possible if the influences of the sensibility had a determining power on man, but which is necessary unless he is to be denied the consciousness of himself as an intelligence, and consequently as a rational cause, energizing by reason, that is, operating freely. This thought certainly involves the idea of an order and a system of laws different from that of the mechanism of nature which belongs to the sensible world; and it makes the conception of an intelligible world necessary (that is to say, the whole system of rational beings as things in themselves). But it does not in the least authorize us to think of it further than as to its *formal* condition only, that is, the universality of the maxims of the will as laws, and consequently the autonomy of the latter, which alone is consistent with its freedom; whereas, on the contrary, all laws that refer to a definite object give heteronomy, which only belongs to laws of nature, and can only apply to the sensible world.

But reason would overstep all its bounds if it undertook to *explain how* pure reason can be practical, which would be exactly the same problem as to explain *how freedom is possible*.

For we can explain nothing but that which we can reduce to laws the object of which can be given in some possible experience. But freedom is a mere *idea* [ideal conception], the objective reality of which can in no wise be shown according to laws of nature, and consequently not in any possible experience; and for this reason it can never be comprehended or understood because we cannot support it by any sort of example or analogy. It holds good only as a necessary hypothesis of reason in a being that believes itself conscious of a will, that is, of a faculty distinct from mere desire (namely, a faculty of determining itself to action as an intelligence, in other words, by laws of reason independently on natural instincts). Now where determination according to laws of nature ceases, there all *explanation* ceases also, and nothing remains but *defense*, that is, the removal of the objections of those who pretend to have seen deeper into the nature of things, and thereupon boldly declare freedom impossible. We can only point out to them that the supposed contradiction that they have discovered in it arises only from this that in order to be able to apply the law of nature to human actions, they must necessarily consider man as an appearance; then when we demand of them that they should also think of him *qua* intelligence as a thing in itself, they still persist in considering him in this respect also as an appearance. In this view it would no doubt be a contradiction to suppose the causality of the same subject (that is, his will) to be withdrawn from all the natural laws of the sensible world. But this contradiction disappears if they would only bethink themselves and admit, as is reasonable, that behind the appearances there must also lie at their root (although hidden) the things in themselves, and that we cannot expect the laws of these to be the same as those that govern their appearances.

The subjective impossibility of explaining the freedom of the will is identical with the impossibility of discovering and explaining an interest* which man can take in the moral law. Nevertheless he does actually take an interest in it, the basis of which in us we call the moral feeling, which some have falsely assigned as the standard of our moral judgment, whereas it must rather be viewed as the *subjective* effect that the law exercises on the will, the objective principle of which is furnished by reason alone.

In order, indeed, that a rational being who is also affected through the senses should will what reason alone directs such beings that they ought to will, it is no doubt requisite that reason should have a power *to infuse a feeling of pleasure* or satis-

---

* Interest is that by which reason becomes practical, that is, a cause determining the will. Hence we say of rational beings only that they take an interest in a thing; irrational beings only feel sensual appetites. Reason takes a direct interest in action, then, only when the universal validity of its maxims is alone sufficient to determine the will. Such an interest alone is pure. But if it can determine the will only by means of another object of desire or on the suggestion of a particular feeling of the subject, then Reason takes only an indirect interest in the action; and as Reason by itself without experience cannot discover either objects of the will or a special feeling actuating it, this latter interest would only be empirical, and not a pure rational interest. The logical interest of Reason (namely, to extend its insight) is never direct, but presupposes purposes for which reason is employed.

faction in the fulfilment of duty, that is to say, that it should have a causality by which it determines the sensibility according to its own principles. But it is quite impossible to discern, that is, to make it intelligible *a priori*, how a mere thought, which itself contains nothing sensible, can itself produce a sensation of pleasure or pain; for this is a particular kind of causality of which, as of every other causality, we can determine nothing whatever *a priori*; we must only consult experience about it. But as this cannot supply us with any relation of cause and effect except between two objects of experience, whereas in this case, although indeed the effect produced lies within experience, yet the cause is supposed to be pure reason acting through mere ideas which offer no object to experience, it follows that for us men it is quite impossible to explain how and why the *universality of the maxim as a law,* that is, morality, interests. This only is certain, that it is not *because it interests* us that it has validity for us (for that would be heteronomy and dependence of practical reason on sensibility, namely, on a feeling as its principle, in which case it could never give moral laws), but that it interests us because it is valid for us as men, inasmuch as it had its source in our will as intelligences, in other words in our proper self, *and what belongs to mere appearance is necessarily subordinated by reason to the nature of the thing in itself.*

The question, then, how a categorical imperative is possible, can be answered to this extent that we can assign the only hypothesis on which it is possible, namely, the idea of freedom; and we can also discern the necessity of this hypothesis, and this is sufficient for the *practical exercise* of reason, that is, for the conviction of the *validity of this imperative,* and hence of the moral law; but how this hypothesis itself is possible can never be discerned by any human reason. On the hypothesis, however, that the will of an intelligence is free, its *autonomy,* as the essential formal condition of its determination, is a necessary consequence. Moreover, this freedom of will is not merely quite *possible* as a hypothesis (not involving any contradiction to the principle of physical necessity in the connection of the phenomena of the sensible world) as speculative philosophy can show; but further, a rational being who is conscious of a causality[15] through reason, that is to say, of a will (distinct from desires), must *of necessity* make it practically, that is, in idea, the condition of all his voluntary actions. But to explain how pure reason can be of itself practical without the aid of any spring of action that could be derived from any other

15 Reading "einer" for "seiner."

source, that is, how the mere principle of the *universal validity of all its maxims as laws* (which would certainly be the form of a pure practical reason) can of itself supply a spring, without any matter (object) of the will in which one could antecedently take any interest; and how it can produce an interest which would be called purely *moral;* or in other words, *how pure reason can be practical*—to explain this is beyond the power of human reason, and all the labor and pains of seeking an explanation of it are lost.

It is just the same as if I sought to find out how freedom itself is possible as the causality of a will. For then I quit the ground of philosophical explanation, and I have no other to go upon. I might indeed revel in the world of intelligences which still remains to me, but although I have an *idea* of it which is well founded, yet I have not the least *knowledge* of it, nor can I ever attain to such knowledge with all the efforts of my natural faculty of reason. It signifies only a something that remains over when I have eliminated everything belonging to the world of sense from the actuating principles of my will, serving merely to keep in bounds the principle of motives taken from the field of sensibility; fixing its limits and showing that it does not contain all in all within itself, but that there is more beyond it; but this something more I know no further. Of pure reason which frames this ideal, there remains after the abstraction of all matter, that is, knowledge of objects, nothing but the form, namely, the practical law of the universality of the maxims, and in conformity with this the conception of reason in reference to a pure world of understanding as a possible efficient cause, that is, a cause determining the will. There must here be a total absence of springs unless this idea of an intelligible world is itself the spring, or that in which reason primarily takes an interest; but to make this intelligible is precisely the problem that we cannot solve.

Here now is the extreme limit of all moral inquiry, and it is of great importance to determine it even on this account in order that reason may not, on the one hand, to the prejudice of morals, seek about in the world of sense for the supreme motive and an interest comprehensible but empirical; and on the other hand, that it may not impotently flap its wings without being able to move in the (for it) empty space of transcendent concepts which we call the intelligible world, and so lose itself amidst chimeras. For the rest, the idea of a pure world of understanding as a system of all intelligences, and to which we ourselves as rational beings belong (although we are likewise on the other side members of the sensible world), this remains always a useful and legitimate idea for the purposes of rational belief, although all knowledge stops at its threshold, useful, namely, to produce in us a lively interest in the moral law by means of the noble ideal of a universal kingdom of *ends in themselves* (rational beings), to which we can belong as members then only when we carefully conduct ourselves according to the maxims of freedom as if they were laws of nature.

CONCLUDING REMARK

The speculative employment of reason *with respect to nature* leads to the absolute necessity of some supreme cause of *the world;* the practical employment of reason *with a view to freedom* leads also to absolute necessity, but only *of the laws of the actions* of a rational being as such. Now it is an essential *principle* of reason, however employed, to push its knowledge to a consciousness of its *necessity* (without which it would not be rational knowledge). It is, however, an equally essential *restriction* of the same reason that it can neither discern the *necessity* of what is or what happens, nor of what ought to happen, unless a condition is supposed on which it is or happens or ought to happen. In this way, however, by the constant inquiry for the condition, the satisfaction of reason is only further and further postponed. Hence it unceasingly seeks the unconditionally necessary, and finds itself forced to assume it, although without any means of making it comprehensible to itself, happy enough if only it can discover a conception which agrees with this assumption. It is therefore no fault in our deduction of the supreme principle of morality, but an objection that should be made to human reason in general, that it cannot enable us to conceive the absolute necessity of an unconditional practical law (such as the categorical imperative must be). It cannot be blamed for refusing to explain this necessity by a condition, that is to say, by means of some interest assumed as a basis, since the law would then cease to be a moral law, that is, a supreme law of freedom. And thus while we do not comprehend the practical unconditional necessity of the moral imperative, we yet comprehend its *incomprehensibility*, and this is all that can be fairly demanded of a philosophy which strives to carry its principles up to the very limit of human reason.

Critique of Practical Reason

Introduction
Of the Idea of a Critique of Practical Reason

The theoretical use of reason was concerned with objects of the cognitive faculty only, and a critical examination of it with reference to this use applied properly only to the *pure* faculty of cognition; because this raised the suspicion, which was afterwards confirmed, that it might easily pass beyond its limits, and be lost among unattainable objects, or even contradictory notions. It is quite different with the practical use of reason. In this, reason is concerned with the grounds of determination of the will, which is a faculty either to produce objects corresponding to ideas, or to determine ourselves to the effecting of such objects (whether the physical power is sufficient or not); that is, to determine our causality. For here, reason can at least attain so far as to determine the will, and has always objective reality in so far as it is the volition only that is in question. The first question here, then, is, whether pure reason of itself alone suffices to determine the will, or whether it can be a ground of determination only as dependent on empirical conditions. Now, here there comes in a notion of causality justified by the critique of the pure reason, although not capable of being presented empirically, viz. that of *freedom;* and if we can now discover means of proving that this property does in fact belong to the human will (and so to the

361

will of all rational beings), then it will not only be shown that pure reason can be practical, but that it alone, and not reason empirically limited, is indubitably practical, consequently, we shall have to make a critical examination, not of *pure practical* reason, but only of *practical* reason generally. For when once pure reason is shown to exist, it needs no critical examination. For reason itself contains the standard for the critical examination of every use of it. The critique, then, of practical reason generally is bound to prevent the empirically conditioned reason from claiming exclusively to furnish the ground of determination of the will. If it is proved that there is a [practical]¹ reason, its employment is alone immanent; the empirically conditioned use, which claims supremacy, is on the contrary transcendent, and expresses itself in demands and precepts which go quite beyond its sphere. This is just the opposite of what might be said of pure reason in its speculative employment.

However, as it is still pure reason, the knowledge of which is here the foundation of its practical employment, the general outline of the classification of a critique of practical reason must be arranged in accordance with that of the speculative. We must, then, have the *Elements* and the *Methodology* of it; and in the former an *Analytic* as the rule of truth, and a *Dialectic* as the exposition and dissolution of the illusion in the judgments of practical reason. But the order in the subdivision of the Analytic will be the reverse of that in the critique of the pure speculative reason. For, in the present case, we shall commence with the *principles* and proceed to the *concepts,* and only then, if possible, to the senses; whereas in the case of the speculative reason we began with the senses, and had to end with the principles. The reason of this lies again in this: that now we have to do with a will, and have to consider reason, not in its relation to objects, but to this will and its causality. We must then, begin with the principles of a causality not empirically conditioned, after which the attempt can be made to establish our notions of the determining grounds of such a will, of their application to objects, and finally to the subject and its sense faculty. We necessarily begin with the law of causality from freedom, that is, with a pure practical principle, and this determines the objects to which alone it can be applied.

¹ The original has "pure," an obvious error.

Book I
The Analytic of Pure Practical Reason

CHAPTER I

OF THE PRINCIPLES OF PURE PRACTICAL REASON

§I—DEFINITION

Practical *principles* are propositions which contain a general determination of the will, having under it several practical rules. They are subjective, or *Maxims*, when the condition is regarded by the subject as valid only for his own will, but are objective, or practical *laws*, when the condition is recognized as objective, that is, valid for the will of every rational being.

Remark

Supposing that *pure* reason contains in itself a practical motive, that is, one adequate to determine the will, then there are practical laws; otherwise all practical principles will be mere maxims. In case the will of a rational being is pathologically affected, there may occur a conflict of the maxims with the practical laws recognized by itself. For example, one may make it his maxim to let no injury pass unrevenged, and yet he may see that this is not a practical law, but only his own maxim; that, on the contrary, regarded as being in one and the same maxim a rule for the will of every rational being, it must contradict itself. In natural philosophy the principles of what happens (e.g. the principle of equality of action and reaction in the communication of motion) are at the same time laws of nature; for the use of reason there is theoretical, and determined by the nature of the object. In practical philosophy, i.e. that which has to do only with the grounds of determination of the will, the principles which a man makes for himself are not laws by which one is inevitably bound; because reason in practical matters has to do with the subject, namely, with the faculty of desire, the special character of which may occasion variety in the rule. The practical rule is always a product of reason, because it prescribes action as a means to the effect. But in the case of a being with whom reason does not of itself determine the will, this rule is an *imperative*, i.e. a rule characterized by "shall," which expresses the objective necessitation of the action, and signifies that if reason completely determined the will, the action would inevitably take place according to this rule. Imperatives, therefore, are objectively valid, and are quite distinct from maxims, which are subjective principles. The former either determine the conditions of the causality of the rational being as an efficient cause, i.e. merely in reference to the effect and the means of attaining it; or they determine the will only, whether it is adequate to the effect or not. The former would be hypothetical imperatives, and contain mere precepts of skill; the latter, on the contrary, would be categorical, and would alone be practical laws. Thus maxims are *principles*, but not *imperatives*. Imperatives themselves, however, when they are conditional (i.e. do not determine the will simply as will, but only in respect to a desired effect, that is, when they are hypothetical imperatives), are practical *precepts*, but not *laws*. Laws must be sufficient to determine the will as will, even before I ask whether I have power sufficient for a desired effect, or the means necessary to produce it; hence they are categorical: otherwise they are not laws at all, because the necessity is wanting, which, if it is to be practical, must be independent on conditions which are pathological, and are therefore only contingently connected with the will. Tell a man, for example, that he must be industrious and thrifty in youth, in order that he may not want in old age; this is a correct and important practical precept of the will. But it is easy to see that in this case the will is directed to something *else* which it is presupposed that it desires, and as to this desire, we must leave it to the actor himself whether he looks forward to other resources than those of his own acquisition, or does not expect to be old, or thinks that in case of future necessity he will be able to make shift with little. Reason, from which alone can spring a rule involving necessity, does, indeed, give necessity to this precept (else it would not be an imperative), but this is a necessity dependent on subjective conditions, and cannot be supposed in the same degree in all subjects. But that reason may give laws it is necessary that it should only need to presuppose *itself*, because rules are objectively and universally valid only when they hold without any contingent subjective conditions, which distinguish one rational being from another. Now tell a man that he should never make a deceitful promise, this is a rule which only concerns his will, whether the purposes he may have can be attained thereby or not; it is the volition only which is to be determined *a priori* by that rule. If now it is found that this rule is practically right, then it is a law, because it is a categorical imperative. Thus, practical laws refer to the will only, without considering what is attained by its causality, and we may disregard this latter (as belonging to the world of sense) in order to have them quite pure.

§II—THEOREM I

All practical principles which presuppose an object (matter) of the faculty of desire as the ground of determination of the will are empirical, and can furnish no practical laws.

By the matter of the faculty of desire I mean an object the realization of which is desired. Now, if the desire for this object *precedes* the practical rule, and is the condition of our making it a principle, then I say (*in the first place*) this principle is in that case wholly empirical, for then what determines the choice is the idea of an object, and that relation of this idea to the subject by which its faculty of desire is determined to its realization. Such a relation to the subject is called the *pleasure* in the realization of an object. This, then, must be presupposed as a condition of the possibility of determination of the will. But it is impossible to know *a priori* of any idea of an object whether it will be connected with *pleasure* or *pain*, or be indifferent. In such cases, therefore, the determining principle of the choice must be empirical, and, therefore, also the practical material principle which presupposes it as a condition.

In the second place, since susceptibility to a pleasure or pain can be known only empirically, and cannot hold in the same degree for all rational beings, a principle which is based on this subjective condition may serve indeed as a *maxim* for the subject which possesses this susceptibility, but not as a *law* even to him (because it is wanting in objective necessity, which must be recognized *a priori*); it follows, therefore, that such a principle can never furnish a practical law.

§III—THEOREM II

All material practical principles as such are of one and the same kind, and come under the general principle of self-love or private happiness.

Pleasure arising from the idea of the existence of a thing, in so far as it is to determine the desire of this thing, is founded on the *susceptibility* of the subject, since it *depends* on the presence of an object; hence it belongs to sense (feeling), and not to understanding, which expresses a relation of the idea *to an object* according to concepts, not to the subject according to feelings. It is, then, practical only in so far as the faculty of desire is determined by the sensation of agreeableness which the subject expects from the actual existence of the object. Now, a rational being's consciousness of the pleasantness of life uninterruptedly accompanying his whole existence is happiness; and the principle which makes this the supreme ground of determination of the will is the principle of self-love. All material principles, then, which place the determining ground of the will in the pleasure or pain to be received from the existence of any object are all of the same kind, inasmuch as they all belong to the principle of self-love or private happiness.

Corollary

All *material* practical rules place the determining principle of the will in the *lower desires,* and if there were no *purely formal* laws of the will adequate to determine it, then we could not admit *any higher desire* at all.

Remark I

It is surprising that men, otherwise acute, can think it possible to distinguish between *higher* and *lower desires,* according as the ideas which are connected with the feeling of pleasure have their origin in the *senses* or in the *understanding;* for when we inquire what are the determining grounds of desire, and place them in some expected pleasantness, it is of no consequence whence the *idea* of this pleasing object is derived, but only how much it *pleases.* Whether an idea has its seat and source in the understanding or not, if it can only determine the choice by presupposing a feeling of pleasure in the subject, it follows that its capability of determining the choice depends altogether on the nature of the inner sense, namely, that this can be agreeably affected by it. However dissimilar ideas of objects may be, though they be ideas of the understanding, or even of the reason in contrast to ideas of sense, yet the feeling of pleasure, by means of which they constitute the determining principle of the will (the expected satisfaction which impels the activity to the production of the object), is of one and the same kind, not only inasmuch as it can only be known empirically, but also inasmuch as it affects one and the same vital force which manifests itself in the faculty of desire, and in this respect can only differ in degree from every other ground of determination. Otherwise, how could we compare in respect of *magnitude* two principles of determination, the ideas of which depend upon different faculties, so as to prefer that which affects the faculty of desire in the highest degree. The same man may return unread an instructive book which he cannot again obtain, in order not to miss a hunt; he may depart in the midst of a fine speech, in order not to be late for dinner; he may leave a rational conversation, such as he otherwise values highly, to take his place at the gaming-table; he may even repulse a poor man whom he at other times takes pleasure in benefiting, because he has only just enough money in his pocket to pay for his admission to the theatre. If the determination of his will rests on the feeling of the agreeableness or disagreeableness that he expects from any cause, it is all the same to him by what sort of ideas he will be affected. The only thing that concerns him, in order to decide his choice, is, how great, how long continued, how easily obtained, and how often repeated, this agreeableness is. Just as to the man who wants money to spend, it is all the same whether the gold was dug out of the mountain or washed out of the sand, provided it is everywhere accepted at the same value; so the man who cares only for the enjoyment of life does not ask whether the ideas are of the understanding or the senses, but only *how much* and *how great pleasure* they will give for the longest time. It is only those that would gladly deny to pure reason the power of determining the will, without the presupposition of any feeling, who could deviate so far from their own exposition as to describe as quite heterogeneous what they have themselves previously brought under one and the same principle. Thus, for example, it is observed that we can find pleasure in the mere *exercise of power,* in the consciousness of our strength of mind in overcoming obstacles which are opposed to our designs, in the culture of our mental talents, etc.; and we justly call these more refined pleasures and enjoyments, because they are more in our power than others; they do not wear out, but rather increase the capacity for further enjoyment of them, and while they delight they at the same time cultivate. But to say on this account that they determine the will in a different way, and not through sense, whereas the possibility of the pleasure presupposes a feeling for it implanted in us, which is the first condition of this satisfaction; this is just as when ignorant persons that like to dabble in metaphysics imagine matter so subtle, so super-subtle, that they almost make themselves giddy with it, and then think that in this way they have conceived it as a *spiritual* and yet extended being. If with *Epicurus* we make virtue determine the will only by means of the pleasure it promises, we cannot afterwards blame him for holding that this pleasure is of the same kind as those of the coarsest senses. For we have no reason whatever to charge him with holding that the ideas by which this feeling is excited in us belong merely to the bodily senses. As far as can be conjectured, he sought the source of many of them in the use of the higher cognitive faculty; but this did not prevent him, and could not prevent him, from holding on the principle above stated, that the pleasure itself which those intellectual ideas give us, and by which alone they can determine the will, is just of the same kind. *Consistency* is the highest obligation of a philosopher, and yet the most rarely found. The ancient Greek schools give us more examples of it than we find in our *syncretistic* age, in which a certain shallow and dishonest *system of compromise* of contradictory principles is devised, because it commends itself better to a public which is content to know something of everything and nothing thoroughly, so as to please every party.[2]

The principle of private happiness, however much understanding and reason may be used in it, cannot contain any other determining principles for the will than those which belong to the *lower* desires; and either there are no [higher][3] desires at all, or *pure* reason must of itself alone be practical: that is, it must be able to determine the will by the mere form of the practical rule without supposing any feeling, and consequently without any idea of the pleasant or unpleasant, which is the matter of the desire, and which is always an empirical condition of the principles. Then only, when reason of itself determines the will (not as the servant of the inclination), it is really a *higher* desire to which that which is pathologically determined is subordinate, and is really, and even specifically, distinct from the latter, so that even the slightest admixture of the motives of the latter impairs its strength and superiority; just as in a mathematical demonstration the least empirical

---

[2] Literally, "to have a firm seat in any saddle." It may be noted that Kant's father was a saddler.
[3] Not in the original text.

condition would degrade and destroy its force and value. Reason, with its practical law, determines the will immediately, not by means of an intervening feeling of pleasure or pain, not even of pleasure in the law itself, and it is only because it can, as pure reason, be practical, that it is possible for it to be *legislative*.

Remark II

To be happy is necessarily the wish of every finite rational being, and this, therefore, is inevitably a determining principle of its faculty of desire. For we are not in possession originally of satisfaction with our whole existence—a bliss which would imply a consciousness of our own independent self-sufficiency—this is a problem imposed upon us by our own finite nature, because we have wants, and these wants regard the matter of our desires, that is, something that is relative to a subjective feeling of pleasure or pain, which determines what we need in order to be satisfied with our condition. But just because this material principle of determination can only be empirically known by the subject, it is impossible to regard this problem as a law; for a law being objective must contain the *very same principle of determination* of the will in all cases and for all rational beings. For, although the notion of happiness is *in every case* the foundation of the practical relation of the *objects* to the desires, yet it is only a general name for the subjective determining principles, and determines nothing specifically; whereas this is what alone we are concerned with in this practical problem, which cannot be solved at all without such specific determination. For it is every man's own special feeling of pleasure and pain that decides in what he is to place his happiness, and even in the same subject this will vary with the difference of his wants according as this feeling changes, and thus a law which is *subjectively necessary* (as a law of nature) is *objectively* a very contingent practical principle, which can and must be very different in different subjects, and therefore can never furnish a law; since, in the desire for happiness it is not the form (of conformity to law) that is decisive, but simply the matter, namely, whether I am to expect pleasure in following the law, and how much. Principles of self-love may, indeed, contain universal precepts of skill (how to find means to accomplish one's purposes), but in that case they are merely theoretical principles;* as, for example, how he who would like to eat bread should contrive a mill; but practical precepts founded on them can never be universal, for the determining principle of the desire is based on the feeling of pleasure and pain, which can never be supposed to be universally directed to the same objects.

Even supposing, however, that all finite rational beings were thoroughly agreed as to what were the objects of their feelings of pleasure and pain, and also as to the means which they must employ to attain the one and avoid the other; still, they could *by no means* set up the *principle of self-love* as a *practical law,* for this unanimity itself would be only contingent. The principle of determination would still be only subjectively valid and merely empirical, and would not possess the necessity which is conceived in every law, namely, an objective necessity arising from *a priori* grounds; unless, indeed, we hold this necessity to be not at all practical, but merely physical, viz. that our action is as inevitably determined by our inclination, as yawning when we see others yawn. It would be better to maintain that there are no practical laws at all, but only *counsels* for the service of our desires, than to raise merely subjective principles to the rank of practical laws, which have objective necessity, and not merely subjective, and which must be known by reason *a priori,* not by experience (however empirically universal this may be). Even the rules of corresponding phenomena are only called laws of nature (e.g. the mechanical laws), when we either know them really *a priori,* or (as in the case of chemical laws) suppose that they would be known *a priori* from objective grounds if our insight reached further. But in the case of merely subjective practical principles, it is expressly made a condition that they rest not on objective but on subjective conditions of choice, and hence that they must always be represented as mere maxims; never as practical laws. This second remark seems at first sight to be mere verbal refinement, but it defines[4] the terms of the most important distinction which can come into consideration in practical investigations.

---

* Propositions which in mathematics or physics are called *practical* ought properly to be called *technical.* For they have nothing to do with the determination of the will; they only point out how a certain effect is to be produced, and are therefore just as theoretical as any propositions which express the connexion of a cause with an effect. Now whoever chooses the effect must also choose the cause.

[4] The original sentence is defective; Hartenstein supplies "enthält."

§IV—THEOREM III

A rational being cannot regard his maxims as practical universal laws, unless he conceives them as principles which determine the will, not by their matter, but by their form only.

By the matter of a practical principle I mean the object of the will. This object is either the determinating ground of the will or it is not. In the former case the rule of the will is subjected to an empirical condition (viz. the relation of the determining idea to the feeling of pleasure and pain); consequently it cannot be a practical law. Now, when we abstract from a law all matter, i.e. every object of the will (as a determining principle), nothing is left but the mere *form* of a universal legislation. Therefore, either a rational being cannot conceive his subjective practical principles, that is, his maxims, as being at the same time universal laws, or he must suppose that their mere form, by which they are fitted for universal legislation, is alone what makes them practical laws.

Remark

The commonest understanding can distinguish without instruction what form of maxim is adapted for universal legislation, and what is not. Suppose, for example, that I have made it my maxim to increase my fortune by every safe means. Now, I have a deposit in my hands, the owner of which is dead and has left no writing about it. This is just the case for my maxim. I desire, then, to know whether that maxim can also hold good as a universal practical law. I apply it, therefore, to the present case, and ask whether it could take the form of a law, and consequently whether I can by my maxim at the same time give such a law as this, that everyone may deny a deposit of which no one can produce a proof. I at once become aware that such a principle, viewed as a law, would annihilate itself, because the result would be that there would be no deposits. A practical law which I recognize as such must be qualified for universal legislation; this is an identical proposition, and therefore self-evident. Now, if I say that my will is subject to a practical law, I cannot adduce my inclination (e.g. in the present case my avarice) as a principle of determination fitted to be a universal practical law; for this is so far from being fitted for a universal legislation that, if put in the form of a universal law, it would destroy itself.

It is, therefore, surprising that intelligent men could have thought of calling the desire of happiness a universal *practical law* on the ground that the desire is universal, and, therefore, also the *maxim* by which everyone makes this desire determine his will. For whereas in other cases a universal law of nature makes everything harmonious; here, on the contrary, if we attribute to the maxim the universality of a law, the extreme opposite of harmony will follow, the greatest opposition, and the complete destruction of the maxim itself, and its purpose. For, in that case, the will of all has not one and the same object, but everyone has his own (his private welfare), which may accidentally accord with the purposes of others which are equally selfish, but it is far from sufficing for a law; because the occasional exceptions which one is permitted to make are endless, and cannot be definitely embraced in one universal rule. In this manner, then, results a harmony like that which a certain satirical poem depicts as existing between a married couple bent on going to ruin, "O, marvellous harmony, what he wishes, she wishes also"; or like what is said of the pledge of Francis I to the Emperor Charles V, "What my brother Charles wishes that I wish also" (viz. Milan). Empirical principles of determination are not fit for any universal external legislation, but just as little for internal; for each man makes his own subject the foundation of his inclination, and in the same subject sometimes one inclination, sometimes another, has the preponderance. To discover a law which would govern them all under this condition, namely, bringing them all into harmony, is quite impossible.

§V—PROBLEM I

Supposing that the mere legislative form of maxims is alone the sufficient determining principle of a will, to find the nature of the will which can be determined by it alone.

Since the bare form of the law can only be conceived by reason, and is, therefore, not an object of the senses, and consequently does not belong to the class of phenomena, it follows that the idea of it, which determines the will, is distinct from all the principles that determine events in nature according to the law of causality, because in their case the determining principles must themselves be phenomena. Now, if no other determining principle can serve as a law for the will except that universal legislative form, such a will must be conceived as quite independent on the natural law of phenomena in their mutual relation, namely, the law of causality; such independence is called *freedom* in the strictest, that is in the transcendental sense; consequently, a will which can have its law in nothing but the mere legislative form of the maxim is a free will.

§VI—PROBLEM II

Supposing that a will is free, to find the law which alone is competent to determine it necessarily.

Since the matter of the practical law, i.e. an object of the maxim, can never be given otherwise than empirically, and the free will is independent on empirical conditions (that is, conditions belonging to the world of sense), and yet is determinable, consequently a free will must find its principle of determination in the law, and yet independently of the matter of the law. But, beside the matter of the law, nothing is contained in it except the legislative form. It is the legislative form, then, contained in the maxim, which can alone constitute a principle of determination of the [free] will.

Remarks

Thus freedom and an unconditional practical law reciprocally imply each other. Now I do not ask here whether they are in fact distinct, or whether an unconditional law is not rather merely the consciousness of a pure practical reason, and the latter identical with the positive concept of freedom; I only ask, whence *begins* our *knowledge* of the unconditionally practical, whether it is from freedom or from the practical law? Now it cannot begin from freedom, for of this we cannot be immediately conscious, since the first concept of it is negative; nor can we infer it from experience, for experience gives us the knowledge only of the law of phenomena, and hence of the mechanism of nature, the direct opposite of freedom. It is therefore the moral law, of which we become directly conscious (as soon as we trace for ourselves maxims of the will), that *first* presents itself to us, and leads directly to the concept of freedom, inasmuch as reason presents it as a principle of determination not to be outweighed by any sensible conditions, nay, wholly independent of them. But how is the consciousness of that moral law possible? We can become conscious of pure practical laws just as we are conscious of pure theoretical principles, by attending to the necessity with which reason prescribes them, and to the elimination of all empirical conditions, which it directs. The concept of a pure will arises out of the former, as that of a pure understanding arises out of the latter. That this is the true subordination of our concepts, and that it is morality that first discovers to us the notion of freedom, hence that it is *practical reason* which, with this concept, first proposes to speculative reason the most insoluble problem, thereby placing it in the greatest perplexity, is evident from the following consideration: Since nothing in phenomena can be explained by the concept of freedom, but the mechanism of nature must constitute the only clue; moreover, when pure reason tries to ascend in the series of causes to the unconditioned, it falls into an antinomy which is entangled in incomprehensibilities on the one side as much as the other; whilst the latter (namely, mechanism) is at least useful in the explanation of phenomena, therefore no one would ever have been so rash as to introduce freedom into science, had not the moral law, and with it practical reason, come in and forced this notion upon us. Experience, however, confirms this order of notions. Suppose some one asserts of his lustful appetite that, when the desired object and the opportunity are present, it is quite irresistable. [Ask him]—if a gallows were erected before the house where he finds this opportunity, in order that he should be hanged thereon immediately after the gratification of his lust, whether he could not then control his passion; we need not be long in doubt what he would reply. Ask him, however—if his sovereign ordered him, on pain of the same immediate execution, to bear false witness against an honourable man, whom the prince might wish to destroy under a plausible pretext, would he consider it possible in that case to overcome his love of life, however great it may be. He would perhaps not venture to affirm whether he would do so or not, but he must unhesitatingly admit that it is possible to do so. He judges, therefore, that he can do a certain thing because he is conscious that he ought, and he recognizes that he is free—a fact which but for the moral law he would never have known.

§VII—FUNDAMENTAL LAW OF THE PURE PRACTICAL

REASON

Act so that the maxim of thy will can always at the same time hold good as a principle of universal legislation.

Remark

Pure geometry has postulates which are practical propositions, but contain nothing further than the assumption that we *can* do something if it is required that we *should* do it, and these are the only geometrical propositions that concern actual existence. They are, then, practical rules under a problematical condition of the will; but here the rule says: We absolutely must proceed in a certain manner. The practical rule is, therefore, unconditional, and hence it is conceived *a priori* as a categorically practical proposition by which the will is objectively determined absolutely and immediately (by the practical rule itself, which thus is in this case a law); for *pure reason practical of itself* is here directly legislative. The will is thought as independent on empirical conditions, and, therefore, as pure will determined by *the mere form of the law,* and this principle of determination is regarded as the supreme condition of all maxims. The thing is strange enough, and has no parallel in all the rest of our practical knowledge. For the *a priori* thought of a possible universal legislation which is therefore merely problematical, is unconditionally commanded as a law without borrowing anything from experience or from any external will. This, however, is not a precept to do something by which some desired effect can be attained (for then the will would depend on physical conditions), but a rule that determines the will *a priori* only so far as regards the forms of its maxims; and thus it is at least not impossible to conceive that a law, which only applies to the *subjective* form of principles, yet serves as a principle of determination by means of the *objective* form of law in general. We may call the consciousness of this fundamental law a fact of reason, because we cannot reason it out from antecedent data of reason, e.g. the consciousness of freedom (for this is not antecedently given), but it forces itself on us as a synthetic *a priori* proposition, which is not based on any intuition, either pure or empirical. It would, indeed, be analytical if the freedom of the will were presupposed, but to presuppose freedom as a positive *concept* would require an intellectual intuition, which cannot here be assumed; however, when we regard this law as *given,* it must be observed, in order not to fall into any misconception, that it is not an empirical fact, but the sole fact of the pure reason, which thereby announces itself as originally legislative (*sic volo sic jubeo*).

Corollary

Pure reason is practical of itself alone, and gives (to man) a universal law which we call the *Moral Law.*

Remark

The fact just mentioned is undeniable. It is only necessary to analyse the judgment that men pass on the lawfulness of their actions, in order to find that, whatever inclination may say to the contrary, reason, incorruptible and self-constrained, always confronts the maxim of the will in any action with the pure will, that is, with itself, considering itself as *a priori* practical. Now this principle of morality, just on account of the universality of the legislation which makes it the formal supreme determining principle of the will, without regard to any subjective differences, is declared by the reason to be a law for all rational beings, in so far as they have a will, that is, a power to determine their causality by the conception of rules; and, therefore, so far as they are capable of acting according to principles, and consequently also according to practical *a priori* principles (for these alone have the necessity that reason requires in a principle). It is, therefore, not limited to men only, but applies to all finite beings that possess reason and will; nay, it even includes the Infinite Being as the supreme intelligence. In the former case, however, the law has the form of an imperative, because in them, as rational beings, we can suppose a *pure* will, but being creatures affected with wants and physical motives, not a *holy* will, that is, one which would be incapable of any maxim conflicting with the moral law. In their case, therefore, the moral law is an *imperative,* which commands categorically, because the law is unconditioned; the relation of such a will to this law is *dependence* under the name of *obligation,* which implies a *constraint* to an action, though only by reason and its objective law; and this action is called *duty,* because an elective will, subject to pathological affections (though not determined by them, and therefore still free), implies a wish that arises from *subjective* causes, and therefore may often be opposed to the pure objective determining principle; whence it requires the moral constraint of a resistance of the practical reason, which may be called an internal, but intellectual, compulsion. In the supreme intelligence the elective will is rightly conceived as incapable of any maxim which could not at the same time be objectively a law; and the notion of *holiness,* which on that account belongs to it, places it, not indeed above all practical laws, but above all practically restrictive laws, and consequently above obligation and duty. This holiness of will is, however, a practical idea, which must necessarily serve as a type to which finite rational beings can only approximate indefinitely, and which the pure moral law, which is itself on this account called holy, constantly and rightly holds before their eyes. The utmost that finite practical reason can effect is to be certain of this indefinite progress of one's maxims, and of their steady disposition to advance. This is virtue, and virtue, at least as a naturally acquired faculty, can never be perfect, because assurance in such a case never becomes apodictic certainty, and when it only amounts to persuasion is very dangerous.

§VIII—THEOREM IV

The *autonomy* if the will is the sole principle of all moral laws, and of all duties which conform to them; on the other hand, *heteronomy* of the elective will not only cannot be the basis of any obligation, but is, on the contrary, opposed to the principle thereof, and to the morality of the will.

In fact the sole principle of morality consists in the independence on all matter of the law (namely, a desired object), and in the determination of the elective will by the mere universal legislative form of which its maxim must be capable. Now this *independence* is *freedom* in the *negative* sense, and this *self-legislation* of the pure, and therefore practical, reason is freedom in the *positive* sense. Thus the moral law expresses nothing else than the *autonomy* of the pure practical reason; that is, freedom; and this is itself the formal condition of all maxims, and on this condition only can they agree with the supreme practical law. If therefore the matter of the volition, which can be nothing else than the object of a desire that is connected with the law, enters into the practical law, *as the condition of its possibility,* there results heteronomy of the elective will, namely, dependence on the physical law that we should follow some impulse or inclination. In that case the will does not give itself the law, but only the precept how rationally to follow pathological law; and the maxim which, in such a case, never contains the universally legislative form, not only produces no obligation, but is itself opposed to the principle of a pure practical reason, and, therefore, also to the moral disposition, even though the resulting action may be conformable to the law.

Remark I

Hence ɩ. practical precept, which contains a material (and therefore empirical) condition, must never be reckoned a practical law. For the law of the pure will, which is free, brings the will into a sphere quite different from the empirical; and as the necessity involved in the law is not a physical necessity, it can only consist in the formal conditions of the possibility of a law in general. All the matter of practical rules rests on subjective conditions, which give them only a conditional universality (in case I *desire* this or that, what I must do in order to obtain it), and they all turn on the principle of *private happiness*. Now, it is indeed undeniable that every volition must have an object, and therefore a matter; but it does not follow that this is the determining principle, and the condition of the maxim; for, if it is so, then this cannot be exhibited in a universally legislative form, since in that case the expectation of the existence of the object would be the determining cause of the choice, and the volition must presuppose the dependence of the faculty of desire on the existence of something; but this dependence can only be sought in empirical conditions, and therefore can never furnish a foundation for a necessary and universal rule. Thus, the happiness of others may be the object of the will of a rational being. But if it were the determining principle of the maxim, we must assume that we find not only a rational satisfaction in the welfare of others, but also a want such as the sympathetic disposition in some men occasions. But I cannot assume the existence of this want in every rational being (not at all in God). The matter, then, of the maxim may remain, but it must not be the condition of it, else the maxim could not be fit for a law. Hence, the mere form of law, which limits the matter, must also be a reason for adding this matter to the will, not for presupposing it. For example, let the matter be my own happiness. This (rule), if I attribute it to everyone (as, in fact, I may, in the case of every finite being), can become an *objective* practical law only if I include the happiness of others. Therefore, the law that we should promote the happiness of others does not arise from the assumption that this is an object of everyone's choice, but merely from this, that the form of universality which reason requires as the condition of giving to a maxim of self-love the objective validity of a law, is the principle that determines the will. Therefore it was not the object (the happiness of others) that determined the pure will, but it was the form of law only, by which I restricted my maxim, founded on inclination, so as to give it the universality of a law, and thus to adapt it to the practical reason; and it is this restriction alone, and not the addition of an external spring, that can give rise to the notion of the *obligation* to extend the maxim of my self-love to the happiness of others.

Remark II

The direct opposite of the principle of morality is, when the principle of *private* happiness is made the determining principle of the will, and with this is to be reckoned, as I have shown above, everything that places the determining principle which is to serve as a law anywhere but in the legislative form of the maxim. This contradiction, however, is not merely logical, like that which would arise between rules empirically conditioned, if they were raised to the rank of necessary principles of cognition, but is practical, and would ruin morality altogether were not the voice of reason in reference to the will so clear, so irrepressible, so distinctly audible even to the commonest men. It can only, indeed, be maintained in the perplexing speculations of the schools, which are bold enough to shut their ears against that heavenly voice, in order to support a theory that costs no trouble.

Suppose that an acquaintance whom you otherwise liked were to attempt to justify himself to you for having borne false witness, first by alleging the, in his view, sacred duty of consulting his own happiness; then by enumerating the advantages which he had gained thereby, pointing out the prudence he had shown in securing himself against detection, even by yourself, to whom he now reveals the secret only in order that he may be able to deny it at any time; and suppose he were then to affirm, in all seriousness, that he has fulfilled a true human duty; you would either laugh in his face, or shrink back from him with disgust; and yet, if a man has regulated his principles of action solely with a view to his own advantage, you would have nothing whatever to object against this mode of proceeding. Or suppose some one recommends you a man as steward, as a man to whom you can blindly trust all your affairs; and, in order to inspire you with confidence, extols him as a prudent man who thoroughly understands his own interest, and is so indefatigably active that he lets slip no opportunity of advancing it; lastly, lest you should be afraid of finding a vulgar selfishness in him, praises the good taste with which he lives:

not seeking his pleasure in money-making or in coarse wantonness, but in the enlargement of his knowledge, in instructive intercourse with a select circle, and even in relieving the needy; while as to the means (which, of course, derive all their value from the end) he is not particular, and is ready to use other people's money for the purpose, as if it were his own, provided only he knows that he can do so safely and without discovery; you would either believe that the recommender was mocking you, or that he had lost his senses. So sharply and clearly marked are the boundaries of morality and self-love that even the commonest eye cannot fail to distinguish whether a thing belongs to the one or the other. The few remarks that follow may appear superfluous where the truth is so plain, but at least they may serve to give a little more distinctness to the judgment of common sense.

The principle of happiness may, indeed, furnish maxims, but never such as would be competent to be laws of the will, even if *universal* happiness were made the object. For since the knowledge of this rests on mere empirical data, since every man's judgment on it depends very much on his particular point of view, which is itself moreover very variable, it can supply only *general* rules, not *universal;* that is, it can give rules which on the average will most frequently fit, but not rules which must hold good always and necessarily; hence, no practical *laws* can be founded on it. Just because in this case an object of choice is the foundation of the rule, and must therefore precede it; the rule can refer to nothing but what is [felt],[5] and therefore it refers to experience and is founded on it, and then the variety of judgment must be endless. This principle, therefore, does not prescribe the same practical rules to all rational beings, although the rules are all included under a common title, namely, that of happiness. The moral law, however, is conceived as objectively necessary, only because it holds for everyone that has reason and will.

The maxim of self-love (prudence) only *advises;* the law of morality *commands.* Now there is a great difference between that which we are *advised* to do and that to which we are *obliged.*

The commonest intelligence can easily and without hesitation see what, on the principle of autonomy of the will, requires to be done; but on supposition of heteronomy of the will, it is hard and requires knowledge of the world to see what is to be done. That is to say, what *duty* is, is plain of itself to everyone;

[5] Reading "empfindet" instead of "empfiehlt."

but what is to bring true durable advantage, such as will extend to the whole of one's existence, is always veiled in impenetrable obscurity; and much prudence is required to adapt the practical rule founded on it to the ends of life, even tolerably, by making proper exceptions. But the moral law commands the most punctual obedience from everyone; it must, therefore, not be so difficult to judge what it requires to be done, that the commonest unpractised understanding, even without worldly prudence, should fail to apply it rightly.

It is always in everyone's power to satisfy the categorical command of morality; whereas it is but seldom possible, and by no means so to everyone, to satisfy the empirically conditioned precept of happiness, even with regard to a single purpose. The reason is, that in the former case there is question only of the maxim, which must be genuine and pure; but in the latter case there is question also of one's capacity and physical power to realize a desired object. A command that everyone should try to make himself happy would be foolish, for one never commands anyone to do what he of himself infallibly wishes to do. We must only command the means, or rather supply them, since he cannot do everything that he wishes. But to command morality under the name of duty is quite rational; for, in the first place, not everyone is willing to obey its precepts if they oppose his inclinations; and as to the means of obeying this law, these need not in this case be taught, for in this respect whatever he wishes to do he can do.

He who has *lost* at play may be *vexed* at himself and his folly; but if he is conscious of having *cheated* at play (although he has gained thereby), he must *despise* himself as soon as he compares himself with the moral law. This must, therefore, be something different from the principle of private happiness. For a man must have a different criterion when he is compelled to say to himself: I am a *worthless* fellow, though I have filled my purse; and when he approves himself, and says: I am a *prudent* man, for I have enriched my treasure.

Finally, there is something further in the idea of our practical reason, which accompanies the transgression of a moral law—namely, its *ill desert*. Now the notion of punishment, as such, cannot be united with that of becoming a partaker of happiness; for although he who inflicts the punishment may at the same time have the benevolent purpose of directing this punishment to this end, yet it must first be justified in itself as punishment, i.e. as mere harm, so that if it stopped there, and the person punished could get no glimpse of kindness hidden behind this harshness, he must yet admit that justice was done him, and that his reward was perfectly suitable to his conduct. In every punishment, as such, there must first be justice, and this constitutes the essence of the notion. Benevolence may, indeed, be united with it, but the man who has deserved punishment, has not the least reason to reckon upon this. Punishment, then, is a physical evil, which, though it be not connected with moral evil as a *natural* consequence, ought to be connected with it as a consequence by the principles of a moral legislation. Now, if every crime, even without regarding the physical consequence with respect to the actor, is in itself punishable, that is, forfeits happiness (at least partially), it is obviously absurd to say that the crime consisted just in this, that he has drawn punishment on himself, thereby injuring his private happiness (which, on the principle of self-love, must be the proper notion of all crime). According to this view the punishment would be the reason for calling anything a crime, and justice would, on the contrary, consist in omitting all punishment, and even preventing that which naturally follows; for, if this were done, there would no longer be any evil in the action, since the harm which otherwise followed it, and on account of which alone the action was called evil, would now be prevented. To look, however, on all rewards and punishments as merely the machinery in the hand of a higher power, which is to serve only to set rational creatures striving after their final end (happiness), this is to reduce the will to a mechanism destructive of freedom; this is so evident that it need not detain us.

More refined, though equally false, is the theory of those who suppose a certain special moral sense, which sense and not reason determines the moral law, and in consequence of which the consciousness of virtue is supposed to be directly connected with contentment and pleasure; that of vice, with mental dissatisfaction and pain; thus reducing the whole to the desire of private happiness. Without repeating what has been said above, I will here only remark the fallacy they fall into. In order to imagine the vicious man as tormented with mental dissatisfaction by the consciousness of his transgressions, they must first represent him as in the main basis of his character, at least in some degree, morally good; just as he who is pleased with the consciousness of right conduct must be conceived as already virtuous. The notion of morality and duty must, therefore, have preceded any regard to this satisfaction, and cannot be derived from it. A man must first appreciate the importance of what we call duty, the authority of the moral law, and the immediate dignity which the following of it gives to the person in his own eyes, in order to feel that satisfaction in the consciousness of his conformity to it, and the bitter remorse that accompanies the consciousness of its transgression. It is, there-fore, impossible to feel this satisfaction or dissatisfaction prior to the knowledge of obligation, or to make it the basis of the latter. A man must be at least half honest in order even to be able to form a conception of these feelings. I do not deny that as the human will is, by virtue of liberty, capable of being immediately determined by the moral law, so frequent practice in accordance with this principle of determination can, at last, produce subjectively a feeling of satisfaction; on the contrary, it is a duty to establish and to cultivate this, which alone deserves to be called properly the moral feeling; but the notion of duty cannot be derived from it, else we should have to sup-pose a feeling for the law as such, and thus make that an object of sensation which can only be thought by the reason; and this, if it is not to be a flat contradiction, would destroy all notion of duty, and put in its place a mere mechanical play of refined inclinations sometimes contending with the coarser. . . .

Critique of Judgement

Part I
Critique of Aesthetic Judgement

PREFACE
TO THE FIRST EDITION, 1790

The faculty of knowledge from *a priori* principles may be called *pure reason,* and the general investigation into its possibility and bounds the Critique of pure reason. This is permissible although 'pure reason,' as was the case with the same use of terms in our first work, is only intended to denote reason in its theoretical employment, and although there is no desire to bring under review its faculty as practical reason and its special principles as such. That Critique is, then, an investigation addressed simply to our faculty of knowing things *a priori.* Hence it makes our *cognitive faculties* its sole concern, to the exclusion of the feeling of pleasure or displeasure and the faculty of desire; and among the cognitive faculties it confines its attention to *understanding* and its *a priori* principles, to the exclusion of *judgement* and *reason* (faculties that also belong to theoretical cognition,) because it turns out in the sequel that there is no cognitive faculty other than understanding capable of affording constitutive *a priori* principles of knowledge. Accordingly the Critique which sifts these faculties one and all, so as to try the possible claims of each of the other faculties to a share in the clear possession of knowledge from roots of its own, retains nothing but what *understanding* prescribes *a priori* as a law for nature as the complex of phenomena—the form of these being similarly furnished *a priori*. All other pure concepts it relegates to the rank of ideas, which for our faculty of theoretical cognition are transcendent: though they are not without their use nor redundant, but discharge certain functions as regulative principles. For these concepts serve partly to restrain the officious pretensions of understanding, which, presuming on its ability to supply *a priori* the conditions of the possibility of all things which it is capable of knowing, behaves as if it had thus determined these bounds as those of the possibility of all things generally, and partly also to lead understanding, in its study of nature, according to a principle of completeness, unattainable as this remains for it, and so to promote the ultimate aim of all knowledge.

Properly, therefore, it was *understanding*—which, so far as it contains constitutive *a priori* cognitive principles, has its special realm, and one, moreover, in our *faculty of knowledge*—that the Critique, called in a general way that of Pure Reason, was intended to establish in secure but particular possession against all other competitors. In the same way *reason,* which contains constitutive *a priori* principles solely in respect of the *faculty of desire,* gets its holding assigned to it by the Critique of Practical Reason.

But now comes *judgement,* which in the order of our cognitive faculties forms a middle term between understanding and reason. Has *it* also got independent *a priori* principles? If so, are they constitutive, or are they merely regulative, thus indicating no special realm? And do they give a rule *a priori* to the feeling of pleasure and displeasure, as the middle term between the faculties of cognition and desire, just as understanding prescribes laws *a priori* for the former and reason for the latter? This is the topic to which the present Critique is devoted.

A Critique of pure reason, i.e. of our faculty of judging on *a priori* principles, would be incomplete if the critical examination of judgement, which is a faculty of knowledge, and, as such, lays claim to independent principles, were not dealt with separately. Still, however, its principles cannot, in a system of pure philosophy, form a separate constituent part intermediate between the theoretical and practical divisions, but may when needful be annexed to one or other as occasion requires. For if such a system is some day worked out under the general name of Metaphysic—and its full and complete execution is both possible and of the utmost importance for the employment of reason in all departments of its activity—the critical examination of the ground for this edifice must have been previously carried down to the very depths of the foundations of the faculty of principles independent of experience, lest in some quarter it might give way, and, sinking, inevitably bring with it the ruin of all.

We may readily gather, however, from the nature of the faculty of judgement (whose correct employment is so necessary and universally requisite that it is just this faculty that is intended when we speak of sound understanding) that the discovery of a peculiar principle belonging to it—and some such it must contain in itself *a priori,* for otherwise it would not be a cognitive faculty the distinctive character of which is obvious to the most commonplace criticism—must be a task involving considerable difficulties. For this principle is one which must not be derived from *a priori* concepts, seeing that these are the property of understanding, and judgement is only directed to their application. It has, therefore, itself to furnish a concept, and one from which, properly, we get no cognition of a thing, but which it can itself employ as a rule only—but not as an objective rule to which it can adapt its judgement, because, for that, another faculty of judgement would again be required to enable us to decide whether the case was one for the application of the rule or not.

It is chiefly in those estimates that are called aesthetic, and which relate to the beautiful and sublime, whether of nature or of art, that one meets with the above difficulty about a principle (be it subjective or objective). And yet the critical search for a principle of judgement in their case is the most important item in a Critique of this faculty. For, although they do not of themselves contribute a whit to the knowledge of things, they still belong wholly to the faculty of knowledge, and evidence an immediate bearing of this faculty upon the feeling of pleasure or displeasure according to some *a priori* principle, and do so without confusing this principle with what is capable of being a determining ground of the faculty of desire, for the latter has its principles *a priori* in concepts of reason. Logical estimates of nature, however, stand on a different footing. They deal with cases in which experience presents a conformity to law in things, which the understanding's general concept of the sensible is no longer adequate to render intelligible or explicable, and in which judgement may have recourse to itself for a principle of the reference of the natural thing to the unknowable supersensible and, indeed, must employ some such principle, though with a regard only to itself and the knowledge of nature. For in these cases the application of such an *a priori* principle for the *cognition* of what is in the world is both possible and necessary, and withal opens out prospects which are profitable for practical reason. But here there is no immediate reference to the feeling of pleasure or displeasure. But this is precisely the riddle in the principle of judgement that necessitates a separate division for this faculty in the Critique, for there was nothing to prevent the formation of logical estimates according to concepts (from which no immediate conclusion can ever be drawn to the feeling of pleasure or displeasure) having been treated, with a critical statement of its limitations, in an appendage to the theoretical part of philosophy.

The present investigation of taste, as a faculty of aesthetic judgement, not being undertaken with a view to the formation or culture of taste, (which will pursue its course in the future, as in the past, independently of such inquiries,) but being merely directed to its transcendental aspects, I feel assured of its indulgent criticism in respect of any shortcomings on that score. But in all that is relevant to the transcendental aspect it must be prepared to stand the test of the most rigorous examination. Yet even here I venture to hope that the difficulty of unravelling a problem so involved in its nature may serve as an excuse for a certain amount of hardly avoidable obscurity in its solution, provided that the accuracy of our statement of the principle is proved with all requisite clearness. I admit that the mode of deriving the phenomena of judgement from that principle has not all the lucidity that is rightly demanded elsewhere, where the subject is cognition by concepts, and that I believe I have in fact attained in the second part of this work.

With this, then, I bring my entire critical undertaking to a close. I shall hasten to the doctrinal part, in order, as far as possible, to snatch from any advancing years what time may yet be favourable to the task. It is obvious that no separate division of Doctrine is reserved for the faculty of judgement, seeing that with judgement Critique takes the place of Theory; but, following the division of philosophy into theoretical and practical, and of pure philosophy in the same way, the whole ground will be covered by the Metaphysics of Nature and of Morals.

Introduction

I. DIVISION OF PHILOSOPHY

Philosophy may be said to contain the principles of the rational cognition that concepts afford us of things (not merely, as with Logic, the principles of the form of thought in general irrespective of the Objects), and, thus interpreted, the course, usually adopted, of dividing it into *theoretical* and *practical* is perfectly sound. But this makes imperative a specific distinction on the part of the concepts by which the principles of this rational cognition get their Object assigned to them, for if the concepts are not distinct they fail to justify a division, which always presupposes that the principles belonging to the rational cognition of the several parts of the science in question are themselves mutually exclusive.

Now there are but two kinds of concepts, and these yield a corresponding number of distinct principles of the possibility of their objects. The concepts referred to are those *of nature* and that *of freedom.* By the first of these a *theoretical* cognition from *a priori* principles becomes possible. In respect of such cognition, however, the second, by its very concept, imports no more than a negative principle (that of simple antithesis), while for the determination of the will, on the other hand, it establishes fundamental principles which enlarge the scope of its activity, and which on that account are called *practical.* Hence the division of philosophy falls properly into two parts, quite distinct in their principles—a theoretical, as *Philosophy of Nature,* and a practical, as *Philosophy of Morals* (for this is what the practical legislation of reason by the concept of freedom is called). Hitherto, however, in the application of these expressions to the division of the different principles, and with them to the division of philosophy, a gross misuse of the terms has prevailed; for what is practical according to concepts of nature has been taken as identical with what is practical according to the concept of freedom, with the result that a division has been made under these heads of theoretical and practical, by which, in effect, there has been no division at all (seeing that both parts might have similar principles).

The will—for this is what is said—is the faculty of desire and, as such, is just one of the many natural causes in the world, the one, namely, which acts by concepts; and whatever is represented as possible (or necessary) through the efficacy of will is called practically possible (or necessary): the intention being to distinguish its possibility (or necessity) from the physical possibility or necessity of an effect the causality of whose cause is not determined to its production by concepts (but rather, as with lifeless matter, by mechanism, and, as with the lower animals, by instinct). Now, the question in respect of the practical faculty: whether, that is to say, the concept, by which the causality of the will gets its rule, is a concept of nature or of freedom, is here left quite open.

The latter distinction, however, is essential. For, let the concept determining the causality be a concept of nature, and then the principles are *technically-practical;* but, let it be a concept of freedom, and they are *morally-practical.* Now, in the division of a rational science the difference between objects that require different principles for their cognition is the difference on which everything turns. Hence technically-practical principles belong to theoretical philosophy (natural science), whereas those morally-practical alone form the second part, that is, practical philosophy (ethical science).

All technically-practical rules (i.e. those of art and skill generally, or even of prudence, as a skill in exercising an influence over men and their wills) must, so far as their principles rest upon concepts, be reckoned only as corollaries to theoretical philosophy. For they only touch the possibility of things according to concepts of nature, and this embraces, not alone the means discoverable in nature for the purpose, but even the will itself (as a faculty of desire, and consequently a natural faculty), so far as it is determinable on these rules by natural motives. Still these practical rules are not called laws (like physical laws), but only precepts. This is due to the fact that the will does not stand simply under the natural concept, but also under the concept of freedom. In the latter connexion its principles are called laws, and these principles, with the addition of what follows from them, alone constitute the second or practical part of philosophy.

The solution of the problems of pure geometry is not allocated to a special part of that science, nor does the art of land-surveying merit the name of practical, in contradistinction to pure, as a second part of the general science of geometry, and with equally little, or perhaps less, right can the mechanical or chemical art of experiment or of observation be ranked as a practical part of the science of nature, or, in fine, domestic, agricultural, or political economy, the art of social intercourse, the principles of dietetics, or even general instruction as to the attainment of happiness, or as much as the control of the inclinations or the restraining of the affections with a view thereto, be denominated practical philosophy—not to mention forming these latter into a second part of philosophy in general. For, between them all, the above contain nothing more than rules of skill, which are thus only technically practical—the skill being directed to producing an effect which is possible according to natural concepts of causes and effects. As these concepts belong to theoretical philosophy they are subject to those precepts as mere corollaries of theoretical philosophy (i.e. as corollaries of natural science), and so cannot claim any place in any special philosophy called practical. On the other hand the morally practical precepts, which are founded entirely on the concept of freedom, to the complete exclusion of grounds taken from nature for the determination of the will, form quite a special kind of precepts. These, too, like the rules obeyed by nature, are, without qualification, called laws—though they do not, like the latter, rest on sensible conditions, but upon a supersensible principle—and they must needs have a separate part of philosophy allotted to them as their own, corresponding to the theoretical part, and termed practical philosophy.

Hence it is evident that a complex of practical precepts furnished by philosophy does not form a special part of philosophy, co-ordinate with the theoretical, by reason of its precepts being practical—for that they might be, notwithstanding that their principles were derived wholly from the theoretical knowledge of nature (as technically-practical rules). But an adequate reason only exists where their principle, being in no way borrowed from the concept of nature, which is always sensibly conditioned, rests consequently on the supersensible, which the concept of freedom alone makes cognizable by means of its formal laws, and where, therefore, they are morally-practical, i.e. not merely precepts and rules in this or that interest, but laws independent of all antecedent reference to ends or aims.

II. THE REALM OF PHILOSOPHY IN GENERAL

The employment of our faculty of cognition from principles, and with it philosophy, is coextensive with the applicability of *a priori* concepts.

Now a division of the complex of all the objects to which those concepts are referred for the purpose, where possible, of compassing their knowledge, may be made according to the varied competence or incompetence of our faculty in that connexion.

Concepts, so far as they are referred to objects apart from the question of whether knowledge of them is possible or not, have their field, which is determined simply by the relation in which their Object stands to our faculty of cognition in general. The part of this field in which knowledge is possible for us, is a territory (*territorium*) for these concepts and the requisite cognitive faculty. The part of the territory over which they exercise legislative authority is the realm (*ditio*) of these concepts, and their appropriate cognitive faculty. Empirical concepts have, therefore, their territory, doubtless, in nature as the complex of all sensible objects, but they have no realm (only a dwelling-place, *domicilium*), for, although they are formed according to law, they are not themselves legislative, but the rules founded on them are empirical, and consequently contingent.

Our entire faculty of cognition has two realms, that of natural concepts and that of the concept of freedom, for through both it prescribes laws *a priori*. In accordance with this distinction, then, philosophy is divisible into theoretical and practical. But the territory upon which its realm is established, and over which it *exercises* its legislative authority, is still always confined to the complex of the objects of all possible experience, taken as no more than mere phenomena, for otherwise legislation by the understanding in respect of them is unthinkable.

The function of prescribing laws by means of concepts of nature is discharged by understanding, and is theoretical. That of prescribing laws by means of the concept of freedom is discharged by reason and is merely practical. It is only in the practical sphere that reason can prescribe laws; in respect of theoretical knowledge (of nature) it can only (as by the understanding advised in the law) deduce from given laws their logical consequences, which still always remain restricted to nature. But we cannot reverse this and say that where rules are practical reason is then and there *legislative,* since the rules might be technically practical.

Understanding and reason, therefore, have two distinct jurisdictions over one and the same territory of experience. But neither can interfere with the other. For the concept of freedom just as little disturbs the legislation of nature, as the concept of nature influences legislation through the concept of freedom. That it is possible for us at least to think without contradiction of both these jurisdictions, and their appropriate faculties, as coexisting in the same Subject, was shown by the Critique of Pure Reason, since it disposed of the objections on the other side by detecting their dialectical illusion.

Still, how does it happen that these two different realms do not form *one* realm, seeing that, while they do not limit each other in their legislation, they continually do so in their effects in the sensible world? The explanation lies in the fact that the concept of nature represents its objects in intuition doubtless, yet not as things-in-themselves, but as mere phenomena, whereas the concept of freedom represents in its Object what is no doubt a thing-in-itself, but it does not make it intuitable, and further that neither the one nor the other is capable, therefore, of furnishing a theoretical cognition of its Object (or even of the thinking Subject) as a thing-in-itself, or, as this would be, of the supersensible—the idea of which has certainly to be introduced as the basis of the possibility of all those objects of experience, although it cannot itself ever be elevated or extended into a cognition.

Our entire cognitive faculty is, therefore, presented with an unbounded, but, also, inaccessible field—the field of the supersensible—in which we seek in vain for a territory, and on which, therefore, we can have no realm for theoretical cognition, be it for concepts of understanding or of reason. This field we must indeed occupy with ideas in the interest as well of the theoretical as the practical employment of reason, but in connexion with the laws arising from the concept of freedom we cannot procure for these ideas any but practical reality, which, accordingly, fails to advance our theoretical cognition one step towards the supersensible.

Albeit, then, between the realm of the natural concept, as the sensible, and the realm of the concept of freedom, as the supersensible, there is a great gulf fixed, so that it is not possible to pass from the former to the latter (by means of the theoretical employment of reason), just as if they were so many separate worlds, the first of which is powerless to exercise influence on the second: still the latter is *meant* to influence the former— that is to say, the concept of freedom is meant to actualize in the sensible world the end proposed by its laws; and nature must consequently also be capable of being regarded in such a way that in the conformity to law of its form it at least harmonizes with the possibility of the ends to be effectuated in it according to the laws of freedom. There must, therefore, be a ground of the *unity* of the surpersensible that lies at the basis of nature, with what the concept of freedom contains in a practical way, and although the concept of this ground neither theoretically nor practically attains to a knowledge of it, and so has no peculiar realm of its own, still it renders possible the transition from the mode of thought according to the principles of the one to that according to the principles of the other.

III. THE CRITIQUE OF JUDGEMENT AS A MEANS OF

CONNECTING THE TWO PARTS OF PHILOSOPHY IN A WHOLE

The Critique which deals with what our cognitive faculties are capable of yielding *a priori* has properly speaking no realm in respect of Objects; for it is not a doctrine, its sole business being to investigate whether, having regard to the general bearings of our faculties, a doctrine is possible by their means, and if so, how. Its field extends to all their pretensions, with a view to confining them within their legitimate bounds. But what is shut out of the division of Philosophy may still be admitted as a principal part into the general Critique of our faculty of pure cognition, in the event, namely, of its containing principles which are not in themselves available either for theoretical or practical employment.

Concepts of nature contain the ground of all theoretical cognition *a priori* and rest, as we saw, upon the legislative authority of understanding. The concept of freedom contains the ground of all sensuously unconditioned practical precepts *a priori,* and rests upon that of reason. Both faculties, therefore, besides their application in point of logical form to principles of whatever origin, have, in addition, their own peculiar jurisdiction in the matter of their content, and so, there being no further (*a priori*) jurisdiction above them, the division of Philosophy into theoretical and practical is justified.

But there is still further in the family of our higher cognitive faculties a middle term between understanding and reason. This is *judgement,* of which we may reasonably presume by analogy that it may likewise contain, if not a special authority to prescribe laws, still a principle peculiar to itself upon which laws are sought, although one merely subjective *a priori*. This principle, even if it has no field of objects appropriate to it as its realm, may still have some territory or other with a certain character, for which just this very principle alone may be valid.

But in addition to the above considerations there is yet (to judge by analogy) a further ground, upon which judgement may be brought into line with another arrangement of our powers of representation, and one that appears to be of even greater importance than that of its kinship with the family of cognitive faculties. For all faculties of the soul, or capacities, are reducible to three, which do not admit of any further derivation from a common ground: the *faculty of knowledge,* the *feeling of pleasure or displeasure,* and the *faculty of desire.** For the faculty of cognition understanding alone is legislative, if (as must be the case where it is considered on its own account free of confusion with the faculty of desire) this faculty,

* Where one has reason to suppose that a relation subsists between concepts, that are used as empirical principles, and the faculty of pure cognition *a priori,* it is worth while attempting, in consideration of this connexion, to give them a transcendental definition—a definition, that is, by pure categories, so far as these by themselves adequately indicate the distinction of the concept in question from others. This course follows that of the mathematician, who leaves the empirical data of his problem indeterminate, and only brings their relation in pure synthesis under the concepts of pure arithmetic, and thus generalizes his solution. I have been taken to task for adopting a similar procedure (*Critique of Practical Reason,* Preface) and fault has been found with my definition of the faculty of desire, as *a faculty which by means of its representations is the cause of the actuality of the objects of those representations:* for mere *wishes* would still be desires, and yet in their case every one is ready to abandon all claim to being able by means of them alone to call their Object into existence. But this proves no more than the presence of desires in man by which he is in contradiction with himself. For in such a case he seeks the production of the Object by means of his representation alone, without any hope of its being effectual, since he is conscious that his mechanical powers (if I may so call those which are not psychological), which would have to be determined by that representation, are either unequal to the task of realizing the Object (by the intervention of means, therefore) or else are addressed to what is quite impossible, as, for example, to undo the past (*O mihi praeteritos,* &c.) or, to be able to annihilate the interval that, with intolerable delay, divides us from the wish-for moment. Now, conscious as we are in such fantastic desires of the inefficiency of our representations, (or even of their futility,) as *causes* of their objects, there is still involved in every *wish* a reference of the same as cause, and therefore the representation of its *causality,* and this is especially discernible where the wish, as *longing,* is an affection. For such affections, since they dilate the heart and render it inert and thus exhaust its powers, show that a strain is kept on being exerted and re-exerted on these powers by the representations, but that the mind is allowed continually to relapse and get languid upon recognition of the impossibility before it. Even prayers for the aversion of great, and, so far as we can see, inevitable evils, and many superstitious means for attaining ends impossible of attainment by natural means, prove the causal reference of representations to their Objects—a causality which not even the consciousness of inefficiency for producing the effect can deter from straining towards it. But why our nature should be furnished with a propensity to consciously vain desires is a teleological problem of anthropology. It would seem that were we not to be determined to the exertion of our power before we had assured ourselves of the efficiency of our faculty for producing an Object, our

as that of *theoretical cognition,* is referred to nature, in respect
of which alone (as phenomenon) it is possible for us to prescribe laws by means of *a priori* concepts of nature, which are
properly pure concepts of understanding. For the faculty of
desire, as a higher faculty operating under the concept of freedom, only reason (in which alone this concept has a place)
prescribes laws *a priori.* Now between the faculties of knowledge and desire stands the feeling of pleasure, just as judgement
is intermediate between understanding and reason. Hence we
may, provisionally at least, assume that judgement likewise contains an *a priori* principle of its own, and that, since pleasure or
displeasure is necessarily combined with the faculty of desire
(be it antecedent to its principle, as with the lower desires, or,
as with the higher, only supervening upon its determination by
the moral law), it will effect a transition from the faculty of
pure knowledge, i.e. from the realm of concepts of nature, to
that of the concept of freedom, just as in its logical employment it makes possible the transition from understanding to
reason.

Hence, despite the fact of Philosophy being only divisible
into two principal parts, the theoretical and the practical, and
despite the fact of all that we may have to say of the special
principles of judgement having to be assigned to its theoretical
part, i.e. to rational cognition according to concepts of nature:
still the Critique of pure reason, which must settle this whole
question before the above system is taken in hand, so as to sub-
stantiate its possibility, consists of three parts: the Critique of
pure understanding, of pure judgement, and of pure reason,
which faculties are called pure on the ground of their being
legislative *a priori.*

IV. JUDGEMENT AS A FACULTY BY WHICH LAWS ARE

PRESCRIBED A PRIORI

Judgement in general is the faculty of thinking the particular
as contained under the universal. If the universal (the rule,
principle, or law) is given, then the judgement which sub-

---

power would remain to a large extent unused. For as a rule we only
first learn to know our powers by making trial of them. This deceit of
vain desires is therefore only the result of a beneficent disposition in
our nature.

sumes the particular under it *is determinant*. This is so even where such a judgement is transcendental and, as such, provides the conditions *a priori* in conformity with which alone subsumption under that universal can be effected. If, however, only the particular is given and the universal has to be found for it, then the judgement is simply *reflective*.

The determinant judgement determines under universal transcendental laws furnished by understanding and is subsumptive only; the law is marked out for it *a priori*, and it has no need to devise a law for its own guidance to enable it to subordinate the particular in nature to the universal. But there are such manifold forms of nature, so many modifications, as it were, of the universal transcendental concepts of nature, left undetermined by the laws furnished by pure understanding *a priori* as above mentioned, and for the reason that these laws only touch the general possibility of a nature, (as an object of sense) that there must needs also be laws in this behalf. These laws, being empirical, may be contingent as far as the light of *our* understanding goes, but still, if they are to be called laws (as the concept of a nature requires) they must be regarded as necessary on a principle, unknown though it be to us, of the unity of the manifold. The reflective judgement which is compelled to ascend from the particular in nature to the universal, stands, therefore, in need of a principle. This principle it cannot borrow from experience, because what it has to do is to establish just the unity of all empirical principles under higher, though likewise empirical, principles, and thence the possibility of the systematic subordination of higher and lower. Such a transcendental principle, therefore, the reflective judgement can only give as a law from and to itself. It cannot derive it from any other quarter (as it would then be a determinant judgement). Nor can it prescribe it to nature, for reflection on the laws of nature adjusts itself to nature, and not nature to the conditions according to which we strive to obtain a concept of it, a concept that is quite contingent in respect of these conditions.

Now the principle sought can only be this: as universal laws of nature have their ground in our understanding, which prescribes them to nature (though only according to the universal concept of it as nature), particular empirical laws must be regarded, in respect of that which is left undetermined in them by these universal laws, according to a unity such as they would have if an understanding (though it be not ours) had supplied them for the benefit of our cognitive faculties, so as to render possible a system of experience according to particular natural laws. This is not to be taken as implying that such an understanding must be actually assumed (for it is only the reflective judgement which avails itself of this idea as a principle for the purpose of reflection and not for determining anything); but this faculty rather gives by this means a law to itself alone and not to nature.

Now the concept of an Object, so far as it contains at the same time the ground of the actuality of this Object, is called its *end,* and the agreement of a thing with that constitution of things which is only possible according to ends, is called the *finality* of its form. Accordingly the principle of judgement, in respect of the form of the things of nature under empirical laws generally, is the *finality of nature* in its multiplicity. In other words, by this concept nature is represented as if an understanding contained the ground of the unity of the manifold of its empirical laws.

The finality of nature is, therefore, a particular *a priori* concept, which has its origin solely in the reflective judgement. For we cannot ascribe to the products of nature anything like a reference of nature in them to ends, but we can only make use of this concept to reflect upon them in respect of the nexus of phenomena in nature—a nexus given according to empirical laws. Furthermore, this concept is entirely different from practical finality (in human art or even morals), though it is doubtless thought after this analogy.

V. THE PRINCIPLE OF THE FORMAL FINALITY OF NATURE IS A TRANSCENDENTAL PRINCIPLE OF JUDGEMENT

A transcendental principle is one through which we represent *a priori* the universal condition under which alone things can become Objects of our cognition generally. A principle, on the other hand, is called metaphysical, where it represents *a priori* the condition under which alone Objects whose concept has to be given empirically, may become further determined *a priori*. Thus the principle of the cognition of bodies as substances, and as changeable substances, is transcendental where the statement is that their change must have a cause: but it is metaphysical where it asserts that their change must have an *external cause*. For in the first case bodies need only be thought through ontological predicates (pure concepts of understanding), e.g. as substance, to enable the proposition of be cognized *a priori;* whereas, in the second case, the empirical concept of a body (as a movable thing in space) must be introduced to support the proposition, although, once this is done, it may be seen quite *a priori* that the latter predicate (movement only by means of an external cause) applies to body. In this way, as I shall show presently, the principle of the finality of nature (in the multiplicity of its empirical laws) is a transcendental principle. For the concept of Objects, regarded as standing under this principle, is only the pure concept of objects of possible empirical cognition generally, and involves nothing empirical. On the other hand the principle of practical finality, implied in the idea of the *determination* of a free *will,* would be a metaphysical principle, because the concept of a faculty of desire, as will, has to be given empirically, i.e. is not included among transcendental predicates. But both these principles are, none the less, not empirical, but *a priori* principles; because no further experience is required for the synthesis of the predicate with the empirical concept of the subject of their judgements, but it may be apprehended quite *a priori.*

That the concept of a finality of nature belongs to transcendental principles is abundantly evident from the maxims of judgement upon which we rely *a priori* in the investigation of nature, and which yet have to do with no more than the possibility of experience, and consequently of the knowledge of nature, but of nature not merely in a general way, but as determined by a manifold of particular laws. These maxims crop up frequently enough in the course of this science, though only in a scattered way. They are aphorisms of metaphysical wisdom, making their appearance in a number of rules the necessity of which cannot be demonstrated from concepts. 'Nature takes the shortest way (*lex parsimoniae*); yet it makes no leap, either in the sequence of its changes, or in the juxtaposition of specifically different forms (*lex continui in natura*); its vast variety in empirical laws is, for all that, unity under a few principles (*principia praeter necessitatem non sunt multiplicanda*)'; and so forth.

If we propose to assign the origin of these elementary rules, and attempt to do so on psychological lines, we go straight in the teeth of their sense. For they tell us, not what happens, i.e. according to what rule our powers of judgement actually discharge their functions, and how we judge, but how we ought to judge; and we cannot get this logical objective necessity where the principles are merely empirical. Hence the finality of nature for our cognitive faculties and their employment, which manifestly radiates from them, is a transcendental principle of judgements, and so needs also a transcendental Deduction, by means of which the ground for this mode of judging must be traced to the *a priori* sources of knowledge.

Now, looking at the grounds of the possibility of an experience, the first thing, of course, that meets us is something necessary—namely, the universal laws apart from which nature in general (as an object of sense) cannot be thought. These rest on the categories, applied to the formal conditions of all intuition possible for us, so far as it is also given *a priori*. Under these laws judgement is determinant; for it has nothing else to do than to subsume under given laws. For instance, understanding says: all change has its cause (universal law of nature); transcendental judgement has nothing further to do than to furnish *a priori* the condition of subsumption under the concept of understanding placed before it: this we get in the succession of the determinations of one and the same thing. Now for nature in general, as an object of possible experience, that law is cognized as absolutely necessary. But besides this formal time-condition, the objects of empirical cognition are determined, or, so far as we can judge *a priori,* are determinable, in divers ways, so that specifically differentiated natures, over and above what they have in common as things of nature in general, are further capable of being causes in an infinite variety of ways; and each of these modes must, on the concept of a cause in general, have its rule, which is a law, and, consequently, imports necessity: although owing to the constitution and limitations of our faculties of cognition we may entirely fail to see this necessity. Accordingly, in respect of nature's merely empirical laws, we must think in nature a possibility of an endless multiplicity of empirical laws, which yet are contingent so far as our insight goes, i.e. cannot be cognized *a priori.* In respect of these we estimate the unity of nature according to empirical laws, and the possibility of the unity of experience, as a system according to empirical laws, to be contingent. But, now, such a unity is one which must be necessarily presupposed and assumed, as otherwise we should not have a thoroughgoing connexion of empirical cognition in a whole of experience. For the universal laws of nature, while providing, certainly, for such a connexion among things generically, as things of nature in general, do not do so for them specifically as such particular things of nature. Hence judgement is compelled, for its own guidance, to adopt it as an *a priori* principle, that what is for human insight contingent in the particular (empirical) laws of nature contains nevertheless unity of law in the synthesis of its manifold in an intrinsically possible experience—unfathomable, though still thinkable, as such unity may, no doubt, be for us. Consequently, as the unity of law in a synthesis, which is cognized by us in obedience to a necessary aim (a need of understanding), though recognized at the same time as contingent, is represented as a finality of Objects (here of nature), so judgement, which, in respect of things under possible (yet to be discovered) empirical laws, is merely reflective, must regard nature in respect of the latter according to a *principle of finality* for our cognitive faculty, which then finds expression in the above maxims of judgement. Now this transcendental concept of a finality of nature is neither a concept of nature nor of freedom, since it attributes nothing at all to the Object, i.e. to nature, but only represents the unique mode in which we must proceed in our reflection upon the objects of nature with a view to getting a thoroughly interconnected whole of experience, and so is a subjective principle, i.e. maxim, of judgement. For this reason, too, just as if it were a lucky chance that favoured us, we are rejoiced (properly speaking relieved of a want) where we meet with such systematic unity under merely empirical laws: although we must necessarily assume the presence of such a unity, apart from any ability on our part to apprehend or prove its existence.

In order to convince ourselves of the correctness of this Deduction of the concept before us, and the necessity of assuming it as a transcendental principle of cognition, let us just bethink ourselves of the magnitude of the task. We have to form a connected experience from given perceptions of a nature containing a maybe endless multiplicity of empirical laws, and this problem has its seat *a priori* in our understanding. This understanding is no doubt *a priori* in possession of universal laws of nature, apart from which nature would be incapable of being an object of experience at all. But over and above this it needs a certain order of nature in its particular rules which are only capable of being brought to its knowledge empirically, and which, so far as it is concerned, are contingent. These rules, without which we would have no means of advance from the universal analogy of a possible experience in general to a particular, must be regarded by understanding as laws, i.e. as necessary—for otherwise they would not form an order of nature —though it be unable to cognize or ever get an insight into their necessity. Albeit, then, it can determine nothing *a priori* in respect of these (Objects), it must, in pursuit of such empirical so-called laws, lay at the basis of all reflection upon them an *a priori* principle, to the effect, namely, that a cognizable order of nature is possible according to them. A principle of this kind is expressed in the following propositions. There is in nature a subordination of genera and species comprehensible by us: Each of these genera again approximates to the others on a common principle, so that a transition may be possible from one to the other, and thereby to a higher genus: While it seems at the outset unavoidable for our understanding to assume for the specific variety of natural operations a like number of various kinds of causality, yet these may all be reduced to a small number of principles, the quest for which is our business; and so forth. This adaptation of nature to our cognitive faculties is presupposed *a priori* by judgement on behalf of its reflection upon it according to empirical laws. But understanding all the while recognizes it objectively as contingent, and it is merely judgement that attributes it to nature as transcendental finality, i.e. a finality in respect of the Subject's faculty of cognition. For, were it not for the presupposition, we should have no order of nature in accordance with empirical laws, and, consequently, no guiding-thread for an experience that has to be brought to bear upon these in all their variety, or for an investigation of them.

For it is quite conceivable that, despite all the uniformity of the things of nature according to universal laws, without which we would not have the form of general empirical knowledge at all, the specific variety of the empirical laws of nature, with their effects, might still be so great as to make it impossible for our understanding to discover in nature an intelligible order, to divide its products into genera and species so as to avail ourselves of the principles of explanation and comprehension of one for explaining and interpreting another, and out of material coming to hand in such confusion (properly speaking only infinitely multiform and ill-adapted to our power of apprehension) to make a consistent context of experience.

Thus judgement, also, is equipped with an *a priori* principle for the possibility of nature, but only in a subjective respect. By means of this it prescribes a law, not to nature (as autonomy), but to itself (as heautonomy), to guide its reflection upon nature. This law may be called *the law of the specification of nature* in respect of its empirical laws. It is not one cognized *a priori* in nature, but judgement adopts it in the interests of a natural order, cognizable by our understanding, in the division which it makes of nature's universal laws when it seeks to sub-ordinate to them a variety of particular laws. So when it is said that nature specifies its universal laws on a principle of finality for our cognitive faculties, i.e. of suitability for the human understanding and its necessary function of finding the universal for the particular presented to it by perception, and again for connexion of varieties (which are, of course, common for each species) in the unity of principle, we do not thereby either prescribe a law to nature, or learn one from it by observation—although the principle in question may be confirmed by this means. For it is not a principle of the determinant but merely of the reflective judgement. All that is intended is that, no matter what is the order and disposition of nature in respect of its universal laws, we must investigate its empirical laws throughout on that principle and the maxims founded thereon, because only so far as that principle applies can we make any headway in the employment of our understanding in experience, or gain knowledge.

VI. THE ASSOCIATION OF THE FEELING OF PLEASURE WITH THE CONCEPT OF THE FINALITY OF NATURE

The conceived harmony of nature in the manifold of its particular laws with our need of finding universality of principles for it must, so far as our insight goes, be deemed contingent, but withal indispensable for the requirements of our understanding, and, consequently, a finality by which nature is in accord with our aim, but only so far as this is directed to knowledge. The universal laws of understanding, which are equally laws of nature, are, although arising from spontaneity, just as necessary for nature as the laws of motion applicable to matter. Their origin does not presuppose any regard to our cognitive faculties, seeing that it is only by their means that we first come by any conception of the meaning of a knowledge of things (of nature), and they of necessity apply to nature as Object of our cognition in general. But it is contingent, so far as we can see, that the order of nature in its particular laws, with their wealth of at least possible variety and heterogeneity transcending all our powers of comprehension, should still in actual fact be commensurate with these powers. To find out this order is an undertaking on the part of our understanding, which pursues it with a regard to a necessary end of its own, that, namely, of introducing into nature unity of principle. This end must, then, be attributed to nature by judgement, since no law can be here prescribed to it by understanding.

The attainment of every aim is coupled with a feeling of pleasure. Now where such attainment has for its condition a representation *a priori*—as here a principle for the reflective judgement in general—the feeling of pleasure also is determined by a ground which is *a priori* and valid for all men: and that, too, merely by virtue of the reference of the Object to our faculty of cognition. As the concept of finality here takes no cognizance whatever of the faculty of desire, it differs entirely from all practical finality of nature.

As a matter of fact, we do not, and cannot, find in ourselves the slightest effect on the feeling of pleasure from the coincidence of perceptions with the laws in accordance with the universal concepts of nature (the Categories), since in their case understanding necessarily follows the bent of its own nature without ulterior aim. But, while this is so, the discovery, on the other hand, that two or more empirical heterogeneous laws of nature are allied under one principle that embraces them both, is the ground of a very appreciable pleasure, often even of admiration, and such, too, as does not wear off even though we are already familiar enough with its object. It is true that we no longer notice any decided pleasure in the comprehensibility of nature, or in the unity of its divisions into genera and species, without which the empirical concepts, that afford us our knowledge of nature in its particular laws, would not be possible. Still it is certain that the pleasure appeared in due course, and only by reason of the most ordinary experience being impossible without it, has it become gradually fused with simple cognition, and no longer arrests particular attention. Something, then, that makes us attentive in our estimate of nature to its finality for our understanding—an endeavour to bring, where possible, its heterogeneous laws under higher, though still always empirical, laws—is required in order that, on meeting with success, pleasure may be felt in this their accord with our cognitive faculty, which accord is regarded by us as purely contingent. As against this a representation of nature would be altogether displeasing to us, were we to be forewarned by it that, on the least investigation carried beyond the commonest experience, we should come in contact with such a heterogeneity of its laws as would make the union of its particular laws under universal empirical laws impossible for our understanding. For this would conflict with the principle of the subjectively final specification of nature in its genera, and with our own reflective judgement in respect thereof.

Yet this presupposition of judgement is so indeterminate on the question of the extent of the prevalence of that ideal finality of nature for our cognitive faculties, that if we are told that a more searching or enlarged knowledge of nature, derived from observation, must eventually bring us into contact with a multiplicity of laws that no human understanding could reduce to a principle, we can reconcile ourselves to the thought. But still we listen more gladly to others who hold out to us the hope that the more intimately we come to know the secrets of nature, or the better we are able to compare it with external members as yet unknown to us, the more simple shall we find it in its principles, and the further our experience advances the more harmonious shall we find it in the apparent heterogeneity of its empirical laws. For our judgement makes it imperative upon us to proceed on the principle of the conformity of nature to our faculty of cognition, so far as that principle extends, without deciding—for the rule is not given to us by a determinant judgement—whether bounds are anywhere set to it or not. For while in respect of the rational employment of our cognitive faculty bounds may be definitely determined, in the empirical field no such determination of bounds is possible.

VII. THE AESTHETIC REPRESENTATION OF THE FINALITY OF NATURE

That which is purely subjective in the representation of an Object, i.e. what constitutes its reference to the Subject, not to the object, is its aesthetic quality. On the other hand, that which in such a representation serves, or is available, for the determination of the object (for the purpose of knowledge), is its logical validity. In the cognition of an object of sense both sides are presented conjointly. In the sense-representation of external things the Quality of space in which we intuite them is the merely subjective side of my representation of them (by which what the things are in themselves as Objects is left quite open), and it is on account of that reference that the object in being intuited in space is also thought merely as a phenomenon. But despite its purely subjective Quality, space is still a constituent of the knowledge of things as phenomena. *Sensation* (here external) also agrees in expressing a merely subjective side of our representations of external things, but one which is properly their matter (through which we are given something with real existence), just as space is the mere *a priori* form of the possibility of their intuition; and so sensation is, none the less, also employed in the cognition of external Objects.

But that subjective side of a representation *which is incapable of becoming an element of cognition,* is the *pleasure* or *displeasure* connected with it; for through it I cognize nothing in the object of the representation, although it may easily be the result of the operation of some cognition or other. Now the finality of a thing, so far as represented in our perception of it, is in no way a quality of the object itself (for a quality of this kind is not one that can be perceived), although it may be inferred from a cognition of things. In the finality, therefore, which is prior to the cognition of an Object, and which, even apart from any desire to make use of the representation of it for the purpose of a cognition, is yet immediately connected with it, we have the subjective quality belonging to it that is incapable of becoming a constituent of knowledge. Hence we only apply the term 'final' to the object on account of its representation being immediately coupled with the feeling of pleasure: and this representation itself is an aesthetic representation of the finality. The only question is whether such a representation of finality exists at all.

If pleasure is connected with the mere apprehension (*apprehensio*) of the form of an object of intuition, apart from any reference it may have to a concept for the purpose of a definite cognition, this does not make the representation referable to the Object, but solely to the Subject. In such a case the pleasure can express nothing but the conformity of the Object to the cognitive faculties brought into play in the reflective judgement, and so far as they are in play, and hence merely a subjective formal finality of the Object. For that apprehension of forms in the imagination can never take place without the reflective judgement, even when it has no intention of so doing, comparing them at least with its faculty of referring intuitions to concepts. If, now, in this comparison, imagination (as the faculty of intuitions *a priori*) is undesignedly brought into accord with understanding (as the faculty of concepts) by means of a given representation, and a feeling of pleasure is thereby aroused, then the object must be regarded as final for the reflective judgement. A judgement of this kind is an aesthetic judgement upon the finality of the Object, which does not depend upon any present concept of the object, and does not provide one. When the form of an object (as opposed to the matter of its representation, as sensation) is, in the mere act of reflecting upon it, without regard to any concept to be obtained from it, estimated as the ground of a pleasure in the representation of such an Object, then this pleasure is also judged to be combined necessarily with the representation of it, and so not merely for the Subject apprehending this form, but for all in general who pass judgement. The object is then called beautiful; and the faculty of judging by means of such a pleasure (and so also with universal validity) is called taste. For since the ground of the pleasure is made to reside merely in the form of the object for reflection generally, consequently not in any sensation of the object, and without any reference, either, to any concept that might have something or other in view, it is with the conformity to law in the empirical employment of judgement generally (unity of imagination and understanding) in the Subject, and with this alone, that the representation of the Object in reflection, the conditions of which are universally valid *a priori*, accords. And, as this accordance of the object with the faculties of the Subject is contingent, it gives rise to a representation of a finality on the part of the object in respect of the cognitive faculties of the Subject.

Here, now, is a pleasure which—as is the case with all pleasure or displeasure that is not brought about through the agency of the concept of freedom (i.e. through the antecedent determination of the higher faculty of desire by means of pure reason)—no concepts could ever enable us to regard as necessarily connected with the representation of an object. It must always be only through reflective perception that it is cognized as conjoined with this representation. As with all empirical judgements, it is, consequently, unable to announce objective necessity or lay claim to *a priori* validity. But, then, the judgement of taste in fact only lays claim, like every other empirical judgement, to be valid for every one, and, despite its inner contingency this is always possible. The only point that is strange or out of the way about it, is that it is not an empirical concept, but a feeling of pleasure (and so not a concept at all), that is yet exacted from every one by the judgement of taste, just as if it were a predicate united to the cognition of the Object, and that is meant to be conjoined with its representation.

A singular empirical judgement, as, for example, the judgement of one who perceives a movable drop of water in a rockcrystal, rightly looks to every one finding the fact as stated, since the judgement has been formed according to the universal conditions of the determinant judgement under the laws of a possible experience generally. In the same way one who feels pleasure in simple reflection on the form of an object, without having any concept in mind, rightly lays claim to the agreement of every one, although this judgement is empirical and a singular judgement. For the ground of this pleasure is found in the universal, though subjective, condition of reflective judgements, namely the final harmony of an object (be it a product of nature or of art) with the mutual relation of the faculties of cognition (imagination and understanding) which are requisite for every empirical cognition. The pleasure in judgements of taste is, therefore, dependent doubtless on an empirical representation, and cannot be united *a priori* to any concept (one cannot determine *a priori* what object will be in accordance with taste or not—one must find out the object that is so); but then it is only made the determining ground of this judgement by virtue of our consciousness of its resting simply upon reflection and the universal, though only subjective, conditions of the harmony of that reflection with the knowledge of objects generally, for which the form of the Object is final.

This is why judgements of taste are subjected to a Critique in respect of their possibility. For their possibility presupposes an *a priori* principle, although that principle is neither a cognitive principle for understanding nor a practical principle for the will, and is thus in no way determinant *a priori*.

Susceptibility to pleasure arising from reflection on the forms of things (whether of nature or of art) betokens, however, not only a finality on the part of Objects in their relation to the reflective judgement in the Subject, in accordance with the concept of nature, but also, conversely, a finality on the part of the Subject, answering to the concept of freedom, in respect of the form, or even formlessness, of objects. The result is that the aesthetic judgement refers not merely, as a judgement of taste, to the beautiful, but also, as springing from a higher intellectual feeling, to the *sublime*. Hence the above-mentioned Critique of Aesthetic Judgement must be divided on these lines into two main parts.

VIII. THE LOGICAL REPRESENTATION OF THE FINALITY OF NATURE

There are two ways in which finality may be represented in an object given in experience. It may be made to turn on what is purely subjective. In this case the object is considered in respect of its form as present in *apprehension* (*apprehensio*) prior to any concept; and the harmony of this form with the cognitive faculties, promoting the combination of the intuition with concepts for cognition generally, is represented as a finality of the form of the object. Or, on the other hand, the representation of finality may be made to turn on what is objective, in which case it is represented as the harmony of the form of the object with the possibility of the thing itself according to an antecedent concept of it containing the ground of this form. We have seen that the representation of the former kind of finality rests on the pleasure immediately felt in mere reflection on the form of the object. But that of the latter kind of finality, as it refers the form of the Object, not to the Subject's cognitive faculties engaged in its apprehension, but to a definite cognition of the object under a given concept, has nothing to do with a feeling of pleasure in things, but only with understanding and its estimate of them. Where the concept of an object is given, the function of judgement, in its employment of that concept for cognition, consists in *presentation* (*exhibitio*), i.e. in placing beside the concept an intuition corresponding to it. Here it may be that our own imagination is the agent employed, as in the case of art, where we realize a preconceived concept of an object which we set before ourselves as an end. Or the agent may be nature in its technic (as in the case of organic bodies) when we read into it our own concept of an end to assist our estimate of its product. In this case what is represented is not a mere *finality* of nature in the form of the thing, but this very product as a *natural end*. Although our concept that nature, in its empirical laws, is subjectively final in its forms is in no way a concept of the Object, but only a principle of judgement for providing itself with concepts in the vast multiplicity of nature, so that it may be able to take its bearings, yet, on the analogy of an end, as it were a regard to our cognitive faculties is here attributed to nature. *Natural beauty* may, therefore, be looked on as the *presentation* of the concept of formal, i.e. merely subjective, finality and *natural ends* as the presentation of the concept of a real, i.e. objective, finality. The former of these we estimate by taste (aesthetically by means of the feeling of pleasure), the latter by understanding and reason (logically according to concepts).

On these considerations is based the division of the Critique of Judgement into that of the *aesthetic* and the *teleological* judgement. By the first is meant the faculty of estimating formal finality (otherwise called subjective) by the feeling of pleasure or displeasure, by the second the faculty of estimating the real finality (objective) of nature by understanding and reason.

In a Critique of Judgement the part dealing with aesthetic judgement is essentially relevant, as it alone contains a principle introduced by judgement completely *a priori* as the basis of its reflection upon nature. This is the principle of nature's formal finality for our cognitive faculties in its particular (empirical) laws—a principle without which understanding could not feel itself at home in nature: whereas no reason is assignable *a priori*, nor is so much as the possibility of one apparent from the concept of nature as an object of experience, whether in its universal or in its particular aspects, why there should be objective ends of nature, i.e. things only possible as natural ends. But it is only judgement that, without being itself possessed *a priori* of a principle in that behalf, in actually occurring cases (of certain products) contains the rule for making use of the concept of ends in the interest of reason, after that the above transcendental principle has already prepared understanding to apply to nature the concept of an end (at least in respect of its form).

But the transcendental principle by which a finality of nature, in its subjective reference to our cognitive faculties, is represented in the form of a thing as a principle of its estimation, leaves quite undetermined the question of where and in what cases we have to make our estimate of the object as a product according to a principle of finality, instead of simply according to universal laws of nature. It resigns to the *aesthetic* judgement the task of deciding the conformity of this product (in its form) to our cognitive faculties as a question of taste (a matter which the aesthetic judgement decides, not by any harmony with concepts, but by feeling). On the other hand judgement as teleologically employed assigns the determinate conditions under which something (e.g. an organized body) is to be estimated after the idea of an end of nature. But it can adduce no principle from the concept of nature, as an object of experience, to give it its authority to ascribe *a priori* to nature a reference to ends, or even only indeterminately to assume them from actual experience in the case of such products. The reason of this is that in order to be able merely empirically to cognize objective finality in a certain object, many particular experiences must be collected and reviewed under the unity of their principle. Aesthetic judgement is, therefore, a special faculty of estimating according to a rule, but not according to concepts. The teleological is not a special faculty, but only general reflective judgement proceeding, as it always does in theoretical cognition, according to concepts, but in respect of certain objects of nature, following special principles—those, namely, of a judgement that is merely reflective and does not determine Objects. Hence, as regards its application, it belongs to the theoretical part of philosophy, and on account of its special principles, which are not determinant, as principles belonging to doctrine have to be, it must also form a special part of the Critique. On the other hand the aesthetic judgement contributes nothing to the cognition of its objects. Hence it must *only* be allocated to the Critique of the judging Subject and of its faculties of knowledge so far as these are capable of possessing *a priori* principles, be their use (theoretical or practical) otherwise what it may—a Critique which is the propaedeutic of all philosophy.

IX. JOINDER OF THE LEGISLATIONS OF UNDERSTANDING AND REASON BY MEANS OF JUDGEMENT

Understanding prescribes laws *a priori* for nature as an Object of sense, so that we may have a theoretical knowledge of it in a possible experience. Reason prescribes laws *a priori* for freedom and its peculiar causality as the supersensible in the Subject, so that we may have a purely practical knowledge. The realm of the concept of nature under the one legislation, and that of the concept of freedom under the other, are completely cut off from all reciprocal influence, that they might severally (each according to its own principles) exert upon the other, by the broad gulf that divides the supersensible from phenomena. The concept of freedom determines nothing in respect of the theoretical cognition of nature; and the concept of nature likewise nothing in respect of the practical laws of freedom. To that extent, then, it is not possible to throw a bridge from the one realm to the other. Yet although the determining grounds of causality according to the concept of freedom (and the practical rule that this contains) have no place in nature, and the sensible cannot determine the supersensible in the Subject; still the converse is possible (not, it is true, in respect of the knowledge of nature, but of the consequences arising from the supersensible and bearing on the sensible). So much indeed is implied in the concept of a causality by freedom, the *operation* of which, in conformity with the formal laws of freedom, is to take effect in the world. The word *cause*, however, in its application to the supersensible only signifies the *ground* that determines the causality of things of nature to an effect in conformity with their appropriate natural laws, but at the same time also in unison with the formal principle of the laws of reason—a ground which, while its possibility is impenetrable, may still be completely cleared of the charge of contradiction that it is alleged to involve.* The effect in accordance with the concept of freedom is the final end which (or the manifestation of which in the sensible world) is to exist, and this presupposes the condition of the possibility of that end in nature (i.e. in the nature of the Subject as a being of the sensible world, namely, as man). It is so presupposed *a priori*, and without regard to the practical, by judgement. This faculty, with its concept of a *finality* of nature, provides us with the mediating concept between concepts of nature and the concept of freedom—a concept that makes possible the transition from the pure theoretical [legislation of understanding] to the pure practical [legislation of reason] and from conformity to law in accordance with the former to final ends according to the latter. For through that concept we cognize the possibility of the final end that can only be actualized in nature and in harmony with its laws.

Understanding, by the possibility of its supplying *a priori* laws for nature, furnishes a proof of the fact that nature is cognized by us only as phenomenon, and in so doing points to its having a supersensible substrate; but this substrate it leaves quite *undetermined*. Judgement by the *a priori* principle of its estimation of nature according to its possible particular laws provides this supersensible substrate (within as well as without us) with *determinability through the intellectual faculty*. But reason gives *determination* to the same *a priori* by its practical law. Thus judgement makes possible the transition from the realm of the concept of nature to that of the concept of freedom.

---

* One of the various supposed contradictions in this complete distinction of the causality of nature from that through freedom, is expressed in the objection that when I speak of *hindrances* opposed by nature to causality according to laws of freedom (moral laws) or of *assistance* lent to it by nature, I am all the time admitting an *influence* of the former upon the latter. But the misinterpretation is easily avoided, if attention is only paid to the meaning of the statement. The resistance or furtherance is not between nature and freedom, but between the former as phenomenon and *the effects* of the latter as phenomena in the world of sense. Even the causality of freedom (of pure and practical reason) is the causality of a natural cause subordinated to freedom (a causality of the Subject regarded as man, and consequently as a phenomenon), and one, the ground of whose determination is contained in the intelligible, that is thought under freedom, in a manner that is not further or otherwise explicable (just as in the case of that intelligible that forms the supersensible substrate of nature).

In respect of the faculties of the soul generally, regarded as higher faculties, i.e. as faculties containing an autonomy, understanding is the one that contains the *constitutive a priori* principles for the *faculty of cognition* (the theoretical knowledge of nature). The *feeling of pleasure and displeasure* is provided for by the judgement in its independence from concepts and from sensations that refer to the determination of the faculty of desire and would thus be capable of being immediately practical. For the *faculty of desire* there is reason, which is practical without mediation of any pleasure of whatsoever origin, and which determines for it, as a higher faculty, the final end that is attended at the same time with pure intellectual delight in the Object. Judgement's concept of a finality of nature falls, besides, under the head of natural concepts, but only as a regulative principle of the cognitive faculties—although the aesthetic judgement on certain objects (of nature or of art) which occasions that concept, is a constitutive principle in respect of the feeling of pleasure or displeasure. The spontaneity in the play of the cognitive faculties whose harmonious accord contains the ground of this pleasure, makes the concept in question, in its consequence, a suitable mediating link connecting the realm of the concept of nature with that of the concept of freedom, as this accord at the same time promotes the sensibility of the mind for moral feeling. The following table may facilitate the review of all the above faculties in their systematic unity.*

List of Mental Faculties	*Cognitive Faculties*
Cognitive faculties.	Understanding.
Feeling of pleasure and displeasure.	Judgement.
Faculty of desire.	Reason.

* It has been thought somewhat suspicious that my divisions in pure philosophy should almost always come out threefold. But it is due to the nature of the case. If a division is to be *a priori* it must be either analytic, according to the law of contradiction—and then it is always twofold (*quodlibet ens est aut A aut non A*)—or else it is *synthetic*. If it is to be derived in the latter case from *a priori* concepts (not, as in mathematics, from the *a priori* intuition corresponding to the concept) then, to meet the requirements of synthetic unity in general, namely (1) a condition, (2) a conditioned, (3) the concept arising from the union of the conditioned with its condition, the division must of necessity be trichotomous.

A priori Principles	*Application*
Conformity to law.	Nature.
Finality.	Art.
Final End.	Freedom.

Metaphysics of Morals: Metaphysical Principles of Virtue

VII. Ethical Duties Are of Broad Obligation; ^{390¹} on the Other Hand, Juridical Duties Are of Strict Obligation

This proposition is a consequence of the foregoing. For if the law can command only the maxim of actions and not the actions themselves, then this is a sign that the law leaves in its obedience (observance) a latitude (*latitudo*) for free choice, i.e., it cannot definitely assign

---

¹ Marginal numbers refer to page numbers in Volume Six of the Königliche Preussiche Akademie der Wissenschaften edition of Kant's works (Berlin, 1902–1938).

in what way and to what extent something should be brought about by an action directed to an end which is at the same time a duty. But by a broad duty is not understood a permission to make exceptions to the maxim of the actions, but only the permission to limit one maxim of duty by another (e.g., the general love of one's neighbor by the love of one's parents); and this in fact broadens the field for the practice of virtue. The broader the duty, the more imperfect, therefore, is one's obligation to an action; and the closer one nevertheless brings the maxim of his observance of this broad duty (in his own mind) to the strict duty (of right), so much the more perfect is his virtuous action.

Imperfect duties are, therefore, merely duties of virtue. The fulfillment of them is merit (*meritum*) = + *a;* but their transgression is not forthwith an offense (*demeritum*) = − *a*, but merely moral unworth = *o*, unless the subject made it a principle not to conform to these duties. The strength of purpose in such fulfillment is alone properly called virtue (*virtus*); the weakness in such transgression is not so much vice (*vitium*) as mere lack of virtue, want of moral strength (*defectus moralis*). (As the word *Tugend* ["virtue"] is derived from *taugen* ["to be good for something"], so *Untugend* ["lack of virtue"] by its etymology signifies "good for nothing.") Every action contrary to duty is called transgression (*peccatum*). Deliberate transgression that has become a principle properly constitutes what is called vice (*vitium*).

Although the conformity of actions to right (i.e., being an upright man) is nothing meritorious, yet the conformity to right of the maxim of such actions regarded as duties, i.e., *respect* for right, is meritorious. For by this latter conformity a man makes the right of humanity or of men his end and thereby enlarges his concept of duty
391 beyond that of indebtedness (*officium debiti*), since another person by his rights can, according to the law, require actions of me but cannot require that the law at the same time contain the incentive of my actions as well. The same thing is true of the universal ethical command, "Act in accordance with duty from duty." [2] To

---

[2] Or, "Act dutifully from a sense of duty." The German is, *Handle pflichtmäßig aus Pflicht.*

establish this disposition of itself and to quicken it is meritorious, as in the above case, because it goes beyond the law of duty for actions and makes the law in itself also the incentive.

But just for this reason, these ethical duties must also be counted as of broad obligation. With regard to such broad obligation there exists a subjective principle of ethical reward (or, rather, of susceptibility to such reward in accordance with the law of virtue) in order that this broad obligation be brought as close as possible to a strict one. This principle is that of a moral pleasure which goes beyond mere satisfaction with oneself (which may be merely negative); and it is proudly said that, in the consciousness of this moral pleasure, virtue is its own reward.

If this merit is the merit of a man with regard to other men, i.e., if it consists in his promoting their natural— and recognized by all men as natural—end, i.e., if it consists in his making their happiness his own, then one might call it sweet merit, the consciousness of which produces a moral enjoyment in which men are by sympathy inclined to revel. On the other hand, the bitter merit of promoting the true good of others when they do not recognize their true good (in the case of the ungrateful and the thankless) usually has no such effect, but engenders only satisfaction with oneself; in this latter case, however, the merit would be even greater.

VIII. Exposition of the Duties of Virtue as Broad Duties

1. ONE'S OWN PERFECTION AS AN END WHICH IS AT THE SAME TIME A DUTY

(a) Physical perfection, i.e., the cultivation of all our capacities in general in order to promote the ends set before us by reason. That this is a duty and therefore an end in itself, and that the effort to bring this about, even without regard to the advantage which such an effort affords us, is based not on a conditional (pragmatic) imperative but on an unconditional (moral) one, can be seen from the following consideration. The capacity to propose an end to oneself is the characteristic of humanity (as distinguished from animality). The rational will [*Vernunftwille*] is therefore bound up with the end of the humanity in our own person, as is also, consequently, the duty to deserve well of humanity by means of culture in general, and to acquire or promote the capacity of carrying out all sorts of ends, as far as this capacity is to be found in man. This is to say that cultivating the crude predispositions of one's nature is a duty, since thus the animal is first raised to man; therefore, it is a duty in itself.

But this duty is only ethical, i.e., of broad obligation. No principle of reason prescribes exactly how far one must go in this effort (in enlarging or correcting one's faculty of understanding, i.e., in knowledge or in technical ability). Besides, the variety of circumstances which men may encounter makes quite optional the choice of the kind of occupation for which one should cultivate his talent. There is here, therefore, no law of reason for actions but only for the maxim of actions, viz., "Cultivate your powers of mind and body so as to be able to fulfill all the ends which may arise for you, uncertain as you may be which ends might become your own."

(*b*) Cultivation of morality within ourselves. The greatest moral perfection of man is to do his duty and to do it, of course, from duty (so that the law is not merely the rule, but also the incentive of his actions). Now, at first sight this certainly seems to be a strict obligation; and the principle of duty seems to command, with the exactness and strictness of a law, not merely the legality of every action but also the morality of it, i.e., the mental disposition. But in fact, even here the law commands only the maxim of the action, namely, that the ground of the obligation is to be sought not in sensible impulses (advantage or disadvantage) but wholly in the law; and so the law does not command the action itself. For it is not possible for man to look so far into the depths of his own heart as ever to be entirely certain, even in one single action, of the purity of his moral purpose and the sincerity of his mental disposition, although he has no doubt at all about its legality. Often the weakness which dissuades a man from the risk of a crime is regarded by him as virtue (which involves the concept of strength). But how many people who have lived a long and blameless life are merely fortunate to have escaped   393 many temptations? With each deed, how much pure moral content might have been in their mental disposition remains hidden even from themselves.

Therefore, this duty to estimate the worth of one's actions not merely according to their legality but also according to their morality (mental disposition) is also only of broad obligation. The law does not command this internal action in the human mind itself but merely the maxim of the action, namely, that one should strive according to every capacity so that in all actions in accordance with duty the thought of duty should of itself be a sufficient incentive.

2. The Happiness of Others as an End Which Is at the Same Time a Duty

(a) Physical welfare. Benevolence can be unlimited, for nothing need be done about it. But the case is more difficult with beneficence, especially when it is not to be done from friendly inclination (love) toward others, but from duty and with the sacrifice and mortification of many an appetite. That beneficence is a duty results from the fact that since our self-love cannot be separated from our need to be loved by others (to obtain help from them in case of need), we therefore make ourselves an end for others; and this maxim can never be obligatory except by qualifying as a universal law and, consequently, through a will to make others our ends. Hence the happiness of others is an end which is at the same time a duty.

But while I should sacrifice a part of my welfare to others without any hope of recompense because it is my duty, yet it is impossible to set definite limits on how far this is to go. Much depends upon what the true need of each one would be according to his own feelings, and it must be left to each one to determine this need for himself. For to sacrifice one's own happiness, one's true needs, in order to promote the happiness of others would be a self-contradictory maxim if made a universal law. Therefore, this duty is only a broad one; it has a latitude within which we may do more or less without being able to assign definite limits to it. The law holds only for maxims, not for definite actions.

394   (*b*) The moral well-being (*salus moralis*) of others also belongs to the happiness of others, which it is our duty to promote; but this duty is only negative. The pain that a man feels from remorse of conscience, though its origin is moral, is nevertheless in its operation physical, like grief, fear, and every other diseased condition. To take care that he should not deservedly encounter this inward reproach is not indeed my duty, but is, rather, his business; but it is my duty to do nothing which, according to human nature, might tempt him to do something for which his conscience might afterward torment him, i.e., it is my duty to give him no occasion for scandal. But there are no definite limits within which this care for the moral satisfaction of others must be kept; it therefore involves only a broad obligation.

IX. What Is a Duty of Virtue?

Virtue is the strength of man's maxim in obeying his duty. All strength is known only by the obstacles it can overcome; and in the case of virtue the obstacles are the natural inclinations, which can come into conflict with moral purpose. And since it is man himself who puts these obstacles in the way of his maxims, virtue is not merely self-constraint (for that might be an effort of one inclination to constrain another), but is, moreover, a constraint according to a principle of internal freedom and, consquently, by the mere representation of his duty according to its formal law.

All duties contain the concept of constraint by law. And indeed ethical duties contain a constraint for which only an internal legislation is possible; juridical duties, on the other hand, contain one for which external legislation also is possible. Both, therefore, include the concept of constraint, either self-constraint or constraint by others. The moral power of self-constraint may be called virtue, and the action springing from such a disposition (respect for the law) may be called a virtuous (ethical) action, though the law expresses a juridical duty. For it is the doctrine of virtue that commands us to consider the rights of men as holy.

But what it is virtuous to do is not on that account properly a duty of virtue. The former can only concern the formal element of the maxims; the latter, however, concerns their matter, namely, an end which is at the same time conceived as a duty. But since the ethical obligation to ends (of which there are several) is only broad, inasmuch as it contains only a law for the maxim of actions, and since the end is the matter (object) of choice, so there are many duties, differing according to the variety of lawful ends. These may be called duties of virtue (*officia honestatis*) just because they are subject only to free self-constraint, not to the constraint of other men, and because they determine an end which is at the same time a duty.

Virtue insofar as it is the agreement of the will with every duty (this agreement being grounded in a firm disposition of mind) is, like everything formal, merely one and the same. But with regard to the end of actions which is at the same time a duty, i.e., with regard to that (the material) which one ought to make an end, there can be several virtues; and since the obligation to the maxim of the end is called a duty of virtue, it follows that there are likewise several duties of virtue.

The supreme principle of the doctrine of virtue is this: "Act according to a maxim whose ends are such that there can be a universal law that everyone have these ends." According to this principle a man is an end to himself as well as to others. And it is not enough that he is not authorized to use either himself or others merely as means (this latter including also the case of his being indifferent to others), but rather, making mankind in general one's end is in itself a duty of every man.

Since this principle of the doctrine of virtue is a categorical imperative, it does not admit of a proof; but it does admit of a deduction[3] from pure practical reason.

---

[3] *Deduktion*, usually translated as "deduction," but might be better translated as "justification." See *Critique of Pure Reason*, B 116 ff.

Whatever can be an end in man's relation to himself and
to others is an end for pure practical reason, since this
latter is a faculty of ends in general. For practical reason
to be indifferent to ends, i.e., to take no interest in them,
would be a contradiction; for then it would not determine the maxims of actions (and the actions always contain an end) and, consequently, would not be practical
reason. Pure reason, however, cannot a priori command
any ends unless it declares these ends to be at the same
time duties; such duties are then called duties of virtue.

396 ## X. The Supreme Principle of the Doctrine of Right Was Analytic; That of the Doctrine of Virtue Is Synthetic

It is clear from the principle of contradiction that external constraint, insofar as it resists any hindrance to
external freedom in conformity with universal law (i.e.,
insofar as it is a hindrance to the hindrance to external
freedom), can be consistent with ends generally. I need
not go beyond the concept of freedom to see this, be
each man's end what he will. The supreme principle of
right is therefore analytic.[4]

On the other hand, the principle of the doctrine of
virtue goes beyond the concept of external freedom, and
according to universal laws connects with that concept
an end which this principle makes a duty. This principle
of the doctrine of virtue is therefore synthetic.[5] Its possi-

[4] The supreme principle of the doctrine of right is found in
§ C of the Introduction to *The Metaphysical Principles of Right*:
"Act externally so that the free use of your choice can coexist
with the freedom of any man according to a universal law."

[5] For Kant's distinction between analytic and synthetic judgments see *Critique of Pure Reason*, B 10 ff.

bility is contained in the deduction (Section IX above).

This extension of the concept of duty beyond the concept of external freedom and of such freedom's restriction by means of the merely formal condition of its thorough harmony puts internal freedom in place of constraint from without, this internal freedom being the power of self-constraint, not with the help of other inclinations but through pure practical reason (which scorns all such help). This extension consists in the following fact, which raises this internal freedom above juridical duty: internal freedom proposes ends from which right altogether abstracts. In the case of the moral imperative and the supposition of freedom which this imperative necessarily involves, the law, the capacity (to fulfill the law), and the will determining the maxim make up all the elements which constitute the concept of juridical duty. But in the imperative which commands the duty of virtue there is added, besides the concept of self-constraint, that of an end. This is not an end that we have, but one that we ought to have, and hence one that pure practical reason has in itself. Pure practical reason's highest, unconditional end (which, however, is always a duty) consists in this, that virtue is its own end and, because of the merit which men accord it, is also its own reward. Herein virtue shines so brightly as an ideal that in human eyes it seems to overshadow even holiness itself, which is never tempted to transgression.* This, however, is an illusion arising 397 from the fact that since we have no measure for degrees of strength except the magnitude of the hindrances which could have been overcome (which are the inclinations within us), we are led to mistake the subjective conditions of estimating a magnitude for the objective conditions of the magnitude itself. But compared with human ends, all of which have hindrances to be combated, it is true that the worth of virtue itself, which is its own end, far outweighs the worth of all the utility and all the empirical

---

* So that one might vary two well-known verses of Haller thus:
> With all his failings man is still
> Better than angels void of will.

[The actual lines from Albrecht von Haller's poem, *Über den Ursprung des Übels* ("Concerning the Origin of Evil," 1734), are:
> For God loves no constraint; the world with its failings
> Is better than a host of angels void of will.]

ends and advantages which virtue may have as consequences.

One may indeed say that man is obligated to be virtuous (to have moral strength). For although the capacity
(*facultas*) to overcome all opposing sensible impulses can
and must be presupposed on behalf of freedom, yet this
capacity as strength (*robur*) is something that must be
acquired by upholding the moral incentive (the representation of the law) both through contemplating (*con-
templatione*) the dignity of the pure law of reason within
us and at the same time through exercise (*exercitio*) as
well.

398 *XI.*

According to the preceding principles, the scheme of
the duties of virtue can be exhibited in the following
way:

the material element of the duty of virtue

	1	2	
internal duty of virtue	my own end, which is at the same time my duty (my own perfection)	the end of others, whose promotion is at the same time my duty (the happiness of others)	external duty of virtue
	3	4	
	the law, which is at the same time an incentive, on which the morality of every free determination of the will rests	the end, which is at the same time an incentive, on which the legality	

the formal element of the duty of virtue

XII. Sensitive Basic Concepts [6] of the Susceptibility of the Mind to Concepts of Duty Generally

These are such moral qualities that, if one does not possess them, there can be no duty to acquire them. These are moral feeling, conscience, love of one's neighbor, and respect for oneself (self-esteem). There is no obligation to have these, because they are subjective conditions of susceptibility to the concept of duty and are not objective conditions of morality. They are all sensitive [*ästhetisch*] and antecedent but natural predispositions (*praedispositio*) of being affected by concepts of duty. Though it cannot be regarded as a duty to have these predispositions, yet every man has them, and it is by means of them that he can be obligated. The consciousness of them is not of empirical origin but can only follow upon the consciousness of a moral law—upon its effect on the mind.

(A) MORAL FEELING

This is the susceptibility to pleasure or displeasure merely from the consciousness of the agreement or disagreement of our action with the law of duty. Every determination of choice proceeds from the representation of the possible action, through the feeling of pleasure or displeasure in taking an interest in the action or in its effect, to the deed; and here the sensitive condition (the affection of the internal sense) is either a pathological or a moral feeling. The former is that feeling which precedes

---

[6] *Ästhetische Vorbegriffe.*

the representation of the law; the latter is that which can
only follow the represen:tation of the law.

Now, there can be no duty to have a moral feeling or
to acquire it; for all consciousness of obligatioɪ presupposes this feeling in order that the constraint which lies
in the concept of duty may be known. Every man (as a
moral being) has this feeling originally within himself;
the obligation can only extend to cultivating it and even
strengthening it through wonder at its inscrutable origin.
This cultivation comes about through seeing how just by
the mere representation of reason this feeling is excited
most strongly, in its purity and apart from every pathological stimulus.

It is not proper to call this feeling a moral sense, for by
the word "sense" is generally understood a theoretical
faculty of perception directed to an object; on the contrary, moral feeling (like pleasure or displeasure in general) is something merely subjective, which yields no
knowledge. No man is devoid of all moral feeling; for if
he were totally unsusceptible to this sensation, he would
be morally dead. And if (to speak in the language of
physicians) the moral vital force could no longer produce
any effect on this feeling, then his humanity would be
dissolved (as if by chemical laws) into mere animality,
and would be irretrievably mixed with the mass of other
natural beings. We ˙ave no special sense for (moral)
good and evil any more than for truth, although such
expressions are often used. However, we do have a
susceptibility of free choice for being moved by pure
practical reason (and its law), and it is this that we call
moral feeling.

(B) CONCERNING CONSCIENCE

Just so, conscience is not something to be acquired,
and there is no duty to provide oneself with a conscience;
but insofar as every man is a moral being, he has it originally within him. Being bound to have a conscience
would be like having a duty to recognize duties. For
conscience is practical reason, holding up before a man
his duty for acquittal or condemnation in every case

under a law. Hence conscience does not relate to an object, but only to the subject (affecting moral feeling by its own act), and thus it is not an obligation and duty, but an inevitable fact. Therefore, when it is said that this man has no conscience, this means he does not heed its dictates. For if he really had none, he would not impute to himself anything done in accordance with duty, nor 401 reproach himself for anything done contrary to it; and thus he would not even be able to conceive of the duty of having a conscience.

I pass by the various divisions of conscience and only take note of a consequence of what has just been said, namely, that there is no such thing as an erring conscience. In the objective judgment of whether or not something is a duty, one can indeed sometimes be mistaken; but I cannot be mistaken in my subjective judgment as to whether I have compared something with my practical (here judicially acting) reason for the sake of such a judgment; for if I were mistaken in that, I would then not have exercised practical judgment at all, and in that case there is neither truth nor error. Unconscientiousness is not lack of conscience but the propensity not to heed its judgment. But when a man is aware of having acted according to his conscience, then as far as guilt or innocence is concerned, nothing more can be demanded. He is only obligated to inform his understanding of what is or is not a duty. But when it comes, or has come, to a deed, then conscience speaks involuntarily and inevitably. To act conscientiously can, therefore, not itself be a duty, since otherwise it would be necessary to have a second conscience to be aware of the act of the first.

The duty here is only to cultivate our conscience, to sharpen our attention to the voice of this internal judge, and to use every means to get it a hearing; hence such a duty is only an indirect one.

(c) CONCERNING THE LOVE OF MANKIND

Love is a matter of sensation, not of willing; and I cannot love because I would, still less because I should (being obligated to love). Hence a duty to love is non-existent. But benevolence (*amor benevolentiae*), as a mode of action, can be subject to a law of duty. Disinterested benevolence toward men is often (though very improperly) called love; indeed, love is spoken of as being at the same time our duty even where the happiness of another is not concerned, but, rather, where the complete and free surrender of all one's ends to those of another (even superhuman) being is involved. But all duty is necessitation, a constraint, even though it might be self-constraint according to a law. And what one does from constraint does not come about from love.

402   It is our duty to benefit other men according to our capacity, whether we love them or not; and this duty loses nothing of its weight even though we must make the sad remark that our species, alas! when we know it more closely, is not such as to be found particularly worthy of love. But hatred of mankind is always odious, even though, without any active hostility, it consists merely in complete withdrawal from mankind (solitary misanthropy). For benevolence remains always a duty, even benevolence toward the hater of mankind, whom we certainly cannot love, but to whom we can nevertheless render good.

To hate vice in men is neither a duty nor contrary to duty, but is merely a feeling of abhorrence, in which the will has no influence on the feeling nor the feeling on the will. Beneficence is a duty. Whoever often exercises this and sees his beneficent purpose succeed comes at last really to love him whom he has benefited. When therefore it is said, "Thou shalt love thy neighbor as thyself," this does not mean you should directly (at first) love and through this love (subsequently) benefit him; but rather, "Do good to your neighbor," and this beneficence will produce in you the love of mankind (as a readiness of inclination toward beneficence in general).

Complaisant love [*Liebe des Wohlgefallens*] (*amor complacentiae*) would alone be direct. But for this (as pleasure immediately connected with the representation of the existence of an object) to be a duty, i.e., being forced to find pleasure in a thing, is a contradiction.

(D) CONCERNING RESPECT

Respect (*reverentia*) is likewise something merely sub-jective; it is a feeling of a special kind and not a judgment about an object which it would be a duty to bring about or to promote. For, if considered as a duty, this feeling could only be represented by means of the respect we have for it. To have a duty to this, therefore, would amount to being obligated to have a duty. Accordingly, it is improper to say that man has a duty of self-esteem; one ought rather to say that the law within him inevitably exacts respect for his own being, and this feeling (which is of a special kind) is the ground of certain duties, i.e., of certain actions consistent with his duty to himself. Thus it cannot be said that he has a duty of self-respect, for he must have respect for the law within himself in order to be able to conceive duty at all.

Index